Performing the Gospels in Byzantium

Tracing the Gospel text from script to illustration to recitation, this study looks at how illuminated manuscripts operated within ritual and architecture. Focusing on a group of richly illuminated lectionaries from the late eleventh century, the book articulates how the process of textual recitation produced marginalia and miniatures that reflected and subverted the manner in which the Gospel was read and simultaneously imagined by readers and listeners alike. This unique approach to manuscript illumination points to images that slowly unfolded in the minds of its listeners as they imagined the text being recited, as meaning carefully changed and built as the text proceeded. By examining this process within specific acoustic architectural spaces and the sonic conditions of medieval chant, the volume brings together the concerns of sound studies, liturgical studies, and art history to demonstrate how images, texts, and recitations played with the environment of the middle Byzantine church.

ROLAND BETANCOURT is Professor of Art History at the University of California, Irvine, where he was awarded the distinction of Chancellor's Fellow from 2019–22. Previously, he spent a year as the Elizabeth and J. Richardson Dilworth Fellow at the Institute for Advanced Study in Princeton. His published books include *Sight, Touch, and Imagination in Byzantium* (Cambridge, 2018) and *Byzantine Intersectionality: Sexuality, Gender, and Race in the Middle Ages* (2020). His ongoing work focuses on Byzantine temporality and simulacral spaces, past and present.

Performing the Gospels in Byzantium

Sight, Sound, and Space in the Divine Liturgy

ROLAND BETANCOURT
University of California, Irvine

CAMBRIDGE
UNIVERSITY PRESS

CAMBRIDGE
UNIVERSITY PRESS

University Printing House, Cambridge CB2 8BS, United Kingdom

One Liberty Plaza, 20th Floor, New York, NY 10006, USA

477 Williamstown Road, Port Melbourne, VIC 3207, Australia

314–321, 3rd Floor, Plot 3, Splendor Forum, Jasola District Centre, New Delhi – 110025, India

79 Anson Road, #06–04/06, Singapore 079906

Cambridge University Press is part of the University of Cambridge.

It furthers the University's mission by disseminating knowledge in the pursuit of education, learning, and research at the highest international levels of excellence.

www.cambridge.org
Information on this title: www.cambridge.org/9781108491396
DOI: 10.1017/9781108868532

First published 2021

Printed in Singapore by Markono Print Media Pte Ltd

A catalogue record for this publication is available from the British Library.

Library of Congress Cataloging-in-Publication Data
Names: Betancourt, Roland, author.
Title: Performing the Gospels in Byzantium : sight, sound, and space in the divine liturgy / Roland Betancourt, University of California, Irvine.
Description: Cambridge ; New York : Cambridge University Press, 2021. | Includes bibliographical references and index.
Identifiers: LCCN 2020039492 (print) | LCCN 2020039493 (ebook) | ISBN 9781108491396 (hardback) | ISBN 9781108812030 (paperback) | ISBN 9781108868532 (epub)
Subjects: LCSH: Illumination of books and manuscripts, Byzantine. | Lectionaries. | Liturgy and art. | Senses and sensation–Religious aspects–Orthodox Eastern Church.
Classification: LCC ND2930 .B48 2020 (print) | LCC ND2930 (ebook) | DDC 745.6/709495–dc23
LC record available at https://lccn.loc.gov/2020039492
LC ebook record available at https://lccn.loc.gov/2020039493

ISBN 978-1-108-49139-6 Hardback

Contents

List of Illustrations

Frontispieces

Figures

Acknowledgments

I have been writing this book on and off for over ten years now. In this time, far too many debts have been incurred, personal, professional, and financial. Taking this moment to acknowledge these dues at the completion of a manuscript is an honor that I am greatly privileged to enjoy at this time.

This volume began as my first paper in graduate school, written for Robert S. Nelson's seminar on word and image in the Middle Ages in the fall of 2009. I recall those days fondly, particularly getting to enjoy a class that was so driven by what drew me to Rob as an adviser and a class that was so clearly marked by Rob's enduring friendship with the late Michael Camille. Bissera Pentcheva and Ioli Kalavrezou's stimulating colloquium at Dumbarton Oaks on phenomenology and aesthetics galvanized my interests, as just weeks before I had discovered the exciting work by Christoffer Weitze et al. on the acoustics of Hagia Sophia, which Bissera herself has fruitfully furthered.

Over time, marked by semesters and chapters written, the paper grew and eventually became the overextended core of my dissertation. In the time that has followed, the project has dilated. My desire has been to not simply produce a study on a manuscript type (i.e., the Byzantine Gospel lectionary), but rather to follow the Gospel from text to image, to recitation and ritual, to sound and architecture – and consider how all these parts come together and play off one another.

While this is the closest book to my dissertation, it was not my first, because I felt that I first had to lay the groundwork on Byzantine perception for this book to make sense. My emphasis on the workings of the imagination as a cognitive faculty in my first book is a key factor in comprehending how the visual analyses and iconographic plays that I outline in this volume are cultivated and sustained by Byzantine viewers, whom I often prefer to call "users" so as to be less optic and more inclusive of the broader sensorium and its perceptual and cognitive dimensions. Therefore, this is volume two of a broader study, which I have long referred to as *The Proleptic Image*. The third book in the trilogy, if I ever finish it, will be the eponymous volume on the ebbs and flow of time.

This is a book marked by access. Access to archives, access to images, and access to resources. Resources used to travel to access archives, to buy photographic equipment to produce photographs, and then more resources to license and publish those images in print. An exorbitant amount in image fees has been paid to the libraries that hold the manuscripts found in this text. And, much time has been consumed with working to gain access to the manuscripts themselves or to images of said manuscripts from institutions across the Mediterranean and the United States.

Much of this access has been based on economic and gender privilege. Therefore, I wish to give special thanks to all those institutions whose collections are open access and charge no fees for images or reproduction. To those who follow ethical models of access with clear and accessible procedures, rather than being restricted by gatekeepers that require tapping into intricate social networks for permitting access. And, to those where all genders are welcomed and able to work with safety, dignity, and respect.

Over the years, I found myself in various libraries, museums, and archives for this project, far more than have even made it into the book itself. But the generosity and care of some do continue to stand out. At the Vatican Library, Paolo Vian granted me access to consult the manuscripts found there and over the years approved many of my requests for images and their reproduction rights. At Dumbarton Oaks, Stephen Zwirn patiently sat in the room with me and read about Byzantine silver while I carefully made my way through their manuscript holdings. And, over the years, various at the Dumbarton Oaks Research Library, including Deb Brown Stewart, Alyson Williams, and Samuel Shapiro, have helped immensely with resources and images rights. At the Metropolitan Museum of Art, Helen Evans gave me all the images I could possibly need of the Jaharis Lectionary, and Christine Brennan helped with details. Special thanks must also be offered to Melanie Holcomb who went out of her way to track down the names and numbers of people who might be able to help me with difficult-to-find images, outside the Met's holdings. At the State Historical Museum in Moscow, Svetlana Bedrak was crucial for gaining image rights and exceptional. At the National Library of Greece, many assisted me with access and rights, including Daniel B. Wallace, Robert Marcello, and Leigh Ann Thompson at the Center for the Study of New Testament Manuscripts in Plano, Texas. At Art Resource, Robbi Siegel has been a true lifesaver over the years, always remembering me and turning around image files and rights in a matter of hours for me. At Monza, several managed to point me in the direction of the recent photography of the ampullae, including their photographer Piero Pozzi and the members of the Fondazione Gaiani. At the Greek Patriarchate in Jerusalem, I must thank Anna Koulouris who graciously took my call and offered to speak to the bishop on my behalf to request images from their august holdings. In Thessaloniki, Pelli Mastora at the Ephorate of Antiquities provided me with impressive images and lush details of the mosaics of Hagios Georgios and Hosios David. Many others have assisted in various capacities, even if only fielding my inquiries to state they didn't know or were unable to help.

For the collections of Mount Athos, I am grateful to Alice Isabella Sullivan, who directed me to Robert W. Allison and the Friends of Mount Athos, who in turn directed me to Anastasios Ntouros at the Mount Athos Center and spoke to Father Symeon of the Dionysiou Monastery to grant me access to their manuscript holdings. At the Dionysiou Monastery, the monk Gabriil graciously showed me codex 587, and informed me about their ongoing digitization projects and the upcoming publication of their facsimile of the manuscript. Because of this impending publication, I was not able to view or publish the new photography of the manuscript. Therefore, I must add to this list of acknowledgments the warm hospitality of Anna G. Lyssikatou at the Patriarchal Institute in Thessaloniki, who presented me with the color slides made for the Athos publications in the 1970s and coordinated their digitization for inclusion in this volume. Early on in my research, Archimandrite John Cotsonis led me to the existence of codex 587's microfilm at the Pennsylvania State University. And, Tony Cutler swiftly ensured that the microfilm was mailed to me so that I could digitize it. I must also acknowledge the landmark and unfinished work of Mary-Lyon Dolezal, whose writing and reconstructions served as a companion to my thinking in its infancy.

Truly, this book would not have been possible without the generous financial support of the UCI Humanities Commons Publication Grant and the award of a three-year Chancellor's Fellowship at UCI. Special acknowledgment is due to Dean Tyrus Miller for comprehending the unique needs of publishing in art history and the nature of my projects and going out of his way to find manners in which to support my research and publishing. Again, without this support, this book would have suffered greatly, being prohibitively expensive and impossible for me to undertake financially on my own. In the Art History Department, Heather Layton and A.J. Lipscomb processed more receipts than they might care to remember and spent many hours contacting foreign institutions, begging for them to accept our payments. Beth Pace oversaw the whole endeavor, offering advice and guidance when most needed.

At Cambridge University Press, Michael Sharp's continuous interest and support for my work gave a home to this volume. Mary Bongiovi served as an industrious content manager. Shaheer Anwarli worked tirelessly as project manager, particularly handling the immense number of images and their complicated typesetting. Damian Love was a diligent and expedient copyeditor, as was Alice Falk and Aleah Hernandez who saw earlier drafts of the manuscript and tended to it. Kate Mertes managed to produce, once again, an exceptional index. I also would like to acknowledge Chris Crochetière for her contribution and inspiration for the cover design. A generous subsidy for the costs of image rights and color publication was provided by a Publication Grant from the Mary Jaharis Center for Byzantine Art and Culture.

My colleagues at Yale University, the Institute for Advanced Study, and the University of California, Irvine have not only offered guidance and advice, but also camaraderie and friendship. Jackie Jung and David Joselit offered insightful feedback on this project in its dissertation phase, encouraging publication as its own book. Nancy Patterson Ševčenko offered encouraging support and interest at a crucial juncture. Jennifer Davis read an early draft of the manuscript, offering critical and motivating advice for its revision and organization. And, Aden Kumler has probably seen more versions of this project than anyone else. For our always riveting conversations, I am deeply grateful.

To my three advisers, Robert S. Nelson, Robert Ousterhout, and Robert Maxwell across graduate school and undergrad. Firstly, and above all, to Rob for his guidance, collegiality, and ethical grounding throughout my doctoral work. Secondly, to Bob for his enthusiastic support and excitement for my future during my final year at UPenn. And, thirdly, to Robert for being a source of inspiration and motivation in my undergraduate years as I sought to find my way as an art historian.

To all my friends, I truly apologize for all the holidays I missed, the birthday parties I skipped, the outings I flaked on, and the shared kitchen tables I filled with books and papers to complete versions of this project over the years. I shall never get those moments back. Perhaps this could have waited a little bit longer.

To Michael Kelleher, finally, who was there at my side at this book's completion and journeyed across Italy, Greece, and Turkey as I finished my research and photography for this book. He valiantly stood in Hagia Sophia for over six hours as I photographed, blocking tourists from entering my shots, coyly shining ring-lights on marbles, enthusiastically propping my camera on the floor for long exposures, holding my various lenses and bags, and even offering to move stanchions, placards, floor coverings, and mountains just so that I could get the perfect shot. I thank him, not only for these gestures of love, but for the fact that when asked what his favorite part of this whole trip was, his answer is always: being in Hagia Sophia with me. That Byzantium beat out gelato and pasta is why I love him. *Tap, tap, tap.*

Introduction

The Gospel Lectionary in the Divine Liturgy

In the Byzantine rite, three key manuscripts were used for the recitation of texts from the Old and New Testaments.[1] The first is the Prophetologion, the liturgical equivalent of the Prophet Book; it contained the readings from the major and minor prophets of the Septuagint excerpted and arranged for their recitation. This reading was customarily done at Vespers or, when it occurred in the liturgy itself, after the Thrice-Holy Hymn, which is the moment at which conciliar decrees would also have been read, immediately before the reading from Acts of the Apostles.[2] While the Prophet Books themselves garnered illuminations, Prophetologia were rarely, if ever, illustrated.[3] The second is the Praxapostolos, which contains the Acts of the Apostles and the Epistles, which were read daily in the Divine Liturgy before the proclamation of the Gospel. Some of these attracted the work of illuminators, who apparently – and fittingly, for a manuscript used in the context of the Divine Liturgy – emphasized actions of reading and recitation.[4] And the third is the Gospel lectionary, which contains excerpts from the four Gospels ordered for daily reading throughout the liturgical year.

The last manuscript type is the focus of this study. The Gospel lectionary would have been read aloud from the ambo of the church during the first half of the Divine Liturgy, known as the Liturgy of the Catechumens, which immediately followed the reading of the "Divine Apostles" (i.e., the reading

[1] For a concise but thorough introduction to the readings, see Job Getcha, "Le système des lectures bibliques du rite byzantin," in A.M. Triacca and A. Pistoia (eds.), *La liturgie, interprète de l'écriture*, vol. 1 (Rome: Edizioni Liturgiche, 2003), 25–56.

[2] Juan Mateos, *Le Typicon de la Grande Église*, 2 vols. (Rome: Pontifical Oriental Institute, 1962–64), 2:282.

[3] See John Lowden, *Illuminated Prophet Books: A Study of Byzantine Manuscripts of the Major and Minor Prophets* (University Park: Pennsylvania State University Press, 1988), 5–7, esp. 5n7. See also Sysse Gudrun Engberg, "The Greek Old Testament Lectionary as a Liturgical Book," *Cahiers de l'Institut de Moyen Âge grec et latin* 54 (1986): 39–48.

[4] See Jeffrey C. Anderson, "The Walters Praxapostolos and Liturgical Illustration," *Δελτίον Χριστιανικής Αρχαιολογικής Εταιρείας* 19 (1997): 9–38. See also K. Juack, "Zu den griechischen Lektionaren und ihrer Überlieferung der Katholischen Briefe," in Kurt Aland (ed.), *Die alten Übersetzungen des Neuen Testaments, die Kirchenväterzitate und Lektionare*, Arbeiten zur neutestamentlichen Textforschung 5 (Berlin: De Gruyter, 1972), 498–589; Irmgard De Vries, *The Epistles, Gospels, and the Tones of the Byzantine Liturgical Year* (Antwerp: Vita et Pax, 1954).

from the Praxapostolos).[5] The lectionary would have been chanted aloud by a skilled reader from the ambo, while the bishop, patriarch, or officiating priest would have listened to it from within the sanctuary and afterward given his homily from that place. The proper chanting of the Gospel text was glossed in the lectionaries by a system of musical markings known as ekphonetic notation, often written in a carmine ink. These chant marks guided the skilled chanter, usually a deacon, who would have given life to the text for an attentive congregation.

Despite the long-standing debate over the codification and standardization of the lectionary as a text, scholars seem to agree that its form more or less stabilized in Constantinople during the tenth century, though the selection of readings included in each manuscript continued to vary depending on the volume's intended use.[6] In the late eleventh century, however, the lectionary began to flourish with figural initials and accompanying marginalia alongside elaborate miniatures. The present book focuses on a group of closely affiliated lectionaries produced in Constantinople around 1100 with extensive illumination programs, covering initials, marginalia, and miniatures.[7]

[5] For a generic survey of the lectionary, see Elisabeth Yota, "The Lectionary," in Vasiliki Tsamakda (ed.), *A Companion to Byzantine Illustrated Manuscripts* (Leiden: Brill, 2017), 287–99.

[6] Alexis Kniazeff, "Le lecture de l'Ancien et du Nouveau Testament dans le rite byzantin," in Bishop Cassien and Bernard Botte (eds.), *Le Prière des heures*, Lex Orandi 35 (Paris: Éditions du Cerf, 1963), 201–51. See also Yvonne Burns, "The Lectionary of the Patriarch of Constantinople," *Studia Patristica* 15:1 (1984): 515–20; Yvonne Burns, "The Historical Events that Occasioned the Inception of the Byzantine Gospel Lectionary," *Jahrbuch der Österreichischen Byzantinistik* 32:4 (1982): 119–27; Bruce Metzger, "Greek Lectionaries and a Critical Edition of the New Testament," in Aland (ed.), *Alten Übersetzungen*, 479–97; Carroll Osburn, "The Greek Lectionaries of the New Testament," in Bart D. Ehrman and Michael W. Holmes (eds.), *The Text of the New Testament in Contemporary Research: Essays on the Status Quaestionis*, 2nd edn (Leiden: Brill, 2013), 93–114.

On illuminated lectionaries, see Mary-Lyon Dolezal, "The Middle Byzantine Lectionary: Textual and Pictorial Expression of Liturgical Ritual," 2 vols., PhD dissertation, University of Chicago (1991). On the evolution of the cathedral rite, see Stefano Parenti, "The Cathedral Rite of Constantinople: Evolution of a Local Tradition," *Orientalia Christiana Periodica* 77 (2011): 449–69. See also Daniel Galadza, "The Jerusalem Lectionary and the Byzantine Rite," in Bert Groen, Daniel Galadza, Nina Glibetić, and Gabriel Radle (eds.), *Rites and Rituals of the Christian East* (Leuven: Peeters, 2014), 181–99; Daniel Galadza, "A Greek Source of the Jerusalem Lectionary: Sinai Gr. N.E. MΓ 8 (10th c.)," in Diliana Atanassova and Tinatin Chronz (eds.), *Synaxis Katholike: Beiträge zu Gottesdienst und Geschichte der fünf altkirchlichen Patriarchate für Heinzgerd Brakmann zum 70. Geburtstag* (Vienna: Lit Verlag, 2014), 213–28; Daniel Galadza, *Liturgy and Byzantinization in Jerusalem* (Oxford University Press, 2018).

[7] While several other lectionaries figure prominently in this story, my focus is on the exemplars of the tradition that prioritize a uniform, coherent, and complex play between text and illuminations. This group is less oriented around a lectionary type or a codification of its readings, as it is dependent on my assessment of their nuanced and compelling use of

These marginal images and initials appear in between silence and sound. While similar images are also featured in Gospel books, psalters, and collections of homilies not necessarily intended for liturgical use, they are particularly numerous in manuscripts produced specifically for public oral performance. In the case of the lectionary, these marginal images deploy a coherent logic – a regularity that has often been summed up as a banal illustration of the text and as such has been undertheorized by scholars. And while a systematic analysis suggests that their use has a coherent logic, it is one that seems replete with subtle iconographic errors and startling exceptions to its own rules. What sets the illuminations in the Gospel lectionary apart from those in other books is their repeated insistence on the oral and aural qualities of the lectionary, and their play with the ways in which readers and listeners alike would have imagined in their minds the excerpted narratives being retold in the Gospels.

The aim of this book is to consider how miniatures, illustrated initials, and marginalia in the Gospel book operate alongside the text and the text's recitation in the Divine Liturgy at the moment of the daily Gospel reading. It looks across manuscript illumination and liturgical space with the goal of contextualizing how image, text, sound, and architecture operate alongside one another to produce what I refer to as "polyvalent images" – images that flicker across multiple readings and spectrums of possibility. Since the lectionaries discussed throughout this work appear to be some of the highest-quality illuminated Byzantine manuscripts of the late eleventh century, they have all come to be associated with the most exquisite centers of manuscript production in Constantinople,

manuscript illustration: Dionysiou Lectionary (Mount Athos, Dionysiou Monastery, Cod. 587); Venice Lectionary (Venice, Istituto Ellenico, Cod. 2); Athens Lectionary (Athens, National Library of Greece, Cod. 68); New York Cruciform Lectionary (New York, Morgan Library, Cod. 692); Dumbarton Oaks Lectionary (Washington, DC, Dumbarton Oaks, Cod. 1); Jaharis Lectionary (New York, Metropolitan Museum of Art, 2007.286); Paris Lectionary (Paris, Bibliothèque nationale de France, supp. gr. 27); Vatican Lectionary (Vatican City, Biblioteca Apostolica Vaticana, gr. 1156); and Hamilton Lectionary (New York, Morgan Library, Cod. 639). See the List of Illustrations for a more comprehensive list of the lectionaries and manuscripts addressed. Other lectionaries of note, but which did not capture the interest of this study given the rather simplistic approaches of their illustration programs, include, but are not limited to, Athens, National Library of Greece, Cod. 190; Istanbul, Patriarchal Library, Cod. 8; Mount Athos, Panteleimon Monastery, Cod. 2; and Mount Athos, Iviron Monastery, Cod. 1 and Cod. 1392. The little-studied Mount Athos, Vatopedi Monastery, Skeuphylakion, Cod. 3 is also omitted because while its historiated initials encourage future attention congruent with the goals of this study, the manuscript itself merits independent study beyond the scope of this book.

possibly produced from within the patriarchal orbit itself and for the church of Hagia Sophia.[8]

This volume will therefore imagine Hagia Sophia as the site for these manuscripts' use. While I employ this setting with critical skepticism and qualification, I also recognize that other contexts of use are lost to us today. Therefore, the second part of this volume will explore what the use of one of these lectionaries might have been like in the space of the "Great Church" of Constantinople. This investigation is opened up by outlining and clearly elucidating the lectionary's liturgical use and the associated theories and practices of divine inspiration, recitation, and performance that contoured the delivery of the daily lection.

Therefore, the second half of this book moves well beyond the manuscripts themselves. My interest here is to understand how the lectionary alters and affects the understanding of architectural decoration, acoustics, and ritual sites within the church. The final two chapters, for example, look at key architectural details and spaces in Hagia Sophia that played with the sonic dimension of the lectionary, its aural and iconographic resonances in the space, and how conventional readings of Hagia Sophia changed over time and over the course of the lections' recitations. Rather than attempting to write a monographic study on the Gospel lectionary itself as a manuscript type, the goal in considering recitation practices and architecture is to demonstrate how liturgical spaces operated with the same level of iconographic play that we can observe across text–image relations.

[8] While many of the manuscripts at the center of my focus overlap with the group of so-called "patriarchal lectionaries," this term is deeply fraught with problems arising from a desire to securely attribute origins of patronage and reconstruct sites of use. Similarly, the very criterion by which these patriarchal lectionaries are identified is tautological, dependent on a group of key readings that are seen as indicators of this manuscript type. The clear coexistence of various lectionary manuscripts in the patriarchate and its orbit suggests that while this group might have been a part of the Constantinopolitan patriarchate and its orbit, others surely also existed alongside these in the same collections, playing on different functions and strengths. Furthermore, while fruitful and generative relations exist within the group, in terms of their illuminations, this category is counterproductive given that the type of marginalia and images that we find in lectionaries both overlaps and also cuts across this group in generative ways that are far more compelling and fruitful avenues of intellectual inquiry than the clear delineation of manuscript category according to an artificially constructed, modern classification for an already relatively small corpus of manuscripts. On the patriarchal lectionary, see Elena Velkovska, "Il lezionario patriarcale Ottoboni gr. 175," in Marco D'Agostino and Paola Degni (eds.), *Alethes Philia: Studi in onore di Giancarlo Prato*, vol. 2 (Spoleto: Fondazione Centro italiano di studi sull'alto Medioevo, 2010), 687–94. For an exceptional survey of recent literature, see Robert S. Nelson, "Patriarchal Lectionaries of Constantinople: History, Attributions, and Prospects," in Derek Krueger and Robert S. Nelson (eds.), *The New Testament in Byzantium* (Washington, DC: Dumbarton Oaks, 2016), 87–115.

The key commitment of this text is to understand how pictures slowly and "procedurally" unfold through their use in the liturgy. This interest in procedurality derives from Ian Bogost's analysis of video games, where he develops the idea of a *procedural rhetoric*: a "practice of authoring arguments through processes."[9] Bogost's concept is indebted to the work of Janet Murray, who defined the procedural – the computer's "defining ability to execute a series of rules" – as one of the key properties of a digital environment.[10] My argument here is that rather than being stably defined, images (that is, miniatures, marginalia, initials in manuscripts or decorative details and spaces in architecture) share with us facets of meaning and spectrums of signification that are perpetually in flux. Rather than being immediately legible or concrete in meaning, these images unfold differently every time they are put to use, determined not only by liturgical ritual and the day of the year, but also by how viewers work through potential readings, getting confused or misdirected by their indeterminacy. Rather than a model of play or complexity for this iconographic approach, the concept of procedurality allows us to appreciate how images are made to elicit different experiences and readings across their usage in ritual.

Art versus Use: The Problem of Illuminating Spoken Text

Most art historians have viewed the riches of Byzantine liturgical manuscripts as some sort of lavish curiosity intended for the cursory glance of a wealthy and elite patron, confined to the scholar's shelf rather than placed on the chanter's lectern. The logic here is that because images in a text intended for recitation could not have been perused and contemplated by the user in any meaningful fashion, these were objects created either as novelties or as lavish displays of conspicuous consumption.

In 2004, Irmgard Hutter attempted to revise some fundamental assumptions about Byzantine illumination, including the practical use of complexly illuminated manuscripts in the liturgical rite. Hutter comments,

> At best, they were studied and admired for a while by those who received them, but I am pretty sure that most of them were a sort of the Byzantine

[9] Ian Bogost, *Persuasive Games: The Expressive Power of Videogames* (Cambridge, MA: MIT Press, 2007), 28–29.

[10] Janet Murray, *Hamlet on the Holodeck: The Future of Narrative in Cyberspace* (New York: Free Press, 1997), 71.

> equivalent to modern coffeetable books, before they were stored away on the shelves or in chests of a library . . . Those illuminated manuscripts which today are regarded as rare and special by modern observers, have been estimated in exactly the same way in Byzantine times, at their time of production as well as at their time of copying up to several hundred years later.[11]

Hutter claims that these manuscripts were not often used in the service and that the "splendid volumes" of Byzantine illumination, from the Paris Gregory of Nazianzus Homilies (Paris, Bibliothèque nationale de France, gr. 510) to the various Octateuchs, were purely objects of admiration: praised a bit upon reception, but ultimately treated as decoration. She assigns to these manuscripts a gaze identical to that of the modern connoisseur: admired for their fine technical skill and beauty but without any function beyond that gaze, intended for no daily or practical use.

The lack of wax stains on these manuscripts' fine pages and their pristine condition suggest for Hutter their status as "fine art" objects in the Byzantine world, showing no evidence of use. Sumptuously illuminated manuscripts are often in better condition than many text-only counterparts that feature extensive use and wear. However, the notion that these illustrated manuscripts lack evidence of use is a deep mischaracterization, perhaps fueled by the fact that many of these manuscripts have been circulated only in highly cropped images of their illustrations. This has only been exacerbated by the fact that access to the manuscripts themselves and even their microfilms has been highly limited or difficult, especially for the Athonite examples wholly denied to female scholars. However, a perusal of one of the best-illuminated examples, the Dionysiou Lectionary (Mt. Athos, Dionysiou Monastery, cod. 587) immediately demonstrates extensive signs of use: smudges in the writing, drips of candle wax, interlinear notes and comments, as well as corrections to the text and the careful stitching of tears in the parchment. These signs demonstrate a class of objects that were carefully handled, respected, and cared for, but this should not negate their functional use and their functional use should not negate their aesthetic complexity.

It was along this division between the aesthetic and the functional that John Lowden, in an article tellingly titled "Luxury and Liturgy:

[11] Irmgard Hutter, "Some Aspects of Byzantine Manuscript Illumination Reconsidered," in E.N. Dobrynina (ed.), *Drevnerusskoe iskusstvo: Iskusstvo rukopisnoi knigi: Vizantiia, Drevniaia Rus'* (Saint Petersburg: Dmitrii Bulanin, 2004), 21–43, at 34, 36.

The Function of Books," distinguishes between two kinds of lectionary.[12] This binary comes to delimit the boundaries of use for images and marginalia in a book such as the illuminated lectionary. From these perspectives, art is fundamentally something to be looked at and contemplated, something ultimately antithetical to so-called practical use.[13] For example, Hutter elsewhere attempts to position the Byzantine illuminator-scribe as a fine artist through a reading of the Greek terms used to describe the use of gold script and illumination in manuscript colophons. She explicitly concludes:

[12] John Lowden, "Luxury and Liturgy: The Function of Books," in R. Morris (ed.), *Church and People in Byzantium* (Centre for Byzantine, Ottoman and Modern Greek Studies, University of Birmingham, 1990), 263–80; cf. John Lowden, "The Luxury Book as a Diplomatic Gift," in J. Shepard et al. (eds.), *Byzantine Diplomacy* (Aldershot: Variorum, 1992), 249–60. See also John Lowden, "Book Production," in Elizabeth Jeffreys, John Haldon, and Robin Cormack (eds.), *Oxford Handbook of Byzantine Studies* (Oxford University Press, 2008), 462–72. On the use of manuscripts in the liturgy, see George Galavaris, "Manuscripts and the Liturgy," in G. Vikan (ed.), *Illuminated Greek Manuscripts from American Collections: An Exhibition in Honor of Kurt Weitzmann* (Princeton University Press, 1973), 20–25.

[13] This division between art and the functional has consistently plagued the modern discipline of art history. One need only recall Svetlana Alpers's comment in her seminal essay "Is Art History?" to see the historiographic anachronism of this thinking: "The question, 'What is art?' and the old answer that defined it as having aesthetic rather than utilitarian appeal never seemed further from anyone's mind." Already in 1977, Alpers labeled the division between artistic value and functionality as obsolete. The epistemic violence of this division once produced the category of "primitive art" and articulated a colonial project through the systematic exclusion of arts whose utilitarian, tribal, and ritual value stood outside of a certain conception of art history. Arnold Rubin's 1989 survey of the arts of Africa, Oceania, and Native America, titled *Art as Technology*, precisely positioned these various arts within art history through the cultural complexity offered by their utilitarian performance. This tactic speaks to the violence of such an exclusion, since Rubin takes on the feature that once served as an exclusionary force – that is, the technological – as the banner under which to unite and resist this excision and erasure from the history of art. See Svetlana Alpers, "Is Art History?" *Daedalus* 106:3 (Summer 1977): 1–13, esp. 4. See also Arnold Rubin, *Art as Technology: The Arts of Africa, Oceania, Native America, and Southern California* (Catskill, NY: Hillcrest Press, 1989).
In Byzantine art history, a similar division has been consciously made. For example, in a special issue of *Gesta* dedicated to the history of medieval art without the concept of "art," in response to Hans Belting's influential tome *Likeness and Presence*, Henry Maguire states that "art," as has been noted by "many recent critics," is for the most part a nineteenth-century invention oriented around individual achievement, monetary value, and detachment from everyday life. However, Maguire does not cite any of these "many recent critics." He tacitly suggests that while we might not know what art was for past audiences, we certainly know what art is for us today, which somehow does not require critical definition or research. Thus, the distinction between the medieval cult image and the modern work of art that Maguire was thus purporting to address was not one of art versus image, but one of "fine" versus "applied" art, "quality versus social function," and "aesthetic beauty versus numinous power." See Henry Maguire, "Medieval Art without 'Art'?: Introduction," *Gesta* 34:1 (1995): 3–4, at 3. For a further instantiation of my argument here, see Roland Betancourt, "Medieval Art after Duchamp: Hans Belting's *Likeness and Presence* at 25," *Gesta* 55:1 (2016): 5–17.

> Art is the extra added to the norm of the manuscript containing text. As a rule, however, art is not deemed worth mentioning [in monastic inventories], because, in a text-oriented book culture, the adornment is part and parcel of the written contents.[14]

This artist-scribe is defined in terms of skill, technique, and command in dealing with the image's material medium, yet it lies outside the realm of possibility that the artist's production is part of a cohesive intellectual project inseparable from the function of the manuscript. In these terms, images are nothing more than additive "ornament," in the word's most pejorative sense. They are not even worth mentioning, given that their expected place is in the embellishment of the text, which is primary. Yet these judgments take for granted the notion that Byzantium was in fact a "text-oriented book culture" without critically considering the status of the "text" in the premodern world: most notably, they ignore that reading the written text was often, if not always, an oral and aural act.

In *Image on the Edge* (1992), even Michael Camille seems to accept this binary of artistic embellishment and use. He writes:

> Of course, the periphery of the written page had existed in earlier periods and had even been the site of pictures, as in Byzantine and Anglo-Saxon Psalters of the tenth century, where the side margins were the locus of often complex text illustrations. But this extra-textual space only developed into a site of artistic elaboration as the idea of the text as written document superseded the idea of the text as a cue for speech. The way monks read was called *meditatio*, in which every word was masticated and digested for memorization by being uttered out loud.[15]

Camille sees the flourishing of marginal illumination as concurrent with the shift in how the text was perceived. While acknowledging the existence of marginal illuminations in Byzantine Psalters as an exception to the model that he proposes, he describes the illuminations in Byzantium as textual illustrations and the later development as artistic elaboration, which emerges in his teleological model alongside the privileging of writing over speech.

As John Lowden observes in his most recent work on lectionaries, images are justifiable in manuscripts intended for private devotion and contemplation, but one using the lectionary would have had "little chance

[14] Irmgard Hutter, "Decorative Systems in Byzantine Manuscripts, and the Scribe as Artist: Evidence from Manuscripts in Oxford," *Word & Image* 12:1 (1996): 4–22, at 5.

[15] Michael Camille, *Image on the Edge: The Margins of Medieval Art* (London: Reaktion, 1992), 18.

to study images."[16] Hence, Lowden perpetuates the same assumptions about the function of marginalia and miniatures in medieval manuscripts as Hutter and, perhaps unintentionally, Camille. However, scholarship to date has not engaged the implicit conundrum here: these images *do* exist within texts primed for liturgical use, and they consciously and self-reflexively deploy the cross-sensory use of a multimedia manuscript as a springboard for comment and reflection. My interest here is how images operate on the peripheries of vision and how they are composed, placed, and designed to work precisely within the context of this focus during recitation, where they are not the subject of direct contemplation.

Another important conundrum must also be confronted. Surveying the corpus of extant Byzantine manuscripts, Nancy Patterson Ševčenko has observed that the majority of Byzantine illustrated books were liturgically oriented: lectionaries, books of the Divine Liturgy, liturgical rolls, Psalters, synaxaria, menologia, saints' lives, hymnbooks, sermons, and homilies.[17] While many of these books may have had religious functions outside the liturgy, they all share a pronounced oral character, either in the performance of the liturgy or in private prayer. Outside of these liturgical manuscripts, the full Bible was rarely illustrated (the only example extant, partially preserved, is the tenth-century Leo Bible), and individual books of the Bible that are illustrated appear to be intended for private devotion. Hundreds of illustrated Gospels exist, although the images are usually limited to portraits of the four Evangelists.[18]

Secular texts and their illustrations may provide the most intriguing information, since they suggest reasons why images were deployed as tools. For example, ancient texts were rarely illustrated. Homer is an exception, but only before the fifth century CE. It is particularly interesting that Old Testament Octateuchs, when illuminated, have more in common with the twelfth-century Madrid Skylitzes, the only illustrated historical chronicle,

[16] John Lowden, *The Jaharis Gospel Lectionary: The Story of a Byzantine Book* (New York: Metropolitan Museum of Art, 2009), 17.

[17] Nancy Ševčenko, "Illuminating the Liturgy: Illustrated Service Books in Byzantium," in Linda Safran (ed.), *Heaven on Earth: Art and the Church in Byzantium* (University Park: Pennsylvania State University Press, 1998), 186–228.

[18] Thus, most of the religious texts that do exist, as Ševčenko aptly notes, suggest a liturgical function or a private devotional function, such as in the case of Psalters; the latter are attested in the work of Georgi Parpulov as well. Georgi Parpulov, "The Psalms and Personal Piety in Byzantium," in Paul Magdalino and Robert Nelson (eds.), *The Old Testament in Byzantium* (Washington, DC: Dumbarton Oaks, 2010), 77–105. See also Georgi Parpulov, "Toward a History of Byzantine Psalters," PhD dissertation, University of Chicago (2004).

than with liturgical manuscripts.[19] These extraliturgical texts appear to take on a different order of illumination that fits their own purposes. Thus, illustration of narrative alone does not convincingly explain why the Gospel lectionary is so often illustrated. The crux of illustration again appears to be connected to its capability to code the use, application, and performance of the information contained in the volume. It is therefore not surprising that the secular texts most frequently illustrated were how-to manuals on farming, hunting, surgery, and siege warfare; herbals; bird and flower books; and geography books. Apparently, the books that occasioned illumination in Byzantium were those whose subject matter had to be visualized to be comprehended and imitated: all – particularly the so-called how-to manuals – were concerned with conditions of practice rooted in process.[20] In other words, there seems to be a correlation between visualization, emulation, and orality that emerges from an implicit comprehension of the image's capability to exist beyond logics of depiction or visual representation, instead enacting a certain unfolding of the subject matter in the user's mind and actions.

Unlike Psalters, Gospel books, collections of homilies, or secular texts that might easily be stereotyped as objects of private devotion or erudite curiosity, the Gospel lectionary in particular undercuts assumptions that these costly volumes must have had some purpose other than daily or at least habitual use in the Divine Liturgy. These volumes are often quite large, intended for the easy recitation of the Gospels from the ambo of the Byzantine church by a chanter; and because they excerpt and organize the Gospels according to liturgical needs, they seem all the less relevant to the realm of private devotion. At the same time, the question remains of how easily miniatures and marginalia would be seen or comprehended by a chanter who must recite the text aloud in a linear manner, rather than having the luxury of meandering across the page during pauses in his personal reading and contemplation.[21] Nevertheless, as this volume will

[19] See John Lowden, "Illustrated Octateuch Manuscripts: A Byzantine Phenomenon," in Magdalino and Nelson (eds.), *Old Testament in Byzantium*, 107–52; John Lowden, *The Octateuchs: A Study in Byzantine Manuscript Illustration* (University Park: Pennsylvania State University Press, 1992). See also Kurt Weitzmann and Massimo Bernabò, *The Byzantine Octateuchs*, 2 vols. (Princeton University Press, 1999). On the Madrid Skylitzes, see Elena Boeck, *Imagining the Byzantine Past: The Perception of History in the Illustrated Manuscripts of Skylitzes and Manasses* (Cambridge University Press, 2015).

[20] For a study of the role of visualizing technical knowledge, see Courtney Roby, *Technical Ekphrasis in Ancient Science and Literature: The Written Machine between Alexandria and Rome* (Cambridge University Press, 2016).

[21] On the reading of the Bible in Byzantium more generally, see Ernst Gamillscheg, "Die Lektüre der Bibel in Byzanz: Kurze Beobachtungen zu einigen griechischen Handschriften mit

show, the design program and its complexities thrive precisely on this type of visuality, in which the errant and contemplative gaze is delimited by the necessities of oral performance.

The Illuminated Lectionary's Audience and Reception

Most studies available on marginal images and manuscripts are premised on a slow hermeneutic, a careful process of reading that enacts the margin's exegetical and subversive potentials. While the monk reads and rests, for example, the monstrous creeps out from the capitals in a cloister, as in Thomas Dale's work on St-Michel-de-Cuxa; or, through the slow process of reading, discussion, and contemplation, the abstract ornamentation in the *Taifa* Palaces of Spain emerges in Cynthia Robinson's studies as a complex paradisiacal vision.[22] After all, the binary-shattering potential of the margin in Michael Camille's own work was revealed through the intervisuality of the center and the periphery. Comprehending the artistic elaboration of the extratextual space requires the ability to look at it closely and over time, something wholly impossible for someone pressing through the linear recitation of the lectionary.

Because it contains the daily readings of the Gospel that are to be proclaimed, the lectionary is an oral text par excellence.[23] What then is the role of reception for such a manuscript, and who composed its audience? For Mary-Lyon Dolezal, for example, the images of the Dionysiou Gospel lectionary "illuminate and enliven" the Gospel passages throughout the liturgical year for the patriarch of Constantinople – and "for him alone."[24] Dolezal's statement betrays an art-historical emphasis on the purely visual,

Bibelkatenen," in Claudia Rapp and Andreas Külzer (eds.), *The Bible in Byzantium: Appropriation, Adaptation, Interpretation* (Göttingen: Vandenhoeck & Ruprecht, 2018), 39–46.

22 Thomas E.A. Dale, "Monsters, Corporeal Deformities, and Phantasms in the Cloister of St-Michel-de-Cuxa," *Art Bulletin* 83:3 (September 2001): 402–36; Cynthia Robinson, "Seeing Paradise: Metaphor and Vision in the *Taifa* Palace Architecture," *Gesta* 36:2 (1997): 145–55; Cynthia Robinson, "Marginal Ornament: Poetics, Mimesis, and Devotion in the Palace of the Lions," *Muqarnas* 25 (2008): 185–214.

23 The Gospel lectionary, out of all manuscript types, is the most orally driven in the intentions of its use; hence according to Michael Camille's model discussed above, it should be the last one to support extensive illuminations. Implicit here is the idea that these images simply illustrate the text, serving as a one-to-one depiction of the words on the page, an aspect of illumination that Kurt Weitzmann discussed at length in his formal genealogy of the Byzantine manuscript's format. See Kurt Weitzmann, *Illustrations in Roll and Codex: A Study of the Origin and Method of Text Illustration* (Princeton University Press, 1947), esp. 130–81.

24 Mary-Lyon Dolezal, "Illuminating the Liturgical Word: Text and Image in a Decorated Lectionary (Mount Athos, Dionysiou Monastery, cod. 587)," *Word & Image* 12:1 (1996): 23–60, at 60.

an assumption that illuminated manuscripts are aesthetic objects, sensually experienced through eyesight alone as works of art. In other words, as suggested above, the illumination of the Gospel lectionary is understood as producing a form of conspicuous consumption for an elite patron.[25]

Given its function in the Divine Liturgy, we must understand that the manuscript would have been put to use by a single reader when he took it from the altar and placed it on the ambo for the daily lection. This is also the only moment at which we have any clear indication that the lectionary would have been opened; when a second lectionary was enthroned upon the patriarch's seat during the Easter and Epiphany vigils, it was presumably kept shut. That one of these lavishly illuminated manuscripts (today still in fairly good condition) might have served this role is always possible. During the Easter vigil, the patriarch also would have read the lectionary from within the sanctuary, and these illuminated lectionaries might have also been put to such uses. But neither circumstance sheds any light on the high quality and large quantity of images in these works. They feature decorative programs covering the course of the entire liturgical year; while important feast days might be given special attention, there is no clear emphasis or sign of priority that could enable us to securely attribute their use to only a particular feast cycle or particular date when they would have had a larger audience.

Thus, this study takes the chanter as these manuscripts' primary user and viewer. In other words, I assume that rather than enlivening the Gospels solely for the patriarch, these images enlivened the Gospel for the reader – but not for the reader alone. Since the reader was often accompanied by subdeacons carrying candles to illuminate the Gospels, they too would have served as a likely audience for these remarkable manuscripts and their illuminations. Indeed, while the chanter would have been following the text carefully in order to declaim the words in

[25] As Kurt Weitzmann described it in 1954, "Considering the importance of the lectionary as the main book of the orthodox service, it is not surprising to find the Greek Church focusing its artistic energies on its embellishment by means of textual illustrations as well as the decoration of its covers with gold, enamels, and jewels." This production-centered argument may be useful from an economic perspective, understanding that the goods and labor necessary to produce a visually elaborate manuscript would increase its cost and thus make it a commodity of limited availability. Kurt Weitzmann, "The Constantinopolitan Lectionary, Morgan 639," in Dorothy Miner (ed.), *Studies in Art and Literature for Belle da Costa Greene* (Princeton University Press, 1954), 358–73, at 358. On Byzantine book covers and their decoration, see John Lowden, "The Word Made Visible: The Exterior of the Early Christian Book as Visual Argument," in W.E. Klingshirn and L. Safran (eds.), *The Early Christian Book* (Washington, DC: Catholic University of America, 2007), 13–47.

conformity with the musical notation, those accessory figures beside him would have been able to contemplate the miniatures and marginalia in a slow and focused manner. Nevertheless, I will argue in what follows that such images were in a sense akin to the chant marks, shaping the ways in which the text was proclaimed by the reader. Like the marginalia, ekphonetic notations lie on the peripheries of the reader's vision, and both require that they be perceived simultaneously with the text. I will show the ways in which the images, by giving visual emphasis to scenes and producing complex permutations of the story, could have molded how the reader himself imagined the scene and thus how he recited it to the congregation. Given that public recitation was the primary manner in which Byzantine audiences consumed texts, the proper delivery of a text was highly prized and valued, particularly in the eleventh century.[26] A good reader had to know the narrative very well in order to give proper emphasis to words and phrases, express the complex emotions of the characters, and communicate the important aspects of the reading.

This approach also suggests that the lectionary's marginal illustrations are in effect not necessarily confined to the page alone. According to Byzantine theories of representation, the goal of a good recitation was precisely to turn listeners into viewers.[27] The late fourth-century rhetorician Aphthonios attracted several commentaries throughout the Byzantine period. In his *Progymnasmata*, Aphthonios defines description or ekphrasis as follows: "Ekphrasis is a descriptive language, bringing what is shown vividly before the eyes" (Ἔκφρασίς ἐστι λόγος περιηγηματικὸς ὑπ᾽ ὄψιν ἄγων ἐναργῶς τὸ δηλούμενον).[28] The key to ekphrasis as a rhetorical technique was a desire to overstep the boundaries of linguistic representation and "bring vividly before the eyes" (ὑπ᾽ ὄψιν ἄγων ἐναργῶς) the things being signified. Yet, as the third-century Nicholas of Myra carefully explains further, ekphrasis "tries to turn hearers into spectators" (ἣ δὲ πειρᾶται θεατὰς τοὺς ἀκούοντας ἐργάζεσθαι).[29]

[26] On Byzantine reading and performance in the eleventh century, see Floris Bernard, *Writing and Reading Byzantine Secular Poetry, 1025–1081* (Oxford University Press, 2014).

[27] For a study on the interplay between rhetorical and visual theories of representation in Byzantium and relevant bibliography on the ancient, late antique, and Byzantine counterparts to these theories, see Roland Betancourt, *Sight, Touch, and Imagination in Byzantium* (Cambridge University Press, 2018).

[28] Aphthonios, *Progymnasmata*, 216.20–24, ed. Hugo Rabe, Rhetores Graeci 10 (Leipzig: Teubner, 1926), 36–37; modified trans. George A. Kennedy, *Progymnasmata: Greek Textbooks of Prose Composition and Rhetoric* (Atlanta: Society of Biblical Literature, 2003), 117.

[29] Nicholas of Myra, *Progymnasmata*, ed. J. Felten, Rhetores Graeci 11 (Leipzig: Teubner, 1913), 68; trans. Kennedy, *Progymnasmata*, 166.

A crucial claim of this book is that these images were not for the reader alone; rather, through the delivery of the Gospel text via the reader's chanting, these images were communicated to the listeners, who were deeply invested in imagining what they heard and visualizing the narratives with careful attention to detail and clarity – the highly valued elements that contributed to the "vividness" (ἐνάργεια) of a story.[30] Thus, when images in the lectionaries display confusion about characters and narrative, they often are reflecting confusions inherent in the excerpted text itself. In other words, the marginalia often literally visualize the Gospel text, even retaining the possible confusions and misreadings of a reader/listener as they slowly make their way through the text. For this reason, this book is divided into two parts, one focusing on the details of the manuscript and its marginalia and the other focusing on the oral recitation of the text and its polyvalence in the liturgical space and architecture of Hagia Sophia.

My premise is that the images on the page were capable of being transmitted per se through orality to an attuned audience whose participation in the liturgy demanded an active perceptual focus, in accordance with the deacon's exhortation before the reading: "Wisdom! Let us attend!" (Σοφία, πρόσχωμεν). This focus on the aural text, which required audience members to visualize and imagine the narratives in their minds, could sort out, interpret, and unify a variety of sensual data into cognitive images. In this fundamental operation of the Gospel's visual and aural representation one confronts the power and implications of what I will refer to as the perceptual habits or *habitus* of Byzantine viewers in the liturgy, which amounted to a sensorial epistemology for understanding spoken word, images, and architectural decoration. The reader's interaction with the manuscript in the Divine Liturgy is only a small part of the existence of the manuscript's images, which are distributed across painting, writing, chant, and the listeners' imaginings.

[30] On vividness in classical theories of representation, see Roos Meijering, *Literary and Rhetorical Theories in Greek Scholia* (Groningen: Egbert Forsten, 1987), esp. 39–44; René Nünlist, *The Ancient Critic at Work: Terms and Concepts of Literary Criticism in Greek Scholia* (Cambridge University Press, 2009), esp. 194–97; Nina Otto, *Enargeia: Untersuchung zur Charakteristik alexandrinischer Dichtung* (Stuttgart: Franz Steiner Verlag, 2009); Alessandra Manieri, *L'immagine poetica nella teoria degli antichi: Phantasia ed enargeia* (Pisa: Istituti editoriali e poligrafici internazionali, 1998). On the endurance of these theories in Byzantium, see Stratis Papaioannou, "Byzantine *Enargeia* and Theories of Representation," *Byzantinoslavica* 3 (2011): 48–60; Betancourt, *Sight, Touch, and Imagination*, 199–242.

This approach thus suggests a means of engagement with the Byzantine Gospel lectionary beyond the historical materialism evident in the language of scholars who view such manuscript illumination practices as a form of conspicuous consumption, thereby denying any function to these manuscripts' images. Rather than offering any further speculation on the potential viewership of such manuscripts, which unduly emphasizes a privileged patron with direct visual access to the manuscript's folios, I seek to move past such a limiting and positivist outlook as I consider how the images depicted on the page could be conjured up in the minds of listeners and in the architectural details of the liturgical space.

The Lectionary in Sound and Architecture

Artifacts have a fungible reality to them that we as perceivers experience with our senses and process through perception. Lectionaries, their images, and the architectures and performances in which they are set are neither static nor isolated but feed off one another and conjure up new and different meanings across their different arrangements. These various artifacts generate habitual understandings and realities that have an effect on our lives and often allow themselves to be understood as agentic and animate. The alleged "turn" in art history that can be haphazardly coined the "phenomenological" (and overlapping with "materiality,"[31] "new

[31] Over the past fifteen years, the phenomenological turn has led scholars to reevaluate our sources critically and also imaginatively recreate lost worlds filled with the textures of sensory effects and affects. In archaeology, for example, this approach grew alongside the exploration of materiality in the first decade of the 2000s in the work of Christopher Tilley, Daniel Miller, Lynn Meskell, and many others. On materiality in archaeology, see, for instance, Christopher Tilley, *A Phenomenology of Landscape: Places, Paths and Monuments* (Oxford: Berg, 1997); Daniel Miller (ed.), *Materiality* (Durham, NC: Duke University Press, 2005); and Lynn Meskell, *Object Worlds in Ancient Egypt: Material Biographies Past and Present* (Oxford: Berg, 2004). See also Tim Ingold, "Materials against Materiality," *Archaeological Dialogues* 14:1 (2007): 1–16; Elizabeth Demarrais, "The Materialisation of Culture," in Elizabeth Demarrais, Chris Godsen, and A. Colin Renfrew (eds.), *Rethinking Materiality: The Engagement of Mind with the Material World* (Cambridge: McDonald Institute, 2004), 11–22; Chris Godsen, "What Do Objects Want?," *Journal of Archaeological Method and Theory* 12:3 (2005): 193–211. For a survey, see Carl Knappett, "Materiality," in Ian Hodder (ed.), *Archaeological Theory Today*, 2nd edn (Cambridge: Polity Press, 2012), 188–207; and Carl Knappett, "Materiality in Archaeological Theory," in Claire Smith (ed.), *Encyclopedia of Global Archaeology* (New York: Springer, 2014), 4700–08.

Materiality was marked by a desire to understand the interchange between the material realities of objects and how those material realities were perceived by the senses. These conversations (albeit largely absent in art-historical discourse until the early 2010s) have led in

materialism,"[32] and the "ontological"[33] is not so much a turn as it is a syncretic push to understand the textures of discursive and cognitive exchange that happens between objects in their full reality. It acknowledges that our objects and things are never just material, never just conceptual, but always inherently both. In this regard, the phenomenological turn has more in common with a structural shift toward interdisciplinarity in academic training than it does with

recent years to the consequential intersection of phenomenology and ontology. Early in art history, see James Elkins, "On Some Limits of Materiality in Art History," *31: Das Magazin des Instituts für Theorie* [Zürich] 12 (2008): 24–30.

32 Moving away from an interest in perception and experience, ideated loosely through the lens (or specter) of figures like Henri Bergson and Maurice Merleau-Ponty, more recent investigations in "phenomenology" have centered on matter and object. They have turned to Martin Heidegger's appropriately enmeshed phenomenological ontology, Jean-Paul Sartre's exploration of consciousness and experience, and the distribution, networking, and dispersal of being and agency, as exemplified in the work of Alfred Gell, Bruno Latour, and Ian Hodder. See Alfred Gell, *Art and Agency: An Anthropological Theory* (Oxford: Clarendon Press, 1998); Bruno Latour, *Reassembling the Social: An Introduction to Actor-Network-Theory* (New York: Oxford University Press, 2005); and Ian Hodder, *Entangled: An Archaeology of the Relationships between Humans and Things* (Malden, MA: Wiley-Blackwell, 2012).

In other branches of the humanities, such as literary studies, the inner lives of things have been theorized by figures like Bill Brown, and Jane Bennett has drawn us to the vitality of matter. See Bill Brown, "Thing Theory," *Critical Inquiry* 28:1 (2001): 1–22; and Jane Bennett, *Vibrant Matter: A Political Ecology of Things* (Durham, NC: Duke University Press, 2010). See also Alex Preda, "The Turn to Things: Arguments for a Sociological Theory of Things," *Sociological Quarterly* 40:2 (1999): 347–66; and Bjørnar Olsen, "Material Culture after Text: Re-membering Things," *Norwegian Archaeological Review* 36:3 (2003): 87–104.

These queries have productively built on earlier studies in anthropology on the social life of objects by Arjun Appadurai and Igor Kopytoff. See Arjun Appadurai (ed.), *The Social Life of Things: Commodities in Cultural Perspective* (Cambridge University Press, 1986); and Igor Kopytoff, "The Cultural Biography of Things: Commoditization as Process," in Appadurai (ed.), *Social Life of Things*, 64–92. This history speaks of the object as a medium for the embodiment of social and cultural change, ventriloquized as life. The phenomenological dimension of these various orientations has been deepened by a matured thinking on animacy, discourse, and the inertial draw of matter itself by queer theorists like Mel Y. Chen, Sara Ahmed, and Karen Barad. See Mel Y. Chen, *Animacies: Biopolitics, Racial Mattering, and Queer Affect* (Durham, NC: Duke University Press, 2012); Sara Ahmed, *Queer Phenomenology: Orientations, Objects, Others* (Durham, NC: Duke University Press, 2006); and Karen Barad, *Meeting the Universe Halfway: Quantum Physics and the Entanglement of Matter and Meaning* (Durham, NC: Duke University Press, 2007). See also Barad, "Posthumanist Performativity: Toward an Understanding of How Matter Comes to Matter," *Signs: Journal of Women in Culture and Society* 28:3 (Spring 2003): 801–31.

33 It must not go without mention that object-oriented ontology has also been an important part of this conversation, found in a plurality of iterations from Ian Bogost to Timothy Morton. This hotly debated approach not only has considered matter and the material, the thing and the object, but also has sought to conceptualize a posthuman methodology for the being of objects, one that is simultaneously material, "thingy," and phenomenological on its own terms. While these latter approaches are most closely culled from Heidegger's phenomenological ontology, they have engaged and grappled with the bounds of scholarship, academic writing, and the

phenomenology, the senses, objects, things, or any single one of these discrete categories.[34]

Therefore, in order to consider the Gospel lectionary as an object whose text and images are partaken of within an oral and embodied performance by a reader before a congregation, it becomes necessary to produce a more expansive and interdisciplinary model of research that can encompass the promiscuous permutations between text and image, orality and aurality, sound and acoustics, architecture and space. The first step is that this book must go beyond looking at manuscript illumination on its own, and consequently also rethink the relations between word and image. It also becomes necessary to consider how chant, liturgical space, and architectural decorations on the peripheries of these lectionaries operated with and alongside the manuscripts. The performance of these texts and the liturgical spaces in which they were used contributed to the spectrums of meaning of these manuscripts' illuminations and vice versa. One crucial observation is that architecture and acoustics operated similarly to the plays found within the miniatures and marginalia of the lectionaries themselves. By sketching out patterns of use and resemblances with how

human interpretant. This has led to conversations around speculative realism, as in the writing of Steven Shaviro. See Ian Bogost, *Alien Phenomenology, or What It's Like to Be a Thing* (Minneapolis: University of Minnesota Press, 2012); and Timothy Morton, *Hyperobjects: Philosophy and Ecology after the End of the World* (Minneapolis: University of Minnesota Press, 2013). See also Graham Harman, *Tool-Being: Heidegger and the Metaphysics of Objects* (Chicago: Open Court, 2002). On speculative realism and its extensive bibliography, see Steven Shaviro, *The Universe of Things: On Speculative Realism* (Minneapolis: University of Minnesota Press, 2014).

On a critique, see Rebekah Sheldon, "You Can't Have Me: Feminist Infiltrations in Object-Oriented Ontology," *Los Angeles Review of Books*, April 8, 2017, https://lareviewofbooks.org/article/you-cant-have-me-feminist-infiltrations-in-object-oriented-ontology; and Jordy Rosenberg, "The Molecularization of Sexuality: On Some Primitivisms of the Present," *Theory & Event* 17:2 (2014): n.p.

34 For a methodological survey of the "phenomenological turn," see Roland Betancourt, "Review of Bissera Pentcheva's *Hagia Sophia: Sound, Space, and Spirit in Byzantium* (University Park: Pennsylvania State University Press, 2017)," *Art Bulletin*, 101:4 (2019): 142–45. In art history, "the phenomenological" has largely served as a catchall term for excavating how sensory experience (beyond and around the visual) fits into a certain history of art. But, the phenomenological turn in the humanities has not been just phenomenological. Or rather, it has not been phenomenology as a misnomer for a return toward aesthetics, as in the work of Jacques Rancière, nor about sense perception alone. The phenomenological turn also should not be seen simply as a push against logocentrism or a crude reeling from the vertigo of poststructuralist deconstruction toward a desperate embrace of the concretely palpable. Instead, this turn in the humanities has taken form as an ongoing reorientation regarding how scholars perform scholarship and understand the vicissitudes of objects, embracing the facts that objects are perceptible matter, or at least relatively partake in it. See Jacques Rancière, *Aisthesis: Scenes from the Aesthetic Regime of Art*, trans. Zakir Paul (London: Verso, 2013).

text, image, performance, and space function, this book proposes a more dynamic way of looking at the intersection of visual culture and performance in the Byzantine world.

This interdisciplinary approach has only become possible over the course of the past two decades with the rise of studies in Byzantine liturgy and musicology. Western scholarship has all but neglected Byzantine music, hymnography, and chant, even though these practices have been a part of a living tradition in Eastern Orthodoxy, actively being preserved and expanded in the post-Byzantine worlds. In the early twentieth century, Egon Wellesz, Carsten Høeg, and H. J. W. Tillyard's foundational scholarship on Byzantine musicology and chant articulated the essential notational signs, rules, and rubrics of this musical tradition.[35] Recently, contributions by scholars such as Christian Troelsgård have continued to expand upon these building blocks, allowing us to approach earlier periods of Byzantine chant, particularly that of Middle Byzantium and its ekphonetic notation and neumes.[36] Simultaneously, the work of Alexander Lingas and Sandra Martani on the intersection of chant and liturgy has established the foundations for understanding the nuanced relationship between ritual, performance, and acoustics.[37]

[35] Egon Wellesz, *A History of Byzantine Music and Hymnography*, 2nd edition (Oxford: Clarendon Press, 1961); Carsten Høeg, *La notation ekphonétique* (Copenhagen: Levin & Munksgaard, 1935); H.J.W. Tillyard, "The Problem of Byzantine Neumes," *Journal of Hellenic Studies* 41:1 (1921): 29–49. See also Jean-Baptiste Thibaut, *Origine byzantine de la notation neumatique de l'Église latine* (Paris: A. Picard et Fils, 1907); and Jean-Baptiste Thibaut, *Monuments de la notation ekphonétique et hagiopolite de l'église Grecque* (Saint Petersburg: Kügelgen, Glitsch, 1913). For a historiographic summary, see Diane Touliatos, "Henry Julius Wetenhall Tillyard," in Helen Damico (ed.), *Medieval Scholarship: Biographical Studies on the Formation of a Discipline*, vol. 3 (New York: Garland, 2000), 153–64; Miloš Velimirović, "Egon Wellesz and the Study of Byzantine Chant," *Musical Quarterly* 62:2 (1976): 265–77.

[36] Christian Troelsgård, *Byzantine Neumes: A New Introduction to the Middle Byzantine Musical Notation* (Copenhagen: Museum Tusculanum Press, 2011).

[37] See Alexander Lingas, "How Musical was the 'Sung Office'? Some Observations on the Ethos of the Byzantine Cathedral Rite," in Ivan Moody and Maria Takala-Roszczenko (eds.), *The Traditions of Orthodox Music: Proceedings of the First International Conference on Orthodox Church Music, University of Joensuu, Finland, 13–19 June 2005* (Joensuu: University of Joensuu & International Society for Orthodox Church Music, 2007), 217–34; Alexander Lingas, "Medieval Byzantine Chant and the Sound of Orthodoxy," in Andrew Louth and Augustine Casiday (eds.), *Byzantine Orthodoxies: Papers from the 36th Spring Symposium of Byzantine Studies* (Aldershot: Ashgate, 2006), 131–50; and Alexander Lingas, "From Earth to Heaven: The Changing Soundscape of Byzantine Liturgy," in Mark Jackson and Claire Nesbitt (eds.), *Experiencing Byzantium: Papers from the 44th Spring Symposium of the Society for the Promotion of Byzantine Studies* (Aldershot: Ashgate, 2013), 311–58. See also Sandra Martani, "The Theory and Practice of Ekphonetic Notation: The Manuscript, Sinait. Gr. 213," *Plainsong and Medieval Music* 12 (2003): 15–42; Sandra Martani, "Words and Music in the Greek Gospel Lectionaries," in Nina-Maria Wanek (ed.), *Psaltike: Neue Studien zur byzantinischen Musik. Festschrift für Gerda Wolfram* (Vienna: Praesens, 2011), 219–31.

In the past decade, the sonic or acoustic turn in Byzantine studies has been led by art historians and literary scholars who have focused on the interplay between the performance of texts and the sonic environments in which performances occur, from the recitation of poetry and theater to the Divine Liturgy.[38] For example, Amy Papalexandrou's research on architecture and acoustics has been ongoing, alongside Bissera Pentcheva's work on Hagia Sophia and "aural architecture" in Byzantium more broadly.[39] Together, this research has radically opened up generative areas of investigation. This work is also being furthered by Sharon Gerstel's "Soundscapes of Byzantium" project, which features not only different approaches to acoustic reconstruction, but also a more sustained interest in the interplay between architectural decoration and acoustics.[40] From literary

[38] This sonic or acoustic turn can also be observed across ancient and Western medieval scholarship, as in the work of Shane Butler, Alex Purves, Maurizio Betini, and Guy Lachenaud. And, although Western medieval musicology has received a great deal of attention across the twentieth century, scholars have been recently interested in studying the intersection of music with art. This interdisciplinary approach also has paid a great deal of attention to the role of site, architecture, and space, therefore seeking to emplace the dynamics of art and music, as seen in the work of Susan Boynton and Diane J. Reilly, Deborah Howard, and Niall Atkinson. On the ancient and medieval worlds, see Shane Butler, *The Ancient Phonograph* (Brooklyn: Zone, 2015); Shane Butler and Alex Purves (eds.), *Synaesthesia and the Ancient Senses* (Durham, NC: Acumen, 2013); Maurizio Bettini, *Voci: Antropologia sonora del mondo antico* (Turin: Einaudi, 2008); and Guy Lachenaud, *Les routes de la voix: L'antiquité grecque et le mystère de la voix* (Paris: Belles Lettres, 2013). On the Western medieval and early modern worlds, see Susan Boynton and Diane J. Reilly (eds.), *Resounding Images: Medieval Intersections of Art, Music, and Sound* (Turnhout: Brepols, 2015); Deborah Howard, *Sound and Space in Renaissance Venice* (New Haven, CT: Yale University Press, 2010); Niall Atkinson, *The Noisy Renaissance: Sound, Architecture, and Florentine Urban Life* (University Park: Pennsylvania State University Press, 2016). See also Henning Laugerud, Hans Henrik Lohfert Jorgensen, and Laura Katrine Skinnebach (eds.), *The Saturated Sensorium: Principles of Perception and Mediation in the Middle Ages* (Aarhus University Press, 2015).

[39] Amy Papalexandrou, "The Past Is Noise: Architectural Contexts and the Soundways of Byzantium," paper presented at Byzantine Studies Conference, University of Pennsylvania, 2010; Amy Papalexandrou, "Perceptions of Sound and Sonic Environments across the Byzantine Acoustic Horizon," in Susan Ashbrook Harvey and Margaret Mullett (eds.), *Knowing Bodies, Passionate Souls: Sense Perception in Byzantium* (Washington, DC: Dumbarton Oaks, 2017), 67–85. Bissera Pentcheva, *Hagia Sophia: Sound, Space, and Spirit in Byzantium* (University Park: Pennsylvania State University Press, 2017); and Bissera Pentcheva (ed.), *Aural Architecture in Byzantium: Music, Acoustics, and Ritual* (London: Routledge, 2018). See also David J. Knight, "The Archaeoacoustics of a Sixth-Century Christian Structure: San Vitale, Ravenna," in Raquel Jiménez, Rupert Till, and Mark Howell (eds.), *Music and Ritual: Bridging Material and Living Cultures* (Berlin: Publications of the ICTM Study Group on Music Archaeology, 2013), 133–46.

[40] Sharon E.J. Gerstel, Chris Kyriakakis, Konstantinos T. Raptis, Spyridon Antonopoulos, and James Donahue, "Soundscapes of Byzantium: The Acheiropoietos Basilica and the Cathedral of Hagia Sophia in Thessaloniki," *Hesperia: The Journal of the American School of Classical Studies at Athens* 87:1 (2018): 177–213. See also Spyridon Antonopoulos, Sharon E.J. Gerstel, Chris

studies, scholars such as Emmanuel Bourbouhakis, Niels Gaul, Stratis Papaioannou, and many others, have called for a more astute ear to the subtleties and realities of Byzantine literature as an oral and aural performance.[41] These concerns have not been new in Byzantine studies given the extensive discussion on reading and orality/aurality from the perspectives of both literary history and textual criticism.[42] In other words, they fit into a longer and well-established interest in the dynamics between texts, images, and spaces in various facets of the Byzantine world.

This project is therefore deeply indebted to this research and the foundation which it has established to look at and consider the dynamics of the Gospel lectionary as a text written upon an illuminated manuscript that is to be performed during the liturgy in a particular architectural space and setting. Conceptually and theoretically, however, this work is most deeply indebted to the rigorous and interdisciplinary research that has been done in and around sound studies, which much of this literature on Byzantine soundscapes does not engage. In conceptualizing models of error, misdirection, and failure, my thinking is deeply indebted to the extensive literature over the past decade on the modern and premodern worlds regarding disharmony, noise, and cacophony.[43] This work, alongside Bogost's theory

Kyriakakis, Konstantinos T. Raptis, and James Donahue, "Soundscapes of Byzantium," *Speculum* 92:S1 (2017): S321–35.

41 Emmanuel Bourbouhakis, "Rhetoric and Performance," in Paul Stephenson (ed.), *The Byzantine World* (London: Routledge, 2010), 175–87; Andrew Walker White, *Performing Orthodox Ritual in Byzantium* (Cambridge University Press, 2015); Niels Gaul, "Performative Reading in the Late Byzantine *Theatron*," in Teresa Shawcross and Ida Toth (eds.), *Reading in the Byzantine Empire and Beyond* (Cambridge University Press, 2018), 215–33; Stratis Papaioannou, "Readers and Their Pleasures," in Stratis Papaioannou (ed.), *Oxford Handbook of Byzantine Literature* (Oxford University Press, forthcoming).

42 See Wolfram Hörandner, *Der Prosarhythmus in der rhetorischen Literatur der Byzantiner* (Vienna: Verlag der Osterreichischen Akademie der Wissenschaften, 1981); Herbert Hunger, *Schreiben und Lesen in Byzanz: Die byzantinische Buchkultur* (Munich: C.H. Beck, 1989); Guglielmo Cavallo, *Lire à Byzance*, trans. P. Odorico and A. Segonds (Paris: Belles Lettres, 2006); Diether Roderich Reinsch, "The History of Editing Byzantine Historiographical Texts," in Stephenson (ed.), *Byzantine World*, 435–44; Mary B. Cunningham, "Messages in Context: The Reading of Sermons in Byzantine Churches and Monasteries," in Angeliki Lymberopoulou (ed.), *Images of the Byzantine World: Visions, Messages and Meanings: Studies Presented to Leslie Brubaker* (Burlington, VT: Ashgate, 2011), 83–98; Vessela Valivitcharska, *Rhetoric and Rhythm in Byzantium: The Sound of Persuasion* (Cambridge University Press, 2013); and Shawcross and Toth (eds.), *Reading in the Byzantine Empire*.

43 See Daniel Heller-Roazen, *The Fifth Hammer: Pythagoras and the Disharmony of the World* (Brooklyn: Zone, 2011); Hillel Schwartz, *Making Noise: From Babel to the Big Bang & Beyond* (Brooklyn: Zone, 2011); Veit Erlmann, *Reason and Resonance: A History of Modern Aurality* (Brooklyn: Zone, 2010); Peter Krapp, *Noise Channels: Glitch and Error in Digital Culture* (Minneapolis: University of Minnesota Press, 2011); and Brian Kane, *Sound Unseen: Acousmatic Sound in Theory and Practice* (New York: Oxford University Press, 2014).

of "procedural rhetoric" (discussed above), not only defines how I conceive of the acoustic dimension of reading, ritual, and space, but it has also left an indelible mark on my own theorization of iconography and the bounds of the image.

Approaching the lectionary as a form of Byzantine "media" is as familiar to us and as different to our expectations as the term "new media" today might suggest. This fact necessitates that we think through fruitful contemporary models that have struggled with understanding "new" media by working to question the newness of "new" media, to demonstrate the ongoing processes of remediation across mediums, and to destabilize the divisions between inscriptive and representative technologies by grounding human agency and performance, as Lisa Gitelman, Jay David Bolter, Richard Grusin, Henry Jenkins, and countless others have explored over the past two decades.[44]

Throughout this book, I repeatedly struggle with terms to encompass the fluid dynamics I see at work here: across different types of images in a manuscript, across the texts into which they are set, across the performances that define, contest, and revise them, and across the architectures and liturgical fixtures that affect their reading and are altered by their reading. Images here become not just the things painted in colors next to handwriting on a page, but rather the flux of painting, oral recitation, aural imagination, and the spaces that symbolize and depict the elements of those stories. By considering the joint operation of images, text, sound, and architecture within the context of the Divine Liturgy, this book asks: How can an image on the edge of a page or an architectural frame abandon its stable identity? Furthermore, how can this operation be enriched through iconographic methods that can richly articulate the role of confusion, misdirection, misunderstanding, and varying interpretations regarding images? The unifying conceptual force in this book is the polyvalence of images.

In this flux across text, image, sound, and architecture, the imagination plays a crucial role, but so too do notions of personhood, identity, and

[44] See Geoffrey B. Pingree and Lisa Gitelman, "What's New about New Media?," in Geoffrey B. Pingree and Lisa Gitelman (eds.), *New Media, 1740–1915* (Cambridge, MA: MIT Press, 2003), xi–xxii; Jay David Bolter and Richard Grusin, *Remediation: Understanding New Media* (Cambridge, MA: MIT Press, 1998); Lisa Gitelman, *Always Already New: Media, History, and the Data of Culture* (Cambridge, MA: MIT Press, 2006); Henry Jenkins, *Convergence Culture: Where Old and New Media Collide* (New York: NYU Press, 2006). See also Lev Manovich, *The Language of New Media* (Cambridge, MA: MIT Press, 2001); Brendan Keogh, *A Play of Bodies: How We Perceive Videogames* (Cambridge, MA: MIT Press, 2018).

community that emerge throughout and across the various chapters of this book. Just as Derek Krueger's work on early Christian and Byzantine subjectivity has drawn our attention to the interplay between writing and holiness, liturgy and subjecthood, this volume also shares an interest in these fundamental matters – namely, the intersection of sound, community, and identity – that have been at the core of sound studies as a discipline since its inception. These questions are not only critical in R. Murray Schafer's notion of the "soundscape," but also have been generatively explored in sound studies around the construction of place-making at the intersection of racial, religious, and cultural identity in the writings of Josh Kun, Charles Hirschkind, and Steven Feld, along with countless others across media, cinema, and queer studies.[45] This literature builds on a long and complex history that looks at the multifaceted and amorphous role of sound in mid-twentieth-century continental philosophy, from Roland Barthes to Michel Chion, but ever-present as well in the works of Michel Foucault and Jacques Derrida.[46] For the sake of my readers, I have purged many of these thinkers from this volume, but their presence still remains.

A Roadmap from Text to Image, Sound to Architecture

This book is divided into two complementary parts, which take as their focus the lectionary as a manuscript and the lectionary as an oral and aural text in the liturgy, respectively. Although a neat division between text, image, and sound would be antithetical to the volume's mission, this structure enables us to delve deeply into a series of case studies that can properly show off the complexities of the lectionary without being

[45] See Josh Kun, *Audiotopia: Music, Race, and America* (Berkeley: University of California Press, 2005); Charles Hirschkind, *The Ethical Soundscape: Cassette Sermons and Islamic Counterpublics* (New York: Columbia University Press, 2006); Steven Feld, "Waterfalls of Song: An Acoustemology of Place Resounding in Bosavi, Papua New Guinea," in Steven Feld and Keith H. Basso (eds.), *Senses of Place* (Santa Fe, NM: School of American Research Press, 1996), 91–135; and Steven Feld, *Sound and Sentiment: Birds, Weeping, Poetics, and Song in Kaluli Expression*, 2nd edn (Philadelphia: University of Pennsylvania Press, 1990).

[46] On the voice, see Roland Barthes, "The Grain of the Voice," *Image-Music-Text*, trans. Stephen Heath (New York: Hill & Wang, 1977), 179–89; Michel Chion, *Audio-Vision: Sound on Screen*, trans. Claudia Gorbman (New York: Columbia University Press, 1994). On discourse, see Michel Foucault, "The Discourse on Language," *The Archaeology of Knowledge; and, The Discourse on Language*, trans. A.M. Sheridan Smith (New York: Pantheon, 1972), 215–38; Jacques Derrida, "Différance," *Speech and Phenomena, and Other Essays on Husserl's Theory of Signs*, trans. David Allison (Evanston, IL: Northwestern University Press, 1973), 129–60.

distracted by a desire for comprehensive or exhaustive coverage of its decorative program or manuscript typology.

In Part I, "The Lectionary: Image and Text," the aim is to introduce the lectionary as a manuscript that was intended to be publicly read and to consider how its various forms of illumination affected the acts of reading, speaking, and imagining the Gospel narratives. Chapter 1 examines the role of public reading during the Divine Liturgy. Specifically, we begin by looking at a homily by the patriarch Photios of Constantinople to consider how the meaning of a text would have slowly unfolded for the congregation as members listened closely. Photios is one of the earliest known promoters of historiated initials in the Byzantine world, and his homily coincides with the early emergence of this decorative typology in the Constantinopolitan sphere. After a brief survey of the origins of these initials, we return to the function of sound, voice, and acoustics in the understanding of texts and images in the post-iconoclastic period. Stressing the importance of figural initials at the cusp between silence and sound at the start of a reading sets the scene for tracing the development of these initials in the period from their introduction in the ninth century to their proliferation in the lectionaries of the late eleventh century. The examples that follow are used to explore the ways in which eleventh-century initials and marginalia play with sonic elements of the text: on the one hand, we will focus on the interplay between initials and miniatures of the Evangelists in a way that stresses the text's orality and transcription; on the other hand, we will see how marginalia play with and emphasize the sound depicted within the Gospel narratives themselves, from Christ's speech to the cock's crow before Peter. Illuminators often went beyond just playing with the written text to home in on slippages between the look of the written text and the sound of the oral text, seemingly commenting on both.

The second chapter takes up the ways in which miniatures, marginalia, and initials encode different types of information for a reader, serving as a visual grammar and syntax. Here, we start by examining the two formulaic epigraphs that begin most of the Gospel lections, and that thus serve as the primary medium for the initial's illuminations. Doing so gives us a handle on the two main approaches taken by artists to these initials and to their corresponding marginalia, as they choose to stress either the aurality of Christ's words or the narrative moment in which the Gospel occurred. There is a particular and complex emphasis on speech, as those listening to Christ are often depicted in the margins as responding to his actions. To put these images into a broader context, we will examine how other types of manuscripts also featured illuminated initials that endeavored to represent in their pictures the very words to which they belonged. We thus see artists' desire to blur the lines between the text and the image it conjures up by presenting the two as one and the same, as when the initial of the word for "Earth" depicts a personification of the land or when the initial of the word for "Said" depicts a figure speaking. The same certainly could be said of other marginalia, which often try to represent the words that they are placed next to or that immediately follow them, in a sense playfully depicting in advance the subjects and characters that the reader is about to meet in the text. From here, the focus shifts as we look at how this logic changes across different types of illuminations. While the depictions in initials are usually fairly literal, miniatures often have the role of marking the feast day being celebrated in the liturgy, or summarizing the overarching narrative of the reading. The chapter concludes by looking briefly at the interplay between reading and the imagination, accentuating the way in which initials and marginalia specifically encourage readers to imagine the texts in their minds. Marginalia thereby make visible on the page the types of images that both the speaking reader and listening hearer would have imagined as they made their way through the Gospel story.

Building on these foundations, Chapter 3 looks at how these various functions of initials, miniatures, and marginalia enabled artists to create deeply complex and nuanced images that pushed at and played with the reader's knowledge of the text.[47] Emphasizing the lectionary's fragmented presentation of texts, the chapter concentrates on the way in which images often betray a self-conscious depiction of the types of misunderstandings and errors that readers might make while visualizing the text, since at times the identity of a character or the narrative details might not be fully explained in the lectionary until later in the reading, if at all. We begin this investigation by looking at the challenge of depicting the Godhead in the initial for John 1:18. I argue here that because initials often strove to depict the immediate things described by their words, Byzantine artists had a great deal of trouble depicting the "God no one has ever seen" – specifically, the opening letter of the word "God" (Θεόν). Working through the theological implications of depicting the Godhead himself and considering other examples in which Byzantine artists had to deal with a similar challenge, I examine how the various lectionaries approached the matter and what solutions they arrived at. The primary focus here is the Dionysiou Lectionary, which resolves this problem by depicting God as the Ancient of

[47] For an earlier and briefer version of this chapter, see Roland Betancourt, "Faltering Images: Failure and Error in Byzantine Manuscript Illumination," *Word & Image* 32:1 (2016): 1–20.

Days, a rare image in Byzantium, along with the Christ-child, placing beneath the image the figure of John the Evangelist gesturing up toward it. The answer here is one to which Byzantine artists since late antiquity commonly resorted: to depict the image of the Godhead as a sort of vision. Yet this investigation addresses the question of John the Evangelist's role here: he is depicted as the author of the Gospel reading, but he also can be textually confused with John the Baptist, whom this excerpt describes only as the John who bears witness to the light of God – a description that clearly resonates with John the Evangelist's own role in bearing witness to the deeds of the incarnate Christ through his Gospel.

Maneuvering through these textual confusions and permutations, the chapter underscores how these marginalia do not simply follow the iconographic tropes of either John but rather consciously and repeatedly play with the potential confusion attached to this figure and others. Special attention is paid to the associations made across the various marginal scenes, initials, and miniatures in the manuscript as they would have been seen over the course of the liturgical calendar. Hence, this chapter carefully unfolds how error, confusion, and misdirection play a critical role in the logic of these marginalia, which are caught between the Gospel text, its reading, and recitation. I take as a concluding example an instance when a scribal mistake tripped up the illuminator so that he produced the wrong scene for one of the readings. Here, I scrutinize how the artist realized the error and then proceeded to carefully correct it, not by fixing the initial mistakes but by conflating and blurring identities elsewhere in the manuscript so as to retroactively rehabilitate the earlier confusion. This reparative and recursive handling of the illuminations is critical to the operation of the lectionary's logic, as it also pays close attention to how the ordering and reading of the lections would have molded the reader's approach to and understanding of the images. This chapter serves as the book's linchpin, using the lessons of the two previous chapters to appreciate the complexity of the lectionary's images.

The aim of Part II, "The Liturgy: Sound and Architecture," is to look at the role and function of reading in a religious context, and to examine how the chanting and ritual use of the manuscript unfolded in the architectural space of Hagia Sophia during the Divine Liturgy. The focus thus shifts from the in-depth unfurling of the interplay between initials, marginalia, and miniatures in the lectionary as a manuscript to the manuscript's presence in the liturgy, as these chapters trace the text from its reading to its aural manifestation and acoustic effects in the church and finally to the effects of these performative elements on our understanding of the very architecture of the church. Like Part I, it begins with a study of liturgy and the action of reading: it examines the start of the performance (i.e., how the lectionary opens the liturgical rite), how the text plays with sound and other images, and, finally, how text, image, and sound work together to unfold the polyvalence of the iconography of an image. But in Part II, the theme of error and faltering gives way to spectrums of meaning and signification operating more broadly through the model of the polyvalent image.

Chapter 4 begins by carefully laying out the uses of the lectionary in the Divine Liturgy; I use primary sources to sketch from start to finish the process of the Liturgy of the Catechumens, during which the daily Gospel lection is read.[48] I then consider the act of reading itself in an attempt to provide a palpable sense of what the lector's Gospel recitation might have looked and sounded like. Here, I draw on a mid-eleventh-century description of a public recitation of a religious text in a Constantinopolitan church by Michael Psellos, comparing its details to those offered by *typika*, *diataxes*, commentaries, and other liturgical sources from the period in order to consider possible commonalities. My aim is to conjecture how the somber readings of the Gospels might have been similar to and different from the potentially more bombastic reading of the lives of saints from the menologion, as recounted in this primary text. The transformative power ascribed to reading and recitation in these sources recalls the classical view of reading as an act of embodied inspiration and divine possession. Looking back to ancient Greek practices of reading and to the characterization of recitation, I trace how notions of divine inspiration and possession continued to have influence well through the eleventh century, when these Gospel lectionaries were produced. I seek to demonstrate how such views appeared not only in written descriptions and more philosophically oriented texts but also in the epigrams, inscriptions, and frontispieces of Gospel books, Psalters, and books of homilies. I even argue for an interplay between notions of divine inspiration and paleographic abbreviations and customs. Attention then shifts back to the lectionary's reading, and an examination of how these ideas came into play within the liturgical performance.

Chapter 5 turns to the other side of reading: namely, its aurality and its sonic and acoustic effects in the space of the church. This chapter is staged as a diptych with Chapter 6, as both consider plaques set over the Imperial

[48] For a full description of the middle Byzantine program of the Divine Liturgy from which parts of this summary derive, see Roland Betancourt, "A Byzantine Liturgical Commentary in Verse: Introduction and Translation," *Orientalia Christiana Periodica* 81:2 (2015): 433–72.

Doorway of Hagia Sophia in the narthex and in the naos. Here, I focus on the plaque set in the narthex of the church in the late tenth century, which depicts an enthroned Gospel lectionary in the apse of the church. Analyzing how the cited verse plays with the entry of the lectionary into the church, how the image diagrams the uses of the manuscript in the church from the vantage point of its site, and how the plaque's iconography compares to that of other depictions of the church and the views from the doorway, I argue that the plaque intricately diagrams the lectionary's liturgical performance over the course of the rite according to tenth-century practices. Intriguingly, despite stressing the paradisiacal salvation of all those who enter through Christ, "the door of the sheep" (John 10:7), and thus playing with its architectural setting over the entrance door, the plaque's text fails to include the promise that anyone who enters "will be saved" (σωθήσεται). After considering the Gospel lectionary depicted in the plaque and the chant marks in contemporaneous lectionaries, I argue that this salvation is in a sense deferred from the plaque to those who resonantly experienced its words proclaimed during the reading of the Gospel itself. In other words, that which is visually missing in the text of the plaque is manifested sonically in the performance of the liturgy. This emphasis on sound and aurality is contextualized in the final section of the chapter, which notes the long-standing role played by metaphors of sound in notions of early Christian community and salvation.

The book concludes by turning its attention to the opus sectile plaque over the Imperial Doorway on the western wall of the naos. Taking into consideration its history and rearrangement, Chapter 6 runs through a series of potential readings of the plaque, which varied over time and depended on the associations that the congregations wished to make with contemporaneous visual culture inside and outside the church. The chapter is deliberately arranged as a litany of potential iconographic associations with the image, thereby stressing the cacophony of interpretations. This method seeks to unfold how the plaque resonates with the salvation guaranteed in the plaque on the other side of the doorway by presenting us a polymorphic image of the Heavenly Jerusalem, the Holy Sepulcher, the Fountain of Life, and the ambo of the church. Through this network of images, and relying in particular on the ambo as a hinge joining these interpretations, the plaque begins to reveal long-standing associations between the reading of the Gospel lectionary and the promised heavenly paradise, the fountains of paradise, and the tomb of Christ. The chapter then shifts from iconography to context, in order to further nuance and flesh out the importance of this plaque across the liturgical year, stressing its visibility, its adjoining images, and its links to the empress and emperor, as well as to other sites in the church associated with the empire. The chapter broadens its focus from the lectionary alone to consider how other chants and hymns affected the understanding of the plaque, underscoring the importance of exploring other ways in which we might think of text, image, and sound in relation to the practices and realities of the Divine Liturgy.

PART I

The Lectionary

Image and Text

1 Beginnings and Initials

Text, Image, and Sound

> If someone endeavored to be silent (Σιγᾶν) through all of his life, now he would strive above all else to be loquacious and exercise his tongue in the arts of rhetoric. Or rather, he will be emboldened to ask, what he did not dare, heretofore, for his lips to be parted with the tongs of the prophet, and for his mouth to speak out with the voice of fiery tongues, being methinks unable to bear the joy in silence, or with still tongue to take pride in this feast.[1]

On March 29, 867, Patriarch Photios presented his Homily 17 for the inauguration of the apse image of the Virgin and Child in Hagia Sophia, following the end of Iconoclasm and the restoration of images after the Triumph of Orthodoxy in 843. Photios began his sermon with silence. Not just with the silence that precedes the act of speech, but by uttering the word "silence" itself. His first word in this important sermon is the infinitive "to be silent" (σιγᾶν). With this utterance, Photios shifts from the acoustic manifestation of silence in the church to the linguistic signification of silence, spoken in the resonant domes of Hagia Sophia. Photios there gives sound to that which is by definition impossible to be made manifest by speech. In speaking, one can only manifest silence through reference and absence.

The meaning of this infinitive, "to be silent" (σιγᾶν), which occurs at the moment that the sermon begins, quickly gives way to the building meaning of the sentence, the paragraph, and the completed homily as the words trail on. As Photios's opening statement unfolds, Σιγᾶν finds itself moved along in understanding: the word is defined first as a linguistic unit whose denotation is provided by its lexical definition, but then comes to be

[1] "Σιγᾶν εἴ τις διὰ παντὸς μελετήσειε τοῦ βίου, νῦν λάλος τις εἶναι καὶ πρὸς ῥητόρων τέχνας παρεσκευάσθαι τὴν γλῶσσαν εἴπερ ἄλλο τι διὰ σπουδῆς ἂν ὅτι μάλιστα ποιήσαιτο: μᾶλλον δὲ προφητικῇ λαβίδι διεστομῶσθαι τὰ χείλη καὶ φωνῇ γλωσσῶν πυρίνων διατρανοῦσθαι τὸ στόμα οὔπω πρότερον θαρρήσας εἰς τόλμαν ἥξει αἰτήσεως, οὐκ ἔχων, οἶμαι, σιγῇ τὴν χαρὰν φέρειν καὶ ἠρεμούσῃ γλώσσῃ τῇ πανηγύρει σεμνύνεσθαι." Photios, *Homiliae*, 17, ed. Basileiou Laourdas, *ΟΜΙΛΙΑΙ* (Thessaloniki: Hetaireia Makedonikōn Spoudōn, 1959), 164; modified trans. Cyril Mango, *The Homilies of Photius Patriarch of Constantinople* (Cambridge, MA: Harvard University Press, 1958), 286.

understood relationally, through the meanings and connotations of subsequent words in the homily. As Photios is speaking, the infinitive is continually expanded and refined in the context of the discourse.

Recalling the booming space of Hagia Sophia, one can conceive Photios's speech lingering in the space. One must imagine how Photios might have allowed the "Silence" of Σιγᾶν to resonate under the structure's reverberating domes before moving on to the next word, almost as if exhorting the congregation themselves to be silent, now that he no longer is. As Bissera Pentcheva and others have demonstrated through reconstructive experiments, this acoustic space would have caused chanters to slow down their pace and actively respond to the resonant vibrations of the room – which doubtless would have varied on any given day, depending on the size and composition of the congregation – so that the words could be comprehended and not drowned out in echoes.[2] These observations demand a method for the textual analysis of homilies that considers a rhetorical structure reliant on the acoustic unfolding of words in space through the slowed process of reading.[3] The flexibility of Greek syntax allows meanings to be constantly constructed, suspended, revised, confirmed, negated, and so on. A literal translation of the first line of Photios's homily hints at this complexity, since one would hear "To be silent, if someone, through all – would have endeavored – of his life, now loquacious he is . . ." (Σιγᾶν εἴ τις διὰ παντὸς μελετήσειε τοῦ βίου, νῦν λάλος τις εἶναι . . .). The opening Σιγᾶν, for example, could be understood at first as the third-person plural present indicative – "they are silent" – rather than the present infinitive. But this understanding is soon contradicted by the conditional "if someone" (εἴ τις), and the words slowly begin to unfold and develop into the text with which we are familiar. As a conditional statement these opening words leave listeners in suspense. They cannot comprehend precisely what type of conditional is being constructed until arriving at the

[2] Bissera Pentcheva, "Hagia Sophia and Multisensory Aesthetics," *Gesta* 50:2 (2011): 93–111; Jonathan Abel et al., "Estimating Room Impulse Responses from Recorded Balloon Pops," paper presented at Audio Engineering Society Convention (November 2010), available at www.aes.org/e-lib/browse.cfm?elib=15594; P. Huang et al., "Reverberation Echo Density of Psychoacoustics," paper delivered at Audio Engineering Society Convention (November 2008), available at www.aes.org/e-lib/browse.cfm?elib=14735. Wieslaw Woszczyk, "Acoustics of Hagia Sophia: A Scientific Approach to the Humanities and Sacred Space," in Pentcheva (ed.), *Aural Architecture in Byzantium*, 176–97.

[3] Diether Roderich Reinsch, in a parallel vein, has called for editing and presenting Byzantine texts in a way that suggests their sensual, sonic performance. See Reinsch, "History of Editing Byzantine Historiographical Texts." For a thorough yet concise summary of homiletic practices in the Byzantine Church, see Cunningham, "Messages in Context."

subordinate clause. By choosing to begin his homily with a conditional construction, Photios thus manifests a certain linguistic playfulness. There is a constant state of tension and anticipation being enacted by the orator as the homily unfolds slowly before the listeners who do not have the written text before them – unlike one who reads a written text, even aloud, since that text hints at its future in the reader's peripheral vision. The orator, however, teases listeners, who are always repositioning themselves in the text in an attempt to grasp its whole meaning. Yet, as the homily unfolds, listeners are always being left in a state of deferral as words, sentences, and paragraphs progress, until eventually the discourse is completed.[4]

In this instance, Photios is leading the listener not only toward the text of his homily, scripted either in the mind or on a page before him, but also to the image of the Theotokos in the apse directly above him. It is this image of the Virgin that breaks the imagined man's vow of silence, causing his "mouth to speak out" as if he were possessed or inspired by divine words. Just as the Theotokos bore forth Christ the Logos, so Photios bears forth the *logos* of his homily by gazing upon this image and by the joy that this image inspires. He concludes the homily not because he has completed his thought but because he has simply run out of time. As he eloquently writes near the homily's end:

> But what is to become of me, driven as I am at the same time to speak and be silent? For such is the charm of the subject before me that I prefer to continue speaking without ever being sated by speech. But time, which flows on and knows no delay, urges me to conclude my speech with silence and turn to another compelling duty. Yet, since time can no longer be grasped once it is passed, and as for the topic, even if we talked all our life about it, no one would succeed in expressing it worthily, so, as it is ill to fail in both respects, I shall do what I can and ought, and at the bidding of time consent to be silent.[5]

[4] For a discussion on this model of hermeneutic repositioning, see Hans-Georg Gadamer, *Truth and Method*, 2nd edn, trans. Joel Weinsheimer and Donald G. Marshall (New York: Crossroad, 1989), 301–02; Martin Heidegger, *Being and Time*, trans. John Macquarrie and Edward Robinson (New York: Harper, 1962), 195.

[5] "Ἀλλὰ γὰρ τί πάθω, λέγειν ἅμα καὶ σιγᾶν συνελαυνόμενος; τῷ θέλγοντι γὰρ τῆς προκειμένης ὑποθέσεως προσλιπαρεῖν τοῖς λόγοις καὶ κόρον οὐκ ἔχειν τοῦ λέγειν προῄρημαι. Ὁ δὲ καιρὸς ῥέων καὶ ἀναμονῆς οὐκ εἰδὼς νόμους, σιγὴν ἐπιθέντας τῷ λόγῳ, ἐφ᾽ ἑτέραν ἡμᾶς ἀπαραίτητον ὑπηρεσίαν προτρέπεται. Πλὴν ἐπειδήπερ τὸν μὲν οὐκ ἔστι λαβεῖν παρελθόντα, τῆς δέ, κἂν ὅλον τις τὸν βίον λόγους ποιῆται, κατ᾽ ἀξίαν εἰπεῖν οὐδεὶς ἐξικνεῖται, ὅτι χαλεπὸν ἀμφοῖν ἐκπεσεῖν, τὸ δυνατὸν ἐμοὶ καὶ πρέπον σιγήσας τῷ καιρῷ καλοῦντι πεισθήσομαι." Photios, *Homiliae*, 17, ed. Laourdas, 171–72; trans. Mango, 295–96.

He must "at the bidding of time consent to be silent," for he understands that he could continue talking without ever being satiated. Paradoxically, Photios is driven both to speak and to be silent because he comprehends that he cannot ever properly encompass the image of the Virgin with words: he thus chooses to embrace silence and continue with the liturgy. In this way, his homily begins and ends in, by, and with silence.

This disclaimer may be understood theologically as recognition of the fundamental human inability to describe adequately the mystery of God, as he elaborates it, but it also speaks to the marvel of the graphic that is available for all to contemplate through the depiction of the Theotokos in the apse: a primary, visual experience that cannot be communicated in speech. This latter reading is problematic, however, since Photios equates images with writing – a common conception in Byzantine iconophile writings. As Photios says, the Virgin is represented "in images just as she is in writings and visions" (ταῖς γραφαῖς ὥσπερ τοῖς λόγοις καὶ ταῖς θεωρίαις).[6] Given the implications of this statement about the nature of perception, the stress here on the failure of discourse is clearly not simply a standard trope or rhetorical flourish.

The Illuminated Initial

That Photios chose to speak "silence" when he ceased to be silent directs me to all those silent images and marks that remain silent even as they are being given voice: namely, images and texts found in manuscripts, like those used for the recitation of homilies and biblical readings. In this book, I would like to consider precisely what the interchange of images and writing does for manuscript illumination. It is in the time of Photios himself that Byzantine artists begin experimenting with the intricacies of the illuminated initial. Like the image of the Virgin and Child, these mute images compel one to speak and be silent at the same time, as they stand at the opening of discourse in the moment when the reader moves from silence into speech. According to Leslie Brubaker, the first "unquestionably Byzantine" manuscript containing painted initials is the ninth-century Homilies of Gregory of Nazianzus (Paris, Bibliothèque nationale de France, gr. 510; Figure 1).[7] Produced in Constantinople between 879 and

[6] Photios, *Homiliae*, 17, ed. Laourdas, 171; modified trans. Mango, 295.

[7] Leslie Brubaker, "The Introduction of Painted Initials in Byzantium," *Scriptorium* 45:1 (1991): 22–46, esp. 22.

Figure 1 Homilies of Gregory of Nazianzus [Paris Gregory] (Paris, Bibliothèque nationale de France, gr. 510), fol. 316^{v}.
(Photo: Bibliothèque nationale de France)

882, the manuscript is generally believed to have been a gift from Photios to the emperor Basil I.[8] Because these illuminated initials had a long history in the West, most scholars suggest that they were imported to Byzantium from Italy via Greek manuscripts produced there.[9] Given the experimental quality of the Paris Gregory and the exegetical function of its images, Brubaker suggests that Photios was keen to use initial letters for a more specific purpose than scribal flourishes.[10] Emma Maayan Fanar's recent study on historiated initials in the ninth and tenth centuries has challenged this neat developmental narrative, however; in particular, she seeks to place the Paris Gregory in a broader context, rather than seeing it as the sole originator of these trends.[11] As she points out, illuminated initials appear in earlier texts – examples include the *Sacra parallela* and Dioscurides's *De materia medica* – and their popularity in more common manuscript types, such as the lectionary, suggests that these contemporary models affected the Paris Gregory's unique program rather than vice versa. Furthermore, Fanar also attempts to establish that their models are not the roughly contemporary Western works to which Brubaker points but rather late antique predecessors.

Yet, as Fanar observes, though the Paris Gregory did not innovate significantly in the initial types used or indeed in simply using initials, it may well be the first manuscript to put initials alongside elaborate miniatures and related marginalia.[12] This fact, while perhaps of only tangential interest to a study focused on initial types themselves, is crucial to a consideration of how initials and marginalia came to work side-by-side around the end of the eleventh century through the twelfth and thirteenth centuries, the period on which I focus in this study. The Paris Gregory therefore becomes important here precisely for the ways in which it is both unique and banal, since it serves as an early exemplar of the types of play

[8] Leslie Brubaker, "Politics, Patronage, and Art in the Ninth Century: The Homilies of Gregory Nazianzus in Paris (B.N. gr. 510)," *Dumbarton Oaks Papers* 39 (1985): 1–13.

[9] Catherine Franc-Sgourdeou, "Les initiales historiées dans les manuscrits byzantins aux XIe–XIIe siècles," *Byzantinoslavica* 2 (1967): 336–54, esp. 336–37; Brubaker, "Introduction of Painted Initials," 41–45.

[10] Leslie Brubaker, *Vision and Meaning in Ninth-Century Byzantium* (Cambridge University Press, 1998), 71–95; Brubaker, "Introduction of Painted Initials," 26. See also Sirarpie Der Nersessian, "The Illustrations of the Homilies of Gregory of Nazianzus, Paris gr. 510," *Dumbarton Oaks Papers* 16 (1962): 197–228; Christopher Walter, "Liturgy and the Illustration of Gregory of Nazianzen's Homilies: An Essay in Iconographical Methodology," *Revue des études byzantine* 29 (1971): 183–212.

[11] Emma Maayan Fanar, *Revelation through the Alphabet: Aniconism and Illuminated Initial Letters in Byzantine Artistic Imagination* (Geneva: La Pomme d'Or, 2011), 33–38, 113–66.

[12] Fanar, *Revelation through the Alphabet*, 34.

between word and image that emerge when miniatures and marginalia operate on the same page. Since historiated initials appear to have achieved popularity within the context of lectionaries and homilies, they have an implicit orality, either in preparing for future vocal enactment or bearing a trace of their previous sonic performance.

The Paris Gregory has 1,617 painted initials, but the majority of these fall under the rubric of "ornamental motifs," such as tendrils, ivies, birds, and fish. Fanar has argued that such initials emerge from aniconic trends rooted in iconoclasm, creating their own forms of apophatic representation and functioning as cues for memory.[13] Most often repeated, however, are thirty-two instances of capital epsilon (E) in which the crossbar (*hasta*) is replaced with a hand, formed in the sign of a blessing.[14] This motif appears to be an early source for the historiated initials of the Gospel lectionary that come to contain full-length figures gesturing toward the text of the lection. Kurt Weitzmann suggested that these figural, historiated, or inhabited initials – as they are variously called – were created specifically for the Gospel lectionary.[15] However, I have no interest in perpetuating a developmental narrative for these various historiated initials. Since there are only four extant lectionaries composed before 1000 (the earliest dating from 967) – although the earliest lectionaries may be dated stylistically to around the eighth and ninth centuries[16] – it is difficult to access the lectionary's early chronology and confidently describe its development or its effects on other manuscripts. Yet what the historian may usefully take from Weitzmann's statement is his implicit understanding of an inescapable connection between the lectionary and this particular brand of historiated initials. Rather than pursue any discussion as to how or why they developed, we should consider how they can be understood within the relation between image, text, and oral performance. For this, we must return to Photios's sermon, in particular his discussion of the Virgin's image.

Looking at the Virgin, Photios again brings up this fundamental question of silence. Gazing at her lips, he comments,

[13] Fanar, *Revelation through the Alphabet*, 33–38.

[14] Brubaker, "Introduction of Painted Initials," 36–41.

[15] Weitzmann, "Constantinopolitan Lectionary," esp. 362–63.

[16] The four lectionaries are Sinai gr. 213 (along with Leningrad, Public Library, gr. 283) from 967; London, British Library, add. Cod. 39602 from 980; Vat. gr. 1238 from 991; London, British Library, Harley 5598 from 995. See Dolezal, "Middle Byzantine Lectionary," 1:81n15. See also Lowden, *Jaharis Gospel Lectionary*, 122n5.

> You might say (εἴποις)[17] she is not incapable of speaking . . . To such an extent have the lips been made flesh by the colors, that they appear merely to be pressed together and stilled as in the mysteries, yet their silence is not at all inert neither is the fairness of her form derivatory, but rather it is the real archetype.[18]

Here one encounters an image that is silent but seems capable of speech, her lips having been made fleshlike through the artist's skill. This statement is not merely a formal praise of mimetic value, as it appears at first glance, but rather a commentary on the role of mimesis and silence in icons during the ninth century's iconomachy.

A criticism of idols often lodged by iconoclastic writers is expressed in an epigram placed below the cross on the Chalke Gate set up by Leo V in 815 at the reestablishment of an iconoclastic policy.[19] The poem begins:

> The Lord does not tolerate that Christ be depicted
> as form voiceless and bereft of breath
> in an earthly manner, which is condemned by the scriptures.[20]

This sentiment about the icon's silence is echoed in the iconophile writings of John of Damascus, who writes of an icon "it does not live, nor does it think, or give utterance, or feel, or move its members."[21] Whereas iconoclasts understood this depiction of Christ as a silent form to be anathematized because scripture prohibited idols, iconophiles like John of Damascus understood this silence as a requisite of the icon, produced by an image that was same in

[17] Cyril Mango translates εἴποις as "think," which is consistent with the notion that the Virgin is perceived as not incapable of speaking (Mango, *Homilies*, 290). But to stress the implicit orality in the act of perception as well that is suggested here, I have altered the translation to make it closer to the original Greek.

[18] "Εἴποις ἂν αὐτὴν (μηδ᾽ εἴ τις ἐπερωτῴη, πῶς δὲ παρθενεύεις καὶ τέτοκας;) μηδ᾽ ἂν τὸ φθέγξασθαι παραιτήσασθαι. Οὕτω διεσαρκώθη τὰ χείλη τοῖς χρώμασιν. <ὥστε> καὶ συνεπτύχθαι μόνον καὶ ἠρεμεῖν ὡς ἐν μυστηρίοις, ἀλλ᾽ οὐκ ἔχειν δι᾽ ὅλου τὴν ἡσυχίαν ἀκίνητον, οὐδὲ μιμήσει τὴν μορφὴν ἐνωραΐζεσθαι, ἀλλ᾽ αὐτόχρημα τυγχάνειν ἀρχέτυπον." Photios, *Homiliae*, 17, ed. Laourdas, 167; modified trans. Mango, 290.

[19] Glenn Peers, "Breathless, Speechless Images: On the Chalke Gate Epigram," in L. Finnete and A.P. Booth *Hommages Margaret Thomson*, Cahiers des études anciennes 34 (Quebec: Université Laval, 1998), 109–12.

[20] "Εἰς τὴν πύλην τῆς Χαλκῆς ὑποκάτω τοῦ σταυροῦ / Ἄφωνον εἶδος, καὶ πνοῆς ἐξηρμένον / Χριστὸν γράφεσθαι μὴ φέρων ὁ δεσπότης." Theodore of Stoudios, *Refutatio poematum iconomachorum*, ed. PG 99:435–78, at 437C; trans. Charles Barber, *Figure and Likeness: On the Limits of Representation in Byzantine Iconoclasm* (Princeton University Press, 2002), 92.

[21] "οὔτε γὰρ ζῇ οὔτε λογίζεται οὔτε φθέγγεται οὔτε αἰσθάνεται οὔτε μέλος κινεῖ." John of Damascus, *Orationes de imaginibus tres*, III.16:10–12, ed. P. Bonifatius Kotter, *Die Schriften des Johannes von Damaskos*, vol. 3, Patristische Texte und Studien 17 (Berlin: De Gruyter, 1975), 125; trans. Andrew Louth, *Three Treatises on the Divine Images* (Crestwood, NY: St. Vladimir's Seminary Press, 2003), 95.

signification as its referent but different in *essence* (οὐσία). Hence, the icon's inability to speak defined it against the heretical animacy of the idol.

In describing the perception of the Virgin's capability of speech, Photios chooses to articulate the idea in a way that mirrors its complexity. He calls her "not incapable of speaking" (εἴποις ἄν αὐτήν ... μηδ' ἄν τὸ φθέγξασθαι παραιτήσασθαι), a construction that stresses the expected silence of the image, but he concludes the thought by stating that this silence is not motionless or inert (ἀκίνητον) and neither is her form beautiful for the sake of imitation (μιμήσει τὴν μορφὴν ἐνωραΐζεσθαι), but straightaway seizes its archetype (αὐτόχρημα τυγχάνειν ἀρχέτυπον). Thus, she is silent, unspeaking as an icon, but in the silence of the image there is still motion – which should be understood as an affective or an imagined movement produced in beholders as they contemplate and grasp the image with their minds.[22] This, we may conclude, is the "not inert" silence that affects Photios and that drives him to speak after gazing upon the image. Because the silence of the icon is transformed into the orality of the viewer, "you might say" that the Virgin is not incapable of speaking.

The painted initial in the Paris Gregory with the blessing hand confronts the manuscript's user with a potent gesture of speech – made silent and vocal at the same time by its placement on the crossbar of the initial epsilon. A blessing is always a speech act, even if it is accompanied by a bodily movement, such as the hand raised to bless. While functioning as a deictic marker that draws attention to what is immediately beside it, this hand in the initial also performs a silent speech act, given the orality tied to the gesture. The *hasta*-hand initial demands that its users not look passively at the page and read silently, but rather read aloud and activate the narratives by visualizing the text in their imagination.

Photios directly compares the transmission of speech through hearing to the transmission of form through sight. He stresses, for example, that to reject images is the same as to reject the Gospel, since both operate on the same level of representation. According to this homily, the deeds recounted in the Gospels are called to remembrance in books, yet they are also seen being performed in pictures – and "it is the spectators more than the hearers who are drawn to emulation" (μᾶλλον τοὺς ὁρῶντας ἢ τοὺς ἀκούοντας πρὸς μίμησιν ἐπιστρέφουσιν).[23] This statement sets the standard for the superiority of images in Byzantium, making clear that it is primarily through images that humans can be made to follow in the path of Christ

22 On language of grasping and comprehension, see Betancourt, *Sight, Touch, and Imagination*, esp. 142–55.

23 Photios, *Homiliae*, 17, ed. Laourdas, 170; modified trans. Mango, 294.

and the saints. It does explicitly declare that seers rather than hearers are turned to mimesis and that sight is superior to hearing, but for reasons here that go beyond a mere categorical ranking of sensual hierarchies. Sight is superior to hearing only in the sense that it removes a step – visualization – required of those who hear. Photios describes this process:

> Has [a person] inclined their ear to the story? Has their intelligence drawn to itself, and imagined the thing heard? Then, judging it with sober attention, they deposit it into the memory . . . Has the mind seen? Has it grasped? Has it imagined? Then, effortlessly it has transmitted the forms to the memory.[24]

These rhetorical questions, which allude to the earlier writings of Patriarch Nikephoros on images,[25] demonstrate that the superiority of vision means only that listeners must be more fully engaged. Because they are not provided with an image, listeners must invest themselves in the things heard so as to visualize them before these things can be impressed upon memory and enact mimetic results in the soul. In this regard, Photios's use of painted initials can be tied to the potent process suggested by his statements here. A manuscript's images function as a process of enacting an active sacred gaze that produces a reader-viewer involved with the image-text.

The Paris Gregory's painted initials provide evidence of a new visuality that intertwines text and image. Through the act of reading aloud, the attentive mind is forced into a process whereby the written text and the speech it governs are materially connected with the homily visualized in the miniatures. On folio 316^{r} (Figure 2), for example, the following

[24] "Ἔκλινέ τις τὸ οὖς εἰς διήγημα; εἵλκυσε φανταζομένη τὸ ἀκουσθὲν ἡ διάνοια; νηφούσῃ μελέτῃ τὸ κριθὲν τῇ μνήμῃ ἐναπέθετο. . . Εἶδεν ὁ νοῦς, ἀντελάβετο, ἐφαντάσθη, τοὺς τύπους ἀκόπως ἐν τῇ μνήμῃ παρεπέμψατο." Photios, *Homiliae*, 17, ed. Laourdas, 170; trans. Betancourt, *Sight, Touch, and Imagination*, 182. For a summary of Photios's theory of sight, see also Roland Betancourt, "Why Sight Is Not Touch: Reconsidering the Tactility of Vision in Byzantium," *Dumbarton Oaks Papers* 70 (2016): 1–23.

[25] In his parallel statement, Nikephoros declares that listeners must instead learn "through analogy" (δι᾽ ἀναλογισμοῦ): "But words themselves are the icons of things, and follow on from them as from their causes. To begin with, they enter hearing; for first the sounds of the things spoken encounter those listening, then, second, the listener achieves understanding of the given facts through analogy. [Painting] directly and immediately leads the minds of the viewers to the facts themselves, as if they were present already, and from the first sight and encounters a clear and perfect knowledge of these is gained" (Ἀλλὰ καὶ οἱ λόγοι ἀυτοὶ εἰκόνες εἰσὶ τῶν πραγμάτων, καὶ ἕπονται αὐτοῖς ὡς αἰτίοις. Καὶ πρώτως μὲν τὴν ἀκοὴν εἰσδύονται: πρότερον γὰρ τὰ ἀπηχήματα τῶν λεγομένων τοῖς ἐνηχουμένοις προσπίπτουσι: δευτέρως δὲ δι᾽ ἀναλογισμοῦ ἐπὶ τὴν τῶν δηλουμένων πραγμάτων κατανόησιν ὁ ἠκουτισμένος ἔρχεται. Ἡ δὲ πρώτως καὶ ἀμέσως ἐπ᾽ αὐτὰ τὰ πράγματα, ὡς παρόντα ἤδη, τὸν νοῦν τῶν ἐνορώντων προσάγει, καὶ ἐκ πρώτης θέας καὶ ἐντεύξεως τρανὴν καὶ ἀπεξεσμένην τὴν γνῶσιν τούτων παρέχεται). Nikephoros I, *Antirrheticus*, ed. PG 100:381C–D; trans. Barber, *Figure and Likeness*, 128.

Figure 2 Homilies of Gregory of Nazianzus [Paris Gregory] (Paris, Bibliothèque nationale de France, gr. 510), fol. 316[r].
(Photo: Bibliothèque nationale de France)

narratives are illustrated: Christ healing the blind man at Siloam, the parable of the widow's mite, Christ healing the paralytic at Capernaum, and Christ raising the widow's son at Nain.[26] The cycle visually repeats Christ four times with the raised hand indexing a moment of speech, each reiterating the place of blessing and healing as performative speech acts. We must note that there is little distinction between the depiction of Christ speaking to the widow and the other scenes of Christ healing or raising individuals – all acts are performed through speech.

The text accompanying Gregory's second letter to Kledonios, a seminal christological text, begins on the verso of the miniature's folio (fol. 316^{v}; see Figure 1). This page contains one example of the blessing-hand initial, which, for the reader turning the page, visually echoes the repetitive images of Christ's performative speech acts. Thus, this hand is not simply a marker or mere embellishment but rather here takes on the performative power of the epistle's oration. In particular, the hand functions to represent the bodily gestures of the speech acts that play a critical role within the epistle. As a metonymic afterimage of Christ's healings and raisings, the hand opens the narrative introduced by the temporal and causal "When/Since" (Ἐπειδή) – a format that loosely echoes one of the two introductory standard phrases of the lections in the Gospel lectionary texts (discussed later). This metonymic hand is a part of the narrative and provides a glimpse of some of the potential uses for historiated initials in the Gospel lectionaries of the eleventh and twelfth centuries, where these initials usually are a direct and literal visualization of the words on the page.

This approach is evident in the logic of the contemporary illuminations of the Khludov Psalter. Psalter illuminations often are intended to Christianize the Old Testament text by demonstrating that the New Testament typologically fulfills the prophecies and teachings of the old law. Thus, many images in the Khludov Psalter can be understood within various rubrics of typological commentary. But some of its marginal images present highly literal illustrations of the text that perplex modern art historians because they do not easily fit into unified exegetical, typological theses. The marginalia surrounding Psalm 72 (folio 70^{v}; Figure 3), for example, appear next to the line regarding the wicked men "who set their mouth against the heaven and their tongue passes over the earth" (Greek Psalm 72:9): they make visible the literal scene being read or heard, rather than attempting to comment exegetically on the words' metaphorical or symbolic meanings. This

[26] Brubaker, *Vision and Meaning*, 273–79.

Figure 3 Khludov Psalter (Moscow, State Historical Museum, Cod. 129), fol. 70v.
(Photo: © State Historical Museum, Moscow)

literalism is found in a variety of the so-called marginal Psalters that resemble the Khludov, such as the eleventh-century Theodore, Barberini, and Bristol Psalters.[27] The Khludov image embodies precisely the visuality that Photios addressed when he asked, "Has the mind seen? Has it apprehended? Has it visualized?"[28] It is as if the procedure itself of textual reading/hearing is being depicted on the page. As Brubaker has noted,

> images can absorb and promote ideologies of what is worth remembering, and demonstrate how it is to be remembered, in some ways more easily than words, precisely because images are inarticulate – they can present the shift "intuitively," without labored explanation.[29]

Brubaker here stresses the power of images as tools of enculturation that forcefully train an intuitive logic of seeing, reading, and hearing, in accordance with the tenets of Byzantine image theory. Yet they are not merely mnemonic devices: they operate outside the bounds of visual commentary and cannot be understood simply as a form of visual exegesis.

Scholars have consistently viewed the illuminations of the Gospel lectionary, the Psalter, and the Gregory Homilies as functioning similarly within the liturgy. Maria Evangelatou, Anthony Cutler, and others have observed that the Khludov manuscript and other similar Psalters bear witness to liturgical use, noting the inclusion of rubrics and divisions that organize and prescribe their chant within the rite.[30] While the Psalms certainly were crucial in ecclesiastical worship, Georgi Parpulov cautions

[27] See Suzy Dufrenne, *L'illustration des Psautiers grecs du Moyen Âge*, vol. 1 (Paris: C. Klincksieck, 1966), 49–66; Jeffrey C. Anderson, "On the Nature of the Theodore Psalter," *Art Bulletin* 70:4 (1988): 550–68; Jeffrey C. Anderson, "The Date and Purpose of the Barberini Psalter," *Cahiers archéologiques* 31 (1983): 35–67; Jeffrey C. Anderson, "The Palimpsest Psalter, Pantokrator Cod. 61: Its Content and Relationship to the Bristol Psalter," *Dumbarton Oaks Papers* 48 (1994): 199–220.

[28] Photios, *Homiliae*, 17, ed. Laourdas, 170; modified trans. Mango, 294.

[29] Leslie Brubaker, "Pictures are Good to Think With: Looking at Byzantium," in Paolo Odorico, Panagiotis A. Agapitos, and Martin Hinterberger (eds.), *L'écriture de la mémoire: La littérarité de l'historiographie* (Paris: École des Hautes Études en Sciences Sociales, 2006), 221–52, at 236. See also Leslie Brubaker, "Image, Meta-Text and Text in Byzantium," in Shoishi Sato (ed.), *Herméneutique du texte d'histoire: orientation, interprétation et questions nouvelles* (Nagoya University, 2009), 93–100.

[30] See Maria Evangelatou, "Liturgy and the Illustration of the Ninth-Century Byzantine Marginal Psalters," *Dumbarton Oaks Papers* 63 (2011): 59–116; Anthony Cutler, "Liturgical Strata in the Marginal Psalters," *Dumbarton Oaks Papers* 34–35 (1980–81): 17–30. See also Nicolas Malickij, "Le Psautier byzantine à illustrations marginales du type Chludov est-il de provenance monastique?," in Gabriel Millet (ed.), *L'art byzantin chez les Slaves: L'ancienne Russie, les Slaves catholiques*, vol. 2 (Paris: P. Guenther, 1932), 235–43; Oliver Strunk, "The Byzantine Office at Hagia Sophia," *Dumbarton Oaks Papers* 9/10 (1955/1956): 175–202, esp. 198–99; Christian Troelsgård, "Psalm: III. Byzantine Psalmody," in Stanley Sadie (ed.), *The New Grove Dictionary*

that out of the six hundred or so extant Psalters that he studied, only six can be said to have served a clear liturgical function.[31] Some have also ascribed to the Homilies of Gregory of Nazianzus a liturgical function; George Galavaris has even gone so far as to postulate that the lectionary was the model for its imagery.[32] The homilies that suggest liturgical use also happen to be the most commonly illustrated, featuring images that respond to the liturgical performance and to the feast days mentioned, as are evident in lectionaries.[33] But the Paris Gregory discussed above possesses none of these features and is unique in both its textual composition and illumination program.[34] Whatever function these various manuscripts may have had – either private or communal – these objects would have been read aloud in keeping with the known habits of reading in the medieval world.[35] As Wolfram Hörandner and Herbert Hunger have both remarked, Byzantine literature and rhetoric are essentially inconceivable without a consideration of their oral performance and aural effects.[36]

Text, Image, and Sound in the Lectionary's Initial

The opening folios of the richly illuminated Dionysiou Lectionary (Mount Athos, Dionysiou Monastery, Cod. 587, fols. 1^v–2^r; Figure 4) demonstrate

of Music and Musicians, 29 vols., 2nd edn (London: Macmillan, 2001), 20:463–66; Herb Kessler, "The Psalter," in Vikan (ed.), *Illuminated Greek Manuscripts from American Collections*, 31–33. On the intersection of Psalters and ritual, see Jeffrey C. Anderson and Stephano Parenti, *A Byzantine Monastic Office, 1105 A.D.* (Washington, DC: Catholic University of America Press, 2016).

31 Parpulov, "Psalms and Personal Piety," 82.

32 Walter, "Liturgy and the Illustration"; George Galavaris, *The Illustrations of the Liturgical Homilies of Gregory Nazianzenus* (Princeton University Press, 1969), 98.

33 Galavaris, *Illustrations of the Liturgical Homilies*, 9–10.

34 Brubaker, *Vision and Meaning*, 13–14.

35 For a summary of the studies on the orality and aurality of Byzantine reading and rhetoric, see Bourbouhakis, "Rhetoric and Performance." See also Cavallo, *Lire à Byzance*. More recently, Shawcross and Toth (eds.), *Reading in the Byzantine Empire*. See also Valivitcharska, *Rhetoric and Rhythm in Byzantium*. Western studies on orality, literacy, and performance also offer useful and convincing comparisons for the Byzantine sphere, particularly given the classical roots of these ideas and the dependence of this research on such sources. See Michael Camille, "Seeing and Reading: Some Visual Implications of medieval Literacy and Illiteracy," *Art History* 8 (1985): 26–49; Mary Carruthers, *The Book of Memory: A Study of Memory in Medieval Culture*, 2nd edn (Cambridge University Press, 2008), 195–233; Brian Stock, *The Implications of Literacy: Written Language and Models of Interpretation in the Eleventh and Twelfth Centuries* (Princeton University Press, 1983), esp. 12–87. Most recently, see Emmanuel Bourbouhakis (organizer), "The Sound of Sense: Orality/Aurality in Byzantine Texts and Contexts," Symposium, Princeton University, May 16–17, 2015.

36 Hörandner, *Prosarhythmus*, 50; Hunger, *Schreiben und Lesen in Byzanz*, 126.

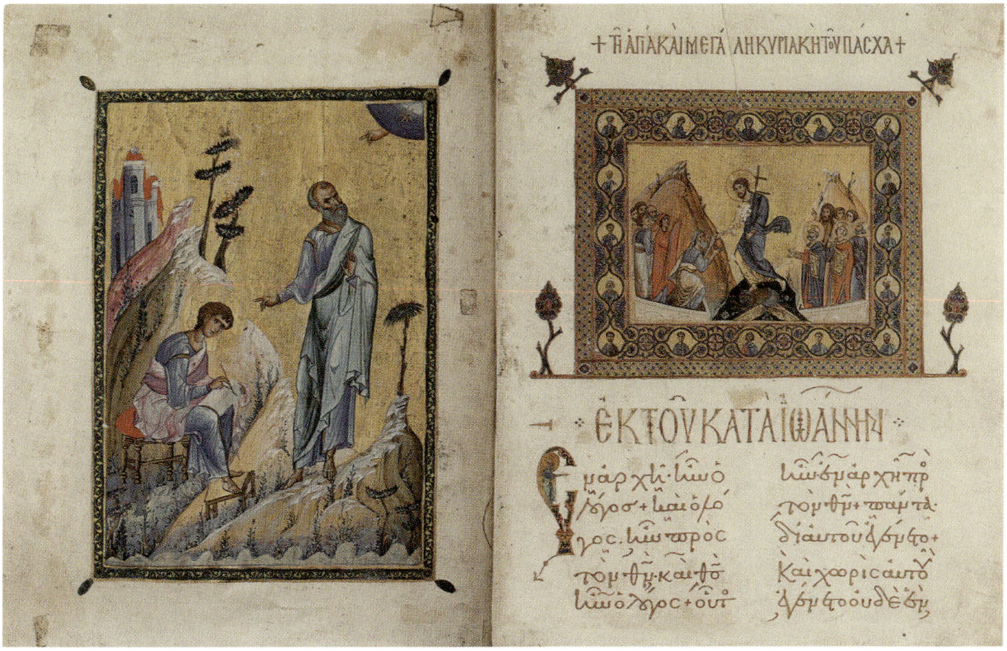

Figure 4 Dionysiou Lectionary (Mount Athos, Dionysiou Monastery, Cod. 587), fol. 1^v. (Photo: after John Lowden, *The Jaharis Gospel Lectionary* [New York: Metropolitan Museum of Art, 2009], 85, fig. 97)

the manuscript's system.[37] The folio on the left portrays John the Evangelist, who, being divinely inspired by the hand of God, points to his scribe Prochoros. These gestures should be read as suggestions of speech, through which the oral message of God is passed on from John, who dictates it to Prochoros. In the initial on the right, we see the figure of John repeated with his arm likewise raised in speech. John stands within a C-shaped, quasi-architectural space that is transformed into a capital epsilon by his raised arm, thereby enacting the opening of John 1: "In the beginning was the Logos." Note that the gesture of the speech act itself is

[37] On the Dionysiou Lectionary, see Dolezal, "Illuminating the Liturgical Word"; John Cotsonis, "On Some Illustrations in the Lectionary, Athos, Dionysiou 587," *Byzantion* 59 (1989): 5–19; Christopher Walter, "The Date and Content of the Dionysiou Lectionary," *Δελτίον Χριστιανικής Αρχαιολογικής Εταιρείας* 4:13 (1985–86): 181–89; John Cotsonis, "New Light on the Dionysiou Lectionary," MA thesis, Pennsylvania State University (1986); Kurt Weitzmann, "An Imperial Lectionary in the Monastery of Dionysiou on Mount Athos: Its Origins and Its Wanderings," *Revue des études sud-est européennes* 7 (1969): 239–53. See also Weitzmann, "Constantinopolitan Lectionary," esp. 362–63.

what completes the epsilon as a textual signifier and hence makes the text readable. It bears witness to the act of dictation to Prochoros depicted in the miniature while playing with the polysemy of the Greek *Logos*, which as is often remarked must be translated not simply as "word," but rather as "utterance" or "discourse."

Since the Gospel lectionary invariably opens with the Easter reading of John 1:1, the epsilon that begins the phrase "In the beginning" (Ἐν ἀρχῆ) stands in that crucial interval between silence and sound, bringing the lectionary's reader into its texts on Easter Sunday. Here, illuminators often stress the interrelations between John's divine inspiration, his utterance of the word, and its transcription by Prochoros. Like the reader who takes up the manuscript to recite the Gospels, here the division between image, sound, and text is made vivid and palpable. Thus, artists often play with the status of John's Gospel, choosing to place emphasis on the polysemy of the Gospel and its various instantiations in image, text, sound, and its performance in the Divine Liturgy.

The power and effect of this resonance, for example, can be seen in a thirteenth-century Gospel book's initial that internalizes the scene of John speaking to Prochoros, thereby depicting the feedback between the archaic Logos and the Gospel's own transcription (Mount Athos, Dionysiou Monastery, Cod. 4, fols. 278^{v}–79^{r}; Figures 5–6). In the miniature on the opposite folio, John turns his attention to the heavens, gesturing to Prochoros – who is diligently transcribing his words, eyes fixed on John – while gazing beyond to the heavenly corner of the page. In the initial, sitting at John's feet, Prochoros diligently transcribes John's words, yet his gaze is directed neither toward John nor toward the parchment upon his left knee. Instead, Prochoros looks out at the text with his eyes fixed on the word that the scribe has carefully placed before him, "λόγος," which likewise abuts the folio upon his lap. This placement of the literal "word" and the image draws a connection not only to the folio upon Prochoros's lap but also to his act of transcribing these words, which now are being offered up to the reader as a text. John similarly directs his visage intently toward the text; yet unlike Prochoros, he stretches out his hand toward the words that he is depicted as pronouncing in this moment. Here, as in most initials that are capital epsilons, that outstretched hand completes the central bar of the E's shape and thus makes it legible; but the hand also speaks to the text's origin as an oral work and its being given voice again by a reader who is now also directing their attention toward this text.

Figure 5 Gospel book (Mount Athos, Dionysiou Monastery, Cod. 4), fol. 278^{v}.
(Photo: after S.M. Pelekanidis et al., *The Treasures of Mount Athos: Illuminated Manuscripts*, vol. 1 [Athens: Ekdotikē Athēnōn, 1974], 55, fig. 25)

A similar arrangement appears in the Venice Lectionary (Venice, Istituto Ellenico, Cod. 2, fol. 4^{r}; Figure 7),[38] where John and Prochoros are both found in the opening initial; yet it replaces altogether the usual

[38] The entirety of the lectionary is available online at the Istituto Ellenico's website (http://www.istitutoellenico.org), under Digital Presentation, listed as "Ευαγγελιστάριο, 13ος αιώνας." While the Venice Lectionary dates to circa 1100, it has also been attributed to the thirteenth century and is listed with that date in the Istituto Ellenico's catalogue. This attribution comes from a note at the end of the codex (fol. 414^{v}), which lists Antonios Malakes as an owner. For discussions using a thirteenth-century attribution, see Andreas Xyngopoulos, "Τὸ ἱστορημένο εὐαγγέλιον τοῦ Ἑλληνικοῦ Ἰνστιτούτου Βενετίας," *Thesaurismata* 1 (1962): 63–88; Eleni D. Kakoulidi, "Κατάλογος τῶν ἑλληνικῶν χειρογράφων τοῦ Ἑλληνικοῦ Ἰνστιτούτου Βενετίας," *Thesaurismata* 8 (1971): 249–73, esp. 251. For discussions following its correct circa 1100 attribution, see Dolezal, "Middle Byzantine Lectionary," 153–82; Boris L. Fonkitch, "Notes paléographiques sur les manuscrits grecs de bibliothèques italiennes," *Thesaurismata* 16 (1979): 153–57; Ioannis Spatharakis, *Corpus of Dated Illuminated Greek Manuscripts to the Year 1453*, vol. 1 (Leiden: Brill, 1981), 76. For a study of Antonios Malakes's collection including the Venice Lectionary, see Robert S. Nelson, "The Manuscripts of Antonios Malakes and the

Figure 6 Gospel book (Mount Athos, Dionysiou Monastery, Cod. 4), fol. 279r.
(Photo: after Pelekanidis et al., *Treasures of Mount Athos*, 57, fig. 27)

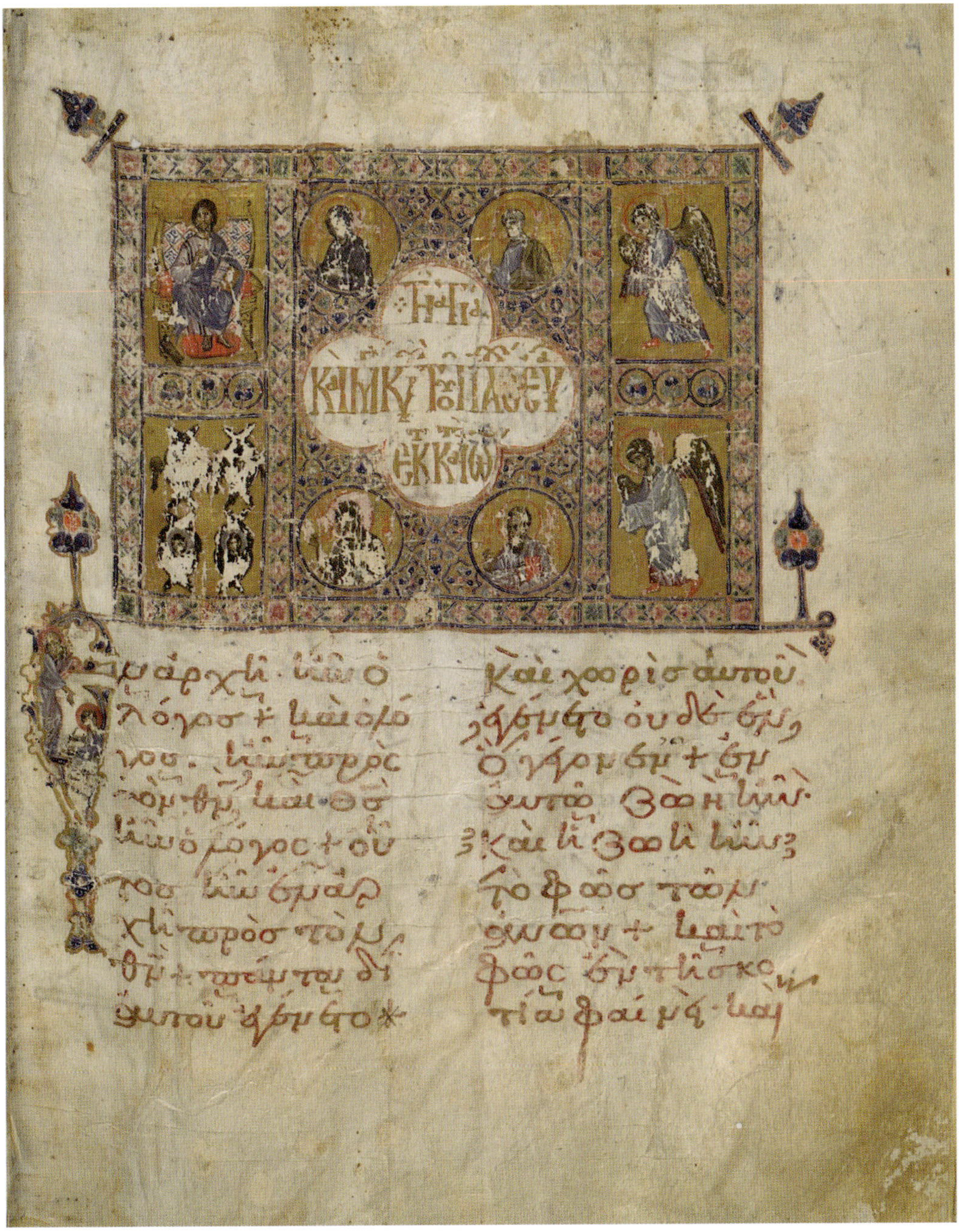

Figure 7 Venice Lectionary (Venice, Istituto Ellenico, Cod. 2), fol. 4r.
(Photo: courtesy of the Hellenic Institute of Byzantine and Post-Byzantine Studies in Venice)

Evangelist portrait on the opposite folio, which features an elaborate carpet. Again sitting at John's feet, Prochoros diligently transcribes his dictations: John gestures in Prochoros's direction, but his eyes are raised above toward the figure of Christ sitting on a lyre-backed throne in the folio's headpiece. In it, a host of angels and holy figures all direct their gaze and bodies toward Christ's odd placement in the upper-left-hand corner of the headpiece. Thus, almost all the attention on the page is directed at Christ, with the remainder diverted down to Prochoros's text through John's gesture in the initial, stressing the transmission of Christ's words and deeds. As before, Prochoros is curiously placed abutting the "word" (λόγος) from the opening verse as he reclines against the bottom lip of the capital epsilon while writing the text upon his lap.

In a thirteenth-century manuscript in Athens, the dynamic of dictation and transcription has been spatialized across the two folios of the open manuscript (Athens, National Library of Greece, Cod. 68, fols. 1^{v}–2^{r}; Figure 8). Here John directs his focus to the icon of Christ in the headpiece, who returns his gaze, while his right index finger is raised, indicating that he is in the process of dictation. In the capital epsilon, the figure of Prochoros, misidentified as John in the library's catalogue, turns his ear back toward John in the miniature on the opposite folio while holding a stylus in his right hand, echoing the latter's gesture of speech. Yet Prochoros here directs his stylus not toward a painted codex or folio before him but rather toward the actual page of the lectionary itself, as if transcribing onto this very folio the divinely inspired words that the user now reads aloud to the congregation. Prochoros is not here transcribing John's words onto some Ur-text that through its chains of transmission was eventually copied into the manuscript being held by some user. Instead, the figure of Prochoros cuts across time and space, as if the transcription of discourse that occurred long ago were occurring now before the reader. By breaking the fourth wall through this depiction of Prochoros writing the text of this lectionary itself, the initial self-reflexively plays with the fluid separation between speech and text, aurality and orality, the graphic and the sonic.

The initial validates and authenticates the Gospel text across time as having been composed by John himself, even if written by his ever-present scribe. However, in the New York Cruciform Lectionary (New York,

Collecting and Appreciation of Illuminated Books in the Early Palaeologan Period," *Jahrbuch der Österreichischen Byzantinistik* 36 (1986): 229–54.

(a)

Figure 8 Athens Lectionary (Athens, National Library of Greece, Cod. 68), fols. 1v–2r.
(Photo: National Library of Greece / The Center for the Study of New Testament Manuscripts, www.csntm.org, digitized NLG 68 at the National Library of Greece)

(b)

Figure 8 (*cont.*)

Figure 9 New York Cruciform Lectionary (New York, Morgan Library, Cod. 692), fol. 2^{v}. (Photo: The Pierpont Morgan Library, New York)

Morgan Library, Cod. 692, fol. 2^{v}; Figure 9),[39] John himself takes the stylus to the page; Prochoros is wholly absent from both the initial and the miniature. In the latter, John is likewise positioned before a lectern and desk, filled with scribal tools; the already written text of his Gospel sits upon his lectern. The oral polyvalences of the text are merely alluded to in the initial, since here the raised arm ends not in an oratorical gesture but rather in a hand clenched around the stylus. The flourish of the epsilon's bottom lip curves inward, slanted toward John as if it were a lectern for a manuscript. At the same time, the top half of this lectern-like flourish extends outward into the text of the lectionary, nearly touching the first omicron of the phrase "the word" (ὁ λόγος). Like a pointing hand, leading the viewer toward the text, this detail again directs attention toward the word, just as we saw earlier in the case of Prochoros's gaze. Nevertheless, the artist here has resolutely chosen to stress John's role as the text's author and to articulate the visual and textual aspects of the lectionary, while still alluding to practices of recitation in the Byzantine world through this

[39] See Jeffrey C. Anderson, *The New York Cruciform Lectionary* (University Park: Pennsylvania State University Press, 1992).

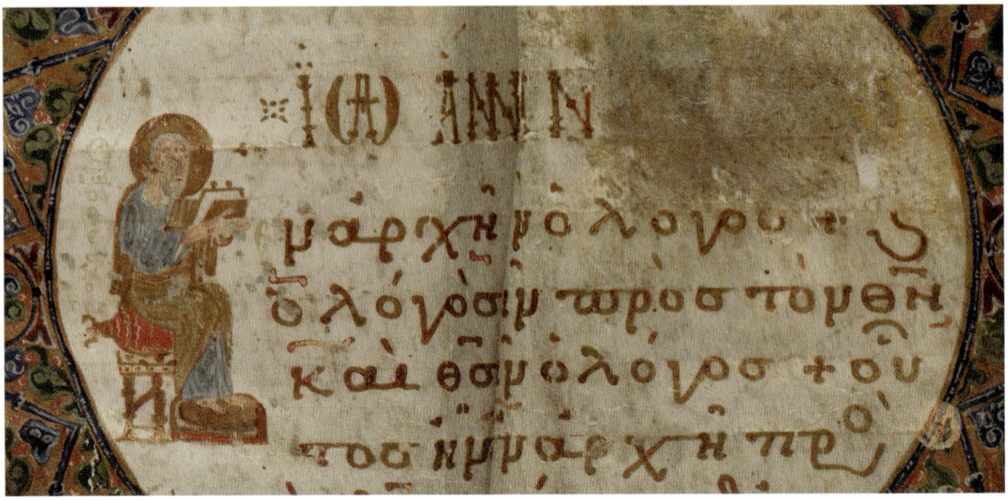

Figure 10 Dumbarton Oaks Lectionary (Washington, DC, Dumbarton Oaks, Cod. 1), fol. 1^{r}. (Photo: © Dumbarton Oaks, Byzantine Collection, Washington, DC)

stance, his extended arm, and the possible visual indeterminacy between a stylus and a pointer, used to help guide a reader reciting a text.

In the Dumbarton Oaks Lectionary (Washington, DC, Dumbarton Oaks, Cod. 1, fol. 1^{r}; Figure 10), we see a resolute focus on the text itself: John is uniquely depicted in the initial as sitting upon a bench with no architectural form to help articulate the body of the epsilon. Looking closely, we can even observe how an uncial epsilon, sized in accordance with the body of the text, has been erased, presumably replaced by this figure of John. Nevertheless, unlike the other cases discussed above, it lacks the definite form of an epsilon. John here holds a Gospel book in his slightly extended hands, rather ineffectively forming the epsilon's crossbar. Furthermore, while the volume's clasps appear to be opened, the codex itself remains closed in his hands, not supporting the dynamic orality of the examples considered thus far. Instead, we see an initial that stresses the body of the text as a physical object rather than playing with the sonic and performative transmutations of this Gospel's composition, recitation, transcription, and liturgical performance.

These various initials thus demonstrate how authors played with the Gospel's various and overlapping understanding as image, text, and sound. Viewed as part of a spectrum of representation, such initials indicate how artists and scribes alike played with word placement and iconographic conventions to articulate the function of the image-text within the acts of reading and recitation in the liturgy. As we consider such a system, we can think about these examples in relation to a twelfth-century Gospel book that was not

Figure 11 Gospel book (Mount Athos, Dionysiou Monastery, Cod. 4), fol. 15^{r}. (Photo: after Pelekanidis et al., *Treasures of Mount Athos*, 53, fig. 20)

designed specifically for liturgical recitation. In the Dionysiou Gospel book (Mount Athos, Dionysiou Monastery, Cod. 4, fol. 15^{r}; Figure 11), the opening B-initial for Matthew 1:1, which reads "Book of the genesis of Jesus Christ" (βίβλος γενέσεως Ἰησοῦ Χριστοῦ), is produced by the figure of the Evangelist Matthew holding his literal book (βίβλος). This strategy pervades the logic of these initials: the illumination represents (and duplicates) the word that it produces, manifesting a harmonious unification of the image-text. However, a paradigm may be gleaned from these various examples.

Compare this uncial B in the Gospel book to one in the same passage of the Dionysiou Lectionary (fol. 126^{r}; Figure 12). Whereas the Gospel book visualizes the word βίβλος itself and clarifies what book this is by showing its author holding it, the lectionary's B opens onto the image conjured by the text's initial words. The book recounting Christ's genesis is visualized in the Dionysiou Lectionary as the literal *genesis of Christ*, as what is shown is a scene of the Nativity – the feast day on which the lection would have been read. However, I would like to propose that the feast day was chosen to be made part of the initial not because of some urge to summarize but rather because of the meaning that the word "genesis" itself would have carried on that day, the feast of the Nativity, when the reader/listener would have imagined it to refer to the scene of Christ's birth – deriving its significance not from its textual but rather its temporal context, uttered on that feast day celebrating the moment in which Christ first was perceived by humanity. The initial then appears as a transparent manifestation of the very

Figure 12 Dionysiou Lectionary (Mount Athos, Dionysiou Monastery, Cod. 587), fol. 126^{r}. (Photo: after Pelekanidis et al., *Treasures of Mount Athos*, 197, fig. 247)

process of reading, whereby the signifier fades and meaning is manifested through the images in the minds of the reader.

The Cock's Crow: The Depiction of Sound

This volume will repeatedly return to the question of how this visual logic operates alongside the sonic manifestation of the Gospel text. To introduce these dynamics here, I wish to focus on one representative strand of marginalia in the lectionary that best exemplifies this traversal of sound across time and space: the scene of the betrayal of Peter based on Matthew 26:74–75, which is recited during the Divine Liturgy on Holy Thursday. This episode is apt for investigating the interrelations of word, recitation, and image because its climactic moment is a sonic event: the cock's crow. The marginalia for the betrayal usually depict the cock on one side of the text while Peter is depicted on the opposite side, reacting to its cry.

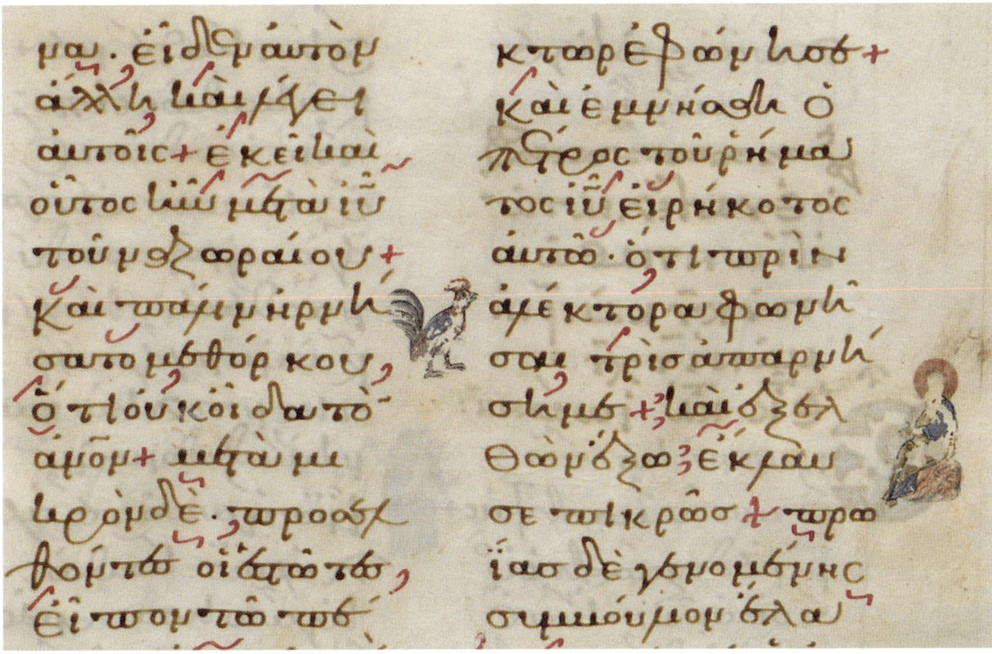

Figure 13 Venice Lectionary (Venice, Istituto Ellenico, Cod. 2), fol. 285r.
(Photo: courtesy of the Hellenic Institute of Byzantine and Post-Byzantine Studies in Venice)

This structure expands from left to right across the page as speech itself traverses through space to its listeners and through time during its reading. In each of the following instances that will be addressed here, the cock is higher than Peter, because the images, as is to be expected, are aligned with the text that refers to them. This organization demonstrates the artists' consistent desires to adhere to the text, rather than produce a unified marginal scene that merely uses a depiction of the event as a framing device.

In the Venice Lectionary (Venice, Istituto Ellenico, Cod. 2, fol. 285r; Figure 13), the cock appears beside its textual signifier – ἀλέκτορα – in the clause where Peter is remembering the words of Christ that foreshadow his third betrayal upon the crow of the cock. The figure of Peter then emerges in the midst of the words that end the verse: "And he went out and wept bitterly." Here, the third-person verb "wept" (ἔκλαυσε) is interrupted by the line break; as the eye reaches the end of the line, seeking and desiring to complete the verb, the now badly eroded figure of Peter weeping appears in the margin, itself completing the verb and its third-person subject. The New York Cruciform Lectionary (New York, Morgan Library, Cod. 692,

Figure 14 New York Cruciform Lectionary (New York, Morgan Library, Cod. 692), fol. 167ᵛ. (Photo: The Pierpont Morgan Library, New York)

fol. 167ᵛ; Figure 14) displays the same approach: the cock is above Peter, placed directly before its verbal signifier. Here, the cock emerges at the instant that Peter has denied Christ a third time, at the beginning of the passage that reads "And immediately the rooster crowed." Peter himself appears just after the word "wept," as in the Venice manuscript. His eyes show distress, and he grasps his pink himation with one hand, while he rubs his weeping eyes with the other. Fifteen folios later in the manuscript (fol. 182ᵛ–83ʳ; Figure 15), the scene reoccurs in the Third Passion lection, which is read on Good Friday (Matthew 26:57–75). This time, however, the illustrations appear across an open spread – emphasizing once again the artist's commitment to the literal intermeshing of the image with the text it represents.

It is worth stressing that in both examples from the New York Cruciform Lectionary, the cock appears beside the sonic act itself that causes Peter to weep. In the Venice Lectionary, in contrast, the cock appears alongside the second reference to it within these two verses – that is, in the portion of the lection that is delivered as an indirect statement of Christ's words (established by the conjunction ὅτι). Therefore, the New York Lectionary highlights the rupture caused by the cock's crow as a sonic event within the narrative, while the Venice example stresses the cock's confirmation of Christ's prophecy.

(a)

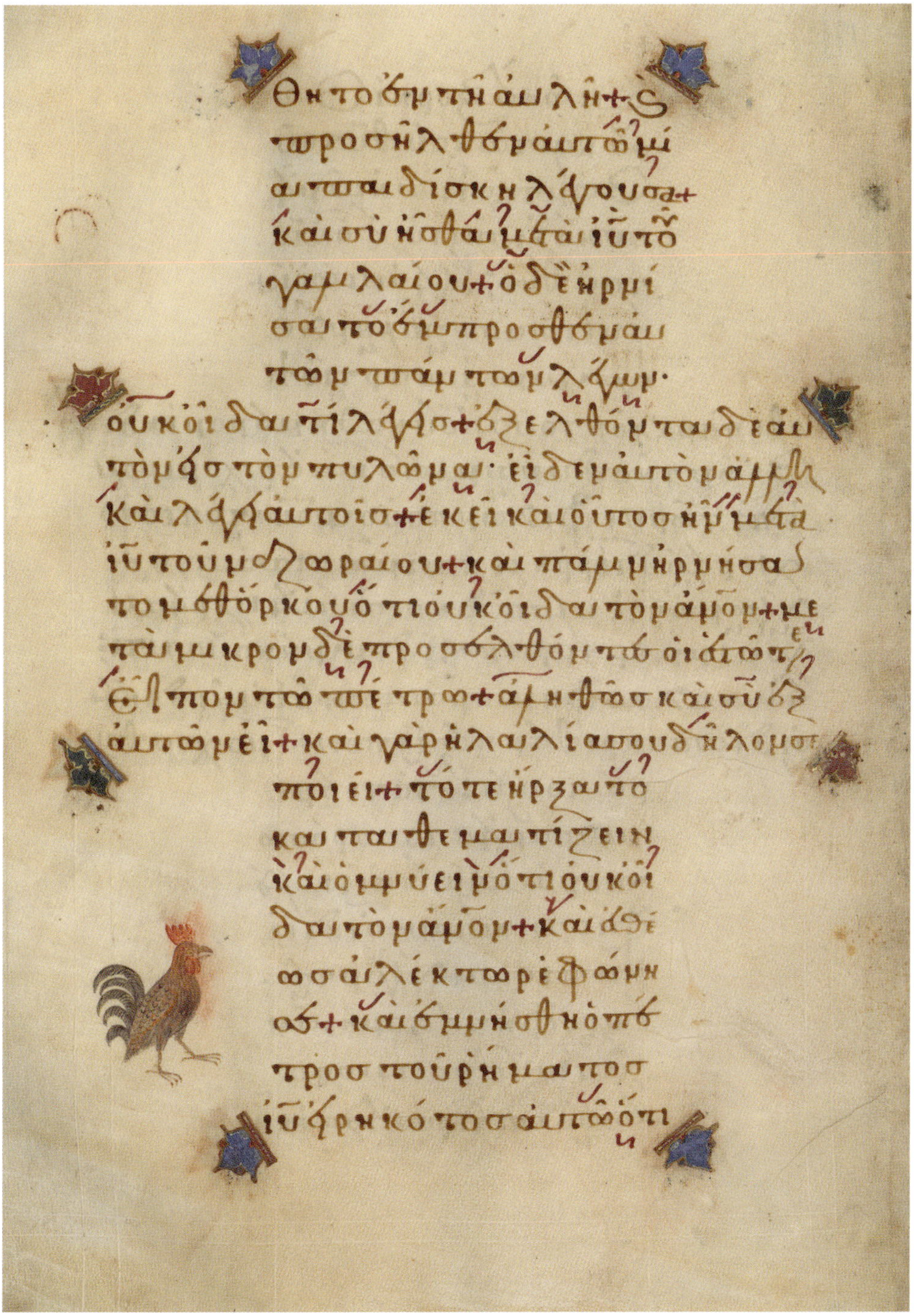

Figure 15 New York Cruciform Lectionary (New York, Morgan Library, Cod. 692), fols. 182v–83r. (Photo: The Pierpont Morgan Library, New York)

(b)

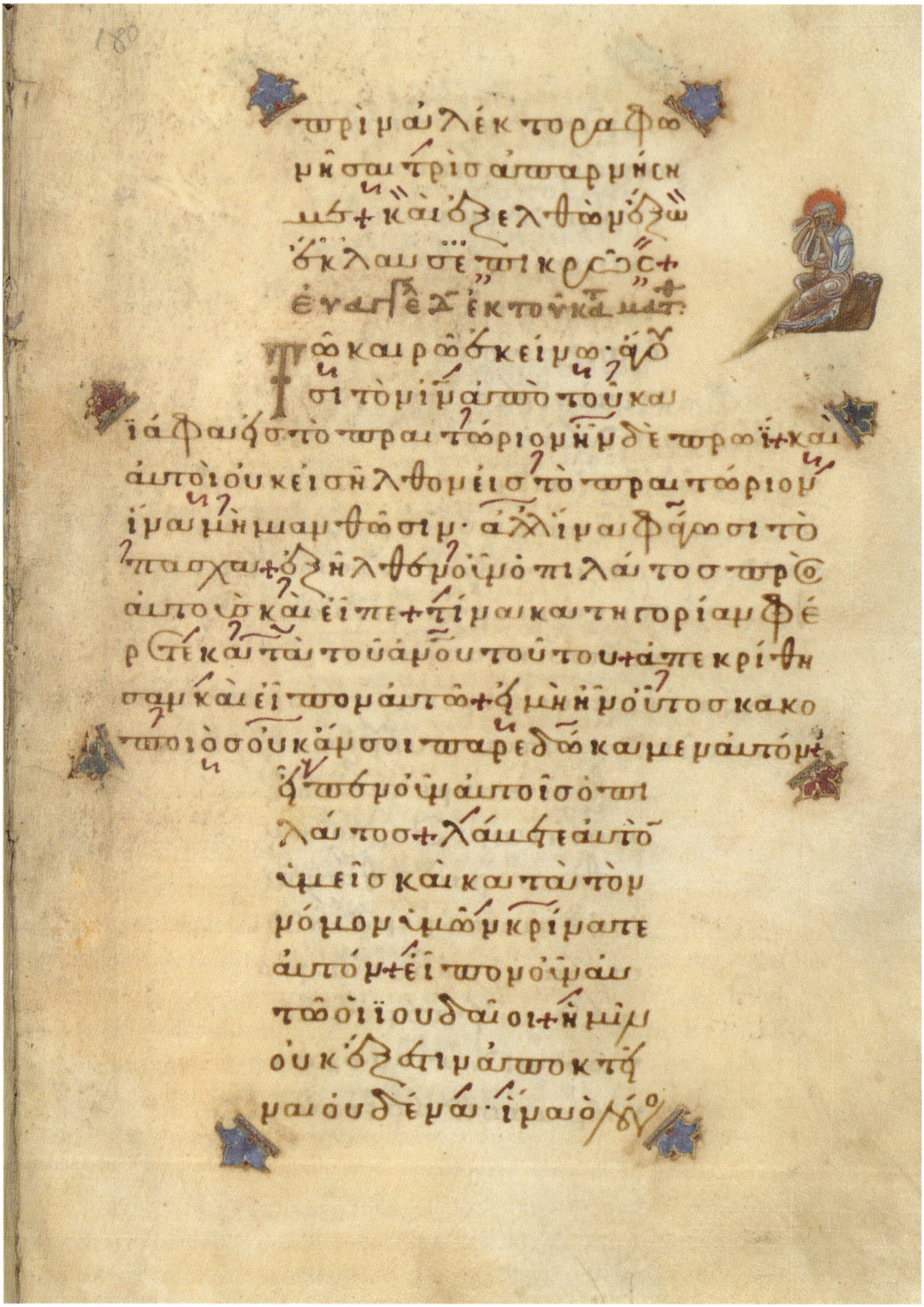

Figure 15 *(cont.)*

Figure 16 New York Cruciform Lectionary (New York, Morgan Library, Cod. 692), fol. 159^{v}. (Photo: The Pierpont Morgan Library, New York)

Interestingly, in the corresponding passage of Luke 22:34 in which Christ prophesies Peter's betrayal, the New York Cruciform Lectionary's artist had already depicted a rooster beside the line, thereby making manifest only in part the events described by Christ (fol. 159^{v}; Figure 16). Hence, the cock's subsequent appearances within the manuscript serve to fulfill that typology set forth in Luke, rather than simply illustrating the betrayal itself or the words of Christ. Luke's passage is read in the morning on Holy Thursday during the orthros – before the recounting of the betrayal of Peter later that day and on Holy Friday. Therefore, when the reader arrives at the illuminations for the betrayal (on the corresponding days in the liturgical calendar) the artist has rendered visually the typology that Luke's passage had previously set forth, demonstrating the typology's own pathology – that is, its effects on the ailing Peter, who is left crying bitterly, pressing his cloak against his face in agony – rather than articulating the indirect statement that prefigures the event. Such prefiguration had already been achieved in the marginal illumination for Luke. Thus, the placement of the cock stresses the sonic fulfillment of the prophesied moment, deriving meaning not from its iconography but rather from its deployment within the relational logic of this particular manuscript.

In the New York Lectionary, the image of the cock's first manifestation functions as a foreshadowing, a prototype (through a form of synecdoche) that is completed and fulfilled by the later addition of its other half: the image of the weeping Peter on the opposite side of the page. The complementary image manifests not individual elements such as the crowing of the cock, the denial, or the remembrance of Christ's words, but rather the completed action of the narrative. This logic of fulfillment suggests that a visual representation is not the only method of transmitting an image: by reading and hearing, the mind can generate its own images of the scenes being described and the various sensory details that they contain.

To grasp the implications of this imagination-driven investment in looking, I wish to examine one other example of the betrayal of Peter scene, which shifts the focus from the representation of sound to a self-reflexive consideration of how sound itself challenges, contests, and plays with visual representation in the lectionary. In the Dumbarton Oaks Lectionary (Washington, DC, Dumbarton Oaks, Cod. 1, fol. 122^{v}; Figure 17), the same scene is approached slightly differently than in the manuscripts examined earlier. In this image the figure of Peter, upon hearing the cock's crow from the other side of the page, remembers

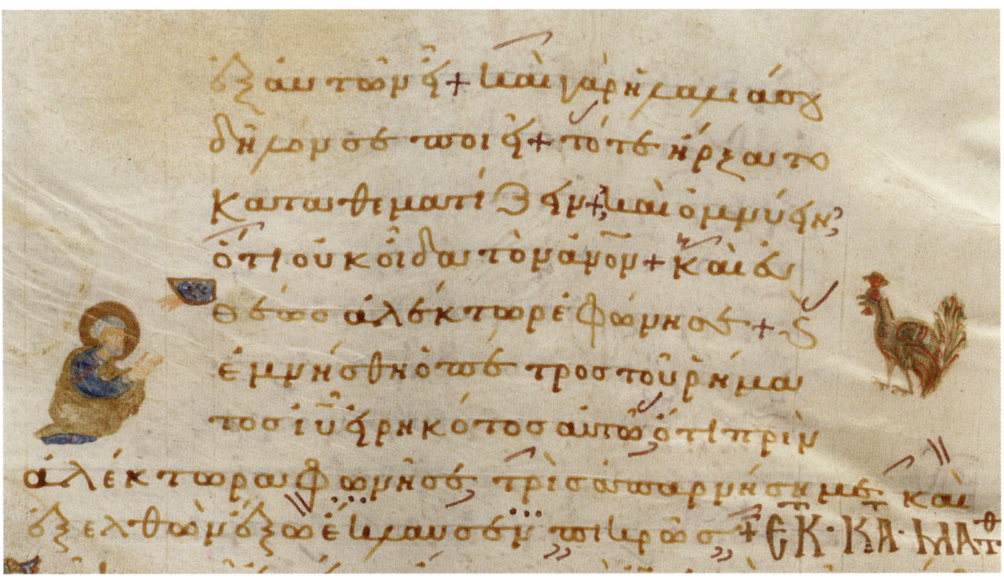

Figure 17 Dumbarton Oaks Lectionary (Washington, DC, Dumbarton Oaks, Cod. 1), fol. 122^{v}. (Photo: © Dumbarton Oaks, Byzantine Collection, Washington, DC)

Christ's words. The emphasis here is not on Peter's weeping but on the realization itself of the betrayal. His remembrance of Christ's words is indicated by the hand of God poking through the heavens, which is formed in a gesture of speech made toward a cowering Peter. The line from Matthew 26:74 reads, "And immediately the rooster crowed" (καὶ εὐθέως ἀλέκτωρ ἐφώνησεν), and after that line is the image of the rooster. On the next line, Peter is adjacent to the words "Peter was reminded" (ἐμνήσθη ὁ Πέτρος). Thus Peter performs the roles of the sentence's subject and verb in advance by manifesting himself before his textual signifier.

The hand of God, however, has a particularly curious position: it appears right beside the word "immediately" (εὐθέως), but that word has been split over two lines, leaving only its second part, "-θέως," next to God. There is something silently compelling about these orthographical choices: a visual pun between the scribe, illuminator, and reader, which revolves around matters of sound, recitation, pronunciation, and memory. Visually, the "θέως" fragment recalls the θεός of God, abutting that illustration of God's hand. However, there is a striking phonetic difference between θέως and θεός, given their accentuation, which would make it nearly impossible to confuse the two aurally. Likewise, the difference between omega and omicron, while deeply connected and assimilated in certain pronunciations of Greek, still would have borne a certain distinctiveness. Nevertheless, there is a resonance here operating between text and image. Note even the manner in which the minuscule epsilon of the θέως pushes the accent of the word to the right, dangling it over the omega, as if the word were accentuated θεώς, almost as if it were phonetically analogous to θεός. There is a play here between phonetics, orthography, narrative, and marginalia that subtly yet potently seeks to unsettle meaning, perhaps even nudging the reader to err if he is not keenly paying attention as he recites the text.

In medieval Greek, a variety of errors and mistakes are attested in the written record that reflect the changing phonetics of the language in this period and its ortho-phonetic flexibility.[40] For example, the late seventh-century sanctuary program at the Koimesis church at Nicaea includes an error in one of its inscriptions, where the Greek term for messenger or angel is spelled ΑΝΓΕΛΟΣ rather than the classical ΑΓΓΕΛΟΣ.[41] In Greek,

[40] See Robert Browning, *Medieval and Modern Greek*, 2nd edn (Cambridge University Press, 1983), 53–87. See also Io Manolessou, "On Historical Linguistics, Linguistic Variation and Medieval Greek," *Byzantine and Modern Greek Studies* 32:1 (2008): 63–79; G.P. Shipp, "The Phonology of Modern Greek," *Glotta* 37 (1958): 233–58.

[41] On the Koimesis church at Nicaea and its iconographic program, see Charles Barber, "The Koimesis Church, Nicaea: The Limits of Representation on the Eve of Iconoclasm," *Jahrbuch*

γγ produces a sound analogous to the English "ng"; thus in the inscription the double gamma is replaced with a nu-gamma combination that renders the word phonetically. The significant phonetic changes to the Greek language in the Byzantine period included shifts in vowel sounds; for example, the pronunciation of eta (η) changed from the classical /ɛ:/, a lengthened *e*, to /i/, the sound of the modern Greek iota (ι). Thus, at times an eta may be replaced in a word by an iota since they are pronounced the same.

Not only did the medieval listeners and readers exist within a soundscape that often manifested what we would call phonetic slippages, but these shifts also enabled the transmutations between text, image, and sound to take on particularly rich meaning. For example, as Bissera Pentcheva notes, in medieval Greek the verse "Taste and see that the Lord is good (Χρηστός)" (Psalm 33:9) would be phonetically indistinguishable from "Taste and see that the Lord is Christ (Χριστός)," given the homophony of the eta and iota as well as the similar accentuation in both words.[42] Thus, when spoken in the context of the liturgy during the Eucharistic rite, the psalm both suggests a gustatory perception of Christ and also demonstrates a phonetic prophecy encoded within the pre-Christian song, which for members of the Greek-speaking Christian world foreshadows the coming of Christ.

The illustration of God beside the "-θέως" engages in similar dynamics. The scene operates on an order somewhere in between orthography, orality, and aurality. The artist-scribe in his writing and illumination deliberately played with the text's use during the process of chanted recitation. Similar play – which bubbles up throughout Byzantine Gospel lectionaries, as this volume will explore – shows us as modern viewers how Byzantine artist-scribes were constantly operating within various coexistent systems of representation and manifestation across different media that encouraged word, image, performance, and sound to riff on one another. This process of unfolding signification demands users who do not passively

der Österreichischen Byzantinistik 41 (1991): 43– 60; Glenn Peers, *Subtle Bodies: Representing Angels in Byzantium* (Berkeley: University of California Press, 2001), 81–88. See also Cyril Mango, "The Date of the Narthex Mosaics of the Church of the Dormition at Nicaea," *Dumbarton Oaks Papers* 13 (1959): 245–52; Paul Underwood, "The Evidence of Restorations in the Sanctuary Mosaics of the Church of the Dormition at Nicaea," *Dumbarton Oaks Papers* 13 (1959): 235–43.

42 "γεύσασθε καὶ ἴδετε ὅτι χρηστὸς ὁ κύριος. . ." (LXX Ps. 33:9; Ps. 34:8). See Bissera Pentcheva, *The Sensual Icon: Space, Ritual, and the Senses in Byzantium* (University Park: Pennsylvania State University Press, 2010), 43.

accept single iconographic readings but who instead actively engage with the text. Doing so requires constant adjustments to their hermeneutic approach, responding to the rules and to the play on those rules in each manuscript's particular design, while also drawing on previous encounters with similar texts that create habituations and feed the users' imagination.

The private visual play in marginalia embodies the in-between spaces that this book explores in subsequent chapters, trailing the Gospel from text and image into the resonant spaces of its performance. My goal is to parse out intriguing instances of such play in order to understand how Byzantine scribes, illuminators, performers, and listeners partook in these dynamics, acknowledging that a text is not simply written or spoken, but rather performed in space. This initiates a trail that begins with the dynamics of text and image relations on the page, on to the reader-viewer's grasp and responses to these cues, and on to the architectural spaces and liturgical performances that contour and define how the congregation listened to these stories, both visualizing them in their imagination and perceiving them in the church spaces around them.

ᾱ + τ̄ + +

ΕΥ͂ ΕΚ ΚΑ ΙΩ͂ :

ν ἀρχῇ· ἦν ὁ λό
γος + καὶ ὁ λόγος
ἦν πρὸς τὸν θν̄
καὶ θσ̄ ἦν ὁ λόγος +
οὗτος ἦν ἐν ἀρχῇ
πρὸς τὸν θν̄ + πά
ντα δι᾽ αὐτοῦ ἐγένε
το + καὶ χωρὶς αὐτοῦ
ἐγένετο οὐδὲ ἕν. ὅ

2 | Miniatures and Marginalia

A Visual Grammar and Syntax

A striking aspect of the Gospel lectionary is the regularity of many of its initials and textual beginnings to each lection. Except when the textual content does not allow, most readings within the lectionary begin with one of two formulaic introductions added to the Gospel text: "Said the Lord" (Εἶπεν ὁ Κ[ύριο]ς; Figure 18) or "At that opportune time" (Τῷ καιρῷ ἐκείνῳ; Figure 19). As a result, many of the historiated initials in lectionaries are "E" or "T"; this predictability makes possible a more cohesive and standardized system of illumination than that which appears in contemporaneous books of homilies, Psalters, or other texts with historiated initials. The illustrations for both formulas often demonstrate a strictly literal depiction of the opening line. The initial does not produce a scene that summarizes the lection or its liturgical function, but rather directly visualizes the text. These initials cannot be treated as distinct iconographic groups or as solutions to pictorial problems. Instead, they lay the groundwork for the complex meaning and semiotic play that occur in the interstices of looking and reading.

This chapter takes a closer look at the Gospel lectionary's illuminations, particularly the relationship between historiated initials, marginalia, and miniatures.[1] Its goal is to sketch out the overall design logic of the types of illuminations found in the lectionary, and articulate some of the formulas and elements that are relatively constant in many of these manuscripts. Using these overarching insights into how initials, marginalia, and miniatures were set up alongside and in contrast to one another, I will sketch a series of rules and conventions that set the lectionary apart from other manuscripts and give it iconographic consistency across various iterations. The next chapter will build on this foundation in order to analyze how artists working on lectionaries purposely and repeatedly overstepped, outplayed, or subverted these rules in their illuminations. In this process, artists accustomed viewers to expect certain things from these illumination

[1] For a brief survey on the relations between word and image in Byzantine lectionaries, see Anna Zakharova, "The Relationship between Text and Image in Byzantine Illuminated Gospel Lectionaries," in Karin Krause and Barbara Schellewald (eds.), *Bild und Text im Mittelalter* (Cologne: Böhlau, 2011), 283–311.

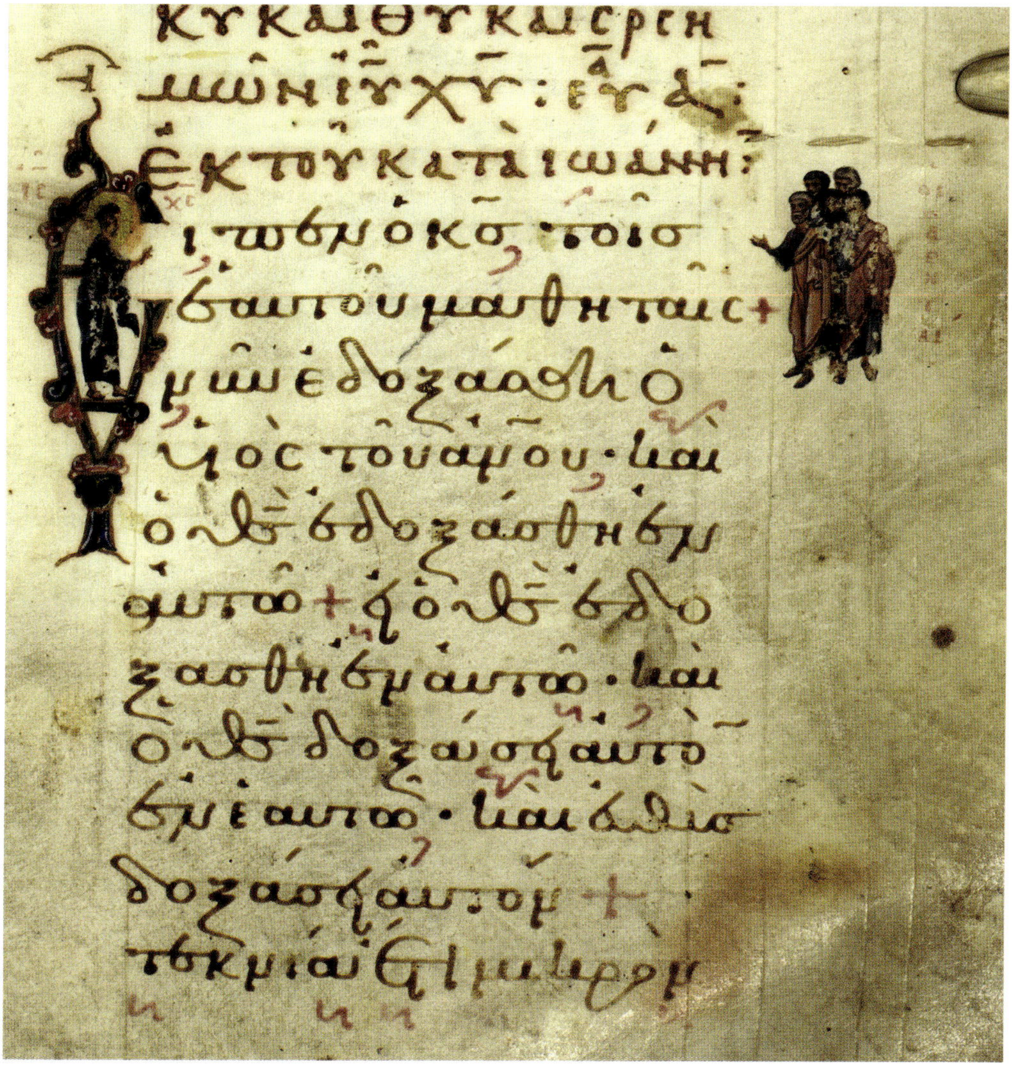

Figure 18 Athens Lectionary (Athens, National Library of Greece, Cod. 68), fol. 123r.
(Photo: National Library of Greece / The Center for the Study of New Testament Manuscripts, www.csntm.org, digitized NLG 68 at the National Library of Greece)

programs and simultaneously challenged those expectations to generate nuanced and complex images that seem to fall somewhere between straightforward iconographic depictions and cryptic puzzles of representation. The following examples demonstrate how the possibilities structured by the illuminations of these formulaic openings train viewers in habits of looking that enable these images to operate outside the logic of their own iconography.

Figure 19 Jaharis Lectionary (New York, Metropolitan Museum of Art, 2007.286), fol. 191^{r}. (Photo: The Metropolitan Museum of Art, New York, Purchase, Mary and Michael Jaharis Gift and Lila Acheson Wallace Gift, 2007, www.metmuseum.org)

The Two Formulas of the Initial

The images for the "E" formula usually depict Christ in a gesture of speech. But variation occurs in its surrounding marginalia, where the recipients of the speech act are often depicted when the formulaic opening itself ("Said the Lord") is appended with an indirect object, such as "to his disciples" (see Athens, National Library of Greece, cod. 68, fol. 123^{r}; Figure 18). Since in the sentence Christ is the subject and also the agent, he is portrayed performing the action described by the words. The epsilon's shell provides a useful, quasi-architectural space within which Christ is shown. The gilded and colorful enclosure echoes the liturgical space as if he were surrounded by mosaics or frescos, the canopy over the altar, and the colonnades of a large ambo, like the one at Hagia Sophia described by Paul the Silentiary in his sixth-century account. However, the "E" itself is completed not by the architectural setting but by the raised hand of the speaking figure within this niche-like structure, which forms the letter's crossbar. The initial's illumination stresses the orality of the image-text and its spatiotemporal performance. Since the subject of the sentence is prescribed by the statement "Said the Lord," this image rarely varies from the figure of Christ; the only rare exception is when it shows the author of the Gospel from which the reading is excerpted.

In one tenth-century lectionary in Athens (Athens, National Library of Greece, cod. 59, fols. 12^{v}, 94^{r}, 61^{r}; Figures 20–22), the resonance between

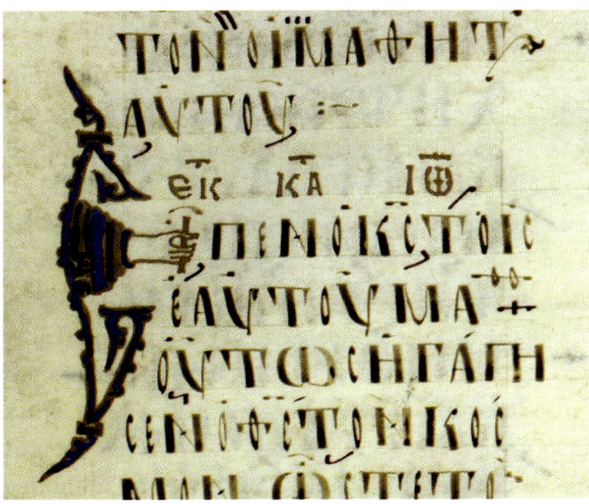

Figure 20 Lectionary (Athens, National Library of Greece, cod. 59), fol. 12^{v}. (Photo: National Library of Greece / The Center for the Study of New Testament Manuscripts, www.csntm.org, digitized NLG 59 at the National Library of Greece)

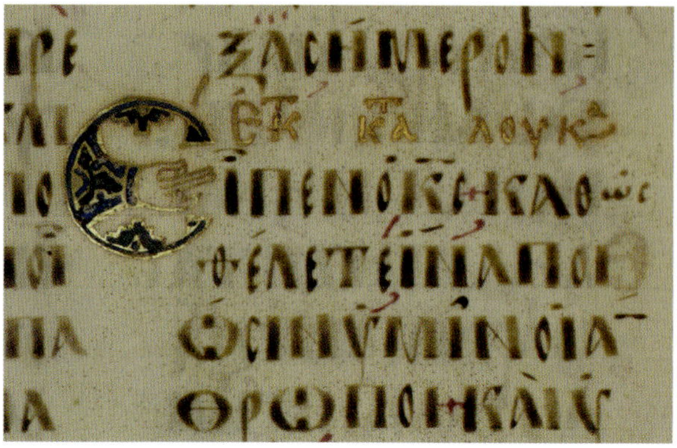

Figure 21 Lectionary (Athens, National Library of Greece, cod. 59), fol. 94r. (Photo: National Library of Greece / The Center for the Study of New Testament Manuscripts, www.csntm.org, digitized NLG 59 at the National Library of Greece)

Figure 22 Lectionary (Athens, National Library of Greece, cod. 59), fol. 61r. (Photo: National Library of Greece / The Center for the Study of New Testament Manuscripts, www.csntm.org, digitized NLG 59 at the National Library of Greece)

word and image, gesture and sound, is made explicit. There, the outstretched hand vacillates between making an oratorical gesture and also grabbing on to the iota beside it. This iota is carefully misaligned with the rest of the letters and slightly larger, tipped at an angle so that it represents a scroll in the grip of the crossbar hand; at the same time, its circumflex and smooth-breathing mark leave no ambiguity about its status as a letter. In other similar instances, the outstretched hand may grasp a scroll and leave the iota untouched, but here the artist chooses to play with the association between speech and scrolls. This link allows artists to embody the orality evoked by the word completed by the iota (that word being Εἶπεν) and underscore that this speech, which the reader now recites, is emerging from a written text. One reason for the scroll's association with speech is that contemporaneous texts, including poems and letters, were often reproduced on loose, single parchment folios, which could easily circulate among small groups and audiences.[2] These loose leaves were often rolled into a scroll (εἰλητάριον)[3] so that they could be distributed, circulated, and eventually performed. Thereby, scrolls suggest the aurality of the oral performance to come.

In the context of the Divine Liturgy, scrolls would have been directly associated with the speech of the clergy, particularly the priests and deacons: bearing scrolls, they would recite the prayers of the rite, both silently and aloud. This act is often represented in the apse of Byzantine churches, where the fathers of the Church, dressed as bishops, bear unfurled scrolls inscribed with their prayers as if partaking in the rite being performed before them. As Sharon Gerstel observes, these "scrolls endow the bishops with the faculty of speech,"[4] enabling them to actively participate in the liturgy. Hence, when depicted within the initial epsilon of Εἶπεν, the scroll not only appears as an indication of speech but alludes to other crucial liturgical manuscripts: namely, the scrolls containing the liturgies of John Chrysostom and Basil the Great and their rites' prayers. In choosing to depict either a hand or figure making an oratorical gesture or holding a scroll (see Vatican City, Biblioteca Apostolica Vaticana, gr. 1157, fols. 39^{v}, 51^{v}; Figures 23 and 24), the artists illuminating this formulaic opening were able to stress the orality of the words spoken within the text as well as the orality of the Gospel text itself during its recitation in the Divine Liturgy.

[2] See Bernard, *Writing and Reading Byzantine Secular Poetry*, 92–96. See also Stratis Papaioannou, "Fragile Literature: Byzantine Letter-Collections and the Case of Michael Psellos," in Paolo Odorico (ed.), *La face cachée de la littérature byzantine: Le texte en tant que message immédiat* (Paris: Centre d'études byzantines, néo-helléniques et sud-est européennes, École des Hautes Études en Sciences Sociales, 2012), 289–328.

[3] On the Greek terminology of books and manuscripts, see Basilios Atsalos, *La terminologie du livre-manuscrit à l'époque byzantine: Termes désignant le livre-manuscrit e l'écriture* (Thessaloniki: Hetaireia Makedonikōn Spoudōn, 1971), esp. 168–69.

[4] Sharon Gerstel, *Beholding the Sacred Mysteries: Programs of the Byzantine Sanctuary* (Seattle: University of Washington Press, 1999), 32. See also Sharon Gerstel, "Liturgical Scrolls in the Byzantine Sanctuary," *Greek, Roman and Byzantine Studies* 35:2 (1994): 195–204.

Figure 23 Lectionary (Vatican City, Biblioteca Apostolica Vaticana, gr. 1157), fol. 39^{v}.
(Photo: © 2019 Biblioteca Apostolica Vaticana. Reproduced by permission of Biblioteca Apostolica Vaticana, all rights reserved)

Figure 24 Lectionary (Vatican City, Biblioteca Apostolica Vaticana, gr. 1157), fol. 51^{v}.
(Photo: © 2019 Biblioteca Apostolica Vaticana. Reproduced by permission of Biblioteca Apostolica Vaticana, all rights reserved)

The "T" formula allows for a wider variety of images, since it presents a spatiotemporal frame: "At that opportune time" (Τῷ καιρῷ ἐκείνῳ). Nevertheless, these images also tend to stress the oral nature of the text. In the Jaharis Gospel Lectionary, at the opening of Luke (fol. 109^{r}; Figure 25), John the Baptist stands before the pseudo-architectural column-like "T" and turns toward the text in a gesture of speech while

Figure 25 Jaharis Lectionary (New York, Metropolitan Museum of Art, 2007.286), fol. 109r.
(Photo: The Metropolitan Museum of Art, New York, Purchase, Mary and Michael Jaharis Gift and Lila Acheson Wallace Gift, 2007, www.metmuseum.org)

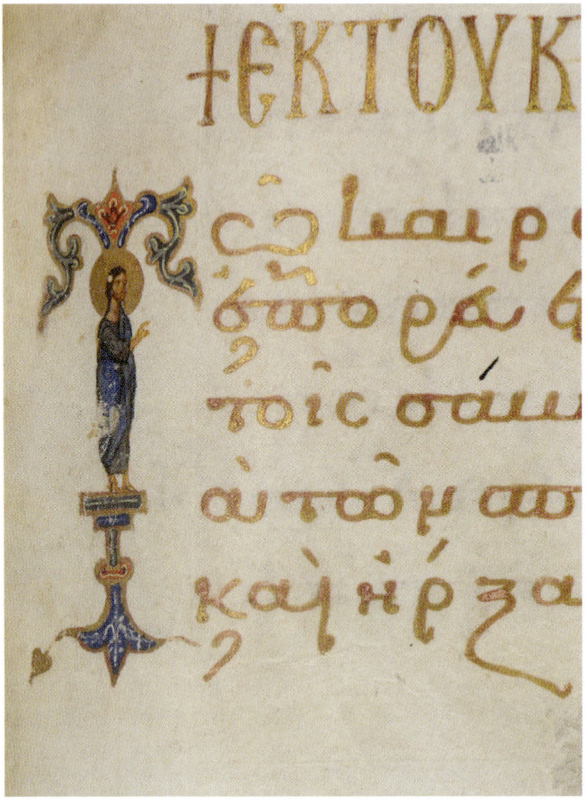

Figure 26 Jaharis Lectionary (New York, Metropolitan Museum of Art, 2007.286), fol. 191^{r}.
(Photo: The Metropolitan Museum of Art, New York, Purchase, Mary and Michael Jaharis Gift and Lila Acheson Wallace Gift, 2007, www.metmuseum.org)

holding a white rolled-up scroll in his left hand.[5] At first glance, the figure could easily be confused with Jesus, given that his garb, posture, and facial expression are very similar to Jesus' as portrayed in the capital tau that opens Mark (fol. 191^{r}; Figure 26). There Christ is dressed in a light blue himation wrapped over a dark blue chiton, as he is in the opening initial for

[5] The Metropolitan Museum of Art's Jaharis Gospel Lectionary (ca. 1100) features figural illuminations only on the opening pages for each of the four Evangelists in the synaxarion, which contains the lections for the movable feast days. The months for the menologion, which contains the fixed feast readings starting on September 1, are merely subdivided by enamel-like headbands. In the four historiated initials presented here, we see an exact adherence with the formula described above. With the exception of the first Evangelist John – always an exception, as discussed elsewhere – the historiated initials illustrate the exact words of the opening of the lections to which they correspond. For a detailed study of this manuscript, see Lowden, *Jaharis Gospel Lectionary*.

Figure 27 Jaharis Lectionary (New York, Metropolitan Museum of Art, 2007.286), fol. 43^{r}.
(Photo: The Metropolitan Museum of Art, New York, Purchase, Mary and Michael Jaharis Gift and Lila Acheson Wallace Gift, 2007, www.metmuseum.org)

Matthew (fol. 43^{r}; Figure 27). He is given a young, round face with a thin, short beard, and his long dark-brown hair is neatly pulled behind him. In the initial for Luke, however, the figure is wearing a brown himation over a yellow chiton. His face is elongated, with a long beard that almost seems to drip off his face in stalactite formations; his hair, while relatively short, appears disheveled, falling behind him in two bundles with two stray wisps at his widow's peak. Hence, by paying close attention to the images – noting particularly the differently colored garb – we clearly distinguish between the figure of John the Baptist here and the similarly positioned Christ figure in the other initials. Across the page on the far-right margin are Herod and Herodias, who are the recipients of John's discourse. The same visual formula is found in the contemporary Gospel lectionary of the Istituto Ellenico in Venice (Venice, Istituto Ellenico, Cod. 2, fol. 144^{r};

Figure 28 Venice Lectionary (Venice, Istituto Ellenico, Cod. 2), fol. 144[r].
(Photo: courtesy of the Hellenic Institute of Byzantine and Post-Byzantine Studies in Venice)

Figure 28), with the addition of a marginal portrait of Saint Luke as the lection's author.

This opening arrangement emerges from the first line of the lection, a verse that in the Bible reads: "And Herod the tetrarch, being reproved by him concerning Herodias the wife of Philip his brother, and concerning all the evils that Herod had done" (Ὁ δὲ Ἡρῴδης ὁ τετραάρχης ἐλεγχόμενος ὑπ' αὐτοῦ περὶ Ἡρῳδιάδος τῆς γυναικὸς τοῦ ἀδελφοῦ αὐτοῦ καὶ περὶ πάντων ὧν ἐποίησεν πονηρῶν ὁ Ἡρῴδης, Luke 3:19).[6] But in the lectionary's text, the scribes have replaced "by him" (ὑπ' αὐτοῦ) with "by John" (ὑπὸ Ἰωάννου) so that the excerpted text will make sense as a lection. Grammatically, the nominative passive participle, ἐλεγχόμενος, which agrees with the nominative subject Ἡρῴδης ὁ τετραάρχης, takes the preposition ὑπό in order to show the personal agency of the person performing the action on the construction's subject. Thus, the initial containing John the Baptist presents not the sentence's grammatical subject but rather its agent. Hence, the initial and marginal illustration visualize not a rigorous, grammatical description of the scene, but rather its directional agency: John is in the initial performing the action while Herod and Herodias are placed in the far-right margin, being reprimanded by him at that opportune time.

[6] John Lowden points out the opening words as placed in the lection read "At that time: Herod the tetrarch, being reproved by him for Herodias . . ." (Lowden, *Jaharis Gospel Lectionary*, 63). In his transcription and translation, however, Lowden has missed an important change to the biblical text. Because he often translates the biblical text rather than the lectionary's text, his versions must always be checked against the wording in the manuscript.

A similar alteration of the Gospel text is evidenced in the opening of Mark in the Jaharis Lectionary (folio 191r; see Figure 19). Again, this lection begins with the "T" formula, but this time Christ is depicted within the architecture of the "T." Like John the Baptist, he raises his hand in a gesture of speech and is turned toward the text. The Christ figure here illustrates the opening words: "At that opportune time: Jesus went (ἐπορεύετο ὁ Ἰ[ησοῦ]ς) on the Sabbath through the cornfields" (Mark 2:23). The Bible has ἐγένετο introducing an indirect statement – whose subject is an accusative (αὐτόν) and verb is an infinitive (παραπορεύεσθαι); whereas the excerpt instead has a middle imperfect of a verb related to the original infinitive (ἐπορεύετο) and specifies the identity of the subject/agent by adding ὁ Ἰησοῦς. These changes serve the practical function of clarifying the reading for the congregation and clearly articulating the figures and stories depicted in the marginal illustrations.

In the opening folio of the readings for the Passion cycle in the Dionysiou Lectionary (fol. 66r; Figure 29), we encounter a similarly deep play with this visual syntax. Here the lection begins with the formula "Said the Lord" and, as is often the case, further specifies the text's audience: "The Lord said to his disciples" (Εἶπεν ὁ Κ[ύριο]ς τοῖς ἑαυτοῦ μαθηταῖς). The initial's architecture constructs the performative space of the verb, with the subject – "the Lord" – performing its action. The indirect object – "his disciples" – appears spread out in groups across the page; the dative plural article "τοῖς" is adjacent to one group, as if the image itself had replaced the words "his disciples," which follow on the next line. Such play occurs frequently in a variety of illuminated lectionaries. In these instances, the image consistently manifests *in advance* what is expected by the reader, foreshadowing the word before its textual appearance.

In the Paris Lectionary (Paris, Bibliothèque nationale de France, supp. gr. 27), an extension of this play across columns of text demonstrates the agility of artists in responding creatively to what the text affords (fols. 60v–61r; Figure 30). There, the readings from Luke begin with the story of Jesus casting out a demon from a man in the temple (Luke 4:31–36). The initial is illuminated with the figure of Christ, holding a closed codex in his left hand and making a gesture of speech with his right, as one would expect, and gazing across the text and the page toward a figure in the left-hand margin of the opposite folio. Here, Christ is the illustration for the opening verse, which in the Bible reads: "And he came down to Capernaum, a city of Galilee, and there he was, teaching them on the Sabbaths" (Καὶ κατῆλθεν εἰς Καφαρναοὺμ πόλιν τῆς Γαλιλαίας. Καὶ ἦν διδάσκων αὐτοὺς ἐν τοῖς σάββασιν). To aid comprehension, the lectionary makes the same kinds

Figure 29 Dionysiou Lectionary (Mount Athos, Dionysiou Monastery, Cod. 587), fol. 66[r].
(Photo: Patriarchal Institute for Patristic Studies in Thessaloniki)

Figure 30 Paris Lectionary (Paris, Bibliothèque nationale de France, supp. gr. 27), fol. 60^{v}–61^{r}. (Photo: Bibliothèque nationale de France)

of alteration to the biblical text that we have already seen, adding Jesus' name to clarify the subject and deleting narrative elements such as the initial "And" (Καί) and the prefix κατά- from κατῆλθεν, which show relationships of time and location that are confusing without the preceding text.

The accusative αὐτούς, referring to those being taught by him, is likewise changed to the dative αὐτοῖς to stress that the teaching is being performed to or for them. The most important indirect object – the man from whom the demon is excised – is cleverly displayed on that opposite folio at which Christ gazes from the initial.

After the demon has been cast out of that person (Luke 4:35), the Gospel continues: "And amazement came upon all, and they were speaking together, with one another, saying, 'What is this word? For with authority and power he commands the unclean spirits, and they come out!'" (Luke 4:36; fol. 61^r^, Figure 31). The figure's right hand is raised in wonder and speech at that final verse, as if responding to Christ across the page. However, he is placed right next to the exclamation of the people in this verse, as if among those speaking these words. At the same time, in order to emphasize that this man is the recipient of Christ's miraculous words, his body encompasses the portion of the exclamation that refers to the exorcism: "For with authority and power he commands the unclean spirits, and they come out" (ὅτι ἐν ἐξουσίᾳ καὶ δυνάμει ἐπιτάσσει τοῖς ἀκαθάρτοις πνεύμασιν, καὶ ἐξέρχονται). In this way, the figure is a synecdoche for the entirety of the crowd that Christ was teaching, that now marvels in his wonders, and is identified as the person benefiting from his miracle. The change of the biblical text to the dative in the lection's opening verse marks him as the indirect object, as part of the dative "them" (αὐτοῖς) to whom or, better yet, for whom Christ taught.

Such marginalia carefully articulate the grammatical and syntactical nuances of the lections through visual play, using placement and hierarchy to visually represent the dynamics of the verses and their actions in literal depictions. The remarkable thing here is that even in their faithful literalism, the lectionaries' artists show a striking and complex creativity as they follow the contours of the written words on the page and play with their possibilities. For example, on the folio in the Jaharis Lectionary discussed above (fol. 43^r^; see Figure 27), the lection initiated by the E formula opens with a line from Matthew 18:10: "Said the Lord: 'See that you do not despise one of these little ones'" (Ὁρᾶτε μὴ καταφρονήσητε ἑνὸς τῶν μικρῶν τούτων). Jesus sits upon a stool with his arm raised in speech, gesturing toward a child below him. The child stands on an added level of the initial, below Christ, looking up at him with hands raised up in supplication. The child naturally appears beside the words "one of these little ones" (ἑνὸς τῶν μικρῶν τούτων), illustrating the object of Christ's statement. Note as well that while Christ's hand is raised to form the epsilon's crossbar, his fingers also curve downward toward the child, stressing the deictic function of the "these" (τούτων) in the phrase "these

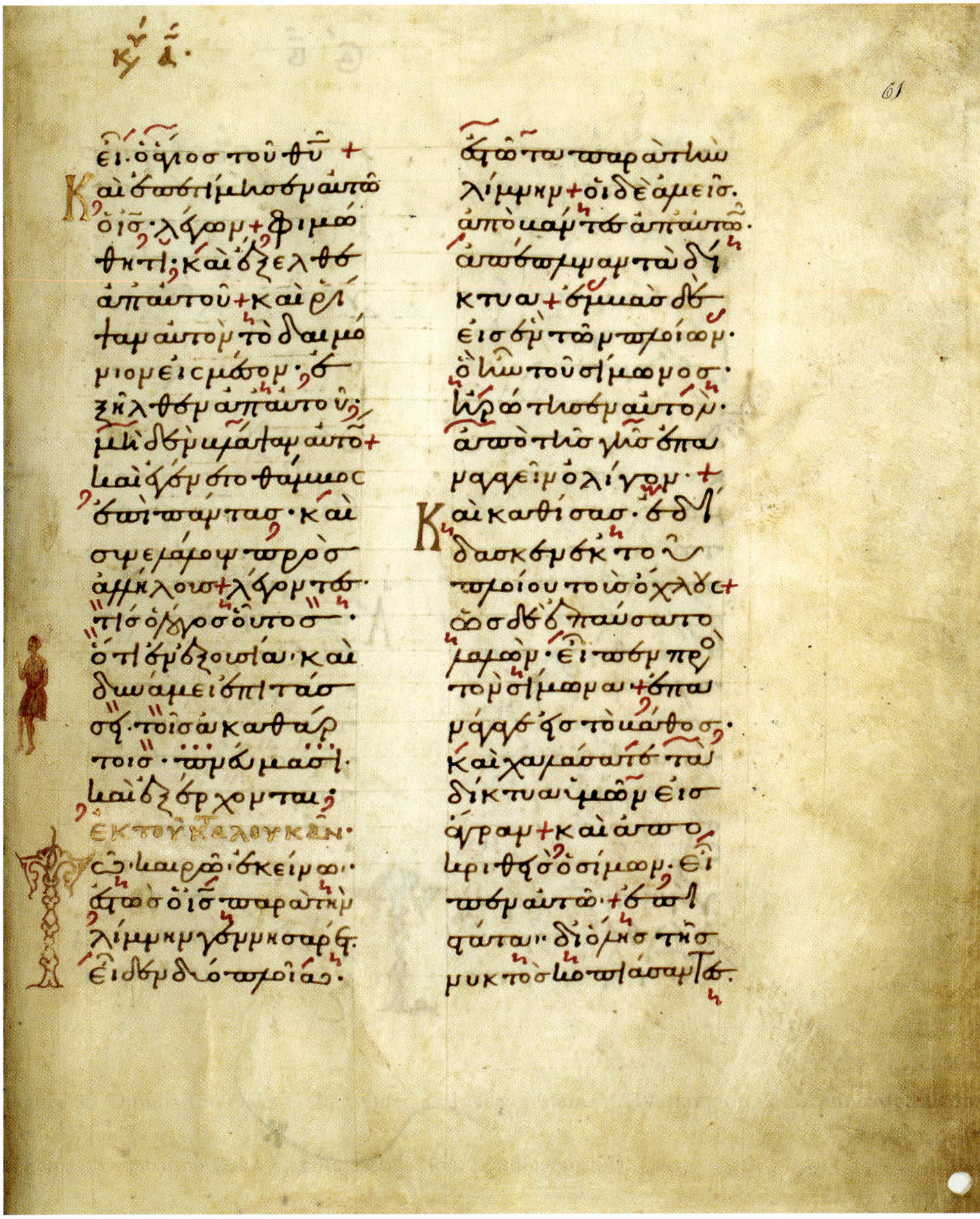

Figure 31 Paris Lectionary (Paris, Bibliothèque nationale de France, supp. gr. 27), fol. 61[r].
(Photo: Bibliothèque nationale de France)

little ones" and indicating within this lection that there is in fact a child present. The deictic "these" and the child's depiction in the initial recall the context of the lection's excerpt: earlier in this biblical passage, Christ had called a child to stand in the midst of the disciples when they asked, "Who is the greatest in the kingdom of heaven?" (Matthew 18:1–2). Hence, the artist has gone beyond what is explicitly stated in the lection both to flesh out the scene and to better explain the demonstrative pronoun. In drawing from other portions of the biblical text, the artist has been careful to bring in the detail of the child only, which helps explain the lection's demonstrative pronoun – much as we saw above in manuscripts in which a third-person personal pronoun in the biblical text is replaced with a proper noun. Word and image work together to clarify and expand upon one another, as the syntax of the lection's verses is articulated visually.

An excellent example of this visual grammar is offered by a historiated initial not from a lectionary but from the *Homilies on the Virgin* of James of Kokkinobaphos, circa 1122–25 (Vatican gr. 1162, fol. 147^{r}; Figure 32).[7] In the miniature introducing this section of the homily, the Virgin is seen resting in the land with a creature that personifies Earth beside her. Below, the homily's text begins with the word "Γῆ" (Earth), and the same creature forms the initial. Jeffrey Anderson, in his discussion of the Sinai Homilies, has referred to this migration of theme from a miniature to a corresponding initial as "reduplication," and it is a common element in these works – see, for example, the reduplication of David across the miniature and initial in the Dumbarton Oaks Psalter, Odes, and New Testament manuscript (Washington, DC, Dumbarton Oaks, Cod. 3, fol. 27^{r}; Figure 33).[8] Robert Nelson, in particular, has elucidated the complex grammatical and oral play found in these and other manuscripts, demonstrating how such texts' visual systems rely on an aural logic tied to their recitation.[9] An analogous approach is taken to select initials from the only extant illuminated grammar book, made for Sebastokratorissa Irene with the text of Theodore Prodromos's *Grammar* (Jerusalem, Greek Orthodox

[7] Jeffrey C. Anderson, "The Illustrated Sermons of James the Monk: Their Dates, Order, and Place in the History of Byzantine Art," *Viator* 22 (1991): 69–120, esp. 96; Kallirroe Linardou, "The Kokkinobaphos Manuscripts Revisited: The Internal Evidence of the Books," *Scriptorium* 61:2 (2007): 384–407. For a more extensive study of the relationships between word and image in the manuscript, there is a new study by Kallirroe Linardou, "Reading Two Byzantine Illustrated Books: The Kokkinobaphos Manuscripts (Vaticanus graecus 1162 and Parisinus graecus 1208)," PhD dissertation, University of Birmingham (2004). See also Irmgard Hutter, "Die Homilien des Mönches Jakobos und ihre Illustrationen," PhD dissertation, University of Vienna (1970); Irmgard Hutter and Paul Canart, *Das Marienhomiliar des Mönches Jakobos von Kokkinobaphos, Codex Vaticanus graecus 1162*, 2 vols. (Vatican, 1991).

[8] Jeffrey C. Anderson, "The Illustration of Cod. Sinai. Gr. 339," *Art Bulletin* 61:2 (1979): 167–85, at 171. See also Viktor Lazarev, *Storia della pittura bizantina*, Italian trans. Gildo Fossati (Turin: G. Einaudi, 1967), fig. 244; Sirarpie Der Nersessian, "A Psalter and New Testament Manuscript at Dumbarton Oaks," *Dumbarton Oaks Papers* 19 (1965): 153–83.

[9] Robert S. Nelson, "The Discourse of Icons, Then and Now," *Art History* 12:2 (1989): 144–57.

Figure 32 James Kokkinobaphos, *Homilies on the Virgin* (Vatican City, Biblioteca Apostolica Vaticana, gr. 1162), fol. 147ʳ.

(Photo:)

Figure 33 Dumbarton Oaks Psalter, Odes, and New Testament (Washington, DC, Dumbarton Oaks, Cod. 3), fol. 27r.
(Photo: © Dumbarton Oaks, Byzantine Collection, Washington, DC)

Patriarchate, Taphou, Cod. 52).[10] When the opening word permits it, the artist has depicted in the initial an image that manifests the meaning of the word, such as two oxen making up the O for Ὁ βοῦς, "The bull" (fol. 38^{v}; Figure 34), or two figures, presumably Nuses, holding what appears to be a red book (perhaps the grammar book itself) to form the H of Ἡ μοῦσα, "The Muse" (fol. 50^{v}; Figure 35). While the latter does not exhibit reduplication of a miniature's theme, in both these examples there is an explicit understanding of the initial as a conduit into the visualization of the words being declaimed – even in books not necessarily intended for liturgical use, such as the grammar book.

Marginalia versus Miniatures: Visualizing Different Types of Information

The Dionysiou Lectionary deserves special attention since the manuscript features an illumination program that complexly and self-reflexively engages with the context of its use and performance in the Divine Liturgy. The various miniatures that open important lections depict the theme of a particular feast day or liturgical event, rather than representing the lection's narrative.[11] The only three headpieces in the manuscript depict the Anastasis for the Easter reading, the Prayer at Gethsemane for the opening of the Passion Week lections, and St. Symeon the Stylite for September 1 at the opening of the fixed-feast readings. These three headpieces emphasize the feast celebrated on that day in the liturgical calendar, yet only the Prayer at Gethsemane has a connection with the actual lection. The use of a headpiece for the Passion cycle lacks a parallel, but it stresses the manuscript's liturgical focus. Despite their marked reflection on the use of the lectionary, the initials themselves never privilege the feast day over the narrative, and marginalia in the Passion cycle are used only when the miniature is oriented toward the feast day and has thus deflected visual emphasis from the literal reading.

[10] Ioannis Spatharakis, "An Illuminated Greek Grammar Manuscript in Jerusalem: A Contribution to the Study of Comnenian Illuminated Ornament," *Jahrbuch der Österreichischen Byzantinistik* 35 (1985): 231–52. On Sebastokratorissa Irene, see Elizabeth Jeffreys, "The Sevastokratorissa Eirene as Literary Patroness: The Monk Iakovos," *Jahrbuch der Österreichischen Byzantinistik* 32:3 (1982): 63–71; Odysseus Lampsidis, "Zur Sebastokratorissa Eirene," *Jahrbuch der Österreichischen Byzantinistik* 34 (1984): 91–105.

[11] See Dolezal, "Illuminating the Liturgical Word," esp. 23–43; Dolezal, "Middle Byzantine Lectionary," 1:149–217.

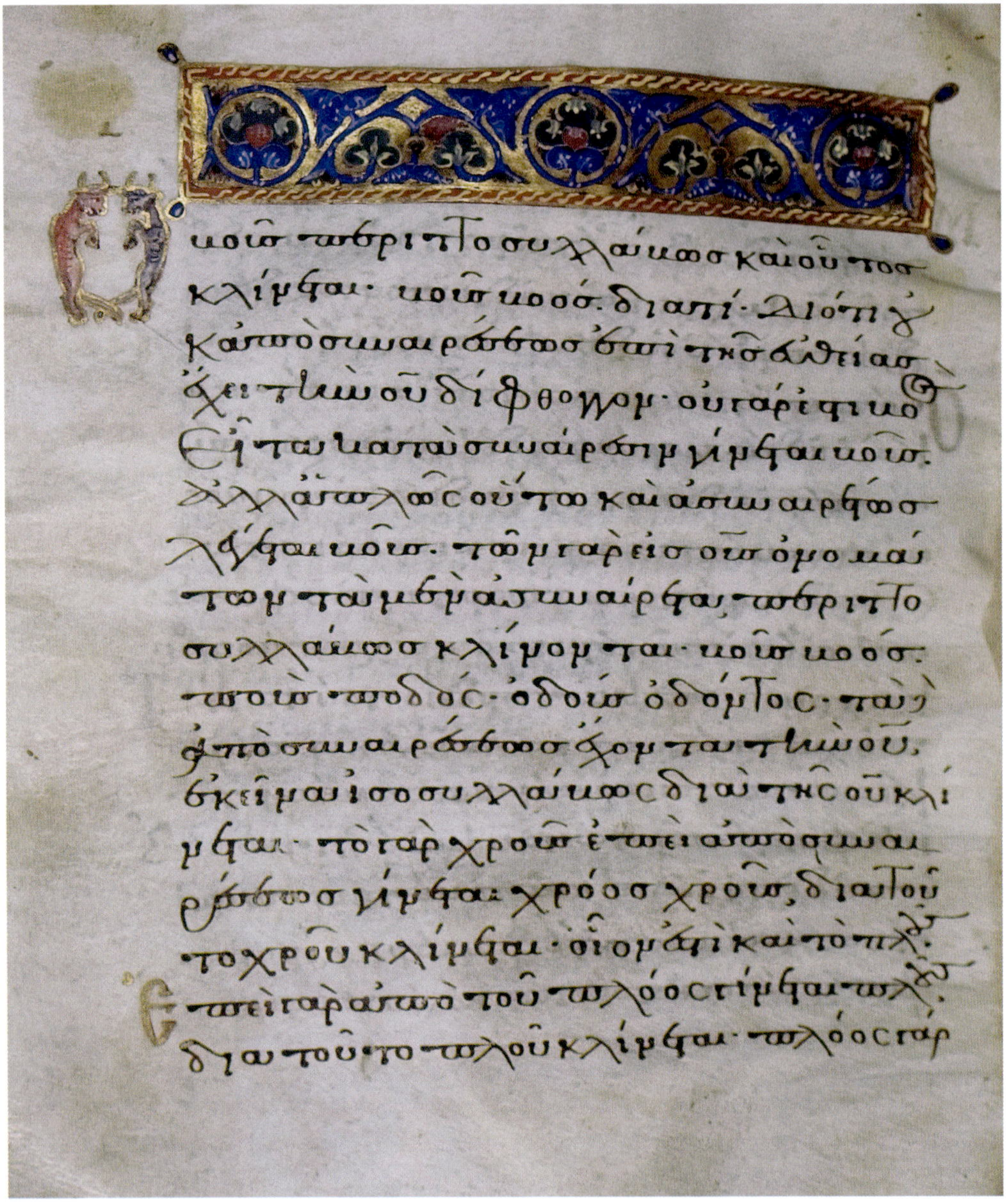

Figure 34 Grammar book (Jerusalem, Greek Orthodox Patriarchate, Taphou, Cod. 52), fol. 38v.
(Photo: Courtesy of the Greek Orthodox Patriarchate of Jerusalem)

Figure 35 Grammar book (Jerusalem, Greek Orthodox Patriarchate, Taphou, Cod. 52), fol. 50v.
(Photo: Courtesy of the Greek Orthodox Patriarchate of Jerusalem)

These aspects of historiated initials demonstrate that they function quite uniquely in the lectionary. Instead of material in the margins commenting on or contesting the content unfurled in the primary text, while the miniature summarizes the reading,[12] in the Byzantine lectionary, the miniature comments on the spatial or temporal context of the reading, while the initials and marginal scenes literally depict (but usually do not summarize) the literal words of the text. The Dumbarton Oaks Lectionary does use the marginal scenes for the reading of the Ascension (fol. 32ʳ; Figure 36) to provide a summary of the narrative rather than depicting the exact words on the page from Mark 16:9–20, read during the orthros on the Thursday of the Ascension. Such exceptions have a curious feature. While the image of Christ being elevated by angels is positioned in the top center of the page, the Apostles who look up at him in awe all are near or next to words that point to them or articulate their spectatorship through demonstrative pronouns and participles denoting sight: thus θεασαμένοις is beside images in the central and right-hand margins at the bottom of the page. As is common in these arrangements, the corresponding article τοῖς is located at the end of one line of text – immediately next to an image, when possible – to play with revealing word and image as one.

A similar layout is found in the Venice Lectionary's treatment of the Transfiguration (fol. 400ʳ; Figure 37). The scene of Christ alongside Moses and Elijah appears atop the page, immediately to the right of the line that refers to Moses and Elijah talking with Jesus (Matthew 17:3). In the central margin, next to the mention of Peter in the left column (Matthew 17:4), is a figure with cropped gray hair who appears to carry a long, thin key, in keeping with contemporaneous depictions of Peter. While he looks up and seemingly gestures toward the Transfiguration, he is in fact pointing to the words in the right column that read "the disciples" (οἱ μαθηταί). To the right of that column are two disciples who mirror these words from Matthew 17:6: "And the disciples having heard, did fall upon their face, and were exceedingly afraid" (καὶ ἀκούσαντες οἱ μαθηταὶ ἔπεσαν ἐπὶ πρόσωπον αὐτῶν καὶ ἐφοβήθησαν σφόδρα). Hence, these two Apostles witnessing the scene embody the actions of the group: falling on their faces (ἔπεσαν ἐπὶ πρόσωπον αὐτῶν) and recoiling in fear (ἐφοβήθησαν σφόδρα), as they seemingly attempt to run off the page. Both appear next to the

12 For western examples of this model, see Camille, *Image on the Edge*. See also Lucy Freeman Sandler, *Studies in Manuscript Illumination, 1200–1400* (London: Pindar Press, 2008); Lilian Randall, *Images in the Margins of Gothic Manuscripts* (Berkeley: University of California Press, 1966).

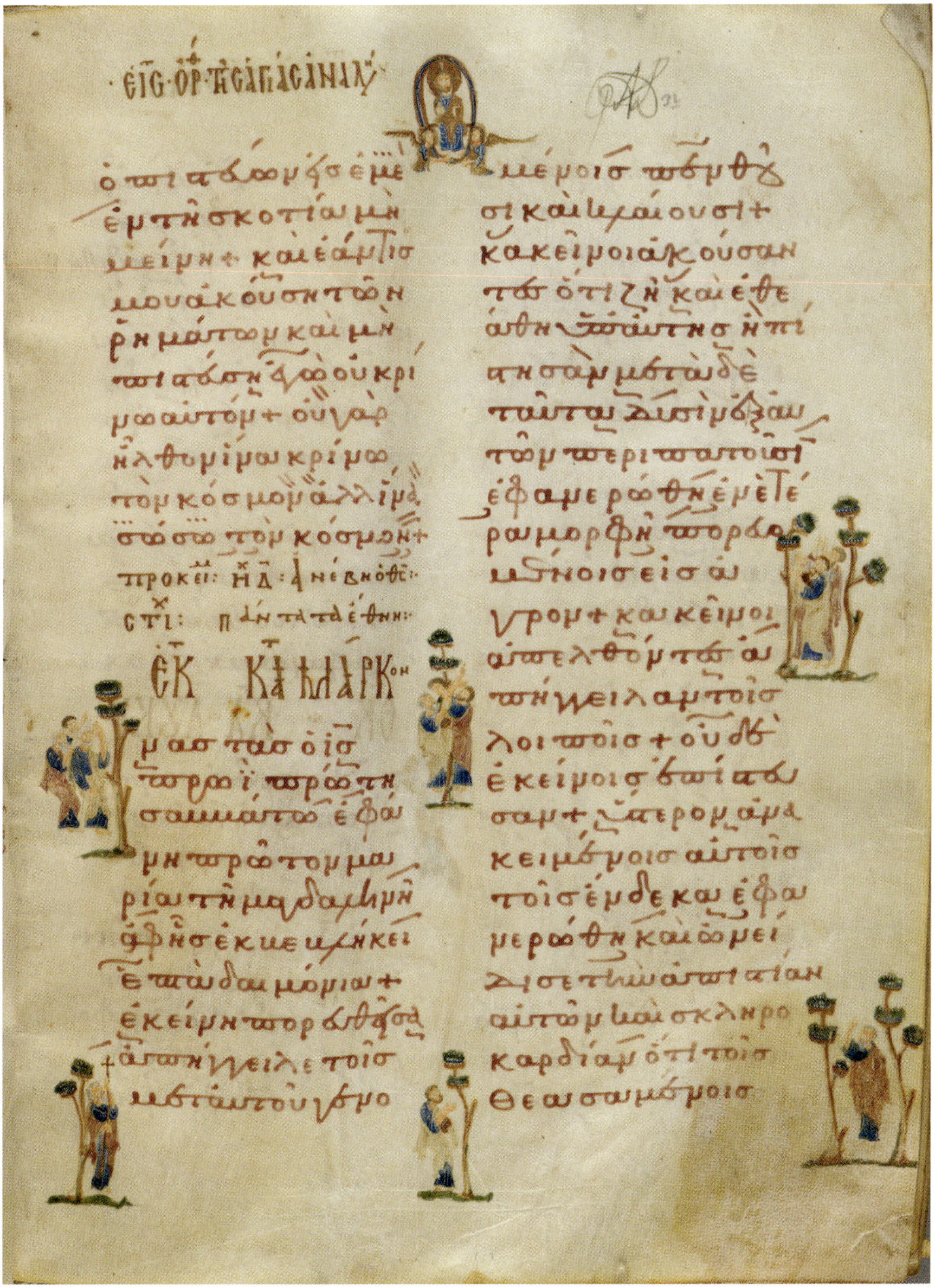

Figure 36 Dumbarton Oaks Lectionary (Washington, DC, Dumbarton Oaks, Cod. 1), fol. 32[r].
(Photo: © Dumbarton Oaks, Byzantine Collection, Washington, DC)

Figure 37 Venice Lectionary (Venice, Istituto Ellenico, Cod. 2), fol. 400r.
(Photo: courtesy of the Hellenic Institute of Byzantine and Post-Byzantine Studies in Venice)

words that describe their actions. Similarly extensive marginal scenes, responding directly to the words beside them and expanding narratives on the page, often occur in lections for the Nativity; examples include the Vatican (fols. 277r–281v; Figures 38–42) and Paris Lectionaries (fols. 172r and 173r; Figures 43–44). Therefore, as the reader moves through the text, such images make visible in advance the words that are to come. In each of these examples, since the passage lacks a discrete miniature, the artist has chosen to unite the functions of both the marginal and initial scenes with the logic of the miniature to construct a *mise-en-page* that plays with elements of both.

In the Vatican Lectionary, the scene of the Ascension in Luke 24:36–53, read during the Divine Liturgy on the Thursday of the Ascension, is not spread over the page but depicted in one scene, in the middle of the right-hand margin (fol. 52r; Figure 45). There, the Ascension is portrayed immediately beside the moment in the lection when Christ ascends into the heavens (Luke 24:51–52). The image encompasses portions of the two verses: "he was carried up into heaven. And they worshipped him and returned to Jerusalem with joy" (ἀνεφέρετο εἰς τὸν οὐρανόν. καὶ αὐτοὶ προσκυνήσαντες αὐτὸν ὑπέστρεψαν εἰς Ἰερουσαλὴμ μετὰ χαρᾶς). As in

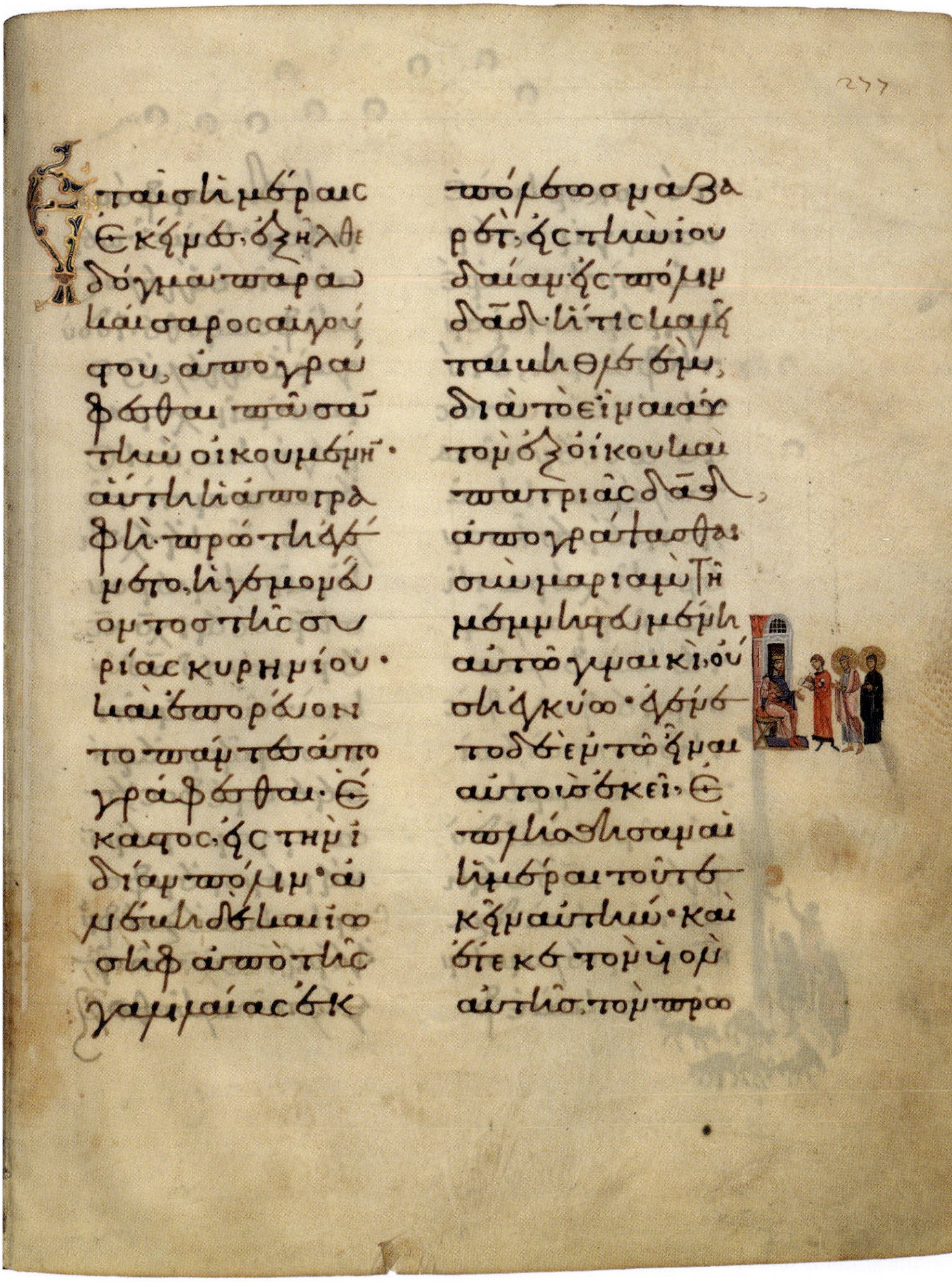

Figure 38 Vatican Lectionary (Vatican City, Biblioteca Apostolica Vaticana, gr. 1156), fol. 277r.
(Photo: © 2019 Biblioteca Apostolica Vaticana. Reproduced by permission of Biblioteca Apostolica Vaticana, all rights reserved)

Figure 39 Vatican Lectionary (Vatican City, Biblioteca Apostolica Vaticana, gr. 1156), fol. 277v–78r.

previous examples discussed, the artist and scribe work as one to play with the relationship between the text and the image. Note how the flourish of the final sigma of "into" (εἰς) extends beyond the text's margin, directing the eye toward Christ in a mandorla borne by angels. Cleverly, here the εἰς abuts the heavenly realm into which Christ is ascending. Thus, as in other examples given, the preposition at the edge of the text column deploys the marginal image to represent in advance the textual signifier that will follow on the coming line, which in this case is "heaven" (τὸν οὐρανόν). The sigma's extension thus makes visible the ineffable space that cannot be represented – the heaven above. Also remarkable is how the placement of the marginalia reveals the interrelation between text and image. While the logic and play of this scene correspond to those seen elsewhere, the text was evidently written with the expectation that an image of the Ascension would be added, since the scribe indented it to accommodate and frame this illumination. Not only does this design support the argument that the

Figure 40 Vatican Lectionary (Vatican City, Biblioteca Apostolica Vaticana, gr. 1156), fol. 278^{v}–79^{r}. (Photo: © 2019 Biblioteca Apostolica Vaticana. Reproduced by permission of Biblioteca Apostolica Vaticana, all rights reserved)

sigma's extension is intended to indicate the heavens and frame the illustration, but it helps us to better grasp how these were intentional and willful moves by artists and scribes alike throughout the manuscript's production.

The historiated initial for the opening of the Dionysiou 587's menologion section depicting St. Symeon on September 1 (fol. 116^{r}; Figure 46) offers a useful point of comparison. Although St. Symeon is depicted in the headpiece and the initial "T" formula would easily be followed if St. Symeon were reduplicated on his column, the manuscript instead illustrates the initial with Christ, identifiable by a cruciform-nimbus and the open book. Here, as we have come to expect, his manifestation matches the words of the lection's opening verse, derived from Luke 4:16: "At that time: Christ came into Nazareth" (ἦλθε[ν] ὁ Ἰ[ησοῦ]ς εἰς τὴν Ναζαρέτ). Thus, he is presented in the initial as the actor in the sentence that opens the lection. The artist has presented him beardless to differentiate him more clearly from the bearded St. Symeon on the column. The image of Christ in the

Figure 41 Vatican Lectionary (Vatican City, Biblioteca Apostolica Vaticana, gr. 1156), fol. 279^{v}–80^{r}.
(Photo: © 2019 Biblioteca Apostolica Vaticana. Reproduced by permission of Biblioteca Apostolica Vaticana, all rights reserved)

initial in this way enacts a re-envisioning of St. Symeon, as Symeon becomes the image of Christ on a column in the initial, and vice versa.

Historiated initials also flourished in eleventh- and twelfth-century manuscripts of the Homilies of Gregory of Nazianzus, such as the well-known mid-twelfth-century Sinai Homilies (Mount Sinai, Saint Catherine's Monastery, gr. 339). This manuscript demonstrates liturgical connections in its format and illuminations, which are attributed to the Kokkinobaphos workshop and associated with the Dumbarton Oaks Psalter, Odes, and New Testament from around 1084 and the Sebastokratorissa grammar book from the second quarter of the twelfth century.[13] When the opening

[13] See Jeffrey C. Anderson, "Cod. Vat. gr. 463 and an Eleventh-Century Byzantine Painting Center," *Dumbarton Oaks Papers* 32 (1978): 175–96. See also Anderson, "Illustration of Cod. Sinai. Gr. 339"; Jeffrey C. Anderson, "The Seraglio Octateuch and the Kokkinobaphos Master," *Dumbarton Oaks Papers* 36 (1982): 83–114.

Figure 42 Vatican Lectionary (Vatican City, Biblioteca Apostolica Vaticana, gr. 1156), fol. 280ᵛ–81ʳ. (Photo: © 2019 Biblioteca Apostolica Vaticana. Reproduced by permission of Biblioteca Apostolica Vaticana, all rights reserved)

letter and words permit it, the artist seizes the opportunity to depict the literal words, as in the initial for the A of "Ἄνδρες ἀδελφοὶ καὶ συμπένητες." The Sinai Homilies, gr. 339 (fol. 341ᵛ; Figure 47), and the Dionysiou Lectionary, Cod. 61, from the late eleventh century (fol. 142ʳ; Figure 48), have depictions of Gregory forming the letter A by turning away from the text and handing out alms to the representations of the poor that form the initial's other side. Here the word "Men" (Ἄνδρες) is manifested literally, while incorporating the elaborations and clarifications that the following words will make to its definition – that is, "Men, brothers and fellow paupers." In the Sinai manuscript, the scene swells to include beggars in the margin, thereby expanding the congregation of these men who emerge first on the periphery of the reader's view and then in the text of Gregory's Homily 14, "On the Love for the Poor."

Artists continued to innovate through the different versions of these initials and images, as the manuscripts considered in George Galavaris's

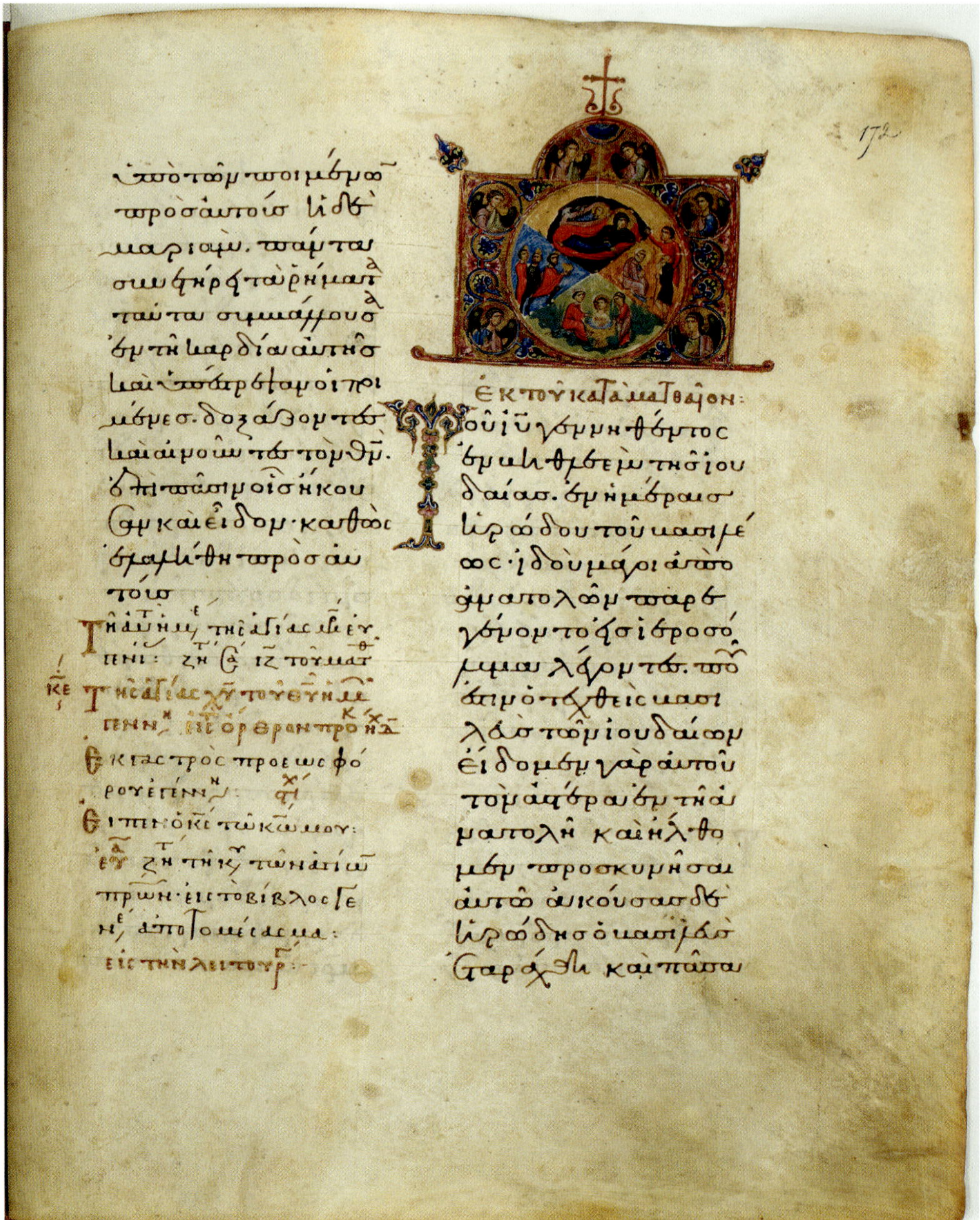

Figure 43 Paris Lectionary (Paris, Bibliothèque nationale de France, supp. gr. 27), fol. 172r.
(Photo: Bibliothèque nationale de France)

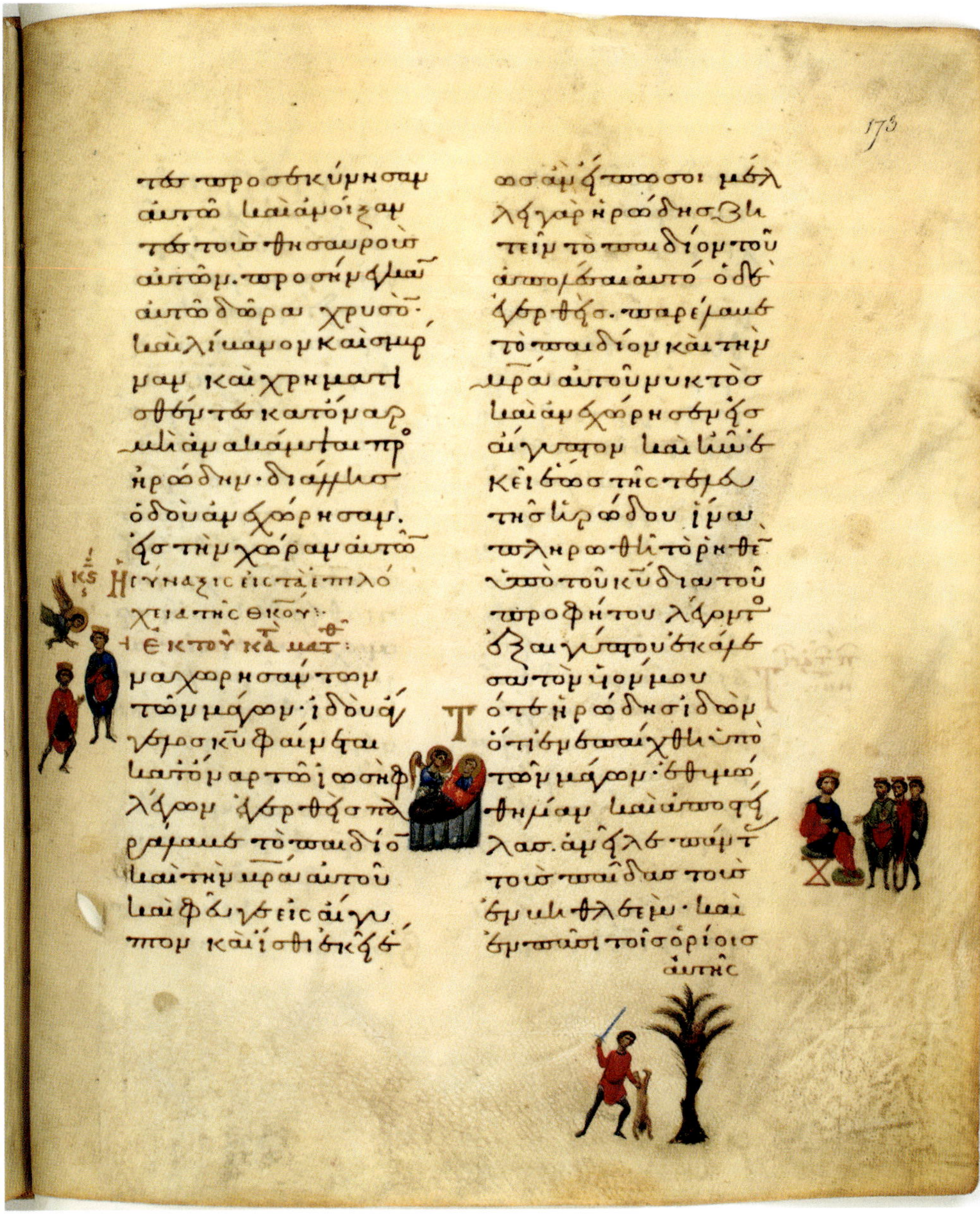

Figure 44 Paris Lectionary (Paris, Bibliothèque nationale de France, supp. gr. 27), fol. 173[r]. (Photo: Bibliothèque nationale de France)

Figure 45 Vatican Lectionary (Vatican City, Biblioteca Apostolica Vaticana, gr. 1156), fol. 52r.
(Photo: © 2019 Biblioteca Apostolica Vaticana. Reproduced by permission of Biblioteca Apostolica Vaticana, all rights reserved)

study of the illuminated homilies demonstrate.[14] In format, these manuscripts are similar to lectionaries in their page composition, with text set in two columns, and their use of historiated initials, marginal scenes, and miniatures. Thus, as we would expect, the miniatures usually make visible the spatiotemporal conditions of the particular homily's performance, reflecting both the feast day and its original context. The best example of

[14] See Galavaris, *Illustrations of the Liturgical Homilies.*

Figure 46 Dionysiou Lectionary (Mount Athos, Dionysiou Monastery, Cod. 587), fol. 116r. (Photo: Patriarchal Institute for Patristic Studies in Thessaloniki)

such visualization is the illumination program for the opening page of Gregory's Homily 44 for the Sunday after Easter, known as the New Sunday or the Sunday of Renewal (Figure 49). In the headpiece miniature, Gregory looks toward St. Mamas, a shepherd, who is sitting on a hill. The

Figure 47 Homilies of Gregory of Nazianzus (Mount Sinai, Saint Catherine's Monastery, gr. 339), fol. 341[v].
(Photo: reproduced by permission of Saint Catherine's Monastery, Sinai, Egypt)

Figure 48 Homilies of Gregory of Nazianzus (Mount Athos, Dionysiou Monastery, Cod. 61), fol. 142r.
(Photo: Patriarchal Institute for Patristic Studies in Thessaloniki)

miniature makes reference not to a date, since the Byzantines celebrated the saint's feast day in September, but to the fact that Gregory's sermon was first delivered at the dedication of a church of St. Mamas.

The date that this sermon is to be read is indicated by another miniature, set beside the upper corner of the headpiece, which depicts the scene of Doubting Thomas – an event commemorated on the Sunday after Easter. A marginal scene above the initial shows the consecration of a church, which appears to heighten the link to St. Mamas in the headpiece and to the context in which the sermon was first composed and uttered. At the same time, it suggests another connection with the first Sunday after Easter.[15] The initial E of Ἐγκαίνια (Renewal) depicts within it a congregation before a church, suggesting that they are commemorating the shrine's consecration as described in the opening lines. This page has thus

15 See Brian Daley, *Gregory of Nazianzus* (London: Routledge, 2006), 154–55.

Figure 49 Homilies of Gregory of Nazianzus (Mount Sinai, Saint Catherine's Monastery, gr. 339), fol. 42^{v}.
(Photo: reproduced by permission of Saint Catherine's Monastery, Sinai, Egypt)

articulately – and wordlessly – delineated the function and use of the homily by encoding various forms of signification in its various scenes, while at the same time directing the reader's performance of the text through its images.

A similar layering of information occurs in the Paris Lectionary's first reading for the synaxarion's lection for September 1 from Luke 4:16–22 (fol. 148[r]; Figure 50): here there are no marginalia surrounding the text and the initial bears no figurative illumination, but the miniature summarizes the reading. Thus, the miniature confronts the reader with the scene of Christ reading and lecturing in the synagogue. This image is appropriately emphasized within the lectionary, since it resonates with the performance of the lection itself and stages the reader's role as akin to that of Christ before him. Yet the miniature is not simply a literal depiction of the lection's first words, as an image of Christ speaking from the initial could have easily achieved. Tasked with summarizing the lection, the miniature presents an ambiguous depiction, making it difficult to ascertain or decide what exact moment is being shown. The miniature alludes to Christ reading from the prophet Isaiah – a lectern stands before him with the text, and a figure points at it as if handing it over to him (Luke 4:16–19) – yet Christ does not engage with the roll directly. Perhaps it is being handed back, since the congregation is clearly staring at him (Luke 4:20). Christ appears not to be reading from the lectern before him: his eyes are fixed on the crowd, and he has raised his right hand as if speaking to them (Luke 4:21–22). Relying on temporal ambiguity, the miniature neatly captures the narrative of the entire lection from start to finish. In order to indicate that this reading occurs on September 1, when Symeon the Stylite is commemorated, the figure of Symeon is flanked by two figures showing reverence to him.

In the Hamilton Lectionary (New York, Morgan Library, Cod. 639, fol. 294[r]; Figure 51), this is resolved somewhat less gracefully. There the miniature contains two scenes – Christ reading in the synagogue and an image of Symeon upon his bier – oddly divided by a speckled-green, marble-like band. This lectionary often uses such dividers: for example, in its opening miniature for Easter Sunday, a blue patterned vertical bar separates the portrait of John the Evangelist and Prochoros from the image of the Anastasis on the left, indicating that the lection is to be performed at Easter in commemoration of the Resurrection (fol. 1[r]; Figure 52).

Other lectionaries resolve these dual demands by indicating the time of a lection's recitation (the feast day) in the marginalia, while the miniatures invariably reflect the text. For example, in Homily 44 from the Sinai

Figure 50 Paris Lectionary (Paris, Bibliothèque nationale de France, supp. gr. 27), fol. 148r.
(Photo: Bibliothèque nationale de France)

Figure 51 Hamilton Lectionary (New York, Morgan Library, Cod. 639), fol. 294^{r}.
(Photo: The Pierpont Morgan Library, New York)

Homilies, the marginalia indicate the day on which the saint is being commemorated while the miniature summarizes the entirety of the lection. In the case of the Ascension scene in the Dumbarton Oaks Lectionary, the combination of marginalia and miniature indicates both the content of the text and the fact that the lection was to be read during the orthros on the Thursday of the Ascension. The Venice Lectionary handled the lection from Matthew 17:1–9 in the same way, depicting the Transfiguration in the top center and placing the disciples in the margins beside their relevant verses (see Figure 37). This combination of central scene and marginal figures across the page simultaneously illustrates the text and indicates that it is to be read during the Divine Liturgy on August 6, the feast day of the Transfiguration.

Consider also the lections in the Vatican Lectionary for the Nativity from Luke 2:1–23, read on the Christmas vigil on December 24 (fols. 277^{r}–78^{v}; see Figures 38–40); from Matthew 2:1–12, read during the liturgy on December 25 (fols. 278^{v}–80^{r}; see Figures 40–41); and from Matthew

Figure 52 Hamilton Lectionary (New York, Morgan Library, Cod. 639), fol. 1r.
(Photo: The Pierpont Morgan Library, New York)

2:13–23, read on December 26 (fols. 280r–81v; see Figure 42).[16] These images lack an introductory miniature, but the lection itself is lavishly illuminated with marginalia that diligently follow the text. In the Paris Lectionary (fols. 172r and 173r; see Figures 43–44), which does use an introductory miniature, the same readings appear in the same order. Here, a miniature depicts the birth of Christ within a circular image, surrounded by adoring angels, which indicates that the sequence is to be read during the commemoration of the Nativity from December 25 to 26. The miniature sets the date of the first lection at December 25, whereas the reading for next day is replete with marginal illuminations but then forgoes a miniature.

Thus we can see that when – as is not always the case – the feast being commemorated overlaps with the content of the lection, allowing both to be represented through marginalia and miniatures, artists often combined the two to unify the function of these classes of images within the lectionary. The congruent and systematic logic of these forms of play, together with their indication of different types of information through different types of images, speaks to the careful calibration of the lectionary as a manuscript type and thus to its ability to generate complexly layered understandings of image and text through subtle nuances and variations. This capacity is what enables the lectionary's readers to be carefully attuned to various details from different types of images as they approach them. As they read and look, readers imagine and visualize the narratives being recited, understanding also the liturgical context and significance of these stories. This process, however, also operates in the minds of listeners as they hear the day's lections during the Divine Liturgy and attempt to visualize those narratives, and the narratives' relations with the images in the church, the celebrations of the day, and the liturgical calendar.

Hearing and Imagination

This survey of anthropomorphic, historiated initials demonstrates a drive toward the visualization of the immediate words on the page, an emphasis on the performance of the image-text, and an interest in the specificity of its spatiotemporal context. These scenes communicate different types of information that simultaneously operate on various levels but can never be

[16] Dolezal, "Middle Byzantine Lectionary," 1:277–82.

ascribed a static meaning. By tacitly making users familiar with these logics, which would have been recognized by anyone skilled in the liturgical arts, these images provide a model of seeing and encourage what Charles Hirschkind calls particular "perceptual habits," which structure how people understand, process, and respond to perceptions.[17] Hirschkind has observed that listening to sermons supports a specific cultural activity that inclines individuals toward certain acts, discourses, gestures, and behaviors.[18] The act of listening is therefore not merely a process of

[17] Charles Hirschkind, "The Ethics of Listening: Cassette-Sermon Audition in Contemporary Egypt," *American Ethnologist* 28:3 (2001): 623–49, esp. 641.

[18] Scholars of Islam have long emphasized the importance of properly reciting the Qur'an. In an eleventh-century treatise, the Persian theologian Al-Ghazali detailed the mental and perceptual processes necessary in reading and listening to the text. These rules demand that speakers ease into the text by focusing the mind on God, who speaks through the text, silencing all internal voices, and giving the appropriate timing to each verse. A series of visual metaphors unpacks the manner in which the so-called "veils" of truth must be lifted through an active investment with the words being heard and through a visualization of their teachings. As Al-Ghazali writes: "The eighth mental task is to feel the Qur'an. This means that the mind of the Qur'an-reader will be affected by different feelings according to the different verses recited. Thus in accordance with what his mind understands, he will be in a state of grief, fear, hope, and so on . . . [W]hen reading a verse which warns and restricts divine forgiveness to those who fulfill certain stipulations, he will make himself so small as if for fear he is about to die. When a verse on the promise of forgiveness is recited he will rejoice as if he flies for joy. When God, His attribute and names are mentioned, he will bow his head in submission to His majesty and in awareness of His greatness." This is a solemn process that requires purposeful concentration as reader and listener alike must invest themselves in the words to visualize the narratives and engage with the emotional states and dispositions of the text, mirroring its actions. Likewise, the reader must pronounce the verses with such emotional fervency and precision that they can elicit their intended affective response. Similarly, in the Byzantine religious sphere, as analyzed in the previous chapter, Photios discusses the difference between hearing scripture and seeing the same deeds represented in icons. See Al-Ghazali, *The Recitation and Interpretation of the Qur'an*, trans. Muhammad Abul Quasem, *The Recitation and Interpretation of the Qur'an: Al-Ghazali's Theory* (London: Kegan Paul International, 1982), 76–77. On Al-Ghazali and recitation, see Gerald L. Bruns, *Hermeneutics Ancient and Modern* (New Haven, CT: Yale University Press, 1992), 124–38; Anna M. Gade, *Perfection Makes Practice: Learning, Emotion, and the Recited Qur'ān in Indonesia* (Honolulu: University of Hawai'i Press, 2004), esp. 138–41. On the recitation and aurality of the Qur'an, see Frederick Denny, "Exegesis and Recitation: Their Development as Classical Forms of Quranic Piety," in Frank E. Reynolds and Theodore M. Ludwig (eds.), *Transitions and Transformations in the History of Religions* (Leiden: Brill, 1980), 91–123; Frederick Denny, "The *Adab* of Quran Recitation: Text and Context," in A.H. Johns (ed.), *International Congress for the Study of the Quran* (Canberra: Australian National University, 1981), 143–60; William A. Graham, "Quran as Spoken Word: An Islamic Contribution to the Understanding of Scripture," in Richard C. Martin (ed.), *Approaches to Islam in Religious Studies* (Tucson: University of Arizona Press, 1985), 23–40; William A. Graham, *Beyond the Written Word: Oral Aspects of Scripture in the History of Religion* (Cambridge University Press, 1987); Kristina Nelson, *The Art of Reciting the Quran* (Austin: University of Texas Press, 1985); Michael Sells, *Approaching the Qur'an: The Early Revelations* (Ashland, OR: White Cloud Press, 1999).

enculturation, a term that suggests passive receptivity, but rather a self-reflexive practice that encourages the desired perceptual habits.[19] Just as seeing is a process, whereby the mind perceives that sensory input and processes it into images, contemplates it, and commits it to memory, so too listening unfolds. Yet the listener must first generate images in the mind to visualize the narratives, before they can be grasped. In this formulation of perception, common to the Byzantine world, text – both written and oral – requires that the person perceiving the story first visualize the narrative.[20] In this regard, marginalia are able to visually manifest words in advance for the mind as it begins to imagine the lections being read.

From 1082 to 1095, there was a fierce disagreement between Leo of Chalcedon and Emperor Alexios I Komnenos over the use of icons, namely arguing about the role of matter and perception in the veneration of icons. And, during this time, Nicholas of Andida composed his liturgical commentary, the *Protheoria*, which relies heavily on Byzantine image theory to articulate the polyvalent meanings of the liturgical rite. As Charles Barber has observed, in this period we encounter a series of texts that "attempt to police one's perception of the icon" by articulating models of behavior toward icons and models of understanding icons.[21] Whereas the ninth-century iconomachy was a debate over whether icons were valid or not, the debates surrounding the Komnenian iconoclasm in the eleventh century were about perception. Certain figures, such as Saint Symeon the New Theologian, may have tried to decenter the primacy of icons, but they did not outright deny their validity.[22] Thus, the debates about icons of the late eleventh and early twelfth centuries focus on the icon's medium and how the icon should be perceived.

It is also during the last two decades of the eleventh century that the curious marginal images that I have been discussing here flourished in the Gospel lectionaries. In my view, this policing of perception by imperial decree was significantly echoed in this widespread popularity of the lectionary's historiated initials. The best-known and most discussed of this period's lectionaries were produced around 1100. For example, Mary-Lyon Dolezal dates the Dionysiou, Cod. 587, to between 1070 and

[19] See Hirschkind, *Ethical Soundscape*.

[20] On Byzantine perception and theories of representation, see Betancourt, *Sight, Touch, and Imagination*.

[21] Charles Barber, *Contesting the Logic of Painting: Art and Understanding in Eleventh-Century Byzantium* (Leiden: Brill, 2007), 1.

[22] Barber, *Contesting the Logic of Painting*, 23–59.

1100;[23] and Jeffrey Anderson even proposes that the Barberini Psalter was commissioned by Alexios Komnenos as partial restitution for the destruction of Church property that incited the debates with Leo of Chalcedon.[24] Interestingly enough, one of the sites to which Alexios had to pay reparations was the church of Christ the Savior in the Chalkoprateia neighborhood, for he had melted down its historiated bronze doors.[25] Known for containing the girdle of the Virgin, this church is also mentioned in an encomium by Michael Psellos as the site where readers would compete in the delivery of religious texts, such as the menologion.[26] It is therefore reasonable to suppose that some of these manuscripts, which are intended for public recitation and which foreground that practice through their illuminations, might have been commissioned for a community that emphasized liturgical recitation and that might also have been used to train those who practiced the art in other churches, including Hagia Sophia. In fact, the man named in Psellos's encomium, Ioannes Kroustoulas, is referred to as *chartoularios*, suggesting that he was a chancery officer in the imperial or patriarchal administration.[27] Without postulating a rigid line of patronage or artistic intention, I propose that this association between the fallout of the Komnenian iconomachy and the flourishing of liturgical manuscripts with historiated initials indicates a generative space for artistic patronage.

Initials, miniatures, and adjoining marginalia ease readers into the images that the text conveys and they help train the perceptual habits of their users, empowering them and reminding them to actively invest their mental faculties in the Gospel so as to make visible the text on the page. For those in the audience, who lacked direct visual contact with these marginal scenes, similar images would crop up in their minds as they listened intently to a chanter's words and imagined the stories being told. Because of their training in ways to perceive and in the established iconographies of Byzantine art, viewers and hearers likely partook in the same mental imagery. This perceptual process is ethically tinged in the salvific play

[23] Dolezal, "Illuminating the Liturgical Word," 59; Weitzmann, "An Imperial Lectionary in the Monastery of Dionysiou."

[24] Anderson, "Date and Purpose of the Barberini Psalter," esp. 56–60.

[25] See Anna Komnene, *Alexias*, 6.3, trans. E.R.A. Sewter, *The Alexiad* (New York: Penguin, 1969), 158.

[26] Michael Psellos, "Encomium for the Monk Ioannes Kroustoulas Who Read Aloud at the Holy Soros," in Charles Barber and Stratis Papaioannou (eds.), *Michael Psellos on Literature and Art: A Byzantine Perspective on Aesthetics* (Notre Dame University Press, 2017), 218–44.

[27] Papaioannou, "Encomium for the Monk Ioannes Kroustoulas," 218.

enacted by the liturgical rite and also in the visuality that such images construct, in effect molding the mind of the reader and training him how to see.[28] Thus, in these historiated initials we see at work the development of perceptual habits through active training, not just passive enculturation or inculcation.

Familiarity with the historiated initial also cultivated a perceptual habitus for approaching text–image relations as well. The images surveyed here encourage viewers to perceive images as mutable forms, morphing back and forth between pictures and utterances. As Maria Evangelatou has argued, in manuscripts illustrating the Book of Job we find that at the moment he is afflicted by sores (Job 2:7), the personified disease is depicted by an E-like monster, modeled after the word Ἕλκος (ulcer or sore; Figure 53).[29] The earliest instances of this imagery appear in the ninth or early tenth century, at the time when Byzantine initials were just beginning to be used. Interestingly, these historiated initials have a literalism much like that of the later initials we have been considering here. Thus, not only could initials become figures, but figures could become initials, demonstrating agile and dynamic interaction between word and image that goes beyond interplay on the page.

I propose that the examples listed here, along with others, molded the perceptual approach taken by readers and listeners of the lectionary's image-text. To be sure, these examples are by no means exhaustive; indeed, no exhaustive treatment is possible, since these images resist the kind of one-to-one iconographic reading needed to summarize them. Instead, initials and marginalia could thrive and function precisely since they were always to a certain extent uncertain. While we might observe the generative creativity that these marginal scenes support, they also confront the art historian with what seem to be illuminators' strange slippages, mistakes, and errors, which at times appear as severe misreadings or misrepresentations of the text that they are intended to depict.

We should note that initials and marginal illuminations often lack *nomina sacra* (the abbreviations of holy names) or any other descriptive words or statements. Such inscriptions identify the image and thereby activate the image for worship – an essential element of the Byzantine icon

[28] See Milton Anastos, "The Ethical Theory of Images Formulated by the Iconoclasts in 754 and 815," *Dumbarton Oaks Papers* 8 (1954): 153–60.

[29] Maria Evangelatou, "From Word into Image: The Visualization of Ulcer in Byzantine Illustrated Manuscripts of the Book of Job," *Gesta* 48:1 (2009): 19–36.

Figure 53 Book of Job (Vatican City, Biblioteca Apostolica Vaticana, gr. 749), fol. 25r.
(Photo: © 2019 Biblioteca Apostolica Vaticana. Reproduced by permission of Biblioteca Apostolica Vaticana, all rights reserved)

as Robert Nelson has remarked.[30] The miniatures of the Dionysiou Lectionary lack these *nomina sacra*, for example. Very rarely, inscriptions appear throughout a manuscript, as in the Morgan Library's late eleventh-century Hamilton Lectionary (Figure 54) and in the Dumbarton Oaks Psalter, Odes, and New Testament (Figure 55). And some instances, like the Dionysiou Homilies, feature historiated initials without *nomina sacra*, yet the miniatures are amply glossed with them. In the Hamilton and Dumbarton Oaks examples, the glosses are done in a red that is unlike

[30] See Robert S. Nelson, "Image and Inscription: Pleas for Salvation in Spaces of Devotion," in Liz James (ed.), *Art and Text in Byzantine Culture* (Cambridge University Press, 2007), 100–19, esp. 101–03.

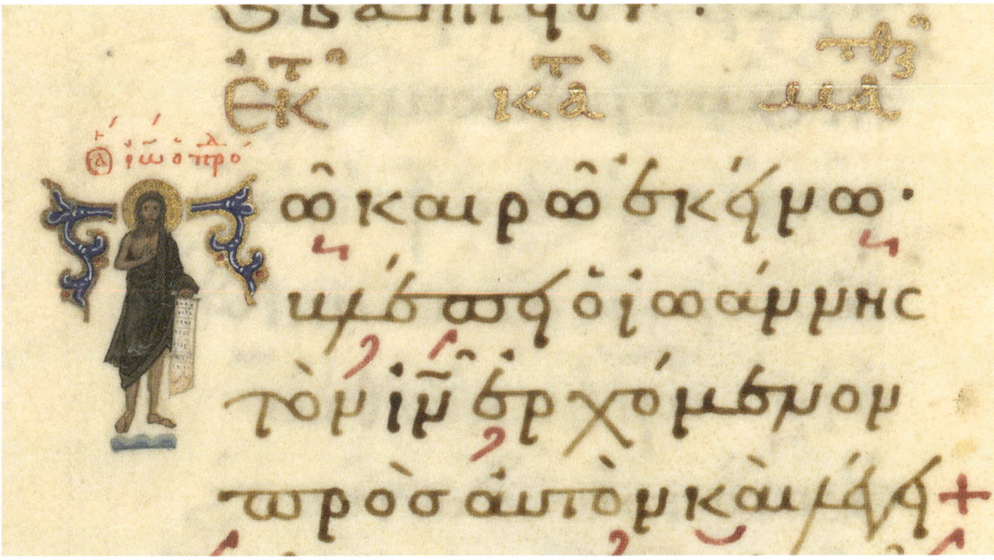

Figure 54 Hamilton Lectionary (New York, Morgan Library, Cod. 639), fol. 332ᵛ.
(Photo: The Pierpont Morgan Library, New York)

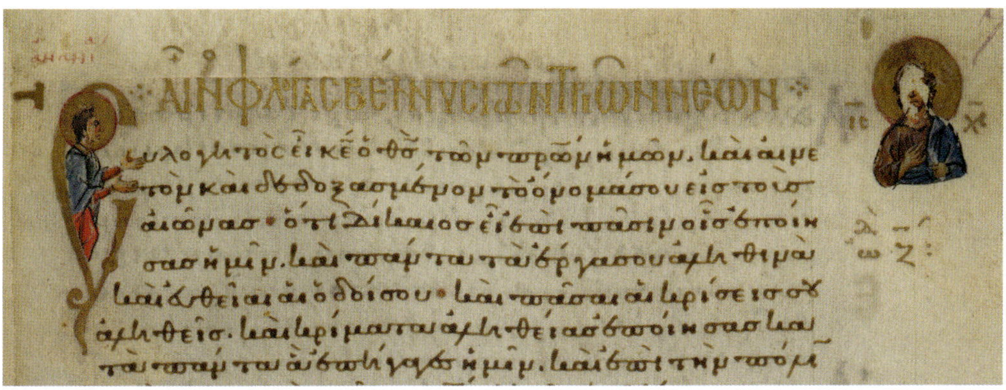

Figure 55 Dumbarton Oaks Psalter, Odes, and New Testament (Washington, DC, Dumbarton Oaks, Cod. 3), fol. 79ʳ.
(Photo: © Dumbarton Oaks, Byzantine Collection, Washington, DC)

the ink in the rest of the manuscript's text but similar to the color used to add rubrics and chant marks in lectionaries. In both of these examples, while the chant marks are written in the same brown or gold ink as the text, these carmine glosses may have had a specific purpose – perhaps curtailing polysemy and attempting to moderate the fertility of the lectionary's system. In my view, the absence of textual glosses and *nomina sacra* on many of these examples demonstrates that these illustrations functioned as proto-images: schematic illustrations of the text that existed on the periphery of both vision and perception, requiring the imagination of the viewer and the text's oral recitation to enliven them into fully fledged images and narratives in the minds of readers and listeners alike.

The complete lack of glosses in the Dionysiou Lectionary (Cod. 587), together with its liturgical emphasis, suggests in this extraordinary case that not even the miniatures were necessarily meant to be venerated as icons in their own right but, rather, that they were contingent on their own fulfillment in the liturgical rite through recitation and performance. In a sense, these images operated as a mere starting point in the liturgical reading for the enactment of the narrative's images in the minds of viewers and listeners. That is, these images are fully realized when image, text, speech, and performance completely merge in an apprehending mind. It demonstrates that rather than being autonomous icons, their iconicity emerges in the moment when the user engages with the lectionary's speech, text, and images.

That the inscriptions on the marginalia of the Hamilton Lectionary are written in the same carmine ink as chant marks often are suggests that these images function analogous to musical notation – a guide for performance that is neither the spoken words, nor the aural song itself, but rather something in between that eludes perception. Since the Byzantines rely not on an absolute tonal system but rather indicate changes in relative pitch, one cannot merely enunciate the chant marks; instead, these graphic signs must be united with the discourse in order to be somehow made manifest. Like chant marks, I propose that these marginal scenes work the same way: that they are imperceptible until they are performed by the reader, who gives voice and imagination to those words during their chant. And, much like chant marks, these images are added after the text, playing on its composition and display, as well as with its meaning and story. Both suggest an artist–scribe dynamic that works in sync to comment and respond to the text laid out before them.

: τ β τῆς διακ :

καὶ κέκραγε λέ-
γων· οὗτος ἦν
ὃν εἶπον· ὁ ὀπί-
σω μου ἐρχόμε-
νος ἔμπροσθέν
μου γέγονεν·
ὅτι πρῶτός
μου ἦν· καὶ ἐκ
τοῦ πληρώ-
ματος αὐτοῦ
ἡμεῖς πάντες
ἐλάβομεν καὶ
χάριν ἀντὶ χά-
ριτος· ὅτι ὁ νό-
μος διὰ Μωϋ-
σέως ἐδόθη· ἡ
χάρις καὶ ἡ ἀλή-

θεια διὰ Ἰησοῦ Χριστοῦ
ἐγένετο·

ΕΚ ΚΑ ΙΩ :

Θεὸν οὐδεὶς
ἑώρακε πώ-
ποτε· ὁ μονο-
γενὴς υἱὸς· ὁ
ὢν εἰς τὸν κόλ-
πον τοῦ πατρὸς
ἐκεῖνος ἐξη-
γήσατο· καὶ αὕ-
τη ἐστὶν ἡ μαρ-
τυρία τοῦ Ἰω-
άννου ὅτε
ἀπέστειλαν οἱ
Ἰουδαῖοι ἐξ Ἱερο-

3 Faltering Images

Iconography between Reading, Error, and Confusion

Marginal illuminations in the Gospel lectionary thrived on the potential for iconographic confusion and misunderstanding, while never attempting to wholly subvert or place themselves in opposition to the Gospel text. My goal in this chapter is to understand how the lectionary cultivates a system of artistic production that, contrary to what one might expect, continuously and systematically presents readers with textual excerpts and illuminations that cause them to falter, err, and become confused as they slowly make their way through the manuscript and through the liturgical year. Paradoxically, while these images adhere closely to iconographic models and motifs, they subtly and critically break the rules, just under the threshold of what a disengaged viewer might notice, and thereby work against one-to-one readings of image and text.

Michael Camille opened *Image on the Edge*, his study of Western medieval marginalia, by explaining to the reader his desire to focus not on clarifying some fixed reading of marginalia but rather on exploring how such images pretended to avoid meaning:

> I could begin, like St. Bernard, by asking what do they all mean, those lascivious apes, autophagic dragons, pot-bellied heads, harp-playing asses, arse-kissing priests and somersaulting jongleurs that protrude at the edges of medieval buildings, sculpture and illuminated manuscripts? But I am more interested in how they pretend to avoid meaning, how they seem to celebrate the flux of "becoming" rather than "being," something I am able to suggest only in the completed sentences and sections of these essays.[1]

These words aptly capture his work's insistence on understanding liminal positions both for the image and for the subjects that the image constitutes. Camille's image was seemingly caught within the very flux of full identification, just as were his queer, subversive subjects. For Camille, marginalia thrived on a relation between center and periphery: in his words, the center was "dependent upon the margins for its continued existence."[2] Thus his

[1] Camille, *Image on the Edge*, 1.

[2] Camille, *Image on the Edge*, 10.

commitment in *Image on the Edge* was to seeing how the margin could do more than merely "play" with the center. In his account, the inherent flux of the margin, and the center's dependence on that margin, produced a system in which the allegedly stable center had to be recursively defined by the elusive margin.

Given the importance of studies on marginal images in the medieval West, I therefore wish to provide here some important qualifications and distinctions regarding the role that these illuminations played in the Byzantine world in the context of lectionaries. In this context, we encounter a different structure of operation, in which the margins do not necessarily subvert the center though this center is nevertheless constituted through their actions. That is, in the lectionaries we do not often find the litany of "lascivious apes, autophagic dragons, pot-bellied heads, harp-playing asses, arse-kissing priests and somersaulting jongleurs" that populated the manuscripts examined by Camille. Instead, we encounter a model closer to that found in Glenn Peers's study of how the sacred is framed in Byzantine art, in which the edges, margins, and borders of the manuscript "mediat[e] viewer response" and serve as that "zone where the most meaningful contact between viewer and viewed" occurs.[3] While we often find in these lectionaries a seemingly slavish and overly literal adherence to the written text and a desire to illuminate precisely the stories that appear immediately next to the illustrations, we will consider how marginalia in Byzantium still enjoy a flux of becoming as they pulsate between various subtle readings, erroneous displays of characters, and confused interpretations of scenes – a subject that has often been overlooked or ignored by art historians. In other words, we will see how images on the edge retained a certain subversive potential, while still framing the viewer's access to the sacred.

In the first two chapters, the task was to lay out a network of motifs, iconographies, and compositional patterns that set up the lectionary to manifest itself as a cohesive system with a clear, articulate, and standardized visual syntax. This produces a manuscript type that is intuitively usable by a viewer who has become familiar with certain repeated tropes and systematized iconographies. Such standardization does not suggest a rote mechanical production, however. On the contrary, it makes possible the emergence of more complex representational strategies as these very rules are built on or violated. This chapter therefore examines how images

[3] Glenn Peers, *Sacred Shock: Framing Visual Experience in Byzantium* (University Park: Pennsylvania State University Press, 2004), 133, 134.

falter or misdirect over the course of reading the text and looking at the illuminations.

I will again undertake a very close reading of images, first observing how those individual images work within the context of various other images in their specific manuscript, and then mapping these operations across different lectionaries and related manuscripts to see how these emerge and interact. In analyzing these nesting units – that is, moving from a specific image to its folio to its manuscript and finally to other similar manuscripts – I intend not to sketch out a single regulating system but rather to diagram how the nexus of these various images operates alongside the imagination and perceptual habitus of their user. In this chapter, I deploy this method to demonstrate how the lectionary builds on shared tropes, iconographies, and habits of looking in order to complicate representation and push the boundaries of iconography. Attention will be paid to how the liturgical calendar alters potential readings by controlling the order of the lections used over the course of the year.

Illuminating What Has Never Been Seen

My concern is with the *procedural* unfolding of images – a term I borrow from Ian Bogost's analysis of videogames. Bogost develops this term to describe a representational system that lies outside the logic of static, mimetic depiction. Bogost calls this a *procedural rhetoric*: a "practice of authoring arguments through processes."[4] One of the best examples of such procedural unfolding in the lectionary emerges in the illumination for the initial Θ of Θεόν for the reading of John 1:18–28 on the Monday after Easter Sunday.[5] This lection begins *without* a formulaic inscription, entering directly into the Gospel text: "God no one has ever seen; the only begotten Son, who is on the bosom of the Father – he did declare" (Θεὸν οὔδεις ἑώρακεν πώποτε: ὁ μονογενὴς υἱὸς ὁ ὢν εἰς τὸν κόλπον τοῦ πατρὸς ἐκεῖνος ἐξηγήσατο). This opening poses a theological problem for the illuminator: although the passage explicitly reads "God no one has ever seen," the intuitive logic of the initial demands that the Θ of Θεόν depict

[4] See Bogost, *Persuasive Games*, 28–29. See also Murray, *Hamlet on the Holodeck*, 71.

[5] For a parallel study of this iconography in the context of exegetical writing, see Gretchen Kreahling McKay, "Illustrating the Gospel of John: The Exegesis of John Chrysostom and Images of the Ancient of Days in Eleventh-Century Byzantine Manuscripts," *Studies in Iconography* 31 (2010): 51–68.

"God" himself. What is required is not necessarily God incarnate but the Godhead, since the passage deliberately contrasts the imperceptibility of the Godhead to the perceptible hypostasis of the incarnate Christ – and it thus provides the New Testament foundation for the prohibition against images of the Godhead.

During Iconoclasm, the argument raised by iconoclasts against the icon was that an earthly form could not manifest the divine image of Christ – it could show only his human form. The iconophiles refuted this claim by proposing that the icon is a site of desire, a present absence, which enjoys the "relative participation" (σχετικῇ . . . μεταλήψει) of the grace and honor of the divine, as Theodore the Studite postulated.[6] For the Byzantine Church, this participation was made possible by the definition of Christ laid out in the Chalcedonian Decree of 451.[7] It enabled the iconophiles to argue that since God had condescended to take up human flesh and form while maintaining two natures in one hypostasis, he had also condescended to be circumscribable by earthly colors and forms. Therefore, since Christ was both fully human and fully divine, the icon depicting the human form of Christ also bore the ineffable divine form.

But in this doctrine of the image, the representation of the Godhead himself remains prohibited. At the official onset of Iconoclasm in 730, Patriarch Germanos wrote to John of Synada that "we figure the image of his human form according to the flesh, and not his incomprehensible and indivisible Godhead (οὐ τῆς ἀκαταλήπτου αὐτοῦ καὶ ἀθεάτου θεότητος), thereby confirming more fully the right faith."[8] Furthermore, as John of Damascus would later explicitly state in his treatise on icons, "For if we

[6] Theodore of Stoudios, *Antirrhetici adversus iconomachus*, 1.12, ed. PG 99: 344C; trans. Catharine Roth, *On the Holy Icons* (Crestwood, NY: St. Vladimir's Seminary Press, 1981), 33.

[7] "Acknowledged in two natures without confusion, without change, without division, without separation – the difference of the natures being by no means taken away because of the union, but rather the distinctive character of each nature being preserved, and [each] combining in one person and hypostasis – not divided or separated into two Persons, but one and the same Son and only-begotten God, Word, Lord Jesus Christ" (ἐν δύο φύσεσιν ἀσυγχύτως ἀτρέπτως ἀδιαιρέτως ἀχωρίστως γνωριζόμενον, οὐδαμοῦ τῆς τῶν φύσεων διαφορᾶς ἀνῃρημένης διὰ τὴν ἕνωσιν, σωιζομένης δὲ μᾶλλον τῆς ἰδιότητος ἑκατέρας φύσεως καὶ εἰς ἓν πρόσωπον καὶ μίαν ὑπόστασιν συντρεχούσης, οὐκ εἰς δύο πρόσωπα μεριζόμενον ἢ διαιρούμενον, ἀλλ᾽ ἕνα καὶ τὸν αὐτὸν υἱὸν μονογενῆ θεὸν λόγον κύριον Ἰησοῦν Χριστόν). Anonymous, *Concilium universale Chalcedonense anno 451*, ed. E. Schwartz, *Acta conciliorum oecumenicorum*, vol. 2.1.2 (Berlin: De Gruyter, 1933), 129–30; trans. Edward Rochie Hardy, "The Chalcedonian Decree," in Edward Rochie Hardy (ed.), *Christology of the Later Fathers* (Louisville, KY: Westminster John Knox Press, 1954; repr., 2006), 371–77, at 373.

[8] "καὶ τῆς κατὰ σάρκα αὐτοῦ ἀνθρωπίνης ἰδέας τὴν εἰκόνα τυποῦντες, καὶ οὐ τῆς ἀκαταλήπτου αὐτοῦ καὶ ἀθεάτου θεότητος, ἐντεῦθεν τὰ τῆς πίστεως παριστᾷν ἐπειγόμεθα." Germanos I, *Epistula domaticae*, 2 (or *Epistula Germani ad Joannem episcopum Synadensem*), ed. J.D. Mansi,

were to make an image of the invisible God, we would really sin; for it is impossible to depict one who is incorporeal and formless, invisible and uncircumscribable."[9] In the eleventh century, even Symeon the New Theologian, who had radically different ideas on icons, reiterated the incomprehensibility and indefinite light of the Godhead, who for Symeon lay beyond sensual perception: only spiritual seeing could allow one to witness him as "no shape or form or impression, but formless light."[10] Thus any attempt to depict the Godhead must be seen as problematic, since such representation was implicitly *and* explicitly forbidden in a wide range of philosophical positions on icons throughout the post-iconoclastic period; its prohibition was one issue on which the iconoclastic and iconophile camps could be said to agree.

In practice, when faced with the challenge of depicting the Godhead himself, artists at times resorted to the trope of the Ancient of Days (ὁ παλαιὸς τῶν ἡμερῶν), an identity that allowed comfortable room for experimentation, semiotic play, and obfuscation.[11] Often understood as a visual manifestation of Christ as an old man, the Ancient of Days appears as an old man, usually enthroned, with long white hair and beard.[12] In their reflections on Daniel's vision (Daniel 7:9–10, 13–14) from which the iconography derives, Christian theologians debated the identity of the Ancient of Days. The Old Testament text suggests that the Son of Man and the Ancient of Days were two discrete entities; the Book of Revelation likens the Ancient of Days to the Son of Man (Revelation 1:9–20) – the eternal manifestation of Christ who has returned to judge humanity; and some Christian commentators in the exegetical tradition, including John

Sacrorum conciliorum nova et amplissima collectio, vol. 13 (Paris: H. Welter, 1902), 101B; trans. Barber, *Figure and Likeness*, 71.

9 "Εἰ μὲν γὰρ τοῦ θεοῦ τοῦ ἀοράτου εἰκόνα ἐποιοῦμεν, ὄντως ἡμαρτάνομεν· ἀδύνατον γὰρ τὸ ἀσώματον καὶ ἀσχημάτιστον καὶ ἀόρατον καὶ ἀπερίγραπτον εἰκονισθῆναι." John of Damascus, *Orationes de imaginibus tres*, II.5; cf. III.2, ed. Kotter, *Die Schriften des Johannes von Damaskos*, 71–72; trans. Louth, *Three Treatises on the Divine Images*, 61.

10 "οὐ σχῆμα ἢ εἶδος ἢ ἐκτύπωμα βλέπουσιν, ἀλλὰ φῶς ἀσχημάτιστον." Symeon the Theologian, *Orationes ethicae*, 1.3.100–01, ed. Jean Darrouzès, *Syméon le Nouveau Théologien, Traites théologiques et éthiques*, Sources chrétiennes 122 (Paris: Éditions du Cerf, 1966), 202; trans. Alexander Golitzin, *On the Mystical Life: The Ethical Discourses*, vol. 1: *The Church and the Last Things* (Crestwood, NY: St. Vladimir's Seminary Press, 1995), 34.

11 For a corpus of Byzantine texts on the Ancient of Days, see Gretchen Kreahling McKay, "The Eastern Christian Exegetical Tradition of Daniel's Vision of the Ancient of Days," *Journal of Early Christian Studies* 7:1 (1999): 139–61.

12 On the related phenomenon of the polymorphism of Christ, depicted as a young, middle-aged, and old man, see Gretchen Kreahling McKay, "Christ's Polymorphism in Jerusalem, Taphou 14: An Examination of Text and Image," *Apocrypha* 14 (2003): 177–91.

Chrysostom, saw the Ancient of Days as clearly suggesting God the Father, since he gives dominion to Christ as the Son of Man.[13] But the Ancient of Days is too common in Byzantium,[14] most likely because such an image comes close to challenging the epistemological foundation of the icon. Indeed, various scholars have grappled with that challenge when confronted with depictions of the Ancient of Days.[15]

The Ancient of Days has an especially complicated history in the Byzantine exegetical and art-historical tradition. Of the twenty-six images surveyed by Gretchen McKay in her study on the appearances of the Ancient of Days in post-iconoclastic Byzantine manuscripts, only one – in a twelfth-century copy of *Barlaam and Joasaph*[16] – is used in conjunction with the text of Daniel's vision; yet the Ancient of Days is deployed elsewhere in a variety of contexts, ranging from the Book of Genesis to the Gospel of John.[17] Demonstrating a semiotic flexibility beyond its textual heritage, this image must be considered as a special case that lends itself to experimentation; an artist could use it to exploit images as a medium coding conditions for representation beyond what is depicted on the page – particularly in moments when such tactics had to be taken to their limits. Therefore, by examining how artists handle this extreme case and how they resolve its complications, we can see more clearly the procedural capacities of the lectionary's marginalia and how this procedurality in turn enabled

[13] McKay, "Daniel's Vision," 149–51. See also Steven Bingham, *The Image of God the Father in Orthodox Theology and Iconography: And Other Studies* (Crestwood, NY: St. Vladimir's Seminary Press, 1995), esp. 1–60; John Collins, *Daniel: A Commentary on the Book of Daniel* (Minneapolis: Fortress, 1993), 304–08; Maurice Casey, *Son of Man: The Interpretation and Influence of Daniel* (London: Society for Promoting Christian Knowledge, 1979), 7–50, 224–40; Julian Morgenstern, "The 'Son of Man' of Daniel 7:13f.: A New Interpretation," *Journal of Biblical Literature* 80:1 (1961): 65–77; A. Feuillet, "Le Fils de l'homme de Daniel et la tradition biblique," *Revue biblique* 60 (1953): 170–202.

[14] Gretchen Kreahling McKay, "Imaging the Divine: A Study of the Representations of the Ancient of Days in Byzantine Manuscripts," PhD dissertation, University of Virginia (1997).

[15] For example, see Kathleen Corrigan, "Visualizing the Divine: An Early Byzantine Icon of the 'Ancient of Days' at Mount Sinai," in Sharon E.J. Gerstel and Robert S. Nelson (eds.), *Approaching the Holy Mountain: Art and Liturgy at St. Catherine's Monastery in the Sinai* (Turnhout: Brepols, 2010), 285–303; André Grabar, *Christian Iconography: A Study of Its Origins*, trans. Terry Grabar (Princeton University Press, 1968), 116; André Grabar, "La représentation de l'intelligible dans l'art byzantin du Moyen Âge," in André Grabar (ed.), *L'art de la fin de l'antiquité et du Moyen Âge*, vol. 1 (Paris: Collège de France, 1968), 51–62; Kurt Weitzmann, *The Monastery of St. Catharine, The Icons* (Princeton University Press, 1976), 41–42.

[16] The Ancient of Days appears as part of a Last Judgment scene immediately prior to the passage where Barlaam quotes the Book of Daniel (Mt. Athos, Iveron Monastery, Cod. 463, fol. 28^{v}). See McKay, "Imaging the Divine," 59–61.

[17] McKay, "Imaging the Divine," 236.

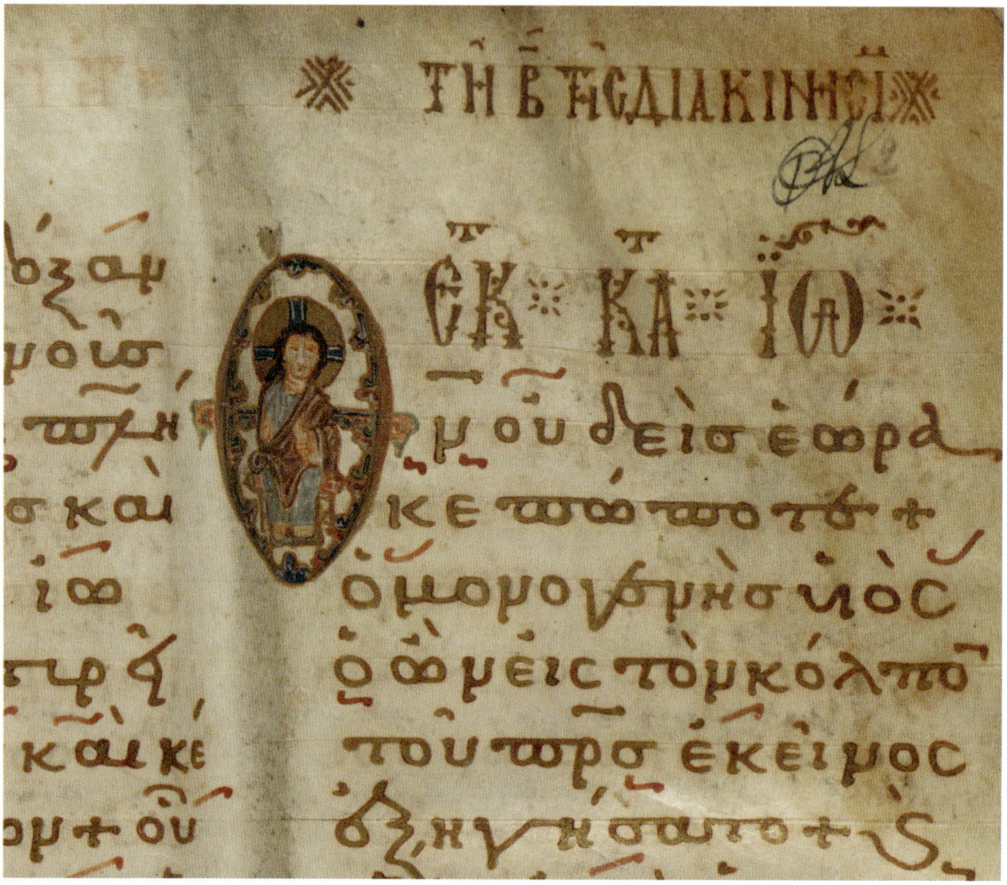

Figure 56 Dumbarton Oaks Lectionary (Washington, DC, Dumbarton Oaks, Cod. 1), fol. 2r.
(Photo: © Dumbarton Oaks, Byzantine Collection, Washington, DC)

artist and user to circumvent the prohibition against representing the Godhead. Because some may suggest that these images have a different ontological status than does a mimetic depiction or representation, we will compare the approaches of a number of manuscripts to the challenge of John 1:18.

In the Dumbarton Oaks Lectionary, the artist has painted an image of Christ with a cruciform halo (fol. 2r; Figure 56) – thereby providing the straightforward answer to this conundrum. After all, the answer to how to depict the God that no one has ever seen was precisely what was at stake in the iconoclastic debates of the eighth and ninth centuries, and the orthodox solution was to use the hypostatic character of the incarnate Christ as a way to manifest God. Such a solution may not entirely satisfy the lectionary's user, who is habituated to expect a literal depiction of the illuminated words. But interestingly, here a scroll is held in Christ's left hand. Thus, the illuminator has managed to depict God in an orthodox manner via the Incarnation, while still capturing the passage's declaration that the "Son is on the bosom of the Father" – that is, showing the Son as the Logos.

In contrast, in the Dionysiou Lectionary the artist literally depicts the imagery of the Gospel text by presenting God the Father as the Ancient of Days with the Son – shown as the youthful Christ "Emmanuel" – on his bosom (fol. 3^{v}; Figure 57).[18] Compare this to the choice by the artist of the Athens Lectionary (Cod. 68) to depict the Christ Emmanuel alone, manifesting through his youth the Incarnation and clearly labeled lest he be mistaken for the Godhead (fol. 2^{v}; Figure 58). In the Dionysiou example, the artist plays with the status of the image by inscribing onto the Ancient of Days a cruciform halo, a feature used to distinguish Christ from other figures. This halo is an attempt to sidestep the problem of his depiction by alluding to the Christ's dual nature. Thus we see that what first appears to be a slavish depiction of the text may in fact be a nonmimetic procedural solution: the connection to Christ suggested by the cruciform halo placed upon the Godhead may be said to exist in the disposition of the viewer toward the icon. When perceiving the incarnate flesh, one is not viewing mere colors or directing one's attention only to that which is circumscribable; rather, one is focusing on the hypostatic union manifested through Christ's icon.

Outside the lectionary, one notable example of such a juxtaposition between the Christ and the Godhead appears in a marginal scene accompanying Stephen's vision in the ninth-century *Sacra parallela* (Paris, Bibliothèque nationale de France, Cod. gr. 923, fol. 40^{r}; Figure 59): Stephen gazes up at the Ancient of Days-type enthroned with the figure of Christ – who, unlike him, bears a cruciform nimbus – at his side.[19] André Grabar has reasoned that this image was made acceptable by the inclusion below it of the visionary Stephen gazing up at the pair enclosed by the mandorla, which stressed the manifestation as an extraordinary, temporary event.[20] Grabar offered a similar interpretation of a theophanic depiction in his reading of the apse mosaic in the fifth- or sixth-century

[18] For a thorough analysis of the various theological permutations enabled by this image, see Cotsonis, "New Light on the Dionysiou Lectionary," 28–36.

[19] Kurt Weitzmann, *The Miniatures of the Sacra Parallela Parisinus graecus 923* (Princeton University Press, 1979), 190.

[20] Grabar, "Représentation de l'intelligible," 54.

Figure 57 Dionysiou Lectionary (Mount Athos, Dionysiou Monastery, Cod. 587), fol. 3v.
(Photo: Patriarchal Institute for Patristic Studies in Thessaloniki)

oratory of Hosios David in Thessaloniki (Figure 60), where two spectators flank the scene of Ezekiel's vision (Ezekiel 1.26–27), the one on the left presumably Ezekiel himself – and where the artist has also included a cruciform nimbus on the central figure to avoid suggesting a depiction of the Godhead.[21] Unlike in the *Sacra parallela*, the cruciform halo is

[21] Grabar, *Christian Iconography*, 116–17. See also Thomas Mathews, *The Clash of Gods: A Reinterpretation of Early Christian Art*, 2nd edn (Princeton University Press, 1999), 116;

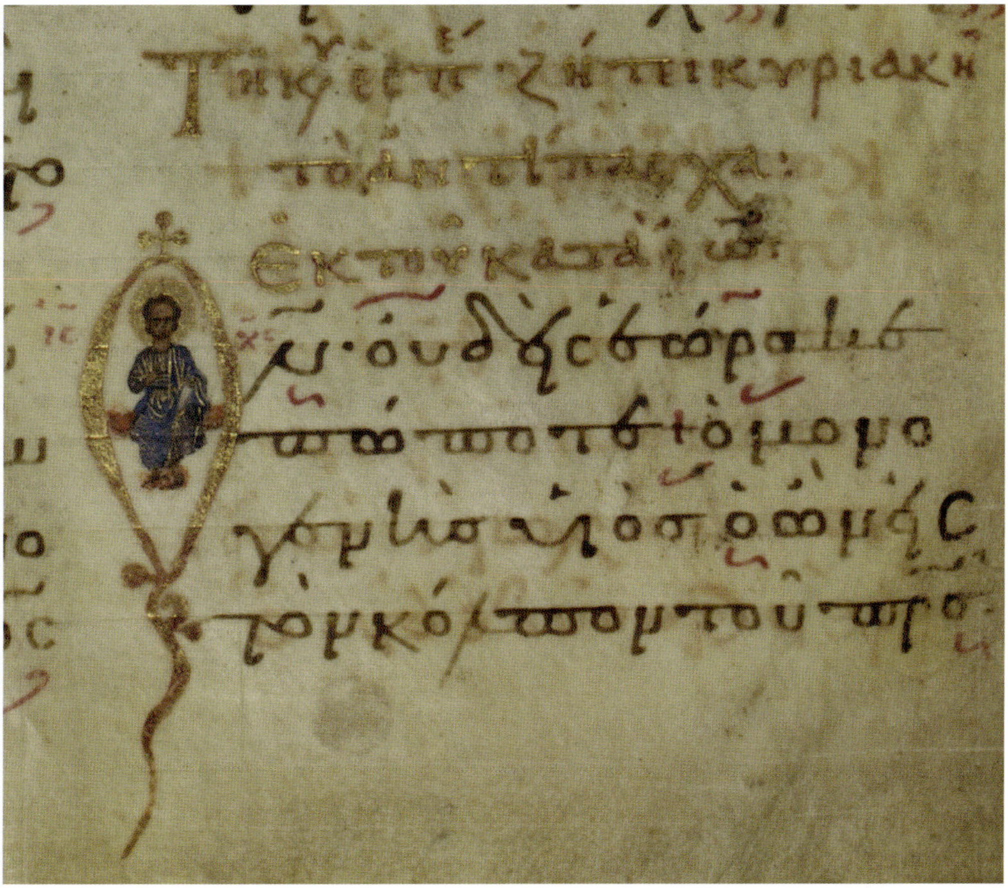

Figure 58 Athens Lectionary (Athens, National Library of Greece, Cod. 68), fol. 2v.
(Photo: National Library of Greece / The Center for the Study of New Testament Manuscripts, www.csntm.org, digitized NLG 68 at the National Library of Greece)

maintained in the Hosios David scene to ensure that God is properly depicted through Christ. In other words, the image makes the Godhead visible indirectly, through the proper channels of the Incarnation. In Grabar's skillful interpretation, the visionary-as-viewer functions to alter the understanding of the scene, which becomes not a manifestation of what was in fact seen by the visionary himself but rather a depiction of the act of seeing. Thus, rather than representing Ezekiel's vision, the image is a procedural outline of a theophanic event.

Robin Cormack, *Writing in Gold: Byzantine Society and Its Icons* (Oxford University Press, 1985), 132–33; James Snyder, "The Meaning of the Maiestas Domini in Hosios David," *Byzantion* 37 (1967): 143–52.

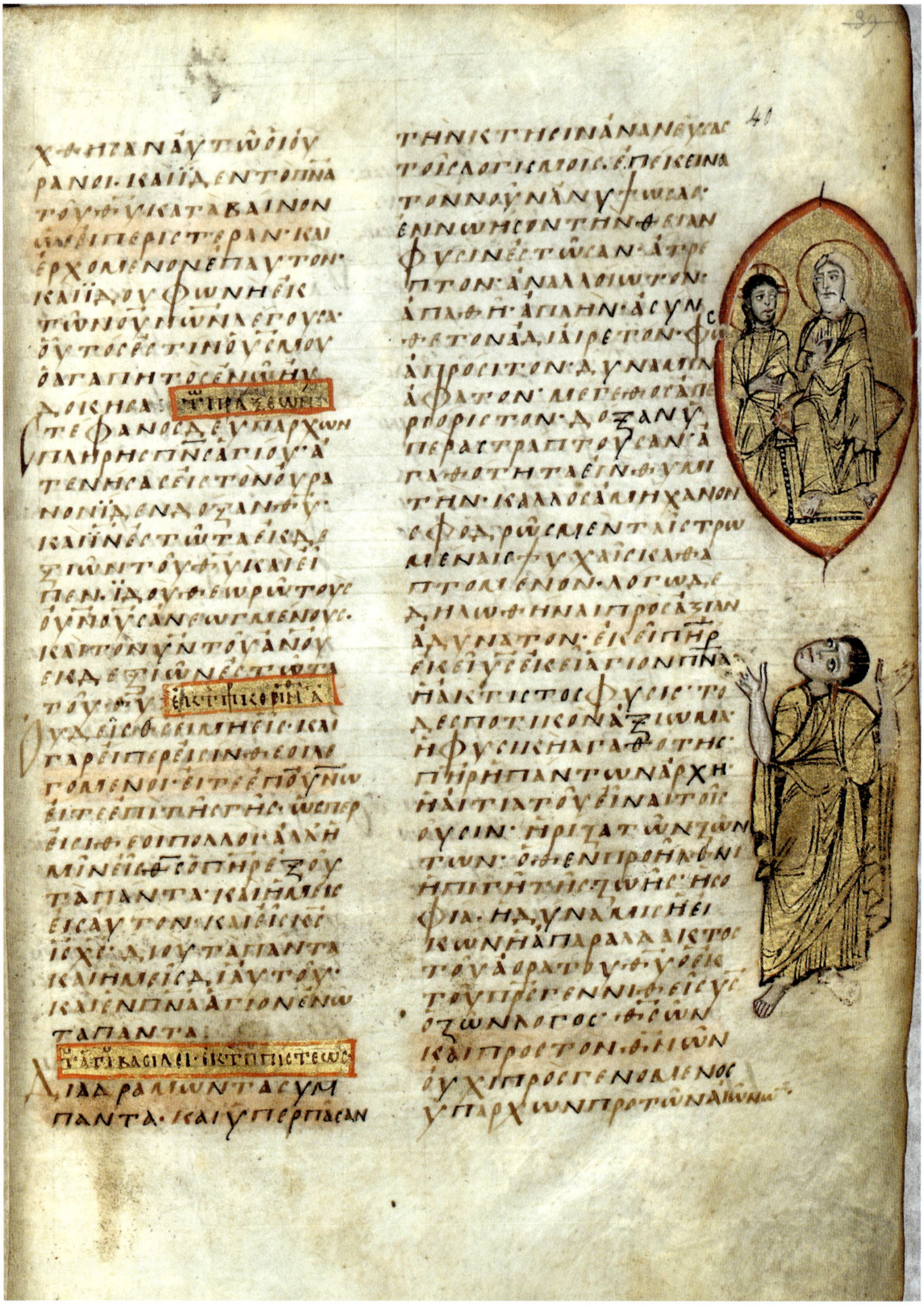

Figure 59 *Sacra parallela* (Paris, Bibliothèque nationale de France, Cod. gr. 923), fol. 40r.
(Photo: Bibliothèque nationale de France)

Figure 60 Hosios David, Thessaloniki, Greece.
(Photo: Ephorate of Antiquities of Thessaloniki, Hellenic Ministry of Culture & Sports – Archaeological Resources Fund)

My argument is that analogously, what the image in the Dionysiou Lectionary's opening for John 1:18 "depicts" is the workings and procedurality of the icon itself: that is, the "relative participation" of the divinity in the incarnate image. Below the Θ-initial, in fact, we see John gesturing up to the Godhead-and-Emmanuel with his left hand while holding his Gospel with his right. But because to depict this so blatantly would undermine the system it seeks to manifest, the halo serves as a protective step taken by the artist – to suggest that in the end the Godhead *himself* has not been depicted. However, since the text being visualized reads "God no one has ever seen," I would argue further that this image exists in a liminal position before representation, *signifying before the signifier* – it is a meta-image of the viewer's necessary disposition toward the icon. As such, the image opens up a possible space of play and enactment rather than presenting something completed. It cannot be said to be a full-fledged image per se; it is instead a foreshadowing on the page of the image that is being imagined – or, rather, fulfilled – as the reader and listeners take in the text.

This structural representation can never be fully portrayed lest it undercut the very system that makes such foreshadowing possible. As Kathleen Corrigan points out in her study on the Ancient of Days icon at Mount

Figure 61 Dionysiou Lectionary (Mount Athos, Dionysiou Monastery, Cod. 587), fol. 34^{v}. (Photo: after Pelekanidis et al., *Treasures of Mount Athos*, 173, fig. 212)

Sinai, depictions of the Ancient of Days and Christ together must always have been quite rare in Byzantium. The juxtaposition of the two figures further complicates the identity of the Ancient of Days by implicitly suggesting that the image operates as a depiction of the Godhead.[22] Notably, in the Dionysiou Lectionary the Ancient of Days appears once again, this time in the opening miniature for John 17:1–13 (fol. 34^{v}; Figure 61) – the lection read on the Seventh Sunday of Eastertide, when the Holy Fathers of the Ecumenical Councils are commemorated. Here, the artist has chosen to depict Christ praying to his Father in the miniature, a rare scene in that it opts for a literal depiction of the difficult opening lines of the lection rather than addressing the feast day, as the Dionysiou

[22] Corrigan, "Visualizing the Divine," 297.

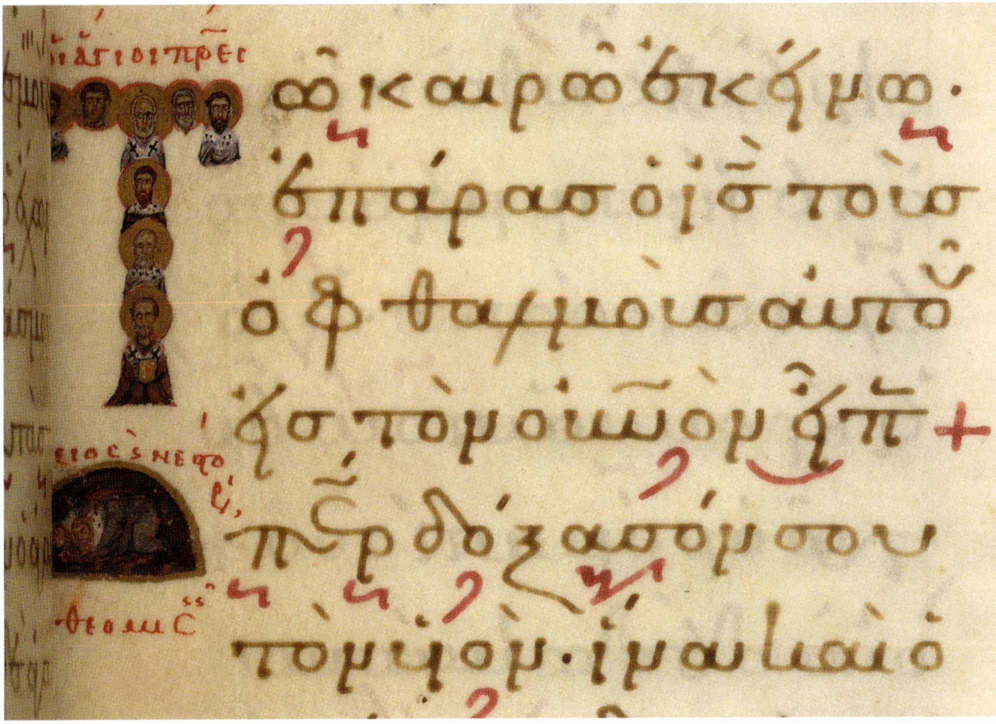

Figure 62 Hamilton Lectionary (New York, Morgan Library, Cod. 639), fol. 42r.
(Photo: The Pierpont Morgan Library, New York)

Lectionary's miniatures – unlike its historiated initials – tend to do. The latter strategy is deployed in the Morgan Library's Hamilton Lectionary, where a historiated T-initial opens the lection with eight portrait busts of Church Fathers, including John Chrysostom and Basil; below them are two heretics of the early Church, Arius and Nestorius, depicted in proskynesis within a cave-like enclosure (fol. 42r; Figure 62).

In the Dionysiou codex, Christ raises his eyes up to the heavens – just as the lection indicates – and prays, "Father, the hour has come. Glorify your Son, so that your Son also may glorify you" (Πάτερ, ἐλήλυθεν ἡ ὥρα. δόξασόν σου τὸν υἱόν, ἵνα καὶ ὁ υἱὸς σου δοξάσῃ σέ). In producing this scene, the artist was again confronted – as in John 1:18 – with the challenge of articulating a difference between Christ and the Father for the sake of literally depicting the text. Elsewhere in the manuscript, when it is necessary to manifest a theophanic presence, Christ is shown within a blue semicircular enclosure of the heavenly realms, similar to the one featuring the bust of the Ancient of Days in this miniature. For example, in the

Figure 63 Dionysiou Lectionary (Mount Athos, Dionysiou Monastery, Cod. 587), fol. 40^{v}.
(Photo: Patriarchal Institute for Patristic Studies in Thessaloniki)

miniature commemorating all saints (fol. 40^{v}; Figure 63) or representing Christ appearing to Saints Kosmas and Damian (fol. 159^{v}; Figure 64), Christ is depicted with a cruciform nimbus while wearing the usual costume he is given in the Dionysiou manuscript: a rich, dark-blue chiton – which sometimes has purple overtones – under a light-blue himation. Within the miniature for John 17:1, the incarnate Christ praying to the Father is clad in this same costume.

Figure 64 Dionysiou Lectionary (Mount Athos, Dionysiou Monastery, Cod. 587), fol. 159^{v}. (Photo: after Pelekanidis et al., *Treasures of Mount Athos*, 214, fig. 269)

In the semicircular enclosure on folio 34^{v} we see the forward-facing bust of the Ancient of Days, who is depicted with the expected long white hair and beard. His chiton and himation are both a dull gold, which echoes the colors of John's himation in this scene. The cruciform halo of the Ancient of Days, indicated by a slight notch in the halo's gilding, can just barely be made out. Therefore, this scene merits further comparison with the figure of the Ancient of Days and the Christ Emmanuel from the Θ of John 1:18. In particular, we must note that in the Θ of John 1:18, the supposed Godhead wears the Dionysiou Lectionary's uniform for Christ – the purple-blue chiton under a lighter blue himation – whereas it is the Christ Emmanuel who is clad in the dull gold chiton-himation combination, which again echoes John's himation.

The Mistaken Identity of John

The miniature on folio 34^{v} features a significant change in the color of John's attire from his previous appearance in the opening miniature for the Gospel of John and his reduplication in the corresponding E-initial for John 1:1 just one folio earlier (fols. 1^{v} and 2^{r}; see Figure 4). In both of those previous appearances, he wore a light-blue himation over a dark-blue chiton. Then, as he bears witness to the theophany of John 1:18 (see Figure 57), gesturing toward that scene much as he gestures toward Christ in the miniature showing Christ's prayer to the Father, his garments echo the blue hues of the Ancient of Day's costume and the golden-brown hues of the Christ Emmanuel's. Rather than varying the colors in their chiton-himation combination, which tends to be the Byzantine preference, the Christ and the Godhead display only a subtle variant in shade, which enables the artist to enfold the dual nature of the incarnate Christ into the figure of John. On the body of John, the brown of the incarnate Christ Emmanuel enfolds the divinity of the Godhead's blue. Thus, this particular image is coded to bear witness to the theophanic body of the Gospel of John, making perceptible the divinity that is itself uncircumscribable. Though he had appeared in John 1:1 in a slightly different color arrangement, the scheme displayed in John 1:18 becomes his signature costume in the manuscript's instances of theophanic witnessing, such as the miniature of Christ's prayer to the Father. Elsewhere, he is usually depicted in the dark-blue chiton and light-blue himation of his initial appearances, often carrying his Gospel book to distinguish him from other Apostles.

Initials also struggle with this theophanic imagery. Illuminations of the Morgan Library's Hamilton Lectionary and the Hellenic Institute's Venice Lectionary enable us to compare several different approaches to dealing with the Θ-initial when the artist has chosen to literalize the lection's text by focusing on the Gospel's apophatic theophany. In the Hamilton Lectionary, the Θ-initial glimmers with apophatic abstraction (fol. 2^{v}; Figure 65): lacking any figural images, it has a shimmering gold frame inset with green and blue and decorated with slight floral flourishes in a pinkish-purple ink with white highlights. The initial is strikingly regular and composed. Here, as in the Venice Lectionary, the abbreviated *nomina sacra*, $\bar{\Theta}\nu$ is separated from the rest of the line by an interpunct, which lends greater visual and phonetic emphasis to the word Θεόν. Above the lection's headline, which indicates its origin from John, is a *labeled* depiction of John the Theologian. John here is clad in sandals and a pink himation wrapped over a blue chiton. This garment is in accord with his

Figure 65 Hamilton Lectionary (New York, Morgan Library, Cod. 639), fol. 2^v.
(Photo: The Pierpont Morgan Library, New York)

depiction in the manuscript's opening miniature (fol. 1^r; Figure 66), where John, inspired by the gesturing hand of God poking out from the heavens, is dictating to Prochoros the scribe. In the marginal scene as well, the hand of God emerges from the heavens, inspiring a John who is performing proskynesis before it. There heaven is sequestered by a gold frame, which both seems to miniaturize the realm of the divine outside the page and which also resonates with the glimmer of the Θ-initial. However, the pink hue of John's himation, while echoing that of the opening John on the previous spread, in fact more closely matches that of Prochoros, his scribe.

Thus, this first miniature operates in two ways. Its marked distancing from the Θ-initial is in itself a visualization of the apophatic statement that no one has seen God; but at the same time, John and his reader have perceived the type of God through the Evangelist's Gospel, which Prochoros has inscribed in letters. Yet in cladding John with the garment of Prochoros, the artist has encoded in this image not merely the event of John's inspiration, but rather the textual body of the Gospel of John. Though it is now hard to make out, the illustration in the Venice Lectionary features the same play with the opening line of John 1:18 (fol. 5^r; Figure 67). In this case, however, the scene set above the statement is transposed vertically into the initial, so that the upper register of the Θ features the divine space of God's inspiring hand and the bottom register features a similarly expectant John with his hands opened in a receptive gesture, just as is depicted in the Hamilton Lectionary.

Figure 66 Hamilton Lectionary (New York, Morgan Library, Cod. 639), fol. 1^{r}.
(Photo: The Pierpont Morgan Library, New York)

In the Venice Lectionary's treatment of the initial, which is similarly worn out, John and Prochoros both wear blue chitons in the opening E of John 1:1 (fol. 4^{r}; Figure 68), while John alone bears traces of a pinkish himation sketched over his body, just as in the Θ-initial. Here, the artist treats emphasizing the identity of the Evangelist as more important than alluding to the written testament composed by John *through* Prochoros. Nevertheless, by drawing the scene into the Θ-initial, he has also stressed the testament of John attested by the opening line, while presenting John's own apophatic theophany as a demonstration of the nonperceptual manifestation of God through his testament rather than through sight alone.

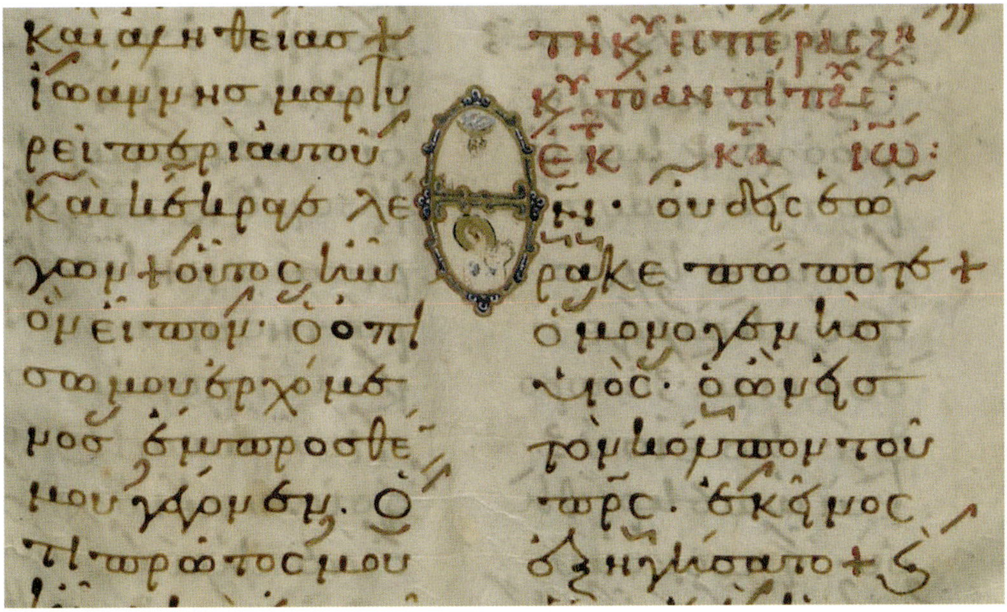

Figure 67 Venice Lectionary (Venice, Istituto Ellenico, Cod. 2), fol. 5r.
(Photo: courtesy of the Hellenic Institute of Byzantine and Post-Byzantine Studies in Venice)

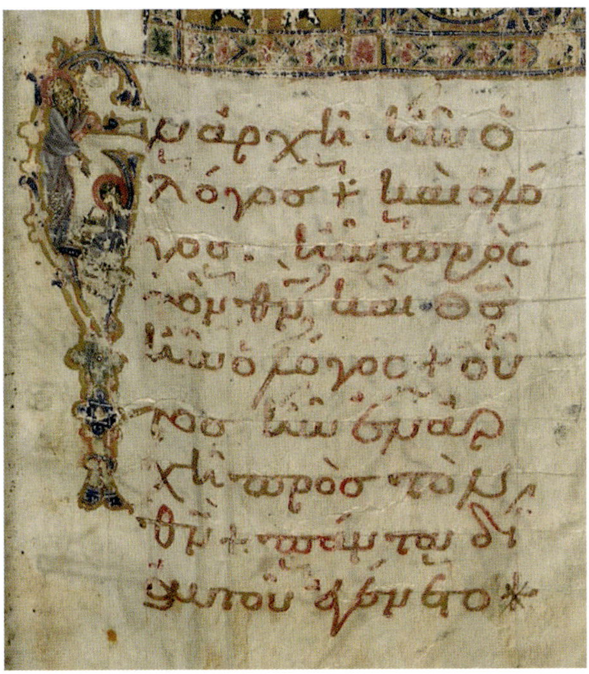

Figure 68 Venice Lectionary (Venice, Istituto Ellenico, Cod. 2), fol. 4r.
(Photo: courtesy of the Hellenic Institute of Byzantine and Post-Byzantine Studies in Venice)

Figure 69 Paris Lectionary (Paris, Bibliothèque nationale de France, supp. gr. 27), fol. 2^r^. (Photo: Bibliothèque nationale de France)

In the Paris Lectionary (Paris, Bibliothèque nationale de France, Supplement gr. 27, fol. 2^r^; Figure 69), a similar conflation of the garbs of John and Prochoros appears with the figure likewise placed above the Θ-initial. The figure above the initial is dressed in a pink himation, with a greenish chiton beneath it whose color, though worn away, seems to be closer to that of John's himation in the miniature on the preceding folio (fol. 1^r^; Figure 70) than to Prochoros's distinctly blue chiton. His face is young, round, and beardless, and his brown hair is neatly cropped. Thus, while we might expect John to occupy this space, as he does in the Hamilton Lectionary, this figure is apparently Prochoros with his hands turned up to the heavens. From that heavenly realm, the figure of Prochoros does not encounter the inspiring hand of God, as John does in the opening miniature; instead, he receives an odd rectangular object, similar to a codex or tablet, that may be understood as John's Gospel text, which is similarly placed in the Hamilton Lectionary.

However, the placement of the marginal figure alongside John 1:17 – "For the law through Moses was given, the grace and the truth through Jesus Christ did come" (ὅτι ὁ νόμος διὰ Μωϋσέως ἐδόθη, ἡ χάρις καὶ ἡ ἀλήθεια διὰ Ἰησοῦ Χριστοῦ ἐγένετο) – suggests another possible identification for this figure. Looking closely, we can note that the heavenly lunette appears in the middle of the interlinear break of the name Moses, encouraging us to read the figure as Moses, who reaches out for the gray tablet of the law from God speaking to him from heaven. The figure's covered hands and profile view are consistent with representations of Moses receiving the law in the Paris Gregory (fol. 438^v^; Figure 71), the tenth-century Leo Bible (Vatican City, Biblioteca Apostolica Vaticana, Reg. gr. 1B, fol. 155^v^;

Figure 70 Paris Lectionary (Paris, Bibliothèque nationale de France, supp. gr. 27), fol. 1r.
(Photo: Bibliothèque nationale de France)

Figure 71 Homilies of Gregory of Nazianzus [Paris Gregory] (Paris, Bibliothèque nationale de France, gr. 510), fol. 438^{v}. (Photo: Bibliothèque nationale de France)

Figure 72), the twelfth-century Rockefeller-McCormick New Testament (University of Chicago, Goodspeed Manuscript Collection, cod. 965, fol. 6^{v}; Figure 73), and the twelfth-century Smyrna Octateuch (Smyrna, Evangelical School Library, cod. A.1, fol. 106^{v}). In this way, the curved ground of the Θ-initial here comes to allude to the topography of Mount Sinai. While the iconography of this manuscript builds on contemporaneous depictions of John, the artist grappling with the apophatic nature of the theta uniquely chose to connect its illumination with the verse that abuts it, rather than following the approach of the Hamilton Lectionary's illuminator, who merely placed John between the two passages.

On the right margin, the artist takes his method further by including Christ upon the crucifix as a representation of the rest of the verse: "the grace and the truth through Jesus Christ did come." In reading the verse, we find that the preposition "through" (διά) appears immediately beside Christ's right hand on the cross. Thus, the image of Christ signifies ahead of the text that salvation has come "through Jesus Christ," as his name

Figure 72 Leo Bible (Vatican City, Biblioteca Apostolica Vaticana, Reg. gr. 1B), 155^{v}.
(Photo: © 2019 Biblioteca Apostolica Vaticana. Reproduced by permission of Biblioteca Apostolica Vaticana, all rights reserved)

follows immediately on the next line. More precisely, the image specifies in advance that the "grace and truth" came through the sacrifice on the cross of Christ, whose resurrection is now being celebrated on Easter Sunday when the verse would have been read, completing the day's lection. Yet we should note that the base of the cross goes beyond the lection and the header for the next lection, ending on the first line of John 1:18, "God no one has ever seen" (θεὸν οὐδεὶς ἑώρακεν πώποτε). Much as Moses stands on the initial dressed in garb that alludes to that of Prochoros on an earlier folio, so the Crucifixion engages with the opening of the next lection and similarly does double duty. While the figure of Moses is somewhat ambiguous in evoking John and Prochoros, particularly for any viewer or artist familiar with the illuminations in other lectionaries, the Christ is both the Christ through which grace and truth came and the God whom no one had ever seen until his revelation through the Incarnation, Crucifixion, and Resurrection. The artist has therefore cleverly produced marginalia here that operate doubly, unfolding with different understandings depending on which lection is being read.

Figure 73 Rockefeller-McCormick New Testament (University of Chicago, Goodspeed Manuscript Collection, cod. 965), fol. 6ᵛ.
(Photo: Special Collections Research Center, University of Chicago Library)

Beyond the initial for John 1:18 being expected to display John, the ending of the previous lection speaks precisely to the witness of John – that is, the Baptist, whose name has not yet been clearly distinguished from that of John the Evangelist in the Gospel text. Together these verses read:

> John testified concerning him. He cried out, saying, "This is the one I spoke about when I said, 'He who comes after me has surpassed me because he was before me.'" Out of his fullness we have all received grace in place of grace already given. For the law was given through Moses; grace and truth came through Jesus Christ. (John 1:15–18)

Hence, we can come to understand the polyvalent play here when we see the figure of John-Prochoros-Moses receiving the inspiration-text-tablet from God; we might also come to conflate John the Evangelist with John the Baptist, since the witness of the Baptist has just been stressed, alongside the authorial witness of John's Gospel. And just as John the Baptist prefigures Christ, so Moses prefigures John the Evangelist – both had communion with God and both subsequently revealed the text of the law, old and new.

Moses serves as the linchpin in this play, given that he experienced a revelation of God in which the sight of God was denied. Though he prefigures the revelation of the Christ, and Christ fulfills the law that was given by God to Moses, Moses was able to converse with God only obliquely, through the clouds. This was an association made in the Divine Liturgy explicitly, as Patriarch Germanos eloquently recounts in his commentary on the Gospel lectionary:

> The Gospel is the coming of God, when He was seen by us: He is no longer speaking to us as through a cloud and indistinctly, as He did to Moses through thunder and lightning and trumpets, by a voice, by darkness and fire on the mountain. Nor does He appear through dreams as to the prophets, but He appeared visibly as a true man. He was seen by us as a gentle and peaceful king who descended quietly like rain upon the fleece, and we have beheld His glory, glory as of the only-begotten Son, full of grace and truth [cf. John 1:14]. Through Him, the God and Father spoke to us face to face, and not through riddles. From heaven the Father bears witness to Him, saying "This is my beloved Son" [Matthew 3:17], wisdom, word, and power, who is foretold to us by the prophets. He is revealed in the gospels, so that all who receive Him and believe in His name might receive the power to become children of God [cf. John 1:12]. We have heard and seen with our eyes that He is the wisdom and word of God, and we all cry "Glory to You, O Lord." And

the Holy Spirit, who was concealed in a bright cloud, now exclaims through a man: "Attend, listen to Him."[23]

Here Germanos draws a connection straight to the experience of Moses, through direct citations of and allusions to material taken from the Easter Sunday lection of John 1:1–17. Thus, we can perceive how these marginalia play with the resonances of their iconography, relying on intertextual meaning and sequential unfolding. Germanos further enables us to understand how the presence of this Moses figure in the margin evokes the revelation of the Gospel lectionary itself during the Divine Liturgy, since it is understood as an analogue of Moses' theophany and a fulfillment of the typologies set forth in his revelation of the old law, which the Gospels now complete through the New Testament. Hence, the identification of the figure on the Θ-initial self-reflexively flits through a variety of identifications and associations that not only articulates a range of its own identities but also figures how the lectionary itself is experienced during the liturgy.

As we can see, none of these images lend themselves to an iconographic reading: instead, they offer parallel, complementary, bifurcating, and at times contradictory permutations that emerge as the user interacts with the image as a pre-semiotic site, caught in a perpetual flux of becoming.[24] These images *unfold* over processes; they are not prescribed by an iconography. Such manic polyvalence of meaning is perhaps best manifested in the Dionysiou Lectionary, whose artists appear to most fully grasp the potential of procedural representation – and which may well be misread in close iconographic studies, which are likely to declare it replete with errors. As has been noted already, below the Θ-initial, John the Evangelist points

[23] "Τὸ εὐαγγέλιον ἐστιν ἡ παρουσία τοῦ Θεοῦ καθ' ἣν ὡράθη ἡμῖν, οὐκ ἔτι διὰ νεφελῶν καὶ αἰνιγμάτων λαλῶν ἡμῖν ὥς ποτε τῷ Μωϋσῇ διὰ φωνῶν καὶ ἀστραπῶν καὶ σαλπίγγων ἤχῳ καὶ γνόφῳ καὶ πυρὶ ἐπὶ τοῦ ὄρους, ἢ τοῖς προφήταις δι' ἐνυπνίων, ἀλλ' ἐμφανῶς ὡς ἄνθρωπος ἀληθινὸς ἐφάνη καὶ ὡράθη ἡμῖν ὁ πραῢς καὶ ἥσυχος βασιλεὺς ὁ πρὶν καταβὰς ἀψοφητὶ ἐν πόκῳ· «καὶ ἐθεασάμεθα τὴν δόξαν αὐτοῦ, δόξαν ὡς μονογενοῦς πλήρης χάριτος καὶ ἀληθείας», δι' οὗ ἐλάλησεν ἡμῖν ὁ Θεὸς καὶ Πατὴρ στόμα πρὸς στόμα καὶ οὐ δι' αἰνιγμάτων, περὶ οὗ ὁ Πατὴρ ἐξ οὐρανοῦ μαρτυρεῖ καὶ λέγει· «οὗτός ἐστιν ὁ Υἱός μου ὁ ἀγαπητός», σοφία, λόγος καὶ δύναμις, ὁ ἐν προφήταις μὲν κηρυχθεὶς ἡμῖν· ἐν εὐαγγελίοις δὲ φανερωθεὶς ἵνα «ὅσοι λάβωσιν αὐτὸν καὶ πιστεύουσιν εἰς τὸ ὄνομα αὐτοῦ λάβωσιν ἐξουσίαν τέκνα Θεοῦ γενέσθαι». Ὃν ἀκηκόαμεν καὶ «ἑωράκαμεν τοῖς ὀφθαλμοῖς ἡμῶν», σοφίαν καὶ λόγον Θεοῦ τοῦτον εἶναι πάντες βοῶμεν· δόξα σοι κύριε. Εἶτα πάλιν τὸ Ἅγιον Πνεῦμα βοᾷ τὸ ἐν νεφέλῃ φωτεινῇ ἐπισκιάζον, νῦν δι' ἀνθρώπου βοᾷ· προσέχετε, «αὐτοῦ ἀκούετε»." Germanos I, *Historia mystica ecclesiae catholicae*, 31, ed. and trans. Paul Meyendorff, *On the Divine Liturgy* (Crestwood, NY: St. Vladimir's Seminary Press, 1984), 80–81.

[24] For a Western medieval case study of an image functioning similarly, see Beate Fricke, "Jesus Wept! On the History of Anthropophagy: A New Reading of a Miniature from the Gospel Book of Otto III as *Kippfigur*," *RES: Anthropology and Aesthetics* 59–60 (2011): 192–205.

toward the Godhead-and-Logos circumscribed by the initial. This marginal image thus seems to follow directly on the final word of the opening, "he did declare" (ἐξηγήσατο), and the second verse of the lection, "And this is the testimony of John" (Καὶ αὕτη ἐστὶν ἡ μαρτυρία τοῦ Ἰωάννου), which appear immediately beside the figure. Hence, it is paralleled by the inspired John of the Hamilton and Venice Lectionaries, suggesting that those figures are responding to this same part of the text. In addition, the image of John here corresponds to the appearance commonly given the Evangelist to which the reading belongs when the artist chooses not to depict the words immediately at hand.

The crux of this marginal image, however, is that the John addressed in the text is John the Baptist, *not* John the Theologian. But at this point in the Gospel, John's identity has yet to be clarified: in the absence of prior knowledge, it is impossible for the reader-listener to determine which is intended. Rather than blaming this uncertainty on a craftsman's mistake or scribal error, one should accept it as a feature of the manuscript's visual epistemology. But a comparison to the face of the John of the Dionysiou Lectionary's opening miniature, repeated in the manuscript's opening initial, makes clear that this is John the Evangelist. The John in the margin does not wear the usual camel-skin robe associated with the Baptist, and he certainly does not look anything like the John the Baptist who is encountered just a few folios later. Yet through the color change to John's himation, the artist continues to connect him to John the Baptist. While the himation resonates with the image of the Christ-and-Godhead above, here John's brown garment – though not his full costume or face – is similar to that of the manuscript's John the Baptist. When John the Baptist first appears in the manuscript after this, he is depicted in his usual camel-skin cloak (fol. 8^r; Figure 74), though not in the costume in which he is seen later performing the baptism in a miniature (fol. 141^v; Figure 75). Interestingly, his cloak in the marginalia (beside said miniature) features a striking blue trim, as if harking back to his earlier manifestation in the guise of the Evangelist. In a similar appearance (fol. 13^v; Figure 76), the trim again appears to be the other side of his himation, as if the figure has enfolded the identities of John the Evangelist and John the Baptist as two sides of the same cloth. His pose, gesture, and gaze strikingly echo those of the image we have taken to be the Evangelist's.

In other lectionaries and Gospel books, we can observe that such framing is often reserved specifically for John the Baptist, as unambiguously shown in the marginal figure clearly labeled "The Holy John the Forerunner" (ὁ ἅγιος Ἰωάννης ὁ Πρόδρομος) in a contemporaneous eleventh-century Gospel book (Vatican City, Biblioteca Apostolica Vaticana, Ross. 138, fol. 4^r; Figure 77). There, John the Baptist appears

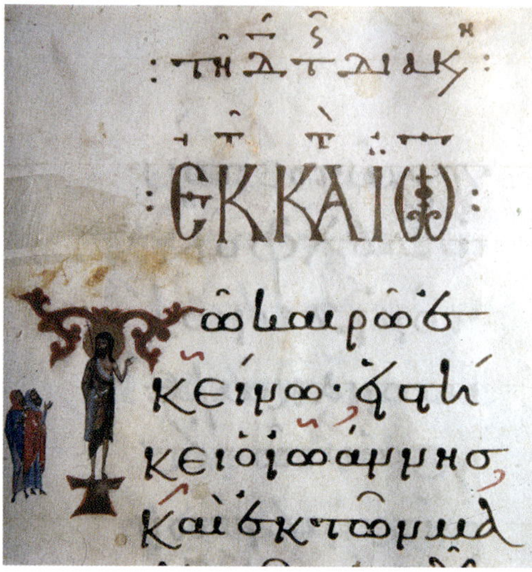

Figure 74 Dionysiou Lectionary (Mount Athos, Dionysiou Monastery, Cod. 587), fol. 8[r].
(Photo: Patriarchal Institute for Patristic Studies in Thessaloniki)

Figure 75 Dionysiou Lectionary (Mount Athos, Dionysiou Monastery, Cod. 587), fol. 141[v].
(Photo: after Pelekanidis et al., *Treasures of Mount Athos*, 203, fig. 255)

Figure 76 Dionysiou Lectionary (Mount Athos, Dionysiou Monastery, Cod. 587), fol. 13[v].
(Photo: Patriarchal Institute for Patristic Studies in Thessaloniki)

Figure 77 Gospel book (Vatican City, Biblioteca Apostolica Vaticana, Ross. 138), fol. 4[r].
(Photo: © 2019 Biblioteca Apostolica Vaticana. Reproduced by permission of Biblioteca Apostolica Vaticana, all rights reserved)

on the right-hand margin as a mirror image of the Dionysiou John: one arm is raised gesturing toward Christ above in the Gospel book's headpiece, toward whom he here gazes rather than toward the viewer, and the other hand is drawn close to his body, almost as if carrying a tome against his chest. The figure acknowledges the iconography of such marginal images of Evangelists, yet it does not seek to create any ambiguity. On the opposite folio (fol. 3ᵛ; Figure 78), John the Evangelist, also clearly labeled, sits at his writing desk in a typical portrait, with his gaze apparently not directed toward Christ in the headpiece; instead, he seems to be lost in thought with his gaze drooping downward toward the marginal figure of John the Baptist alone on the other folio, a spatial play across the open spread of the book that draws on the interrelations between the various images – a feature typical of such marginalia, as we have seen in many examples.

The hermeneutic ambiguity that the Dionysiou Lectionary cultivates, as did the Paris Lectionary in the case of Moses, determines how the linear progression of a reader-listener through the text unfolds slowly as they learn and relearn the narrative over time, testing their assumptions and revising earlier givens. The reader and listener to this point know only one John – the Evangelist. This mistaken identification thus demonstrates an engagement with the lectionary's text as an oral act, as a spatiotemporal utterance, in which the user is constantly generating images through their own hermeneutic processes, imagining and reimagining as the text progresses. Since the lection begins with the statement "According to John," above which the Hamilton Lectionary places the scene of the inspired John, the reader or listener would come to understand this John as the Evangelist and would imagine his features and appearance accordingly. As the reader speaks the lection, this implicit "mistake" occurs. In the image, however, the painter evokes the identity of the Baptist, changing the color of the figure's outer garment to brown in order to foreshadow the John that will soon emerge. This ambivalence is inherent in the text itself, since the Evangelist's Gospel, like the Baptist's preaching, is a testimony of Christ.

To grasp the extent of this system, consider one other image where I am inclined to see John the Evangelist: the miniature for Christ's prayer to the Father at John 17:1–13 (fol. 34ᵛ; Figure 61). Not coincidentally, it is the only other instance in the manuscript where the Godhead is depicted through the guise of the Ancient of Days, as mentioned above. Here, Christ is figured with his hands raised in prayer to God the Father, shown within the blue realm of heaven and clad all in gold. One can barely make out, underneath the thick gilding on the halo of the Ancient of Days, the faint tracings of a cruciform. Behind Christ stands a selected assortment of

Figure 78 Gospel book (Vatican City, Biblioteca Apostolica Vaticana, Ross. 138), fol. 3v–4r. (Photo: © 2019 Biblioteca Apostolica Vaticana. Reproduced by permission of Biblioteca Apostolica Vaticana, all rights reserved)

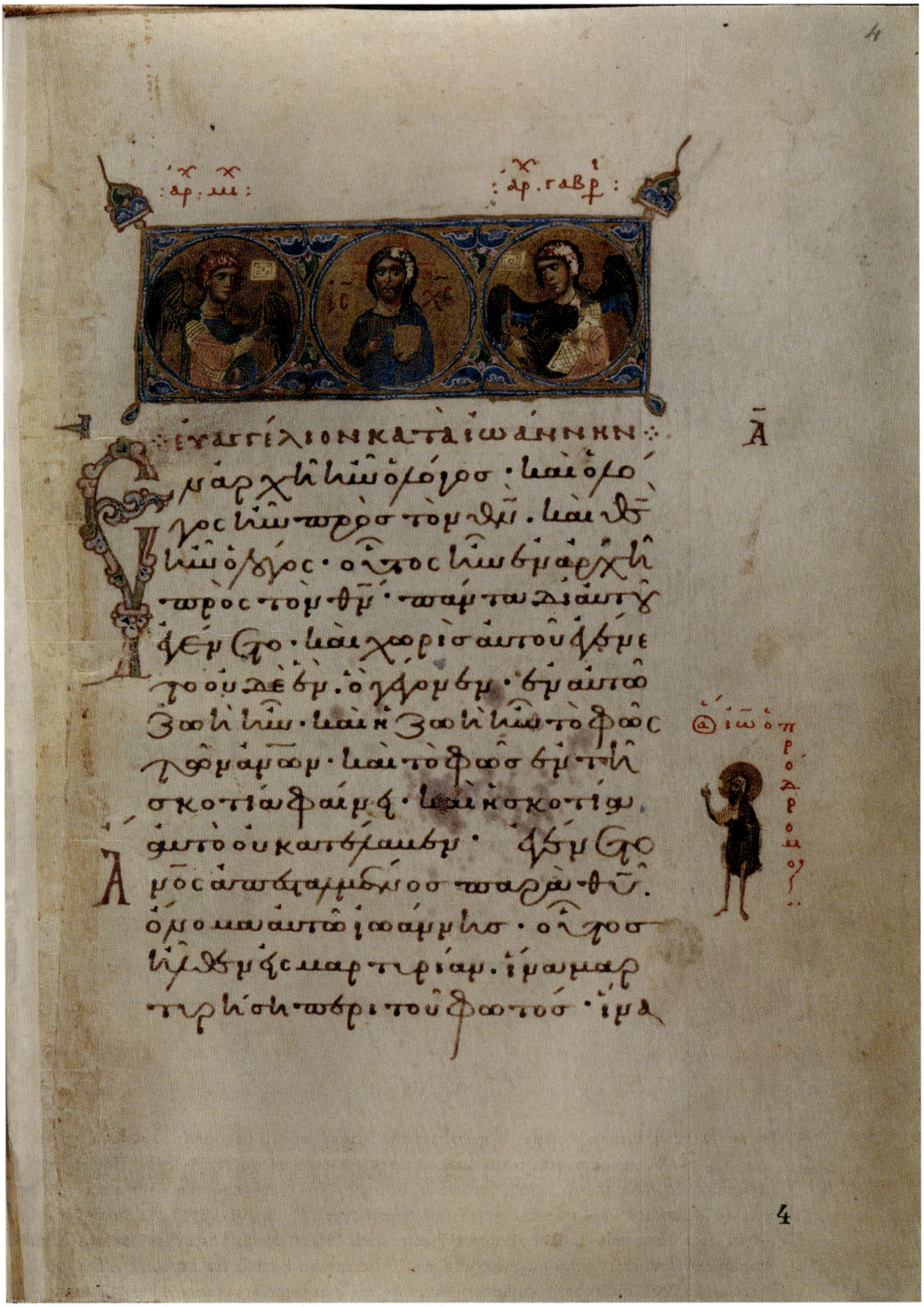

Figure 78 (*cont.*)

Apostles, led by a bearded figure with a gold himation wrapped over a blue chiton, apparently accompanied by Peter among the others behind him. His angular beard and garb should remind the viewer of the enigmatic John who bears witness to the theophany. Here again, this figure seems to direct the viewer's attention to Christ and the Father, as if underscoring his authorship of the lection that is to come – which, like his gesturing hand, leads to that scene. This structure is actually quite common in the manuscript: the gesturing Evangelist in the miniature often is the corresponding lection's author. Throughout the Dionysiou Lectionary, the Apostles follow a fairly coherent iconographic type, as a survey of a few scenes suggests (fols. 14^{v}, 31^{r}, 32^{v}, 36^{v}, and 52^{r}; Figure 79). In particular, John (usually depicted to the far left of Christ) is often symmetrically echoed by another Evangelist on his far right. They often – though not always – wear matching color combinations. However, John is distinguished from this figure by his receding hairline; thus we conclude that the other figure is not John but Matthew. This identification is confirmed not only by looking at typical representations of the four Evangelists found in contemporary Byzantine sources, but also by examining this manuscript for the figure's successive appearances in miniatures and in author-portrait initials: John has the most strictly regulated appearance of all the Apostles (cf. fols. 1^{v}, 3^{v}, 12^{r}, 14^{v}, 26^{v}, 31^{r}, 32^{v}, 36^{v}, 52^{r}, 53^{r}, 153^{v}, 158^{v}, and 167^{r}; Figure 80); Peter, who is always depicted in a brownish-gold himation over a blue chiton, is almost as constrained. Like Mark and Luke, Matthew demonstrates some variety in the color of his himation, though his facial features vary little. He is often played off John not only in the composition of the Apostle groups but also in the possible slippage between the two figures due to their formal similarities: we are more likely to err in identifying Matthew as John than vice versa.

The prayer scene, which illuminates a reading from John, certainly is one of those instances when error is possible (the same misidentification seems possible in several other miniatures as well). We should note that in the select group of Apostles, John is not depicted, while the readily identifiable Peter – who is often paired with John – stands prominently behind Matthew. For these reasons, I initially identified Matthew as John. When we keep in mind the notable appearances of John discussed above, Matthew here might be understood precisely as another manifestation of the theophany that John both witnessed and bore witness to; hence his himation is here again changed to a light gold, resonating with the garb of Christ and the Godhead – a color choice *almost* as rare for Matthew as it is for John in the manuscript.

Figure 79 Dionysiou Lectionary (Mount Athos, Dionysiou Monastery, Cod. 587), fols. 14^{v}, 31^{r}, 32^{v}, 36^{v}, and 52^{r}.
(Photo: after Pelekanidis et al., *Treasures of Mount Athos*, 167, 172, 171, 174, and 182, figs. 199, 210, 206, 213, and 223)

A similar confusion is possible, if not encouraged, in the miniature for the first reading of the *Eothina*: the eleven Gospel passages detailing the appearance of Christ after the Resurrection (fol. 167^{r}; Figure 81). Here, in Jesus' appearance in Galilee, Matthew is prominently depicted, his Gospel book sketched in one hand while he gestures toward Christ with the other. This portrait is only to be expected: because the miniature opens the

Figure 80 Dionysiou Lectionary (Mount Athos, Dionysiou Monastery, Cod. 587), fols. 1^{v}, 3^{v}, 12^{r}, 14^{v}, 26^{v}, 31^{r}, 32^{v}, 36^{v}, 52^{r}, 53^{r}, 153^{v}, 158^{v}, and 167^{r}.
(Photo: after Pelekanidis et al., *Treasures of Mount Athos*, 162, 164, 165, 167, 171, 172, 174, 182, 183, 212, 213, and 216, figs. 189, 191, 195, 199, 206, 207, 210, 213, 223, 224, 266, 267, and 273)

reading of Matthew 28:16–20, it is fitting for Matthew to direct the user's gaze to Christ and carry his Gospel book. That Matthew's himation here is light green rather than gold makes the confusion of this figure with John – dressed as he is in John's usual colors – even more likely. In addition, this Matthew is nearly identical in facial features, posture, and gesture to Matthew as depicted in the prayer scene, where – in a crucial difference – the artist omitted the Gospel book. Hence, it is clear that while the artist is quietly playing with confusion on several levels, he never relinquishes control of the absolute identification of the figure in the prayer scene – demonstrating that while it might be read *as if* it were John, it is indeed Matthew. Nevertheless, we must also note that in this scene Matthew cleverly gestures with his right hand, blocking the view of his left arm, which appears to be raised *as if* he were carrying a Gospel book. The viewer is thus momentarily tricked, forced to reconsider the scene, look for further clues, and recalibrate his understanding. In the miniature on folio 167^{r}, the

Figure 81 Dionysiou Lectionary (Mount Athos, Dionysiou Monastery, Cod. 587), fol. 167[r].
(Photo: Patriarchal Institute for Patristic Studies in Thessaloniki)

same kind of play occurs through Matthew's garb, even as the Gospel book and his hairline define him as Matthew. The crucial difference from the prayer scene is that here John the Evangelist, wedged between Matthew and Luke, stares back at the viewer, as if forcing them to confront their initial error and recognize the complex system of representation at work in the manuscript.

As demonstrated throughout this analysis, these images operate on multiple levels of intervisual citation and commentary: they play with the image of the Ancient of Days and Christ Emmanuel across the manuscript, and also with the identities of John the Evangelist and John the Baptist. Through the intricacies of the Dionysiou Lectionary's image program, and costumes deployed with consistency, these images appear to have produced a complex interactive web that has plainly exposed the system's method. Here, the liminality of these images on the edge of becoming emerges most openly. Therefore, we can say not that an image adheres to an iconographic logic but rather that it echoes the reader-listener's imagining of the text as it unfolds over the course of the liturgy. Here the procedural rhetoric of the image operates on two levels. First, the artist himself is performing within a procedural system insofar as he illuminates the manuscript as if playing within certain rules – that is, what is given to him by the text and by his artistic tradition. But second, the artist is also operating within a procedural system insofar as his images cannot be said to be complete representations until their coding is processed by a user. Thus the elements that we would normally consider iconographic, such as color, style, and the figure's dress or face, all become lines of code within a complex program that relies on the habitus of the lectionary's readers to be its operating system.

In this way, John's direct gaze here operates as a tactic that makes the user indisputably aware of how the lectionary's artist is shaping a self-reflexive medium by pushing the strategies and tactics of Byzantine iconography to their very limits. In the depiction of the appearance of Jesus in Galilee near the end of the manuscript, the artist in effect encapsulates the tactics deployed throughout the manuscript by confronting its user head-on with John's piercing stare. Note that the manuscript text opened by this miniature explicitly declares in the first sentence that the *eleven* disciples went to Galilee:

> Then the eleven disciples went to Galilee, to the mountain where Jesus had told them to go. When they saw him, they worshiped him; but some doubted. Then Jesus came to them and said, "All authority in heaven and on earth has been given to me. Therefore go and make disciples of all nations, baptizing them in the name of the Father and of the Son and of the Holy Spirit, and teaching them to obey everything I have commanded you. And surely I am with you always, to the very end of the age." (Matthew 28:16–20)

However, there are only *ten* disciples in the cluster depicted here. I believe that the missing Apostle is Thomas – an alteration that encourages us to confuse this scene with the parallel event in the narrative of Doubting Thomas from John's Gospel, which is read during the Divine Liturgy on the First Sunday *after* Easter. This passage from Matthew, however, is read during the morning matins *on* Easter Sunday. If we view the lectionary as a linear text, we might see this confusion as another way for the artist to summarize his tactics near the end of the volume. However, if we consider the liturgical unfolding of the manuscript, we will realize that our crucially enigmatic John from John 1:18 would be seen the day *immediately after* this reading. Following the prescriptions from the *Typikon* of Hagia Sophia (where this manuscript was intended to be used), during the orthros rite on Easter Sunday, the reader would encounter this John with his half-shielded face within this miniature with its discreet mistake; *then*, on the next day during the Divine Liturgy he would confront the layered enigma of John the Evangelist playing the role of John the Baptist.[25] Hence, in literally covering John's body with the figure of Matthew, who here wears the usual garments and color combination of the John the Evangelist (as seen in the opening miniature), the artist has cleverly sketched and hinted at the complex system of play that would be encountered the next day in John 1:18.

In fact, the placement of the indeterminant John in Dionysiou Lectionary explicitly taunts the reader as he is confused, perhaps perplexed by the marginal figure. This taunting happens not by the text for the day's reading of John 1:18, but by the verse that stands directly to the left of the marginal John. Abutting him is the line spoken by John the Baptist, explaining Christ, but in a sense explaining his own identity in the margin through John 1:15: "He who after me is coming, hath come before me, for he was before me" (Ὁ ὀπίσω μου ἐρχόμενος ἔμπροσθέν μου γέγονεν, ὅτι πρῶτός μου ἦν). But particular emphasis is given to "before" (πρῶτός) as the sigma's top line dramatically curves up pointing directly at John's face in the margin, as if demonstrating that this is the John that comes "before" the Christ, as he similarly came before in the previous lection. Such careful, astute, and rigorous play demonstrates an artist-scribe working carefully between word and image, producing tricks and traps for the reader to stumble and work through as they read, recite, or learn the text. But this is not a play that must reveal itself all at once or that is fundamental to the understanding of the text or the images; the whole point is that they reveal themselves across iterations of use, pricking the attention of the reader even at their most focused.

I do not wish to suggest that this logic of illumination operates merely as a slowly unfolding, hermeneutic process that eventually leads to a static, fully achieved image that has already – *and always already* – been depicted on the page. Instead, I propose that such images thrive precisely in this intermediate space – on this literal medium – between various possibilities

[25] Anonymous, *Typicon Magnae Ecclesiae*, ed. Mateos, *Typicon de la Grande Église*, 2:170.

of semiotic manifestation. It is a format of signification before the signifier, in the sense that the iconographic signifiers on the page are themselves constantly in flux – as if the neat boundaries of a structuralist semiotics, dependent on interrelation difference, are always shifting and thereby producing a space of synchronic signification that seems to encompass various temporalities and languages all at the same time. In this way, these images offer up spectrums of possibilities for generating meaning and not merely semiotic play, as if the signifier presented itself in flashes of multiplicity. This is to say that rather than drawn-out and focused contemplation resulting or climaxing in a final revelation, all the confusions and slippages that occur throughout the manuscript coexist alongside the biblical identity of the figure or scene. Hence, the possible identification of Matthew in the prayer scene as John is not an erroneous reading per se, nor is it an understanding that must fade once we realize that textually he *should be* Matthew. Instead, we must see this process as one where the artist understands the limitations set forth by the biblical text, adhering to its prescriptions while treating those bounds as his medium as he encodes variations and doublings within the image. It is thus through error that we can reparatively articulate the creativity and innovation of Byzantine artists.

I have chosen to focus on a very particular manuscript illumination because I see this image as a noteworthy site of revelation within the lectionary's artistic production – and also because this focus has enabled me to construct my argument through a close iconographic analysis. My purpose was to demonstrate procedurally the method's own undoing, caused by its need for constant corrections, revisions, and alternative permutations. What I am proposing is that rather than merely being composed iconographically from circulating models, the lectionary's marginalia, initials, and miniatures were authored through processes that reflected how they were continuously and repetitively used. Like a participant in a game, the user is always offered an extensive series of permutations and possibilities to embrace within the coding of the system. The liturgical context and Gospel text establish the rules of the artists' games, which played out every time each set out to paint an icon. Kurt Weitzmann once characterized the relationship of images to text as "illustrations," but here I see both falling under the notion of *play* within a *medium*.[26] Following Rosalind Krauss, by *medium* I mean not something providing physical or technical support for the work of art but rather the conceptual

[26] Weitzmann, *Illustrations in Roll and Codex*, 130–81.

playing field of an artist, who operates in accordance with the rules of their trade.[27] My argument suggests how these images themselves go on to support further procedural play. Thus, what we would call iconography comprises not the elements of a realized image but rather a set of graphic rules with which a user must play so as to formulate an image in their imagination – through reading and seeing, but also through listening.

Error and Reparative Seeing

In this chapter, I have used close, visual analysis to show that purported instances of error and failure in Byzantine illumination in fact reveal clever and remarkably complex strategies of play. But what then do we make of an actual, explicit error in the lectionary? And how might we come to understand an artist's own reparative engagement with their mistake? The Dionysiou Lectionary offers one prominent example of such an error: the illumination for the opening of the lection read on the Tuesday of Renewal, just two days after Easter (Luke 24:12–35) (fol. 5ʳ; Figure 82). The artist has depicted, as is to be expected, the content of the lection's initial lines – Peter's discovery of the empty tomb:

> And Peter having risen, did run to the tomb, and having stooped down he seeth the linen clothes lying alone, and he went away to his own home, wondering at that which was come to pass. And, lo, two of them were going on during that day to a village, distant sixty furlongs from Jerusalem, the name of which is Emmaus. (Luke 24:12–13)

Peter stands beside his name, gesturing toward it and beyond to the tomb. There, a figure peers into that tomb. Yet the peering figure is not Peter but John the Evangelist – dressed precisely as he was in the opening image of the manuscript and displaying his signature facial features and hairline. In the comparable illumination in the Venice Lectionary (fol. 6ʳ; Figure 83), the scene is split between Peter on the left running toward the tomb and his duplicated figure on the right gazing into the open and empty tomb.

The Dionysiou Lectionary differs because of a critical scribal error, which marked this reading as coming from the version in the Gospel of John (John 20:1–10), rather than from the actual source, the Gospel of Luke, as the later correction evidences. Hence, the artist has illuminated the

[27] See Rosalind Krauss, *Under Blue Cup* (Cambridge, MA: MIT Press, 2011), 1–50.

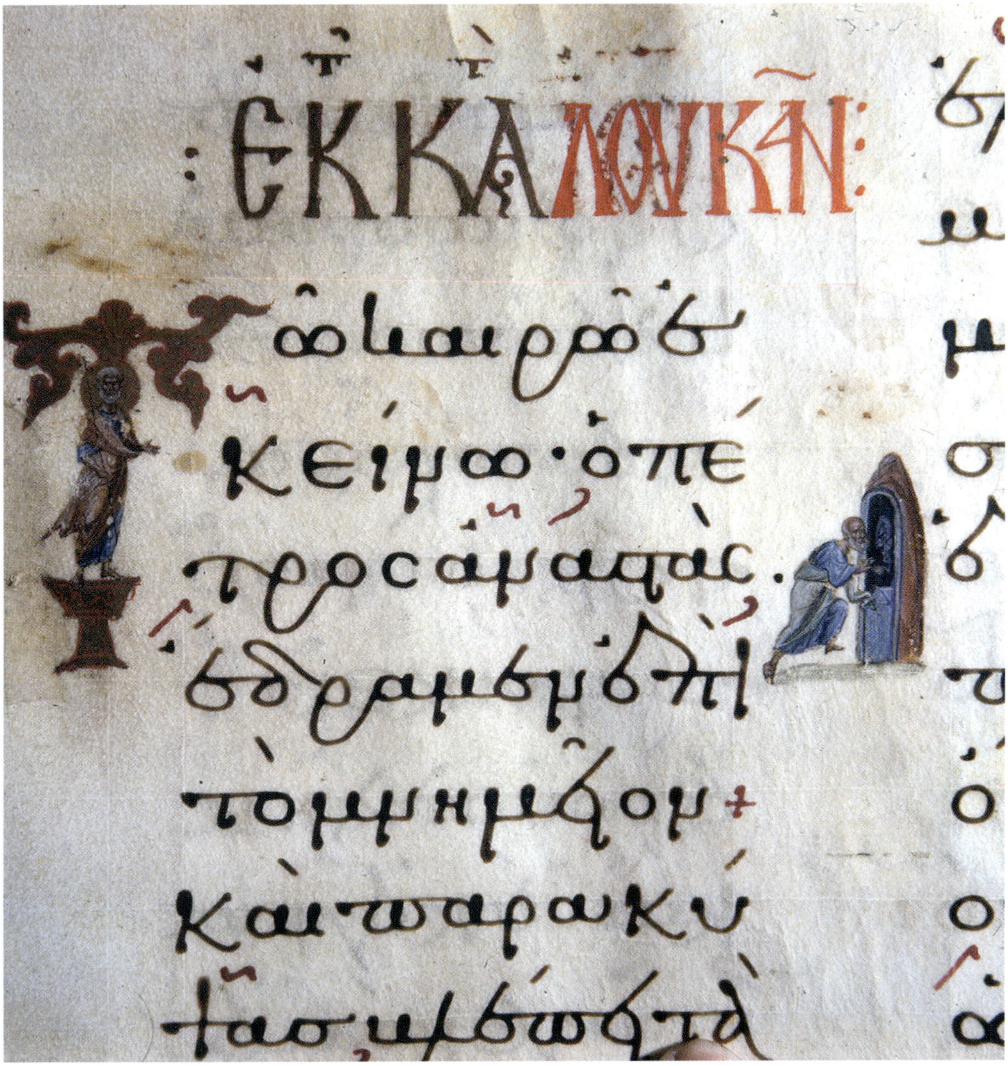

Figure 82 Dionysiou Lectionary (Mount Athos, Dionysiou Monastery, Cod. 587), fol. 5r.
(Photo: Patriarchal Institute for Patristic Studies in Thessaloniki)

text according to the story told in John, which he knew from memory, in which "the other disciple" beats Peter to the tomb. While this other disciple is not named, the artist illuminated him as John – a reasonable choice, since the passage emerges from the Gospel of John. Thus, we are seeing an artist who is working dynamically at the intersection of his training, his memory, and the text before him. While he is picking out words and lines to illuminate, and demonstrating a grasp of the expected iconographies, his

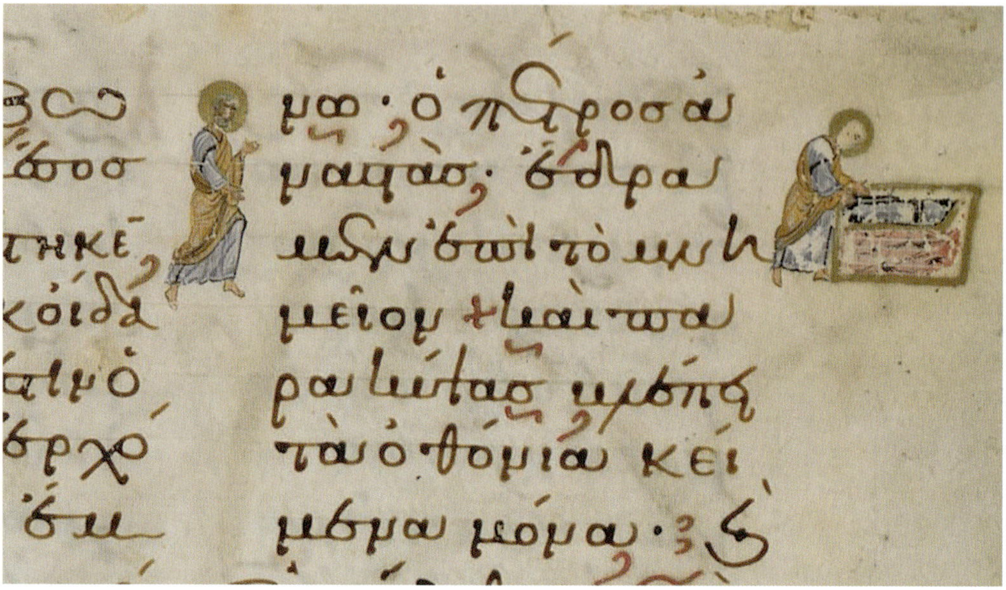

Figure 83 Venice Lectionary (Venice, Istituto Ellenico, Cod. 2), fol. 6r.
(Photo: courtesy of the Hellenic Institute of Byzantine and Post-Byzantine Studies in Venice)

illumination of the scene comes from his memory of the biblical texts; and the artist is not afraid to play with the established iconography and alter it as he sees fit, as he apparently did when he noticed that, rather than featuring the passage from Luke here, this lectionary allegedly contained the reading from John, and thus he inserted this second Apostle arriving at the tomb before Peter. What should we make of such an error?

I believe that the artist realized what he had done, but only after illuminating the scene. It is even possible that the artist himself later corrected the scribal error. Note that a similar acid-red color to the corrected incipit's ink glimmers in the outlining of the gilded T-initial, suggesting that the ink used to outline the initial was also used to correct the text. Even with firsthand observation of the manuscript it is difficult to confirm this assessment without more technical analysis of the pigments. Nevertheless, the ink originally used underneath for the original attribution of the incipit was a duller carmine, the same as that used for the chant marks. A more significant clue is the handling of the miniature for the proper appearance of the text from John at the end of the manuscript (fol. 170v; Figure 84), which appears as the seventh reading of the *Eothina* (John 20:1–10). This miniature captures the

Figure 84 Dionysiou Lectionary (Mount Athos, Dionysiou Monastery, Cod. 587), fol. 170v. (Photo: Patriarchal Institute for Patristic Studies in Thessaloniki)

opening of the scene from John properly: the two disciples encounter Mary Magdalene at the tomb, who explains what has happened. In the Gospel of Luke, by contrast, the women are said to go elsewhere to tell all the disciples, causing Peter to rise and run to the tomb. What is crucial here is the division of the narrative and its handling of the lines related to the discovery of the empty tomb:

> Peter, therefore, went forth, and the other disciple, and they were coming to the tomb, and the two were running together, and the other disciple did run forward more quickly than Peter, and came first to the tomb, and having stooped down, seeth the linen clothes lying, yet, indeed, he entered not. (John 20:3–5)

Here, the artist has essentially duplicated his earlier mistaken image, since now it is proper to show John reaching the tomb before Peter. He portrays the face of John in both depictions in the sequence; however, the artist has changed his attire between the moment that he speaks with the women and his arrival at the tomb. When John peers into the empty tomb, he is wearing Peter's brown himation. Not only does the artist gesture toward his error with this odd and deliberate costume change, but he generates a useful slippage between their two identifications to his advantage: by producing two visually confused figures at the tomb across the manuscript, he helps rectify his earlier error. In essence, the artist has produced this image as a reparative reading of his earlier mistake. Yet this is not the only costume change undertaken: John is not wearing his usual greenish-blue himation in the first sequence of the scene, but instead is dressed in the garb that the manuscript often associates with the figure of Luke, as seen in earlier and subsequent initials (fols. 146^{r}, 32^{v}, and 117^{v}; Figure 85). Hence, the artist has carefully and meticulously encoded his earlier confusion of the passage from Luke in this one by placing the lection's correct author, John, in Luke's garb, pointing to the earlier confusion of authorship, and the second John is in Peter's garb, pointing to the earlier confusion of John for Peter. In a sense, the artist deliberately echoes his mistakes, seizing on and overcoming those earlier errors by making them a generative medium for this image. This logic of illumination is so meticulously intricate, so deeply complex and critically self-reflexive, that I am inclined to doubt my initial reading and attribution of error.

In the Byzantine illuminations of the Gospel lectionary, the moments of failure and error are what enable the image to forsake its stable being and enjoy the flux of multiple and contradictory states of becoming – to stand on the edge of becoming itself. The uniqueness, resonance, and so-called faults of the images discussed in this chapter open up spaces where such slippage, confusion, and misdirection *are* possible – and it is this possibility that most interests me as a methodological imperative. That is, I wish to consider the manner in which a Byzantine artist could have cultivated

Figure 85 Dionysiou Lectionary (Mount Athos, Dionysiou Monastery, Cod. 587), fols. 146ʳ, 32ᵛ, and 117ᵛ.
(Photo: after Pelekanidis et al., *Treasures of Mount Athos*, 208, 171, and 187, figs. 260, 208, and 231)

ample room for failure by pushing and pulling at the strictures of what contemporary art historians have come to articulate as an iconography. My argument is therefore bifurcated between two temporalities: that of my Byzantine artist-scribe and that of my present subject position as an art historian, trained in the methods and narratives of Byzantine art.

PART II

The Liturgy

Sound and Architecture

λόγος κη' περὶ τῆς ἱερᾶς καὶ μητρὸς τῶν ἀρετῶν.

Προσευχή ἐστι. κατὰ μὲν τὴν αὐτῆς
ποιότητα. συνουσία καὶ ἕνωσις ἀνθρώπου
καὶ θεοῦ· κατὰ δὲ τὴν ἐνέργειαν.
κόσμου σύστασις· θεοῦ καταλλαγή· δα-
κρύων μήτηρ. καὶ πάλιν θυγάτηρ· ἁμαρ-
τημάτων ἱλασμός· πειρασμῶν γέφυ-
ρα· θλίψεων μεσότοιχον· πολέ-
μων θραῦσις· ἀγγέλων ἔργον· ἀ-

μακαρίας προσευχῆς:

4 | The Reading of the Lectionary

Recitation, Inspiration, and Embodiment

In the tenth-century *Book of Ceremonies*, which prescribed the social performances of the imperial court, the Gospel lectionary was described as coming in through the narthex of Hagia Sophia and entering the naos via the central door, also known as the Imperial Doorway.[1] A greeting would be exchanged in the narthex before the entry by the emperor and the patriarch, but the emperor would greet the Gospel lectionary first, as it was treated as equivalent to God. In the Constantinopolitan rite, it was only after the dignitaries passed into the church following this ceremony that the rest of the congregation was allowed to enter.[2] The procession would move toward the sanctuary of the church, presumably ascending and descending up and down the ambo, and go on through the solea to the doors of the sanctuary; the lectionary would have been set upon the altar and kissed in reverence. During the reading itself, candles would be lit for the Gospel – even in daylight – to express the joy of the coming of the word of God, and the emperor would remove his crown. A deacon or designated reader would chant the Gospel from the ambo of the church amidst the people who stood and came close to listen to the Logos. Meanwhile, the patriarch would sit on the synthronon in the inner sanctuary, behind the iconostasis, and listen carefully to lection; he then would give his sermon from the synthronon.

This process occurred during the first portion of the liturgy. The bringing in of the Gospel text was called the First or Little Entrance; its counterpart in the second part of the liturgy is the Second or Great Entrance, when the offerings for the Eucharistic service are brought into the sanctuary. The liturgy is therefore so structured that the Gospel lectionary and the Eucharist echo one another. The uninitiated catechumens, allowed to witness only the liturgy centered on the Gospel, would be dismissed at the beginning of the Eucharistic service. Hence, for those

1 See Thomas Mathews, *The Early Churches of Constantinople: Architecture and Liturgy* (University Park: Pennsylvania State University Press, 1971), 139–49.

2 See Robert F. Taft, *The Great Entrance: A History of the Transfer of Gifts and Other Pre-anaphoral Rites of the Liturgy of St. John Chrysostom*, Orientalia Christiana Analecta 200 (Rome: Pont. Institutum Studiorum Orientalium, 1975), 192n51.

who could not ingest the Eucharist (or witness it – primarily, hear it) the Gospel instructed those men and women through the grace and indwelling of the Logos.

In order to properly grasp the reading of the lectionary, it is necessary to first sketch out the context of its recitation. What follows is a description of the rite as depicted in an anonymous liturgical commentary in verse. This poem, produced in southern Italy in the twelfth or thirteenth century, largely adapts in verse Nicholas and Theodore of Andida's *Protheoria*, which dates to the late eleventh century and follows the rite of Hagia Sophia.[3] It thus presents us with the most concise and careful discussion of the middle Byzantine rite as it would have looked in the late eleventh century – the time when the lectionaries discussed in this volume were produced.

The Divine Liturgy itself is begun with the Liturgy of the Catechumens, or the Liturgy of the Word: this is the portion of the rite in which those preparing for baptism may participate, as it is centered on the reading of the Gospel. It begins with the Great Litany of petitions and prayers, also known as the Great Synapte or the Eirenika.[4] Originally, this litany was placed after the Little Entrance and before the Trisagion, the "Thrice Holy" Hymn; yet it begins to move in the eleventh century, and by the end of the thirteenth century it is securely located before the Little Entrance, where it remains in the practices of the modern Church.[5] The litany contains nine intercessions asking for God's aid and a final tenth petition for the salvation and protection of humanity.

It is followed by the "Divine Antiphons," which represent the thirty years of Christ's secret ministry: that is, the time from his birth to his manifestation as the Christ in his baptism.[6] During the third antiphon, dedicated to Christ, the Little Entrance begins and the Gospel lectionary is brought in.[7] Meanwhile the priest silently recites the Prayer of the Entrance, which asks that the terrestrial and celestial hosts come together to begin the liturgy and sing together, uniting the earthly and celestial liturgies as one in the Little Entrance.

The Little Entrance manifests the revelation of Christ upon the Jordan during the baptism; hence it is appropriate that the third antiphon uses

[3] See Betancourt, "Byzantine Liturgical Commentary in Verse," esp. 445–47.

[4] On the Great Litany, see Juan Mateos, *La célébration de la parole dans la liturgie byzantine: Étude historique* (Rome: Pont. Institutum Studiorum Orientalium, 1971), 29–31.

[5] Mateos, *Célébration de la parole*, 30.

[6] On the antiphons, see Mateos, *Célébration de la parole*, 34–45.

[7] On the Little Entrance, see Mateos, *Célébration de la parole*, 71–90.

Psalm 94(95):1–3 to convey the congregation's confrontation with the presence of the Lord:

> O come, let us rejoice in the Lord; let us make a joyful noise to God our savior! Let us anticipate his face with acknowledgment, and with melodies let us make a joyful noise to him, because the Lord is a great God and a great King over all the gods.[8]

The words of the psalm harmonize with the coming of Christ in the form of the Gospel lectionary, just as the words of the Psalms more generally harmonize with the teachings of the Gospel, since they predicted the coming of Christ.[9] Before the reading of the Gospel, the Trisagion is sung: "Holy God, Holy Mighty, Holy Immortal, have mercy on us."[10] This hymn signifies the hypostases of the Father, the Son, and the Holy Spirit in its three repetitions of "holy": each descriptor is unique, yet paradoxically they all refer to one God.[11] Sometimes, when appropriate, after the Trisagion an excerpt from the Prophetologion or a conciliar decree would have been read.[12]

The Trisagion is followed by the recitation of the "Divine Apostles," which represents the calling of the Apostles.[13] This refers to the reading of the Epistles, which customarily precedes the reading of the Gospel in the liturgy; it is accompanied by the singing of the Alleluia three times, manifesting the threefold person of the Holy Trinity.[14] All these actions are completed with the customary "seal" (σφραγίς) of the priest: that is, the making of the sign of the cross. Next, incense is offered in honor of the Gospel so as to represent the grace given to the Apostles through their calling and the indwelling of the Holy Spirit within them.[15] Since there are seven "graces" or gifts of the spirit listed in Isaiah 11:2, it is offered seven times in the course of the rite.

The deacon charged with the task of reciting the Gospel reading takes the lectionary from the altar to the ambo, while the rest of the clergy

[8] For translations of the Septuagint, see A. Pietersma and B.G. Wright (eds.), *A New English Translation of the Septuagint* (Oxford University Press, 2007), 595.

[9] On the role of the Gospel book in the Little Entrance, see Mateos, *Célébration de la Parole*, 82–85, 88–89.

[10] On the Trisagion, see Mateos, *Célébration de la parole*, 91–126.

[11] On the Trinitarian understanding of the Trisagion, see Mateos, *Célébration de la parole*, 101–02.

[12] Anonymous, *Typicon Magnae Ecclesiae*, ed. Mateos, *Typicon de la Grande Église*, 2:282–83.

[13] On the reading of the Epistle and the Gospel, see Mateos, *Célébration de la parole*, 127–47.

[14] On the use of the Alleluia Hymn in conjunction with the reading of the Gospel, see Mateos, *Célébration de la parole*, 134–35.

[15] On the use of incense before the Gospel reading, see Mateos, *Célébration de la parole*, 135–39.

remains within the sanctuary. He is escorted up the ambo by subdeacons carrying candles. The deacon then exhorts the audience to become more attentive in preparation for the reading, proclaiming: "Wisdom, let us attend!" (Σοφία, πρόσχωμεν). During the Easter vigil, the *Typikon* of Hagia Sophia (late ninth or early tenth century) prescribes that the Gospel lectionary be read by the patriarch from the synthronon, and that the deacon upon the ambo repeat what he says, verse by verse.[16] Unfortunately, we know little about the actual conditions of the chanting of the lection itself. Other than these brief details from exceptional feast days, the primary liturgical sources offer little information on how the reading was conducted. We do understand that it would have been chanted in accordance with the ekphonetic musical notation found in the lectionaries, and that therefore the chanter would have played with the resonances and acoustics of the space, not only to heighten melodic effect but also to ensure that the words could be comprehended.

The Liturgy of the Catechumens is drawn to a close through the prayers and intercessions of the Ektene, or the Litany of Supplication, which follows the Gospel reading and precedes the Great Entrance with the Cherubic Hymn at the start of the Liturgy of the Faithful.[17] In these closing rites, a prayer is offered on behalf of the catechumens preparing themselves for baptism, so that they may be divinely instructed and deemed worthy of their initiation, having already been attracted and inspired by the miraculous deeds of Christ as recounted in the Gospel.[18] The Prayer of the Catechumens, which outlines the precepts of a Christian sense of community, asks that the catechumens be instructed, drawn together, and united in the Church through the teachings of Christ as manifested in the Gospel.

The Act of Reading

This account of the entrance of the lectionary matches and is informed by the descriptions found in the *typika*, *diataxes*, commentaries, and other liturgical sources from the middle Byzantine period. However, these sources uniformly lack any details regarding the recitation itself, silent here

[16] Anonymous, *Typicon Magnae Ecclesiae*, ed. Mateos, *Typicon de la Grande Église*, 2:94–96.

[17] On the prayers and litanies following the Gospel reading at the conclusion of the Liturgy of the Catechumens, see Mateos, *Célébration de la parole*, 148–73. See also Taft, *Great Entrance*, 329–32.

[18] On the Prayer for the Catechumens, see Mateos, *Célébration de la parole*, 156–59.

as they are on many other liturgical matters that are assumed to be well known to their practitioners. The lectionaries' ekphonetic notation, which guided the reader's chanting of the biblical lessons, relied on this preexisting knowledge of musical practice and indicated only changes in relative pitch, intonation, and emphasis. We can thus glean some understanding of the text's sonic contours, without being able to wholly or accurately reconstruct it (a subject to which we will return in the following chapter). However, there is little to convey a sense of the reader's actions during the course of the reading or what this performance looked like. This chapter focuses on the embodied aspects of reading the Gospel lections and considers the spiritual and metaphorical role played by the act of reading in the Byzantine world.

One of the more insightful sources on religious recitation to come down to us from the eleventh century is by Michael Psellos. In his encomium for the monk Ioannes Kroustoulas, Psellos preserves a glimpse into the public recitation of a religious text in a church setting – Kroustoulas's reading of saints' lives in the church of the Virgin in the Chalkoprateia neighborhood of Constantinople, near Hagia Sophia.[19] Identified by Psellos as a chancellor, possibly in the patriarchal administration, Ioannes Kroustoulas is described as wearing a common monastic attire in what seems to be a competitive recital of such texts held in this and nearby churches, including the church of the Virgin in the *Ta Kyrou* neighborhood. In this intriguing sketch of religious recitation, Psellos portrays it as a popular event that attracted throngs from all echelons of Constantinopolitan society into the packed church, where Kroustoulas – apparently something of a celebrity – read.

Although his performance was a religious event held in a church, we cannot simply transfer the actions of Kroustoulas to the practices of the Gospel lectionary. But some notable continuities and consistencies deserve our attention. Psellos portrays a crowd that values and emphasizes the powers of recitation to enliven stories of holy figures. The Gospel reading was not just a common practice in late eleventh-century Constantinople but part of a culture in which the recitation of texts was highly valued and garnered a healthy and diverse following. In other words, while we know little about these readers or how they performed the texts, we must understand that the most august readings in Christendom in the most revered church of the empire, Hagia Sophia, would certainly have been

[19] Michael Psellos, *Oratoria minora*, 37, ed. A.R. Littlewood, *Oratoria minora* (Leipzig: Teubner, 1985), 137–51; trans. Papaioannou, *Michael Psellos on Literature and Art*, 218–44.

entrusted to highly skilled readers who may have been much sought after for their oratorical and chanting skills. Keeping in mind this point, however pedantic or simple, helps us avoid the notion that the task was a rote and charmless one, performed by a random member of the clergy.

Just as we are told that readers of the Gospel would light tapers before the reading, even in daylight, so the same detail appears in Psellos's description, which notes the reader's taking up of the candle as a transformative moment. Early on, Psellos observes how Kroustoulas's entire demeanor changed at the moment when he took up the candle to begin his reading:

> For, as soon as he stepped on the space from which he would read, he did not remain the same man. Nor did he retain the same solemn figure or the reserved, in every respect, manner. Rather, as if putting on the virility of a wild animal . . . he took the candle and showed himself to be strong-willed – all but speaking with his body language, he offered a model of how a reader should act. He had not yet read the title of his text, and he had indicated everything.[20]

Psellos communicates the sense that when Kroustoulas picked up the candle, he became the forms he sought to depict. Later Psellos comments that "whenever he might enter a church and approach the book, take a candle, and start the divine narration, he seems to be some other nature, different from human."[21] The act of reading is thus a process of almost divine possession, a notion that, as we will see in the following section, flourished in the Byzantine period and had deep roots in antiquity.

Psellos describes the manner in which the reader carried himself earlier in approaching the site of the reading, possibly the ambo of the church: "When he came in, with that wondrous walk, his usual and universal solemnity, with his eyes looking down, oh what charm! What unpretentiousness!"[22] These words recall the deacon's solemn procession to the ambo with the lectionary, soberly exhorting the congregation to be more

[20] "οὐδὲ γὰρ τοιοῦτος ἦν ὁποῖος εἰσέδυ τὸν τόπον πατήσας τῆς ἀναγνώσεως, οὐδὲ μετὰ τοῦ σεμνοῦ παρέμενε σχήματος καὶ τοῦ συνεσταλμένου πρὸς πάντα φρονήματος, ἀλλὰ θηρὸς ὥσπερ μεταμφιασάμενος γενναιότητα . . . καὶ τὸν κηρὸν λαβὼν σταθηρὸς τὴν γνώμην ἐδέδεικτο, μονονουχὶ διὰ τοῦ σχήματος προσφθεγγόμενος καὶ τυπῶν ὁποῖον δεῖ πάντως τὸν ἀναγινώσκειν ὀφείλοντα γίγνεσθαι· οὔπω γὰρ τοῦ λόγου τὴν ἐπιγραφὴν εἴρηκε καὶ τοῦ παντὸς ἐδεδώκει τὴν δήλωσιν." Michael Psellos, *Oratoria minora*, 37.62–70, ed. Littlewood, 139–40; trans. Papaioannou, 226.

[21] "ὁπηνίκα δὲ εἰς νεὼν εἰσέλθοι καὶ τῇ βίβλῳ προσπλησιάσει καὶ τὸν κηρὸν λαβὼν τῆς θείας ἀπάρξεται διηγήσεως, ἑτέρα τις φύσις δοκεῖ τῆς ἀνθρωπίνης ἀλλότριος." Michael Psellos, *Oratoria minora*, 37.329–31, ed. Littlewood, 148; trans. Papaioannou, 239.

[22] "ἐπεὶ δὲ οὗτος εἰσεληλύθει μετὰ τοῦ θαυμασίου ἐκείνου βαδίσματος, μετὰ τῆς συνήθους καὶ παγκοσμίου σεμνότητος, μετὰ τοῦ κάτω βλέποντος ὄμματος, βαβαὶ τῆς χάριτος ἐκείνης καὶ τῆς

attentive to the wisdom of the Gospels. We can thus appreciate that conducting such recitations incorporated a certain religiously inflected habit, moving from solemnity to the potent virility of the reader's booming voice in the resonant space of the church. Attention to minutiae here thus enables us to draw parallels between this reading and that of the Gospel, which was prefaced by candles and the customary recitation of the heading of the text about to be read. Without a word, the reader is already able to prepare the audience for the day's reading.

Psellos's praise for Kroustoulas focuses largely on his technical skill and expertise, often alluding to classical and late antique commentaries on rhetoric and style to detail what made Kroustoulas such an exceptional reader. For example, Psellos points to Kroustoulas's ability to "punctuate correctly, and turn a period or lengthen a colon, double a word and show amplification, and indicate the force of a preface and its references."[23] Repeatedly, he remarks on the ways in which a skilled reader can mold and shape the punctuation, articulation, and arrangement of words, precisely to stress the narrative's key points, when he has a deep understanding of the entirety of the text's story line. Over and over again, such skill is shown to be dependent on the reader's bodily mastery of recitation, which enabled him to "read long passages in one breath" and "use the right intonation."[24] Psellos extols the virtue of the reader who can recognize the "opportune time" (καιρόν) for exhortations – a phrase that recalls one of the formulaic openings of a lection, which sets the scene in "that opportune time."[25] Kroustoulas's opposite, of course, was the reader who had a poor grasp of the whole of the text and its parts, who lacked skill and training in speaking, and who was constantly distracted by random aspects of the text.[26]

Overall, we can appreciate what elements Psellos values in a reader, since they were in accordance with the teachings of antiquity that constituted the rhetorical and musical instruction of the period. Notably, a skilled reader is able to treat the text as a malleable object, especially in its declamation,

ἁπλότητος." Michael Psellos, *Oratoria minora*, 37.55–58, ed. Littlewood, 139; trans. Papaioannou, 226.

23 "διαστεῖλαι δεόντως καὶ περιόδους στρέψαι καὶ μακρῦναι τὸ κῶλον καὶ διπλῶσαι τὸ ὄνομα καὶ τὴν περιβολὴν δεῖξαι καὶ τὰς ἐνεργείας τῶν προοιμίων καὶ τὰς ἀναφορὰς δηλῶσαι." Michael Psellos, *Oratoria minora*, 37.105–07, ed. Littlewood, 141; trans. Papaioannou, 227.

24 "πνεῦμά τε γὰρ παρεῖχε τῷ λόγῳ, καὶ ἐποίει τόνους ἐτραχύνετό." Michael Psellos, *Oratoria minora*, 37.150–51, ed. Littlewood, 142; trans. Papaioannou, 230.

25 Michael Psellos, *Oratoria minora*, 37.103, ed. Littlewood, 140.

26 See Michael Psellos, *Oratoria minora*, 37.377–419, ed. Littlewood, 149–50; trans. Papaioannou, 241–42.

which seems to have depended to a great extent on intonation, pacing, breathing, emphasis, and the general handling of structure and punctuation. By declaiming, the reader clarifies obscure matters in the text and is able to better convey to the audience both the key narrative elements of the text and its lessons. This operation recalls the logic of the lectionary's marginalia: a reader is able to clarify the identities of persons, convey generative confusions, and vividly articulate the scenes of the text to listeners, much as marginalia enact similarly varied processes for the manuscript's viewer.

I believe we should see such marginalia as significantly shaping how that skilled reader performed the Gospel text in the liturgy, by presenting him with graphic images that enlivened the text as he was reading it, bringing the scenes described on the page into his mind so that he could adequately communicate their nuances through his intonations, stresses, and handling of the Gospel's breaks and punctuation. Psellos's depiction of recitation has a particularly striking visual dimension, as he recounts how the reader transformed himself into the various figures of the stories. Vocally, Kroustoulas impersonated tyrants and mimicked different languages – sometimes the tongue of barbarians, including Armenian words.[27] He performed visually, as well: the audience had their eyes fixed on him as "he transformed and refashioned himself, altering his face into different forms."[28] The latter observation echoes late antique descriptions of dancers and performers on stage who could morph into different characters without even a change of costume. As Ruth Webb has shown, late antique performers were often described as being able to readily change between roles and gender presentation by simply altering their gesture, gait, and posture.[29]

Such descriptions give us much to think about when we consider how the Gospel text might have been performed. Though it is difficult to believe that a reader would interrupt the august Gospels with his own musings, clarifications, or rearrangement of words, we have seen in previous chapters that the lections often made small alterations to the Gospels so that the text would work better as an excerpt. In other words, those writing the

[27] Michael Psellos, *Oratoria minora*, 37.287–93, ed. Littlewood, 146–47; trans. Papaioannou, 237.

[28] "τεχνικῶς μετεμορφοῦτο καὶ διεπλάττετο καὶ τὸ πρόσωπον εἰς ἰδέας ἀνομοίους μετήλλαττεν." Michael Psellos, *Oratoria minora*, 37.122–23, ed. Littlewood, 141; trans. Papaioannou, 228.

[29] Ruth Webb, *Demons and Dancers: Performance in Late Antiquity* (Cambridge, MA: Harvard University Press, 2008), esp. 77–79. See also Regine May, "The Metamorphosis of Pantomime: Apuleius's *Judgment of Paris* (*Met.* 10:30–34)," in Edith Hall and Rosie Wyles (eds.), *New Directions in Ancient Pantomime* (Oxford University Press, 2008), 338–62.

lections acknowledged the need for clarifications when only a portion of text from a larger narrative was recited. To be sure, the homily that followed was intended to do the explanatory work needed to better frame and enliven the Gospel reading. But we should not overlook the ekphonetic notations in any given lectionary, which would have helped to systematize, if not also standardize, some of the aspects of emphasis and stress that burdened Kroustoulas when he was reciting the saints' lives. This is by no means to say that the ekphonetic notations made his task simple, since they require a great deal of training in musical practice to perform well, but they certainly would have helped prescribe the shape of how words, phrases, and passages were delivered before the congregation.

Thus, we can appreciate how the Gospel lectionary internalizes some of these oral practices, altering the text to make it more readily accessible and providing a guide to the proper stresses, intonations, and emphases of the readings. In other words, such liberties are not entirely left up to the individual reader: they are at work in the lectionary and are enshrined in the manuscript itself through textual emendations and the musical notation. The same could be said about the more theatrical, visual aspects of the reader's recitation. Certainly, the recitation of the Gospel in the Divine Liturgy must have taken a more somber approach than the reading of the saints' lives, which might involve somewhat bawdy, violent, and graphic narratives. Yet its stories, too, would have been brought to life by the gestures, postures, and facial expressions of the reader. The marginalia might have also provided suggestions for how to present and embody the Gospels' stories.

Structurally, we see parallels between Kroustoulas's performance and the Gospel's reading, from the carrying of candles and the presumed setting on the ambo to his wearing of ecclesiastical garb. As the climax of the Liturgy of the Catechumens, the Gospel reading must have been a tour de force in its own right: it wove narrative storytelling and musical chant into a single action, and it garnered the attention of visual artists, who lavishly illuminated the books that were part of this production. Over the course of the reading, the reader would have become a vessel for the various characters and for divine grace, protean and malleable as he depicted the various holy figures and stories. Tellingly, in the closing sentences of his encomium, Psellos describes Kroustoulas as an "instrument of the Spirit" or "spirited instrument" (πνευματικὸν ὄργανον),[30] suggesting once again a connection

[30] Michael Psellos, *Oratoria minora*, 37.458, ed. Littlewood, 151; trans. Papaioannou, 228.

between the act of reading and divine inspiration. In this account, the body relinquishes its agency and self-identity, taken over by the actions of those diverse characters and stories that it serves as a vessel to relate.

Reading as Inspiration

In his study of reading habits in the ancient Greek world, Jesper Svenbro sets forth a model of recitation that casts the process as an almost violent practice of possession, whereby the agency of the reader's soul (ψυχή) is suspended and the text temporarily takes hold of him as an "inspirited instrument" (ὄργανον ἔμψυκον). He writes:

> What is reading? From the Greeks' point of view, it is the act in which the reader's vocal apparatus is controlled not by his own ψυχή (except in an intermediary fashion) but by the written inscription that he sees before him, so as to produce a particular sequence of sounds that will be intelligible to the ear. To be read is to take control of somebody else's vocal apparatus, to exercise power over the body of the reader, even from a distance, possibly a great distance both in space and time ... The writer who is successful in getting himself read makes use of the internal organs of someone else, even from beyond the grave, making them serve him as an ὄργανον ἔμψυκον or an *instrumentum vocale*, so as to broadcast his own name and his own words.[31]

In the ancient Greek world, as in the Byzantine world, reading was primarily an oral and aural act on the part of the reader and his audience. The body of the reader served as an apparatus, an intermediary site *of* and *for* the manifestation of discourse. Svenbro's insight draws our attention to the bodily practices of recitation and to the religious implications of this somatic process whereby a human actor lends his voice to the agency of the text: again, we must recognize the importance of performance in the chant and recitation of lectionaries and other religious texts.

Svenbro does not directly engage the process of inspiration that motivates the ancient reader to recite the text. One can note, however, striking resemblances between his characterization of recitation and Plato's own understanding of inspiration and mediation in relation to the rhapsodes who recite the works of the great poets. In his famous metaphor presented

[31] Jesper Svenbro, *Phrasikleia: An Anthropology of Reading in Ancient Greece*, trans. Janet Lloyd (Ithaca, NY: Cornell University Press, 1993), 142; I have replaced the text's transliterations with the Greek terms.

in *Ion* 533d1–535a1, comparing inspiration to a magnetic power, rhapsodes who traveled reciting the works of Homer and other poets were merely a link in a long chain of divine inspiration and possession that came down from the gods through the Muses to the poets, and then continued on through lineages of reciters and listeners.[32] Thus the transmission of

[32] "For, as I was saying just now, this is not an art in you, whereby you speak well on Homer, but a divine power, which moves you like that in the stone which Euripides named a magnet, but most people call 'Heraclea stone.' For this stone not only attracts iron rings, but also imparts to them a power whereby they in turn are able to do the very same thing as the stone, and attract other rings; so that sometimes there is formed quite a long chain of bits of iron and rings, suspended one from another; and they all depend for this power on that one stone. In the same manner also the Muse inspires men herself, and then by means of these inspired persons the inspiration spreads to others, and holds them in a connected chain. For all the good epic poets utter all those fine poems not from art, but as inspired and possessed, and the good lyric poets likewise . . . For the poets tell us, I believe, that the songs they bring us are the sweets they cull from honey-dropping founts in certain gardens and glades of the Muses – like the bees, and winging the air as these do. And what they tell is true. For a poet is a light and winged and sacred thing, and is unable ever to indite until he has been inspired and put out of his senses, and his mind is no longer in him: every man, whilst he retains possession of that, is powerless to indite a verse or chant an oracle . . . For not by art do they utter these things, but by divine influence; since, if they had fully learnt by art to speak on one kind of theme, they would know how to speak on all. And for this reason God takes away the mind of these men and uses them as his ministers, just as he does soothsayers and godly seers, in order that we who hear them may know that it is not they who utter these words of great price, when they are out of their wits, but that it is God himself who speaks and addresses us through them . . . For the god, as it seems to me, intended him to be a sign to us that we should not waver or doubt that these fine poems are not human or the work of men, but divine and the work of gods; and that the poets are merely the interpreters of the gods, according as each is possessed by one of the heavenly powers."

(ἔστι γὰρ τοῦτο τέχνη μὲν οὐκ ὂν παρὰ σοὶ περὶ Ὁμήρου εὖ λέγειν, ὃ νυν δὴ ἔλεγον, θεία δὲ δύναμις ἥ σε κινεῖ. ὥσπερ ἐν τῇ λίθῳ ἣν Εὐριπίδης μὲν Μαγνῆτιν ὠνόμασεν, οἱ δὲ πολλοὶ Ἡρακλείαν. καὶ γὰρ αὕτη ἡ λίθος οὐ μόνον αὐτοὺς τοὺς δακτυλίους ἄγει τοὺς σιδηροῦς, ἀλλὰ καὶ δύναμιν ἐντίθησι τοῖς δακτυλίοις, ὥστ᾽ δύνασθαι ταὐτὸν τοῦτο ποιεῖν ὅπερ ἡ λίθος, ἄλλους ἄγειν δακτυλίους, ὥστ᾽ ἐνίοτε ὁρμαθὸς μακρὸς πάνυ σιδηρίων καὶ δακτυλίων ἐξ ἀλλήλων ἤρτηται: πᾶσι δὲ τούτοις ἐξ ἐκείνης τῆς λίθου ἡ δύναμις ἀνήρτηται. οὕτω δὲ καὶ ἡ Μοῦσα ἐνθέους μὲν ποιεῖ αὐτή, διὰ δὲ τῶν ἐνθέων τούτων ἄλλων ἐνθουσιαζόντων ὁρμαθὸς ἐξαρτᾶται. πάντες γὰρ οἵ τε τῶν ἐπῶν ποιηταὶ οἱ ἀγαθοὶ οὐκ ἐκ τέχνης ἀλλ᾽ ἔνθεοι ὄντες καὶ κατεχόμενοι πάντα ταῦτα τὰ καλὰ λέγουσι ποιήματα, καὶ οἱ μελοποιοὶ οἱ ἀγαθοὶ ὡσαύτως . . . λέγουσι γὰρ δήπουθεν πρὸς ἡμᾶς οἱ ποιηταὶ ὅτι ἀπὸ κρηνῶν μελιρρύτων ἐκ Μουσῶν κήπων τινῶν καὶ ναπῶν δρεπόμενοι τὰ μέλη ἡμῖν φέρουσιν ὥσπερ αἱ μέλιτται, καὶ αὐτοὶ οὕτω πετόμενοι: καὶ ἀληθῆ λέγουσι. κοῦφον γὰρ χρῆμα ποιητής ἐστιν καὶ πτηνὸν καὶ ἱερόν, καὶ οὐ πρότερον οἷός τε ποιεῖν πρὶν ἂν ἔνθεός τε γένηται καὶ ἔκφρων καὶ ὁ νοῦς μηκέτι ἐν αὐτῷ ἐνῇ: ἕως δ᾽ ἂν τουτὶ ἔχῃ τὸ κτῆμα, ἀδύνατος πᾶς ποιεῖν ἄνθρωπός ἐστιν καὶ χρησμῳδεῖν . . . οὐ γὰρ τέχνῃ ταῦτα λέγουσιν ἀλλὰ θείᾳ δυνάμει, ἐπεί, εἴπερ περὶ ἑνὸς τέχνῃ καλῶς ἠπίσταντο λέγειν, κἂν περὶ τῶν ἄλλων ἁπάντων: διὰ ταῦτα δὲ ὁ θεὸς ἐξαιρούμενος τούτων τὸν νοῦν τούτοις χρῆται ὑπηρέταις καὶ τοῖς χρησμῳδοῖς καὶ τοῖς μάντεσι τοῖς θείοις, ἵνα ἡμεῖς οἱ ἀκούοντες εἰδῶμεν ὅτι οὐχ οὗτοί εἰσιν οἱ ταῦτα λέγοντες οὕτω πολλοῦ ἄξια, οἷς νοῦς μὴ πάρεστιν, ἀλλ᾽ ὁ θεὸς αὐτός ἐστιν ὁ λέγων, διὰ τούτων δὲ φθέγγεται πρὸς ἡμᾶς. . . ἐν τούτῳ γὰρ δὴ μάλιστά μοι δοκεῖ ὁ θεὸς ἐνδείξασθαι ἡμῖν, ἵνα μὴ διστάζωμεν, ὅτι οὐκ ἀνθρώπινά ἐστιν τὰ καλὰ ταῦτα ποιήματα οὐδὲ ἀνθρώπων, ἀλλὰ θεῖα καὶ θεῶν, οἱ δὲ ποιηταὶ οὐδὲν ἀλλ᾽ ἢ

information occurred as texts were distributed through human apparatuses, such as rhapsodes and readers. To sketch this process, Plato uses a series of words that metaphorically articulate the inspiration and possession of bodies (ἔνθεοι ὄντες καὶ κατεχόμενοι) and their own proliferation and dissemination (ἐνθουσιαζόντων) through networks of transmission. In this respect, Plato provides a critical language for the spread of inspiration through networked interfaces and users.

This picture resonates with the almost magical description of reading and listening captured by Psellos in his learned encomium on Kroustoulas:

> Such was the charm dripping from his lips, so harmonious was his voice, in such a way he enchanted (κατέθελγε) his listeners and cast a spell (κατεκήλει) on those willing, that, even if someone . . . were to receive the tribulations of Odysseus, even such tribulation would fill his entire heart with joy.[33]

Psellos alludes to a notion of recitation that takes hold of listeners by enchanting and casting a spell over them, even drawing parallels with reciting and listening to Homeric epic. Here, the willing and consenting listeners give themselves up to be possessed and enchanted by the reader's words, just as the divine force took hold of the poet's audience in Plato's *Ion*. Reading, in other words, is a process of inspiration in which listener, reader, text, and the divine are all caught in a chain of divine possession and inspiration – as aptly stressed by Psellos's characterization of Kroustoulas as an "instrument of the Spirit" (πνευματικὸν ὄργανον).

Similar notions of reading as a divine possession often appear in middle Byzantine texts on reading.[34] For example, in the *Life of Nikephoros of Miletos* from around 1000, Ioannes Sikeliotes provides a dramatic description of what it was like to witness the holy figure read: "If you heard him read (as those who had heard him attest), you would say that he was snatched away; with his soul suspended from the words, he journeyed

ἑρμηνῆς εἰσιν τῶν θεῶν, κατεχόμενοι ἐξ ὅτου ἂν ἕκαστος κατέχηται.) Plato, *Ion*, 533d1–535a1, ed. Albert Rijksbaron, *Ion, Or: On the Iliad* (Leiden: Brill, 2007), 80–82; modified ed. and trans. W.R.M. Lamb, *Statesman. Philebus. Ion*, Loeb Classical Library 164 (Cambridge, MA: Harvard University Press, 1925), 421–25. On the date and authorship of the *Ion* dialogue, see also John D. Moore, "The Dating of Plato's *Ion*," *Roman and Byzantine Studies* 15:5 (1974): 421–39.

33 "τοσαύτη γὰρ χάρις τῶν τούτου χειλέων ἀπέσταζε καὶ τοιοῦτος ὑπῆρχε τὴν φωνὴν ἐναρμόνιος καὶ οὕτως κατέθελγε τοὺς ἀκούοντας καὶ κατεκήλει τοὺς εὔφρονας, ὥστε, κἂν εἴ ποτέ τις. . . τὰς τοῦ Ὀδυσσέως εἶχε κακότητας ἀπολαβεῖν, αὐτὰς αὐτίκα καὶ θυμηδίας ἐμπλῆσαι τὴν ψυχὴν ἅπασαν." Michael Psellos, *Oratoria minora*, 37.159–64, ed. Littlewood, 142–43; trans. Papaioannou, 231.

34 See Papaioannou, "Readers and Their Pleasures." I thank Stratis Papaioannou for sharing this text with me. See also Niels Gaul, "The Letter in the *Theatron*: Epistolary Voice, Character, Soul and Their Audience," in Alexander Riehle (ed.), *A Companion to Byzantine Epistolary* (Leiden: Brill, forthcoming).

toward heaven."[35] The act of reading is akin to "abduction" or "seizure" (ἁρπάζεσθαι), a forceful possession of a person's body; yet the one who hears is being taken off to heaven, moved by every word. And earlier, Gregory of Nazianzus described reading Basil the Great as an experience that caused him to be "transformed and brought into harmony, and become another from another, changed by a divine alteration."[36] Like the transformation of Kroustoulas when he takes up the candle, reading for Gregory is a "divine alteration" (θείαν ἀλλοίωσιν), melodic and intellectual – and it happens precisely through the harmony and rhythm (ῥυθμίζομαι) of reading. Michael Psellos elsewhere writes of a letter's hold over its reader, "In what way did it not attract the reader, like a magnet the iron?"[37] Extolling the various pleasures of receiving a letter and delving into its words, Psellos here speaks to the possession of the reader by the text and perhaps alludes to Plato's use of the magnet metaphor in *Ion*.

Of particular interest in the *Ion* is the term ἔνθεος; usually translated as "divinely inspired," it could be literally rendered as *engodded* to stress that this act of inspiration operates through a form of *indwelling* by the divinity. In Byzantium, the term is often used to describe holy texts, their material embodiments, and holy figures such as the Evangelists or Church Fathers.[38] For example, the term is used in the epigram surrounding one of the opening miniatures in the eleventh-century Psalter formerly known as the "Berlin Psalter," now at the Hermitage (formerly Berlin, Berlin University's Christian

[35] "Εἰ δὲ διήκουσας ἀναγινώσκοντος, ὡς οἱ ἀκηκοότες φασίν, εἶπες ἂν ἁρπάζεσθαι τοῦτον καὶ τὴν ψυχὴν ἀποκρέμασθαι τῶν λογίων καὶ πρὸς οὐρανὸν μετεωροπορεῖν." John Sikeliotes, *Vita Nicephori archiepiscopi Mileti*, 28.5–7, trans. Papaioannou, "Readers and Their Pleasures"; ed. H. Delehaye, "Vita S. Nicephori," *Der Latmos. Milet* 3.1 (Berlin: Reimer, 1913), 157–71. See Stratis Papaioannou, "Sicily, Constantinople, Miletos: The Life of a Eunuch and the History of Byzantine Humanism," in Theodora Antonopoulou, Sofia Kotzabassi, and Marina Loukaki (eds.), *Myriobiblos: Essays on Byzantine Literature and Culture* (Berlin: De Gruyter, 2015), 261–84.

[36] "μεθαρμόζομαι καὶ ῥυθμίζομαι καὶ ἄλλος ἐξ ἄλλου γίνομαι, τὴν θείαν ἀλλοίωσιν ἀλλοιούμενος." Gregory of Nazianzus, *Orations*, 43.67.3 (or, *Funebris oratio in laudem Basilii Magni Caesareae in Cappadocia episcopi*), ed. F. Boulenger, *Discours funèbres en l'honneur de son frère Césaire et de Basile de Césarée* (Paris: Picard, 1908), 58–230, at 200.

[37] "Μᾶλλον δὲ τίνι οὐκ ἐφείλκετο τὸν ἀναγινώσκοντα ὥσπερ μαγνῆτις τὸν σίδηρον." Michael Psellos, *Epistulae*, ed. Stratis Papaioannou, *Epistulae* (Leipzig: Teubner, 2019); modified trans. Papaioannou, "Readers and Their Pleasures."

[38] For a general discussion of Byzantine authorship and divine inspiration, see Claudia Rapp, "Holy Texts, Holy Men and Holy Scribes: Aspects of Scriptural Holiness in Late Antiquity," in Klingshirn and Safran (eds.), *Early Christian Book*, 194–222; Derek Krueger, *Writing and Holiness: The Practice of Authorship in the Early Christian East* (Philadelphia: University of Pennsylvania Press, 2004), esp. 1–14.

Figure 86 Berlin Psalter (now at the Hermitage; formerly: Berlin University's Christian Museum, 3807), fol. 2[v].
(Photo: after Stuhlfauth, "Greek Psalter," 316, fig. 7).

Museum, 3807, fol. 2^v; Figure 86).[39] In the top register of the miniature, the Virgin and Child are depicted flanked by the archangels Michael and Gabriel. Below them, in the bottom register, Saints Nicholas, John Chrysostom, and Basil are depicted bearing their sacred codices. The inscription immediately below this scene reads: "The foremost of the prelates, all three of them, holding the inspired books in their hands" (τῶν ἱεραρχῶν ἀκρότης οἱ τρεῖς πάνυ: ἐν χερσὶ βίβλους φέρουσιν ἐνθέους).[40] In this opening image, the artist plays with the chains of divine inspiration that motivate religious writing – from God, through incarnation in the Virgin, and on to the Evangelists and theologians, their scribes, and so on. In the divine space of the top register, the Christ-child looks to his mother, the Theotokos, and loosely drops his right hand bearing a scroll, which directs one's eye down to the field of the Church Fathers below.

In particular, John Chrysostom stands in the center, directly beneath Christ. As is typical, his name is heavily abbreviated to the chi-rho ligature for the Chryso- (Χρυσο-) of his epithet "John of the golden-mouth" (Ἰωάννης ὁ Χρυσόστομος), which praised his rhetorical skill. Heightened in this particular context, there is a playful intervisuality that connects the X-P of Χρυσόστομος with the popular and visually identical X-P monogram of Christ (Χριστός). Graphically, Christ is manifested here as dwelling within the name of the divinely inspired Chrysostom, who is directly below Christ's image. This play is heightened by the word order of the inscription's last line, "ἐν χερσὶ βίβλους φέρουσιν ἐνθέους": the act of bearing the inspired books "in their hands" (ἐν χερσί) is paralleled by the "in-spiration" (ἐνθέους) of the books themselves through epanalepsis, as the action of "in" (ἐν) is repeated at the beginning and end of the statement. This rhetorical device literalizes the notion of indwelling suggested by the term ἔνθεος through the metaphor of carrying a book in one's hand, while likewise demonstrating the long chain of divine inspiration that occurs through the action of the Logos's indwelling within the Virgin's flesh, reaching down into the Evangelists and Holy Fathers, then into their books, and eventually to their readers and listeners – a process analogous to Plato's magnetized chains of inspiration in the *Ion*.[41]

39 Georg Stuhlfauth, "A Greek Psalter with Byzantine Miniatures," *Art Bulletin* 15:4 (1933): 311–26. Forthcoming is the promising volume, Yury Pyatnitsky and Nadezhda Kavrus-Hoffmann, *The Hermitage Psalter: The Amazing Journey of an Exceptional Byzantine Manuscript* (Ann Arbor, MI: Legacy Press, forthcoming).

40 Stuhlfauth, "A Greek Psalter," 316 (fig. 7), 321.

41 Margaret Mitchell in her study of John Chrysostom and Pauline interpretation cites the *Ion* dialogue in passing in her conclusion as a manner of characterizing John Chrysostom's relation to Paul as a "hermeneutics of inspiration." Mitchell deploys the *Ion* as a metaphor to summarize the relationship between John Chrysostom and Paul that she has carefully articulated throughout her work. In particular, Mitchell examines at length (particularly in chapters 3

But these chains of inspiration operate in the literature beyond mere metaphor, demonstrating a profound concern with the indwelling of texts in bodies that transmit them. Take, for example, the use of the term ἔνθεος in an eleventh-century Gospel book in Paris (Paris, Bibliothèque nationale de France, gr. 219, fol. 3^{v}), which bears an opening inscription parallel to that of Michael the Monk's Gospel in Istanbul (Istanbul, Ecumenical Patriarchate, Cod. 3, fols. 131^{v}–32^{r}).[42] The term appears as part of a longer poem written in large, gold uncials within a decorated border. Though the adjective is absent from the Istanbul version, the Paris Gospel uses ἔνθεος to describe the text itself:

> You, who gush forth the boundless-depth of the divinely-inspired words (ἐνθέων λόγων),
> flowing from the tongues of your initiates as if from a spring,
> My soul is parched in that opportune-time of judgment,
> May you allow me to drink a new immortal draught,
> Which you said to your disciples to drink from at that time.[43]

Here, the engodded *logos* (ἐνθέων λόγων) is paired with the imagery of an endlessly flowing fountain, whose streams satiate the thirst of humanity much as does the blood of the Eucharistic wine. The trope of the inspiration of the Logos as a perpetual fountain is common in Byzantium, as epigraphic and iconographic evidence attests.[44] Hence, the chain of inspiration is articulated through a process of bodily ingestion and consumption,

and 5) John's fascination with Paul's chains, which at times take hold of him and drag him away, as in his homily on Ephesians 9 (PG 62:69), and his belief that Paul might be "taking possession" (κατέχειν) of him, as in his homily on Isaiah 45 (PG 56:146). See Margaret Mitchell, *The Heavenly Trumpet: John Chrysostom and the Art of Pauline Interpretation* (Louisville, KY: Westminster John Knox Press, 2002), 408, cf. 176–85, 69.

42 Robert S. Nelson, "Michael the Monk and His Gospel Book," *Actes du XVe congrès international d'études byzantines*, vol. 2 (Athens: Association Internationale des Études Byzantines, 1981), 575–82, esp. 580–81.

43 "ἀλλ' ὦ βλύσας ἄβυσσον ἐνθέων λόγων·/ὡς ἐκ κρήνης ῥεύσασαν σῶν μυστῶν γλώττης·/ψυχὴν ἐμὴν ἄνικμον ἐν καιρῷ δίκης·/εἴης ποτίζων καινὸν ἄμβροτον πόμα·/ὃ σοὺς μαθητὰς εἶπας ἐκπίνειν τότε." For transcription, see Annonymous, *Byzantine Book Epigrams*, 23121, ed. Maria Tomadaki and Paulien Lemay, "Occurrence 23121," in Kristoffel Demoen et al. (eds.), *Database of Byzantine Book Epigrams*, www.dbbe.ugent.be/occurrences/23121. See also Nelson, "Michael the Monk," 580 (n.b. this transcription has minor errors).

44 For epigraphic evidence, see A. Kominis, "Συναγωγὴ ἐπιγραμμάτων εἰς τοὺς τέσσαρας Εὐαγγελιστάς," *Ἐπετηρὶς Ἑταιρείας Βυζαντινῶν Σπουδῶν* 21 (1951): 254–79. For iconographic examples, see George Galavaris, "'Christ the King': A Miniature in a Byzantine Gospels and Its Significance," *Jahrbuch der Österreichischen Byzantinistik* 21 (1972): 119–26; Tania Velmans, "L'iconographie de la 'Fontaine de Vie' dans la tradition byzantine a la fin du Moyen Âge," in André Grabar and Jean Hubert (eds.), *Synthronon* (Paris: C. Klincksieck, 1968), 119–34; Paul Underwood, "The Fountain of Life in Manuscripts of the Gospel," *Dumbarton Oaks Papers* 5 (1950): 41–138.

Figure 87 'Menologion' of Basil II (Vatican, Biblioteca Apostolica Vaticana, gr. 1613), fol. 78ʳ. (Photo: © 2019 Biblioteca Apostolica Vaticana. Reproduced by permission of Biblioteca Apostolica Vaticana, all rights reserved)

literalizing the operation of the term *engodded* as a physical insertion of the divinity within human flesh similar to what happens in the Eucharistic rite.

Compare these interconnected metaphors to a miniature from the Menologion of Basil II (976–1025) that depicts Romanos the Melodist receiving the inspiration for his hymn on the birth of Christ. In this image, the Theotokos literally inserts words into the composer's mouth by giving him a scroll to eat (Vatican City, Biblioteca Apostolica Vaticana, gr. 1613, fol. 78ʳ; Figure 87). This follows a tradition (feasibly, derived from Ezekiel 3:3) according to which Romanos was fed the words to his hymns by the Virgin, as an epigram on the silver revetment of an icon of the Theotokos *Kyriotissa* attests:

> To Romanos, Lady, your worshipper of old
> You gave a written document to eat,

> Now fill my cup, O Virgin, to the brim
> With the sweet vintage draughts of wisdom
> For I so thirst to drink my fill of them
> That they may irrigate my arid mind.[45]

Thus the body of Romanos becomes a vessel and container for the Logos, like that of the Theotokos before him. At the same time, as demonstrated in the Paris Gospel's opening poem, the act of inspiration is connected to its own proliferation. In some scenes, an audience literally drinks from streams that flow from the writings of the Church Fathers, and the iconography often appears next to the canon tables of the Four Gospels.[46] In the epigram, it is the Virgin's icon that enables the profuse flow of drinkable wisdom, which will in turn inspire further deeds and divinely inspired works. As Bissera Pentcheva has argued, the acts of transmitting the *logos* become manifest through visual and textual metaphors of ingestion and pregnancy that resonate with representations of Evangelists and Church Fathers in manuscripts and icons – as well as with liturgical spaces and their architecture, where the *logos* is continually born through the Divine Liturgy.[47]

The notion of indwelling suggested by such models of inspiration appears repeatedly in the Akathistos Hymn, attributed to Romanos the Melodist himself. The Akathistos is replete with various metaphors of indwelling, inspiration, and containment to describe the Incarnation of the Christ. Perhaps most pertinent in this regard is the verse "Hail, womb of the divinely inspired incarnation" (Χαῖρε, γαστὴρ ἐνθέου σαρκώσεως).[48] This line resonates with a parallel notion elaborated throughout the Akathistos, where the Theotokos is characterized as the "ensouled temple" (ἔμψυχον *ναόν*) or the "container of the uncontainable God" (θεοῦ

[45] "'Ρωμανῷ δέσποινα, τῷ λάτρει πάλαι/τόμον φαγεῖν δέδωκας ἐγγεγραμμένον,/ἐμοῦ δὲ τὸν κρατῆρα πλῆσον, παρθένε,/τῶν τῆς σοφίας γλυκερῶν κερασμάτων./Δίψω γὰρ αὐτοῦ ἐκροφῆσαι πλησμίως,/ὡς ὑγρανεῖ μου τὴν κατάξηρον φρένα." Anonymous, *Anthologia Marciana*, 344, ed. S. Lampros, "'Ο Μαρκιανὸς κῶδιξ 524," *Neos Hellenomnemon* 8:2 (1911): 123–92, at 181; trans. Paul Magdalino, "The Liturgical Poetics of an Elite Religious Confraternity," in Shawcross and Toth (eds.), *Reading in the Byzantine Empire and Beyond*, 116–32, at 126. I thank Foteini Spignou for her help with the *Anthologia Marciana*, here and before.

[46] Tania Velmans and Paul Underwood discuss these dynamics of flowing streams of wisdom and inspiration in their respective surveys of the "Fountain of Life" motif, to which we shall return in the subsequent chapters. See Velmans, "L'iconographie de la 'Fontaine de Vie'," 119–27; Underwood, "The Fountain of Life."

[47] Bissera Pentcheva, "Visual Textuality: The Logos as Pregnant Body and Building," *RES: Aesthetics and Anthropology* 45 (2004): 225–38.

[48] Romanos the Melodist (dub.), *Ἀκάθιστος ὕμνος*, 1.15, ed. and trans. Leena Peltomaa, *The Image of the Virgin Mary in the Akathistos Hymn* (Leiden: Brill, 2001), 4–5.

ἀχωρήτου χώρα).[49] Such phrases connect the womb and the temple to the incarnational topography of the Virgin's flesh, likening those sites to the bodies of the holy persons who bear forth the *logos* by producing their divinely inspired writings or by reciting such texts.

As noted in the previous chapter, the act of reading and visualizing within the Gospel lectionary unfolds procedurally through its reading, as users – readers and listeners – imagine its narratives unfolding in their minds as the lection progresses. Both the *Ion* and Byzantine sources describe the process of writing and reading as entailing the relinquishing of agency on the part of the reader, who serves as an apparatus for the text. I suggest here that the unfolding of the icon in the imagination is intimately linked to such notions of inspiration, as these image-texts seek a medium for manifestation through mental and somatic acts of incarnation. This point is perhaps made most vividly in an epigram for an icon composed by Manuel Philes, who was active in the first three decades of the fourteenth century in Constantinople:

> In order that every man contemplating a shadow [i.e., the icon]
> May learn from it to not be dismayed [by] life
> I represent [a shadow] according to that of myself for you, O Stranger.
> For I will borrow speech (λόγον) from the living,
> Pouring into me (ἐγχέαντά μοι) a little the power of breath.[50]

This epigram eloquently captures the dynamics of oral reading in Byzantium: the icon's inscription articulates both the silence of the painting and the rhetorical violence of the text, which takes hold of the reader's power of speech so as to *nearly* endow the image with a voice of its own. As Amy Papalexandrou stresses in her study of orality and monumental inscriptions, "Even in the private sphere, then, the written word is presented as something verbal and audible rather than intimate and silent."[51] Playing with this understanding of the act of reading, the epigram captures this dynamic by deploying the first person. In the act of reading, the "I" of the speaker belongs not to the reader but to the text and its agent, forcibly

[49] Romanos the Melodist (dub.), *Ἀκάθιστος ὕμνος*, 23.2 and 15.6, ed. and trans Peltomaa, *Image of the Virgin Mary*, 18–19 and 13–14.

[50] "Ἵνα δὲ πᾶς ἄνθρωπος ἐντεῦθεν μάθῃ / σκιὰν θεωρῶν μὴ πτοεῖσθαι τὸν βίον, / τὰ κατ' ἐμαυτὴν ζωγραφῶ δή σοι, ξένε. / Δανείσομαι γὰρ ἀπὸ τῶν ζώντων λόγον, / μικροῦ πνοῆς δύναμιν ἐγχέαντά μοι." Manuel Philes, *Carmina*, 180.8–12, ed. E. Miller, *Carmina*, vol. 1 (Paris: Excusum in Typographeo Imperiali, 1855), 88. See also Alice-Mary Talbot, "Epigrams of Manuel Philes on the Theotokos tes Peges and Its Art," *Dumbarton Oaks Papers* 48 (1994): 135–65.

[51] Amy Papalexandrou, "Text in Context: Eloquent Monuments and the Byzantine Beholder," *Word & Image* 17:3 (2001): 259–83, esp. 262.

taking hold of the reader's voice, agency, and identity – even if only for an instant.[52]

The Reading of the Lectionary

In the act of recitation, the Gospel lectionary takes hold of the reader, who gives breath to its written words and its literal images that unfold through his interaction with the image-text. In relinquishing his own "I" for that of Christ the Logos, the reader becomes an inspirited instrument for the Word of God. The lectionary is thus the object that mediates and enables that moment of divine ensoulment, operating as a proxy for Christ. In a passage already quoted in Chapter 3, Patriarch Germanos identified the coming of the Gospel lectionary with a theophanic manifestation of Christ through the Incarnation:

> The Gospel is the coming of God, when He was seen by us: He is no longer speaking to us as through a cloud and indistinctly, as He did to Moses through thunder and lightning and trumpets, by a voice, by darkness and fire on the mountain. Nor does He appear through dreams as to the prophets, but He appeared visibly as a true man.[53]

Not only does the Gospel make possible the representation of the deeds of Christ the Logos, it is also a technology for the sonic and visual manifestation of the Logos within the performance of the liturgy. The Gospel lectionary therefore takes on the role of the incarnated Logos within the church by virtue of what it signifies *and* also how it signifies. The Gospel lectionary is an inspirited secondary agent, and its ability to incarnate, to give bodily manifestation to Christ as Logos, makes the manuscript itself particularly well suited to stand in for Christ. For example, at the Council of Ephesus in 431, according to Cyril of Alexandria, the Gospels were enthroned to represent the enduring presence of Christ.[54] Just as the Virgin's body enabled the perception

[52] See Ivan Drpić, *Epigram, Art, and Devotion in Later Byzantium* (Cambridge University Press, 2016), 67–117.

[53] Germanos I, *Historia mystica ecclesiae catholicae*, 31, ed. and trans. Meyendorff, 80–81.

[54] Cyril of Alexandria, *Apologeticus ad Theodosium*, ed. E. Schwartz, *Acta conciliorum oecumenicorum* 1.1.3 (Berlin: De Gruyter, 1927), 83. In addition, an image of the enthroned Gospels at the Council of Constantinople (381) in Hagia Sophia appears in the mid-tenth-century Paris Gregory (Paris, Bibliothèque nationale de France, gr. 510, fol. 355^{r}). See Christopher Walter, *L'iconographie des conciles dans la tradition byzantine*, Archives de l'orient chrétien 13 (Paris: Institut Français d'Études Byzantines, 1970), esp. 147–48; Christopher

of the divinely inspired Logos, so the reader from the ambo of the Byzantine church can be said to make the divinely inspired Logos perceptible to the minds of the congregation in a manner that echoes the dynamics of the Incarnation and Eucharistic rite itself.[55] As in the Akathistos Hymn's characterization of the body of the Theotokos as a living temple – a trope found in many texts, including Athanasios's *On the Incarnation* – the reading of the Gospel manifests Christ the Logos within the naos of the church, thus constructing liturgical space that, like the Theotokos, contains the Logos.[56]

This desire to associate Christ with the literal realities of the Gospel lectionary as a physical manuscript is also suggested in another hymn attributed to Romanos, in which Christ is specifically depicted as a living book. In his Hymn on Peter's Denial, assigned in the manuscript tradition to Good Friday or Holy Thursday,[57] Romanos imagines Christ saying to Peter:

> Having taken in [my hand] a reed, I am starting to write a pardon for all Adam's descendants. My flesh, which you see, becomes for me like paper and my blood like ink, where I dip my pen and write as I distribute an unending gift to those who cry . . .[58]

Walter, "Icons of the First Council of Nicaea," *Δελτίον Χριστιανικής Αρχαιολογικής Εταιρείας* 16 (1991–92): 209–18, esp. 210–11.

55 A similar idea has been explored in Pentcheva, "Visual Textuality." See also Andrew Mellas, "Melismatic Events," *Phronema* 23 (2008): 67–85.

56 "Although being himself powerful and the creator of the universe, he prepared for himself in the Virgin the body as a temple, and made it his own, as an instrument, making himself known and dwelling in it" (Αὐτὸς γὰρ δυνατὸς ὢν καὶ δημιουργὸς τῶν ὅλων, ἐν τῇ παρθένῳ κατασκευάζει ἑαυτῷ ναὸν τὸ σῶμα, καὶ ἰδιοποιεῖται τοῦτο ὥσπερ ὄργανον, ἐν αὐτῷ γνωριζόμενος καὶ ἐνοικῶν). Athanasios of Alexandria, *De incarnatione verbi*, 8.3, ed. Charles Kannengiesser, *Sur l'incarnation du Verbe*, Sources chrétiennes 199 (Paris: Éditions du Cerf, 1973); trans. John Behr, *On the Incarnation* (Yonkers, NY: St. Vladimir's Seminary Press, 2011), 66–67.

57 For the hymn's liturgical prescription, see José Grosdidier de Matons, *Romanos le Mélode: Hymnes*, vol. 4, Sources chrétiennes 128 (Paris: Éditions du Cerf, 1967), 100. See also Alexander Lingas, "The Liturgical Place of the Kontakion in Constantinople," in Constantine C. Akentiev (ed.), *Liturgy, Architecture, and Art in the Byzantine World: Papers of the XVIII International Byzantine Congress (Moscow, 8–15 August 1991) and Other Essays Dedicated to the Memory of Fr. John Meyendorff* (Publications of the Saint Petersburg Society for Byzantine and Slavic Studies, 1995), 50–57; José Grosdidier de Matons, "Liturgie et hymnographie: Kontakion et canon," *Dumbarton Oaks Papers* 34–35 (1980–81): 31–43.

58 "ταύτῃ γὰρ κάλαμον λαβών, ἄρχομαι γράφειν/συγχώρησιν πᾶσι τοῖς ἐκ τοῦ Ἀδάμ:/ἡ σάρξ μου, ἣν ὁρᾷς, ὥσπερ χάρτης γίνεταί μοι,/καὶ τὸ αἷμά μου μέλαν ὅθεν βάπτω καὶ γράφω,/δωρεὰν νέμων ἀδιάδοχον τοῖς κράζουσι·" Romanos the Melodist, *Cantica*, 34.7, ed. José Grosdidier de Matons, *Hymnes*, 4:120; trans. Ephrem Lash, "On Peter's Denial," *On the Life of Christ: Kontakia* (San Francisco, CA: Harper Collins, 1995), 129–38, at 132.

Thus, the Gospel lectionary is endowed with christological weight, not only in its reading, which echoes the Eucharist rite, but also in its very materiality as flesh and ink, the body and blood of Christ the Logos. The Gospel lectionary thereby serves simultaneously as an image and as a medium for images, as discussed above in the context of its illuminations. It is a material analogue to the body of Christ, given breath and speech via the inspirited reader.

The candles' flickering over the manuscript would have had a dramatic effect on the gold leaf of the painted initials, miniatures, and script, particularly as the reader turned the page, which would have caused striking motion in its miniatures; its gilt, metal-adorned covers would have seemed to be truly living images, nearly capable of speech, just as Bissera Pentcheva and Rico Franses have noted in their studies of icons.[59] All these features would have contributed to the sensual understanding of the animism and lifelike quality of these images, an element that has figured prominently in Byzantine art historiography: they have contributed greatly to the crucial notion of "ensouled painting" (ἔμψυχος γραφή), for instance.[60]

In both Byzantine and classical sources, the act of representation is enacted as a *logos* that demands and desires a body for manifestation: the action is fulfilled by the reader, who lends breath and imagination to enliven the words. In the chapters that follow, I wish to turn our attention

[59] Rico Franses, "When All that Is Gold Does Not Glitter: On the Strange History of Looking at Byzantine Art," in Antony Eastmond and Liz James (eds.), *Icon and Word: The Power of Images in Byzantium. Studies Presented to Robin Cormack* (Aldershot: Ashgate, 2003), 13–24; Bissera Pentcheva, "Moving Eyes: Surface and Shadow in the Byzantine Mixed-Media Relief Icon," *RES: Anthropology and Aesthetics* 53 (2009): 223–34.

[60] Throughout the sources that I have surveyed, there exist many interrelated terms associated with the process of artistic representation as an event. Terms such as ἔνθεος (divinely inspired), ἔμψυχος (ensouled), ἔμπνους (breathing), ἔνυλος (material), ἔνσαρκος (incarnate), or ἔνοικος (indwelling) articulate the crucial concepts of inspiration, life, and incarnation by using the prefix ἐν-/ἐμ-, itself derived from the preposition ἐν (in). Here, the prefix does double duty, suggesting both that an exterior condition or entity such as breath (ἔμ-πνους) or God (ἔν-θεος) dwells within a person or thing and also the converse – that a certain condition or entity, particularly the divinity, takes on material form such as flesh (ἔν-σαρκος) or matter (ἔν-υλος). Each term alludes to a hypostatic condition, for it suggests an *indwelling* rather than a *transformation*: therefore, the combination retains a dual nature as, for example, both fully material and fully spirited, as in the phrases "ensouled painting" (ἔμψυχος γραφή) and "inspirited adornment" (κόσμος ἔμπνους). For a survey of these terms and their relationship to middle Byzantine artistic, literary, and liturgical representation, see Roland Betancourt, "Representation as Indwelling: Contextualizing Michael Psellos's *empsychos graphe* across Artistic, Liturgical, and Literary Theory," *Byzantine and Modern Greek Studies* (forthcoming). For a study of the term κόσμος ἔμπνους and related notions of ornament and adornment in Byzantium, see Drpić, *Epigram, Art, and Devotion*, 67–117.

to the spaces in which the lectionary was performed and in which these practices and images unfolded. My aim is to understand how architecture and church fixtures responded to these dynamics of inspiration, recitation, and performance, while also considering how said performance destabilized the built environment and nuanced the reading of the space and its decoration.

✠ ΕΙΠΕΝ Ο ΚϹ
ΕΓΩ ΕΙΜΙ
Η ΘΥΡΑ ΤΩΝ
ΠΡΟΒΑΤΩΝ
ΔΙ ΕΜΟΥ
ΕΑΝ ΤΙϹ
ΕΙϹΕΛΘΗ
ΕΙϹΕΛΕΥϹΕΤ
ΕΙϹΕΛΕΥϹΕΤ
ΚΕΞΕΛΕΥϹΕΤ
ΚΝΟΜΗΝ
ΕΥΡΗϹΕΙ

5 The Sound of the Lectionary

Chant, Architecture, and Salvation

Over the Imperial Doorway, on the eastern wall of the narthex of Hagia Sophia, a relief plaque is set into the passageway's bronze lintel (Figure 88). It has been dated on epigraphic grounds not to the sixth-century construction of the building but to the late tenth century. It was probably set up during the church's restoration, which was completed in 994 under Basil II, following the destructive earthquake of 989.[1] The relief appears to have been added to the lintel, which apparently does date back to the original Justinianic program: its design fits in with the bosses on the lintel's frame, overlapping its decorative bands. Furthermore, two dowel marks beside the relief on the top suggest that some earlier element was removed so that the plaque could be inserted. The plaque depicts an arch supported by two stylized Corinthian columns. Under the arch and echoing its shape is a round-backed throne, upon which stands an open book onto which is descending the Holy Spirit.

The text within the book is clearly legible, written in a clear, uncial script with common abbreviations:

+ Εἶπεν ὁ Κ(ύριο)ς	Ἐάν τις
Ἐγώ εἰμι	εἰσέλθῃ
Ἡ Θύρα τῶν	Εἰσελεύσετ(αι)
Προβάτων	Κ(αὶ) ἐξελευσετ(αι)
Δι᾽ ἐμοῦ	Κ(αὶ) νομὴν
	Εὑρήσει

The text here derives from the Gospels, but with some important alterations to the Gospel text, which is essentially John 10:9 with a few words borrowed from John 10:7 to clarify the excerpt:

[1] Paul Underwood, "Notes on the Work of the Byzantine Institute in Istanbul: 1957–1959," *Dumbarton Oaks Papers* 14 (1960): 205–22, esp. 212–13. See also William Emerson and Robert L. Van Nice, "Hagia Sophia: Construction of the Second Dome and Its Later Repairs," *Archaeology* 4:3 (1951): 162–71. On the earthquakes of the late tenth century, see Glanville Downey, "Earthquakes at Constantinople and Vicinity, A.D. 342–1454," *Speculum* 30:4 (1955): 596–600, esp. 599–600.

Figure 88 Metal relief panel over Imperial Doorway in the narthex of Hagia Sophia, Constantinople (Istanbul, Turkey).
(Photo: Roland Betancourt)

+ Said the Lord:	If anyone,
I am	Enters, [(they) will be saved,]
The door of the	(They) will go in,
Sheep, [John 10:7]	And (they) will go out,
Through me,	And pasture
	(They) shall find. [John 10:9][2]

The introductory "Said the Lord" (Εἶπεν ὁ Κ(ύριο)ς), one of the two customary openings for a reading in the lectionary, suggests that the panel is depicting a Gospel lectionary. Furthermore, rather than simply using John 10:9, which begins, "I am the door. Through me," the artist has instead opted to clarify the text by borrowing from the end of John 10:7, "I am the door of the sheep." In the Gospel lectionary, such minor changes to the text of the day's lection are quite common, since the lectionary often must clarify the subjects in the opening lines of the excerpted

[2] N.B. I am using the singular, gender-neutral "they" here.

Figure 89 Imperial Doorway mosaic in the narthex of Hagia Sophia, Constantinople (Istanbul, Turkey). (Photo: Roland Betancourt)

reading – usually by replacing pronouns with proper names, as discussed in Chapter 2. Thus, we can understand that the Gospel text being cited here is John 10:9 proper, with "τῶν προβάτων" borrowed for the sake of narrative clarity.

The relief plaque thus does not merely depict a generic book since it carries a greater specificity than the open manuscript depicted above it in the imperial mosaic of Christ (Figure 89). There Christ sits on a lyre-back throne, holding a book inscribed "+Peace onto you all. I am the light of the world" (+Εἰρήνη ὑμῖν. Ἐγώ εἰμι τὸ φῶς τοῦ κόσμου), the latter sentence taken from John 8:12. But this inscription, too, alludes indirectly to the Gospel lectionary, for it recalls what the patriarch says to the reader after that deacon concludes the day's lection, "Peace to you" (Εἰρήνη σοι). The echo suggests a subtle mimetic relationship between Christ and patriarch connected to the central theme of the Gospel lectionary.

All these details clearly indicate that the manuscript depicted in the relief is not simply a Gospel book but specifically a Gospel lectionary. Indeed, this image is unique in representing an identifiable manuscript type rather than a closed book with its bejeweled cover, as is often depicted in scenes of

Christ Pantokrator. The plaque can be seen not only from the space of the narthex but also from directly below the lintel thanks to its beveled surface, enabling it to remain visible to the imperial procession as it entered the naos through the doorway. As the tenth-century *Book of Ceremonies* of Constantine Porphyrogennetos recounts, the imperial entourage would enter the narthex from the Horologion at the south and the emperor would remove his crown at the entrance to the narthex. Meanwhile, the patriarch and his own entourage would await the emperor at the Imperial Door. First those entering perform proskynesis before the Gospel lectionary held by the archdeacon, and then they greet the patriarch with a kiss. They next go up through the Imperial Doorway, performing proskynesis three times with candles while giving thanks to God. Finally, the Patriarch recites a prayer, and the Little Entrance begins.[3] Thus the plaque would have directly evoked the preparatory and participatory rites that initiated the Divine Liturgy, rites whose focal point was the bringing in of the Gospel lectionary.

My aim in this chapter is to use this panel as a case study to explore how liturgical space oriented itself around the reading of the Gospel text and to examine the role of the lectionary at the center of that action. I will set the scene by describing and examining how the relief plaque diagrammed the liturgical space and the architectures of the Gospel's recitation and homiletic response, serving to foreshadow the rites focused on the lectionary that would have followed after the procession passed the Imperial Doorway's threshold with the manuscript. I will then consider how the plaque itself played with the sonic utterance of the lections in the liturgy, concentrating on the plaque's curious omission of the salvation promised in John 10:9 and arguing that this salvation is in a sense deferred to those participating in the liturgy. Finally, I will reflect on the critical role played by sound and hearing in notions about the construction of a Christian community oriented around the teachings of the Word. Thus, this chapter elucidates how the lectionary's aural effects would have resonated with the architectural details of Hagia Sophia, from its ritual procession and recitation through its being chanted and on to its construal of salvation and community for the listeners.

[3] See Constantine VII Porphyrogennetos, *De cerimoniis aulae Byzantinae*, 1.1, ed. and trans. Ann Moffatt and Maxeme Tall, *The Book of Ceremonies*, 2 vols. (Canberra: Australian Association for Byzantine Studies, 2012), vol. 1, 14–16. In the latter, the Greek edition is reproduced with a reprint of J.J. Reiske, *De ceremoniis byzantini*, 3 vols. (Bonn: Weber, 1829–40), 14–16; cf. ed. and French trans. A. Vogt, *Le livre des cérémonies*, 4 vols. (Paris: Les Belles Lettres, 1935–39), 1:10–12.

Diagramming Liturgical Space

There appears to be a striking parallel between this tenth-century plaque and the anachronistic depiction of the Council of Constantinople of 381 found in the ninth-century Homilies of Gregory of Nazianzus in Paris, which features an enthroned Gospel in the apse of Hagia Sophia (Paris, Bibliothèque nationale de France, gr. 510, fol. 355^{r}; Figure 90).[4] The two thrones are clearly similar: the back of each is curved back and ends on each side with a round finial. Likewise, in both the book rests on a lofty cushion, while a rich silky fabric drapes over the front of the chair. While the triangular flourishes visible on the throne depicted on the metal plaque appear to be missing from the Paris Gregory throne's top finials, similar ornaments do seem to be present on the orbs of the lower finials. To be sure, the two thrones are not identical: they differ slightly in their proportions and more markedly in their perspectives – the Paris Gregory throne is squarer and seemingly two-dimensional, presenting a frontal view, while the plaque conveys the impression of a three-dimensional object. Indeed, it seems cleverly designed to spring out from the space of the arch, high above the viewer, in response to the spatial concerns of its site of display above the Imperial Doorway.

It is also crucial to note that the image of the throne in the Paris Gregory is flanked by members of the Council sitting on a sigma- or lunette-shaped stepped platform. In this context, we can read this architectural feature as alluding to the synthronon of Hagia Sophia, where the clergy sat during the liturgical rite; thus we should understand the images presented by the Paris Gregory and by the metal plaque as representations of the bishop's seat in Hagia Sophia. The awkward architectural elements framing the Paris Gregory's throne appear to invoke synecdochically the apse of Hagia Sophia (Figure 91). The central window of the apse has been left out, presumably to give primacy to the enthroned Gospel at the center of the synthronon, but the two flanking windows, framed by marbles colored

[4] On the use of the image in the Paris Gregory, see Brubaker, *Vision and Meaning*, 210–17; Brubaker, "Politics, Patronage, and Art," esp. 4–5. On the depictions of the Church Councils, see Walter, *L'Iconographie des conciles*, 147–48, and esp. 235–39; Walter, "Icons of the First Council of Nicaea." For an introductory survey of uses of the Gospel book in religious and secular ritual, see Dorina Miller Parmenter, "The Iconic Book: The Image of the Bible in Early Christian Rituals," in James W. Watts (ed.), *Iconic Books and Texts* (Sheffield: Equinox, 2013), 63–92. See also Susannah Fisher, "Formulating Viewer Response: Early Medieval Treasury Bindings," in Elise Louviot (ed.), *La formule au Moyen Âge* (Turnhout: Brepols, 2012), 295–313; David Ganz, *Buch-Gewänder: Prachteinbände im Mittelalter* (Berlin: Reimer, 2015).

Figure 90 Homilies of Gregory of Nazianzus [Paris Gregory] (Paris, Bibliothèque nationale de France, gr. 510), fol. 355^{r}.
(Photo: Bibliothèque nationale de France)

Figure 91 Apse of Hagia Sophia, Constantinople (Istanbul, Turkey).
(Photo: Roland Betancourt)

Figure 91 (*cont.*)

pink, green, and a dull mustard-gold, recall the multicolored marble revetments used in the apse of Hagia Sophia. In particular, the gold bands and the gold cornice that tip the two rectangular architectural elements in the manuscript echo both the marbled band running over the three arched windows and the marble cornice that divides the lower register of windows in the apse from those above.

Note that for a viewer standing in the narthex and looking through the doorway, the arch that frames the image of the enthroned lectionary would be duplicated as the arch of the apse and its cupola (Figure 92). The synthronon, where the patriarch sat in the apse throughout the liturgy, is indicated within the plaque by the round-back throne, which when viewed in conjunction with the Paris Gregory might give us some sense of what this chair looked like in the late tenth century. Furthermore, the placement of the open lectionary on the throne in the apse may be shorthand for the location of the Gospel lectionary on the ambo in the middle of the naos, or the allusion may be specifically to the Easter and Epiphany vigils, when the lectionary would have been put on the patriarch's seat. We might even argue that its ensoulment as it is chanted during the reading of the day's lection is likewise symbolically represented in the relief by the descent of the Holy Spirit to the sacred manuscript, though some might be inclined to disregard the motif as common iconography – for example, in representations of the *hetoimasia*, common throughout Byzantine church programs.[5] This image appears on the arch of the apse in Hagia Sophia, but it was not added until the fourteenth century.

Over the course of the liturgical year, the Gospel lectionary itself would be enthroned at least twice upon the synthronon. The *Typikon* of Hagia Sophia, for example, prescribes the use of multiple lectionaries for the Christmas and Epiphany vigils. In the Christmas vigil on December 24, according to the *Typikon*, the patriarch sits to the left of his usual seat, for on that day one Gospel lectionary is enthroned upon the synthronon and another is placed on the altar. Later, the patriarch gives to the deacon charged with reading the Gospel lection for the day the lectionary from the

[5] The *hetoimasia* functions as a hieratical image of the Holy Trinity or of the Incarnation of Christ the Logos, while displaying the Prepared Throne of the Second Coming. Even if the relief plaque were viewed merely as a variant of the *hetoimasia*, the image over the Imperial Doorway would be just as enigmatic, because the iconography of the *hetoimasia* demands polyvalent and complex contextual and procedural unfolding. See Natalia Teteriatnikov, "The Mosaics of the Eastern Arch of Hagia Sophia in Constantinople: Program and Liturgy," *Gesta* 52:1 (2013): 61–84.

Figure 92 View into the nave from the narthex of Hagia Sophia, Constantinople (Istanbul, Turkey). (Photo: Roland Betancourt)

synthronon, from which he recites.[6] On the Epiphany vigil on January 5, three lectionaries are put into play: one is placed on the altar, another is given to the deacon for the recitation of the Gospel lection, and the third is enthroned upon the synthronon, with the patriarch once again sitting beside it.[7] Thus, the depiction of the enthroned lectionary not only makes reference to its symbolic manifestation of the presence of Christ, but it also speaks to those liturgical moments before Christmas and Epiphany when the lectionary itself would have been enthroned upon the patriarch's seat.

On the one hand, if we view this image as a spatial diagram, then we see that it takes the line of sight framed by the doorway and flattens it into a two-dimensional representation of the space that unfolds spatially and temporally within the naos: the ambo with the Gospel book, the synthronon within the sanctuary in the apse, and the larger, framing element of the apse itself. In this way, the image functions as a diagram of the temporal and spatial experience of the liturgy.[8] We have already encountered similar architectural shorthand in the Paris Gregory's depiction of the Council of Constantinople; we may likewise see such diagrammatic representations of liturgical space in the headpieces of liturgical scrolls made for the recitation of the liturgy by the priest.

On the other hand, if we view the metal relief as a temporally proleptic image – that is, as an image that foreshadows moments of the liturgy that are to come – then the descent of the Holy Spirit in the relief indicates the action of reading the Gospel from the ambo of the church. Through that reading, the Holy Spirit instructs the catechumens and enacts the actions of divine grace, which inspired the Apostles and now inspires the men and women participating in the Divine Liturgy. As the Holy Spirit (Ἅγιον Πνεῦμα), its descent manifests the literal process of giving breath (πνεῦνα) to the divinely inspired Gospels as text being performed within the liturgical space. In conjunction with the reading of the Gospel, as the *Protheoria* attests, incense would be burned in order precisely to demonstrate the action of the Holy Spirit: before the reading of the Gospel and after the reading of the Epistles,

[6] Anonymous, *Typicon Magnae Ecclesiae*, ed. Mateos, *Typicon de la Grande Église*, 1:152–55.

[7] Anonymous, *Typicon Magnae Ecclesiae*, ed. Mateos, *Typicon de la Grande Église*, 1:180–81.

[8] For a discussion of this type of temporal and spatial play in other liturgical manuscripts, especially liturgical scrolls, see Roland Betancourt, "Extended in the Imagination: The Representation of Architectural Space in Byzantium," in Vasileios Marinis, Amy Papalexandrou, and Jordan Pickett (eds.), *Architecture and Visual Culture in the Late Antique and Medieval Mediterranean. Studies in Honor of Robert G. Ousterhout* (Turnhout: Brepols, 2020).

> The censer (θυμιατός), in the proper time of the Hallelujah, is moved with the burning of incense (μετὰ θυμιάματος κινούμενος), [thus] manifesting the grace of the Holy Spirit, which having been given to the disciples sent them off for the healing of all sickness and all weakness in Israel.[9]

Incense, together with the proclamation (ἐκφώνησις) of the Gospels, makes palpable the gifts of the Holy Spirit.

In this manner, the Holy Spirit's presence is intimately tied with the reading of the Gospel, making its depiction alongside the lectionary a fitting visual representation of the proclamation of the Gospel. In these respects, the relief plaque over the door is connected to a variety of actions that pertain to the Gospel as a textual and physical object within the unfolding of the rite. The *Protheoria*, which does not aim to provide simple one-to-one understandings of liturgical moments, objects, or iconographies, precisely allows one to articulate the various facets that this image would have been capable of revealing. As the *Protheoria* explains,

> the entrance of the archpriest alludes (ὑπαινίττεσθαι) to the demonstration (ἀνάδειξιν) on the Jordan and the manifestation (φανέρωσιν) of our Christ and God. From this now, as it seems fitting, the dark and narrow laying of marbles in the floor of the Great Church [i.e., Hagia Sophia], orderly arranged and divided between mutually measured intervals, are called rivers. For until the entrance, the archpriest was coming, but not visible and known to all. After having risen in the middle, he completes the supernatural and extraordinary [things]. But the priest, seizing the right time, stands in the middle of the altar before the entrance of the archpriest just as the Forerunner executed the baptism for the sake of repentance.[10]

Given the relief's location at the site where the Little Entrance is initiated and its depiction of the lectionary, in it the descent of the Holy Spirit can be seen to directly allude to the baptism – the descent of the Spirit upon Jesus,

[9] "ὁ δὲ θυμιατὸς ὁ ἐν τῷ καιρῷ τοῦ Ἀλληλούϊα μετὰ θυμιάματος κινούμενος τὴν χάριν τοῦ ἁγίου Πνεύματος δηλοῖ, τὴν δεδομένην τοῖς μαθηταῖς, ὅτε τούτους ἀπέστειλε, τοῦ ἰάσασθαι πᾶσαν νόσον καὶ πᾶσαν μαλακίαν ἐν τῷ Ἰσραήλ." Nicholas and Theodore of Andida, *Προθεωρία Κεφαλαιώδης*, 17, ed. PG 140:440.

[10] "Δοκοῦμεν γὰρ τὴν ἐπὶ τοῦ Ἰορδάνου ἀνάδειξιν καὶ φανέρωσιν τοῦ Χριστοῦ καὶ Θεοῦ ἡμῶν τὴν τοῦ ἀρ[χ]ιερέως εἴσοδον ὑπαινίττεσθαι. Ἐκ τούτου οὖν, ὡς ἔοικε, ποταμοὶ ὀνομάζονται τὰ ἐν τῷ ἐδάφει τῆς Μεγάλης Ἐκκλησίας κείμενα μα[ρ]μάρινα στενὰ καὶ μέλανα δίκην ὀρδίνων, καὶ μεταξὺ μετρίων διαστημάτων ἀλλήλων διαιρούμενα: μέχρι γὰρ τῆς εἰσόδου, εἰ καὶ ἦν ἀρχιερεύς, ἀλλ' οὐχὶ πᾶσι δῆλος καὶ γνώριμος: εἰ δὲ εἰς μέσον ἑστώς, καὶ τὰ ὑπερφυῆ καὶ ἐξαίσια διατελῶν: ἀλλ' ὁ τὸν καιρὸν λαβὼν ἱερεύς, [ὁ] καὶ μέσον τοῦ θυσιαστηρίου ἱστάμενος, πρὸ τῆς εἰσόδου τοῦ ἀρχιερέως, ὡς Πρόδρομος ἐνήργει τὸ διὰ μετανοίας βάπτισμα." Nicholas and Theodore of Andida, *Προθεωρία Κεφαλαιώδης*, 14, ed. PG 140:436.

making the demonstration and manifestation of the Christ known, which is a common motif in the iconography.

The plaque simultaneously depicts an abstracted image of the baptism of Jesus, with the enthroned Gospel standing in for Christ, and also depicts the manner in which the entrance procession moved through the space: entering the naos and ascending through the ambo, on through the solea, and into the sanctuary – with the archpriest finally ascending again to take his place on his chair on the synthronon.[11] The *Protheoria* describes the ascent to the synthronon as "the ascent from the earth to heaven, and the [ascent] from the groveling ministry of the Jews, and the [ascent] from the law of the Old Testament," and similarly it visualizes "the reception of Divine Grace at the Baptism of Christ."[12] Thus, we can understand the relief above the Imperial Doorway of Hagia Sophia as a summary or diagram of liturgical space and time focused on the Little Entrance, which is initiated in this particular space – a function heightened by the slant of the lintel, which makes the plaque visible at the very instant that the patriarch, the lectionary, a processional cross, candle-bearing deacons, and the emperor become manifest within the liturgical space. The relief is an emblem of the temporal ritual enacted in that entryway.

In the twelfth century, Michael, the *protecdicus* of the church of Thessalonica and later deacon of Hagia Sophia, described the entryway of the Imperial Door (see Figure 93) in his ekphrasis of Hagia Sophia:

> There being, symbolically, a triple entry yawning out of the middle of the *protemenisma* (for the holy places are accessible to those who have been taught that there is one God in the Trinity) towards him who passes by the great quantity of silver which at once meets him near the doors, the building lies open forming an immense space, having a hollowness so capacious that it might be pregnant with many thousand bodies and a height so great as to turn the head, and make the eyes stop still as it were at the zenith.[13]

11 On the liturgical topology of Hagia Sophia, see Stephen G. Xydis, "The Chancel Barrier, Solea, and Ambo of Hagia Sophia," *Art Bulletin* 29:1 (1947): 1–24. See also Mathews, *Early Churches of Constantinople*, 139–49.

12 "τὴν ἀπὸ γῆς εἰς οὐρανὸν ἄνοδον, καὶ τὴν ἀπὸ τῆς χαμαιρεποῦς πολιτείας τῶν Ἰουδαίων, καὶ τὴν ἐκ τοῦ νόμου καὶ τῆς Παλαιᾶς Διαθήκης συγκαταβατικῶς ἐγχωρηθείσης ἀυτοῖς, δηλοῖ μετάβασιν: ὡς ἐντεῦθεν δῆλον ὅτι μετὰ τὴν ἀνάδειξιν τοῦ βαπτί[σ]ματος ἀρχὴν λαμβανούσης τῆς θείας χάριτος." Nicholas and Theodore of Andida, *Προθεωρία Κεφαλαιώδης*, 15, ed. PG 140:437.

13 "ἐκ μέσου γὰρ τοῦ προτεμενίσματος συμβολικῶς εἰσόδων ἀναστομουμένων τριπλῶν (βατὰ γὰρ τὰ θεῖα τοῖς ἐν τριάδι τὸν ἕνα δεδιδαγμένοις Θεόν) τῷ τὸν πολὺν ἄργυρον παραμείψαντι, ὃς ὑπαντᾷ πρὸς ταῖς εἰσόδοις εὐθύς, ὡς εἰς τὸ ἀχανὲς ὁ οἶκος ἀνέῳγε, κύτους μὲν εὐρύτητα ἔχων ὡς πολλὰς ἂν σωμάτων μυριάδας ἐγκυμονεῖν, ὕψους δὲ ὅσον τὴν κεφαλὴν ἀνατρέψαντα κορυφὴν οἶσν [sic]

Figure 93 Imperial Doorway in the narthex of Hagia Sophia, Constantinople (Istanbul, Turkey). (Photo: Roland Betancourt)

Here, Michael casts this entryway as a manifestation of the Trinity: its three doors all lead into one common space, manifesting the unity of God. Significantly, he characterizes the massive, resounding space of Hagia Sophia by using a metaphor of pregnancy, which recalls the metaphors used in the Akathistos Hymn to describe the Theotokos (ἔμψυχος ναός), as well as the incarnational logic according to which reading the Gospel is an act of divine indwelling and possession.

Returning to the tenth-century panel in the narthex, we should note that the relief and the imperial mosaic above it bear analogous inscriptions, which guarantee salvation for those who follow the literal path of Christ. The imperial mosaic's inscription on the open Gospel abridges John 8:12, which reads in full: "Then Jesus spoke out again, 'I am the light of the world. The one who follows me will never walk in darkness, but will have the light of life.'" This resonates with the inscription on the open lectionary

στῆσαι τοὺς ὀφθαλμούς." Michael the Deacon, *Ekphrasis of Hagia Sophia*, ed. and trans. Cyril Mango and John Parker, "A Twelfth-Century Description of St. Sophia," *Dumbarton Oaks Papers* 14 (1960): 233–45, at 237.

in the metal relief, which guarantees that those who enter through Christ, "the door of the sheep," will be saved: "they will go in, and they will go out, and pasture they shall find." The inscription literalizes salvation through the act of entering and exiting the church, despite an important omission. The artist has left out the crucial word that guarantees salvation, σωθήσεται – "they will be saved." One might argue that the metaphorical "pasture," reached through the "door of the sheep," sufficiently represents salvation. Perhaps the epigrapher was seeking to save room, given that the right side of the depicted lectionary is quite cramped; even without the word σωθήσεται, the artist resorted to smaller script and included a sixth line of text to fit in the inscription. Yet this answer is unsatisfying, for the artist could have easily used six lines on both sides of the book's spread, rather than only five on the left. In fact, the artist has paid close attention to the textual unfolding of the inscription: for example, he deliberately sets the cognates "entering" (εἰσέλθῃ), "going in" (εἰσελεύσεται), and "exiting" (ἐξελεύσεται) on successive lines to suggest a parallelism between these various actions. In his study of the Imperial Doorway's mosaic above the relief, Robert Nelson has carefully unpacked the ways in which this language of entering and exiting articulates how literate viewers themselves, reading the inscription, would have been transformed into light, doorway, and threshold through the language of its shifters (I/ἔγω) as they passed through the passageway into the luminous space of Hagia Sophia.[14]

The skillful wordplay and parallelism suggest that the epigrapher has quite consciously decided to stress motion in and out of the naos for this particular image, an emphasis appropriate for its location on the lintel and for the various liturgical implications that have already been addressed. Hence, the decision to omit σωθήσεται seems to have been a conceptual choice in highlighting the context of the image – a site of transit and movement.[15]

[14] Robert S. Nelson, *Hagia Sophia, 1850–1950: Holy Wisdom Modern Monument* (University of Chicago Press, 2004), 12.

[15] The attention to context in the imperial mosaic above the lintel has garnered much scholarly interest. Scholars in particular have argued about whether the emperor in proskynesis is meant to represent a particular individual, such as Emperor Leo VI, or a generic model of the emperor whose identity is malleable and interchangeable over time. The latter seems far more likely to me: rather than prescribing a static iconographic definition, the image responds to its various users and contexts. As I have argued, it is clear that these images thrive on spectrums of meaning, which simultaneously coexist with and contradict one another, as we saw in Chapter 3. See Nicolas Oikonomides, "Leo VI and the Narthex Mosaic of Saint Sophia," *Dumbarton Oaks Papers* 30 (1976): 151–72; Nelson, *Hagia Sophia*, 1–28.

The Missing Salvation

By focusing on the omission of σωθήσεται on the metal plaque, we can consider the implications and consequences of such a crucial revision of the Gospel lectionary's text. Likewise, we can consider what such an omission reveals about the logic of the image, the lectionary's performance, and the architectural, acoustic context within which it is set. The verb "to be saved" (σωθήσεται) has a curious treatment in the vocal performance of the Gospel lectionary. Often it is set off by *bareiai* (\) – an ekphonetic notation that indicates to the chanter that he should lower the pitch of his voice and give emphasis to the word or phrase bracketed by the apostrophe-like marks.[16] *Bareiai* differ from *apostrophoi* (↗), which indicate a similar lowering in pitch but without any emphasis. In addition, the verb is at times flanked by interpuncts – punctuation marks that look like raised periods. In the lectionaries without chant marks, these separate the verses of lections; when chant marks are used, the interpunct is covered over with a small cross, called a *teleia* (+), indicating a longer pause between verses. It is also added within verses to stress certain words by setting them off with what are assumed to be briefer pauses than those prescribed by the *teleia*. While the interpuncts are written in the same color ink as the text, the crosses along with the other ekphonetic notations are usually in a carmine ink (though occasionally entire pages have gilt lettering or are written in a single color for some specific reason). In some of the lectionaries surveyed, the interpuncts are even used in conjunction with the *bareiai* to accentuate the verb σωθήσεται.

As Sysse Engberg has noted, ekphonetic notation "helps to visualise the structure of the text," thus ensuring order and homogeneity in recitation and control over the practices of the *anagnostes* or reader.[17] But also, as she notes, these chant marks emerge amidst the end of Iconoclasm and the introduction of minuscule script with careful accentuation and

[16] I am grateful to Alexander Lingas for his helpful advice on these matters. For a survey of Byzantine ekphonetic notations and the function of the various chant marks, see Høeg, *Notation ekphonétique*, esp. 15–42; Wellesz, *History of Byzantine Music*, 249–60; Sysse Gudrun Engberg, "Greek Ekphonetic Notation: The Classical and the Pre-Classical Systems," in Jørgen Raasted and Christian Troelsgård (eds.), *Palaeobyzantine Notations: A Reconsideration of the Source Material* (Hernen: A.A. Bredius Foundation, 1995), 33–55; Martani, "Theory and Practice of Ekphonetic Notation"; Martani, "Words and Music in the Greek Gospel Lectionaries." See also H.J.W. Tillyard, *Handbook of the Middle Byzantine Musical Notation* (Copenhagen: Levin & Munksgaard, 1935).

[17] Engberg, "Greek Ekphonetic Notation," 53.

breathings.[18] Therefore, this trajectory is marked by a radical reorientation in inscriptive and performative practices that are occurring in the empire, many of which have been the focus of this volume: the newfound centrality of images and their capabilities (including the rise of historiated initials), minuscule script, chant marks, and the lectionary itself. By looking at the intersection between the lectionary's textual and paratextual inscription, its representation in architecture, and the oral and acoustic dimensions of the recitation of the lectionary, a single word here is able to demonstrate for us the dynamic relationship between text, image, performance, architecture, and perception. In order to tease out how the verb is deployed in a specific context, I will focus on one manuscript used in Hagia Sophia and compare its appearance in the relevant verse with another appearance of the word chosen at random. My starting point is the Jaharis Lectionary, a manuscript that John Lowden argues was made for use in Hagia Sophia and that has been discussed in Chapter 2.[19]

Before we look at the verse itself and delve deeper into chant marks, let us consider simply the pauses and breaks in a portion of a lection: Mark 16:13–20, verses prescribed for the Day of Ascension (fol. 34[v]; Figure 94). The transcription of the text and its rests reads as follows (verse numbers are indicated in superscripts):

> \+ κἀκεῖνοι ἀπελθόντες ἀπήγγειλαν τοῖς λοιποῖς + οὐδὲ ἐκείνοις ἐπίστευσαν
> \+[13] Ὕστερον ἀνακειμένοις αὐτοῖς τοῖς ἕνδεκα · ἐφανερώθη καὶ ὠνείδισεν τὴν
> ἀπιστίαν αὐτῶν καὶ σκληροκαρδίαν · ὅτι τοῖς θεασαμένοις αὐτὸν
> ἐγηγερμένον οὐκ ἐπίστευσαν + [14] καὶ εἶπεν αὐτοῖς + Πορευθέντες εἰς τὸν
> κόσμον ἅπαντα κηρύξατε τὸ εὐαγγέλιον πάσῃ τῇ κτίσει +[15] ὁ πιστεύσας
> καὶ βαπτισθείς · σωθήσεται · ὁ δὲ ἀπιστήσας κατακριθήσεται +[16] σημεῖα δὲ
> τοῖς πιστεύσασιν ταῦτα παρακολουθήσει + ἐν τῷ ὀνόματί μου δαιμόνια
> ἐκβαλοῦσιν · γλώσσαις λαλήσουσιν καιναῖς+[17] ὄφεις ἀροῦσιν + κἂν
> θανάσιμόν τι πίωσιν οὐ μὴ αὐτοὺς βλάψῃ + ἐπὶ ἀρρώστους χεῖρας
> ἐπιθήσουσιν καὶ καλῶς ἕξουσιν +[18] Ὁ μὲν οὖν κ(ύριο)ς · μετὰ τὸ λαλῆσαι
> αὐτοῖς · ἀνελήμφθη εἰς τὸν οὐρανὸν καὶ ἐκάθισεν ἐκ δεξιῶν τοῦ θ(εο)ῦ +[19]
> ἐκεῖνοι δὲ ἐξελθόντες ἐκήρυξαν πανταχοῦ + τοῦ κ(υρίο)υ συνεργοῦντος · καὶ
> τὸν λόγον βεβαιοῦντος · διὰ τῶν ἐπακολουθούντων σημείων+[20]

As noted above, *teleiai* (+) and interpuncts (·) are used to mark pauses in the utterance of the written word. Some scribal errors in this lectionary, such as on folio 229[v], suggest that the various chant marks were added after

18 Engberg, "Greek Ekphonetic Notation," 53–55.
19 Lowden, *Jaharis Gospel Lectionary*, 15–41.

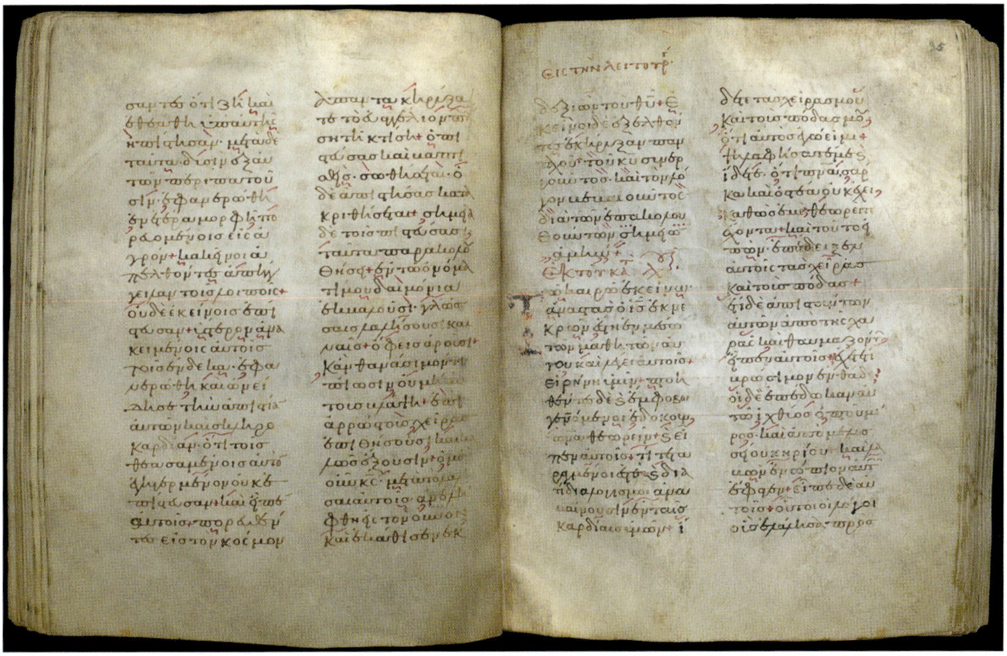

Figure 94 Jaharis Lectionary (New York, Metropolitan Museum of Art, 2007.286), fols. 34[v]–35[r]. (Photo: The Metropolitan Museum of Art, New York, Purchase, Mary and Michael Jaharis Gift and Lila Acheson Wallace Gift, 2007, www.metmuseum.org)

the written text was produced, with spaces for the crosses either left blank or saved with interpuncts. On folio 229[v], constricted space has prevented the scribe from covering the brown interpunct; thus the carmine cross overlaps it but does not obscure it.

Upon close inspection, all the *teleiai* in the Jaharis lectionary appear to overlap preexisting interpuncts. This is quite common across lectionaries. Thus, we may conclude that they were added later – perhaps even by another scribe who was more familiar with the ekphonetic system and used it to achieve the particular tone desired for the lections. My analysis reveals a great deal of similarity among the major lections, particularly in those lectionaries whose illuminations have been discussed above. The guiding principle of the ekphonetic notations appears to be to stress and bring out the narrative of the story, responding astutely to the syntax and composition of the verses. Thus minor variants in a given manuscript can heighten certain words, concepts, or ideas – and their rarity makes such subtle changes all the more noticeable and significant, while also speaking to a certain uniformity of the liturgy's sonic experience in a place like Hagia Sophia.[20]

In the first portion of the excerpt from Mark (quoted above), the lection's *teleiai* are used only in the divisions between the different verses, as indicated by the superscripts. In the Jaharis example, *teleiai* appear at the end of one formulaic opening, "Said the Lord," but rarely at the end of the other, "At that time," where usually only an interpunct is used. It is not until Mark 16:15, where the lection reads "and he [Christ] said to them," that *teleiai* begin to appear within verses – during Christ's speech. That the logic of the *teleiai* here is governed by the incipit formulas suggests that there is a well-established tradition concerning its particular use in relation to the speech of Christ. There are only three places in the excerpt above where a cross appears within a verse (underlined), and one is the moment before Christ begins to speak ("And he said to them"). The other two interruptions both occur while Christ is speaking, before "in my name demons they will throw out" and, a few words later, before "and if any deadly [thing] they might drink it shall not hurt them." These are both potent instances when Christ's pronouncements have a performative action, protecting believers from poison and banishing demons, in or by means of his name. Thus, these visual cues indicate a performative speech act *within* the text, which translates sonically to an extended pause. The written form of these pauses – small, squat cross-like shapes – emphasizes the performativity of Christ's speech visually as well as sonically, requiring the reader on the ambo to pause slightly and allow his voice to resonate in the sonorous domes of Hagia Sophia.

Recent experimental studies seeking to recreate the sonic environment of Hagia Sophia have suggested that when empty, the building would have reverberated for about ten seconds.[21] This number is misleading, however, as Hagia Sophia would have never been empty for the reading of the liturgy, especially on major feast days. The estimated length of

20 These markings might have also indicated physical gestures, in hand movements known as *cheironomia*. However, these were particularly associated with a form of conducting the choir, and thus they were unlikely to be used in the context of reading the Gospel. It is always possible that some of these elements might have served to enliven the performance, and making the sign of the cross for *teleiai* would certainly seem appropriate, but the evidence for such gesturing is limited. See Neil Moran, *Singers in Late Byzantine and Slavonic Painting* (Leiden: Brill, 1986), 38–47.

21 Christoffer Weitze et al, "The Acoustical History of Hagia Sophia Revived through Computer Simulation" (2002), accessed 1 November 2009, www.odeon.dk/pdf/ForumAcousticum2002.pdf. See also Pentcheva, "Hagia Sophia and Multisensory Aesthetics," esp. 102–04. For a study of these acoustic effects and the church, see Pentcheva, *Hagia Sophia*.

reverberation when the church was full is roughly about four seconds, which is significant but would have allowed the words of the liturgy to be intelligible rather than drowned out in a flood of echoes. Thus, we can imagine the effect of the Gospel's reading as it echoes strategically in the space of Hagia Sophia.

Below are the transcriptions for John 10:9 from the lections for September 3, John 10:9–16 (fol. 254r; Figure 95), and for November 13, John 10:1–9 (fol. 267r; Figure 96), respectively:

Εἶπεν ὁ κσ̄+ ἐγώ εἰμι ἡ θύρα+ δι᾽ ἐμοῦ ἐάν τις εἰσέλθῃ σωθήσεται.

Καὶ εἰσελεύσεται · καὶ ἐξελεύσεται καὶ νομὴν εὑρήσει+

+ ἐγώ εἰμι ἡ θύρα+ δι᾽ ἐμοῦ ἐάν τις εἰσέλθῃ · σωθήσεται ·

Καὶ εἰσελεύσεται καὶ ἐξελεύσεται · καὶ νομὴν εὑρήσει+

These transcriptions contain a number of notations. Some of the most notable are the *bareia*, *teleia*, and *apostrophoi*, discussed above, followed by the *kathiste*, *oxeia*, and *syrmatike*. The tight tilde-like mark (⌐), which in the lection appears below the line, is known as a *kathiste* and indicates a narrative style without emphasis. The slanting upward line with a hook at top (↗) is an *oxeia*, and it indicates a relative rise in pitch that should be maintained until the end of the phrase marked by the second *oxeia*. The elongated wave-like *syrmatike* (∼) denotes an undulating movement of the voice, imitating per se the notation's shape.

The doubled *apostrophoi* (”) used at the end of the lection set out the "shall find" (εὑρήσει), and indicate a lowering of the voice without any added emphasis. This combination of the double apostrophoi with doubled *oxeia* (⫽) produces an *apeso exo*, which indicates a raise in pitch only at the very end of εὑρήσει, used here to bring the narrative to a resolve. Immediately before those words, we note that the "and pasture" (καὶ νομὴν) – the object of the "shall find" (εὑρήσει) – is set apart by the three dots of the *kentemata* (∴) at the start and beginning of the two words. The *kentemata* can be used to give dramatic emphasis, producing a transition to a lower pitch. In the segment that precedes this the "And going in and

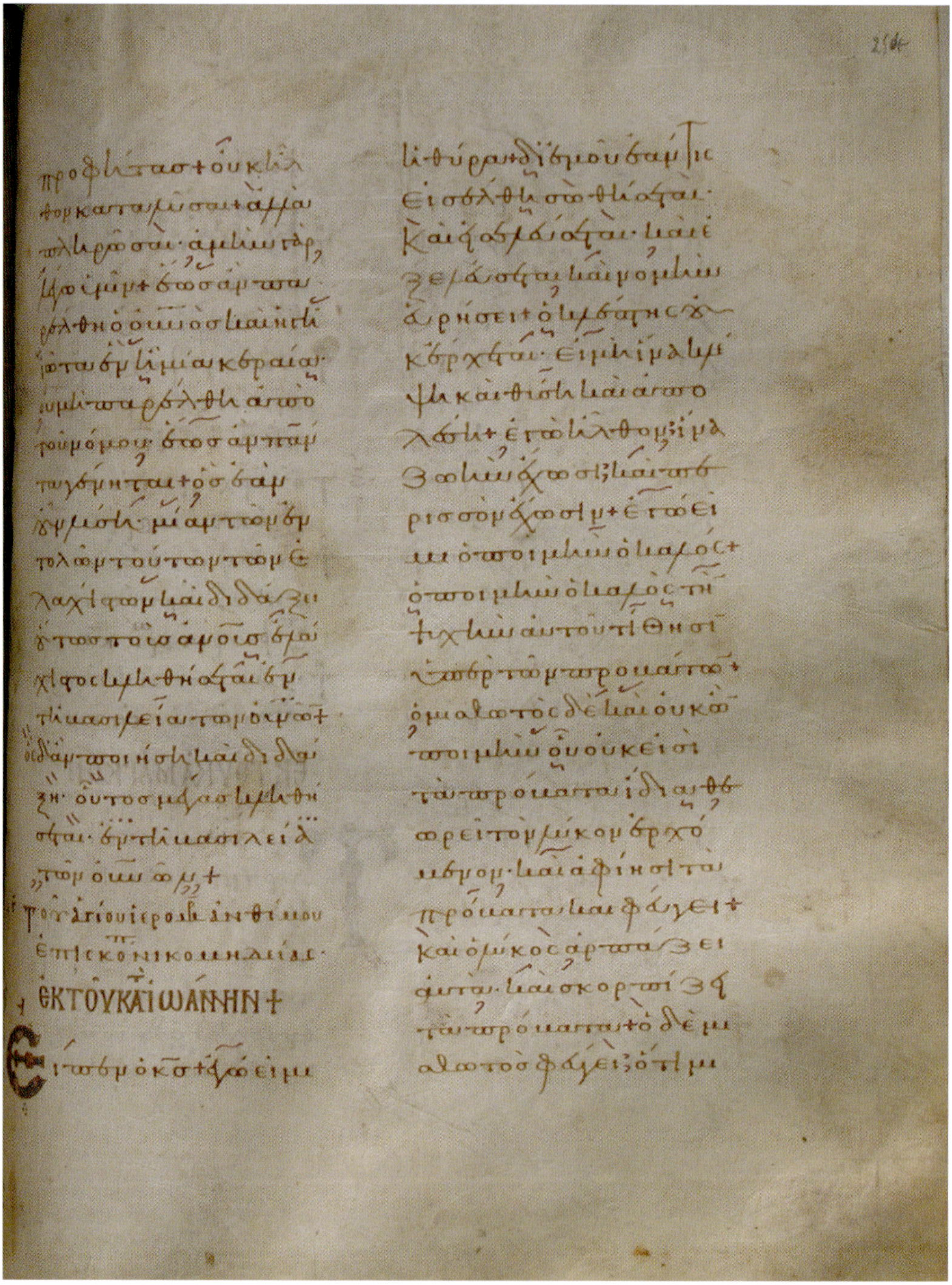

Figure 95 Jaharis Lectionary (New York, Metropolitan Museum of Art, 2007.286), fol. 254[r].
(Photo: The Metropolitan Museum of Art, New York, Purchase, Mary and Michael Jaharis Gift and Lila Acheson Wallace Gift, 2007, www.metmuseum.org)

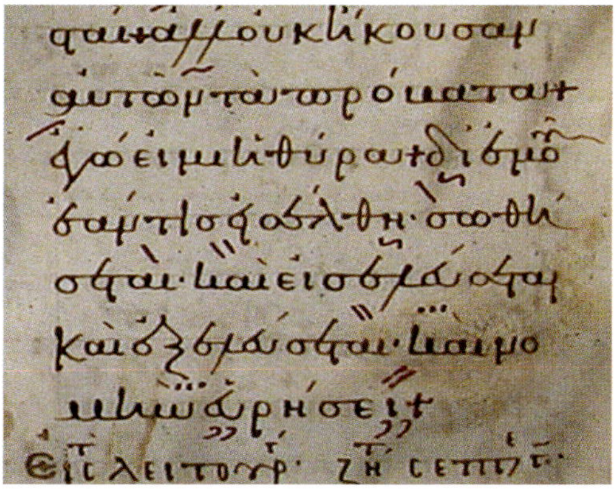

Figure 96 Jaharis Lectionary (New York, Metropolitan Museum of Art, 2007.286), fol. 267r.
(Photo: The Metropolitan Museum of Art, New York, Purchase, Mary and Michael Jaharis Gift and Lila Acheson Wallace Gift, 2007, www .metmuseum.org)

going out" (Καὶ εἰσελεύσεται καὶ ἐξελεύσεται) is bracketed by double *bareiai* (⑊), preceded immediately before that by the σωθήσεται set off both by the pause of the interpuncts and the single *bareiai* that flank it. This emphasis is significant for a singular word, especially having followed the "through me, if someone enters" (δι' ἐμοῦ ἐάν τις εἰσέλθῃ) set off on both ends by a staid and sober *kathiste*.

The doubling of notations that we witness in the November 13 reading is because this verse appears at the end of the day's reading, where we see the doubling of ekphonetic signs that indicates to a reader that the ending of the lection is coming and that his intensity should increase to lend an emotional valence akin to expressive singing. This similarly prepared the congregation as well, urging them to respond to the lection with the formula, "Glory to God" (Δόξα τῷ Θεῷ).[22] This format, as Egon Wellesz and Carsten Høeg noted long ago, is quite typical for the conclusion of lections, but is often deployed quite meticulously for dramatic effect.[23] This formula is used not only for the recitation of Gospel lections, but also in the context of imperial texts meant for public recitation, such as a synodikon.[24]

In a mid-eleventh-century manuscript, featuring the *horos* of the various Church Councils with ekphonetic notations for recitation, one encounters

[22] Wellesz, *History of Byzantine Music*, 251.
[23] Wellesz, *History of Byzantine Music*, 251; Høeg, *Notation ekphonétique*, 128–32.
[24] For a textual analysis of an excerpt from a synodikon that takes into consideration how it would have been chanted, see Wellesz, *History of Byzantine Music*, 259–60.

the same emphasis given to σωθήσεται used for the list of anathemas (Oxford, Bodleian Library, Holkham gr. 6, fol. 44ᵛ).[25] There, the synodikon of the Council of Chalcedon similarly begins with the somber narrative style of the *kathiste*, just as that which is used for the Τῷ καιρῷ ἐκείνῳ that opens certain lections. But, then, this swiftly transitions to the dramatic drop of the single *bareia* framing the word "anathema" itself: ⌐ Ὅλοις τοῖς αἱρετικοῖς⌐ · ˋ ἀνάθεμαˋ.[26] This is similar to the handling of σωθήσεται in the lections, both for September 3 and November 13 readings, where the chant marks read: ⌐δι' ἐμοῦ ἐάν τις εἰσέλθῃ⌐ · ˋ σωθήσεταιˋ. This similar handling reiterates the emphasis provided by this delivery, especially since a synodikon such as this would also have been read during the liturgy (i.e., the Synodikon of Orthodoxy on the Sunday of Orthodoxy, discussed in Chapter 6).[27]

Other appearances of σωθήσεται also evidence an exact handling. For example, consider the notations in Mark 16:16, in the excerpt above: "⌐He who believed and is baptized⌐ · ˋwill be savedˋ · but ˊ he who did not believe will be condemned+." The narrative thus begins soberly, then drops in pitch to emphasize σωθήσεται and rises as the verse ends to give sonic resolution to the line. Overall, the ekphonetic notations on this folio are sparse, appearing only every couple of lines. Hence, the use here of two interpuncts to frame σωθήσεται (underlined in the transcription) stands out. The utterance "will be saved" is given an emphasis in its utterance, and its sonorous drop in pitch gives it added gravitas as it reverberates in the space of the church. This pause demonstrates how the sound was carefully engineered so that the scripture's potent implications could literally resonate with the congregation, enabling them to set their minds intently on the words and carefully visualize the narratives as they were spoken.

[25] The scribal hand of this portion of the manuscript is attributed to Theophylaktos and dated to 1050/1052. See Ruth Barbour, "Summary Description of the Greek Manuscripts from the Library at Holkham Hall," *Bodleian Library Record* 6 (1960): 591–613; Nadia Kavrus-Hoffmann, "Catalogue of Greek Medieval and Renaissance Manuscripts in the Collections of the United States of America. Part V.1: Harvard University, The Houghton Library," *Manuscripta* 54 (2010): 64–147. See also Ewald Kislinger, "Nikolaos Episkopos Lakedaimonias: Chronologische Präzisierungen zur Bischofsliste im Bodleianus Holkham gr. 6," *Jahrbuch der Österreichischen Byzantinistik* 57 (2007): 27–33.

[26] Wellesz, *History of Byzantine Music*, 260.

[27] On the Synodikon of Orthodoxy in Holkham gr. 6, see Romilly J.H. Jenkins and Cyril Mango, "A Synodicon of Antioch and Lacedaemonia," *Dumbarton Oaks Papers* 15 (1961): 225–42; Antonio Rigo, "Le *Synodikon de l'Orthodoxie* et le Palamisme: La forme primitive de P (1351 – avant 1360): Les sources et les témoins," in I.A. Biliarsky (ed.), *Laudator temporis acti: Studia in memoriam Ioannis a. Božilov*, vol. 2 (Sofia: Gutenberg, 2018), 227–41.

As the recordings of Cappella Romana's reconstructions of Byzantine chant show, for example, because any given hymn or lection progresses slowly, the listener must make a considerable effort to comprehend the words that are being delivered by a singer playing with acoustic resonances and the text's phonetics. Bissera Pentcheva's work on chant insightfully stresses the role that "reverberation and aural obfuscation" play both in a text's performance and also in the listener's comprehension and contemplation.[28] This slow unfolding requires an involved listener who can tease out meaning from this acoustic space, requiring time for the imagination to visualize the words. Over a longer time, the listener must construct perceptual habits that will aid this process.

The two appearances of John 10:9 in the Jaharis Lectionary display an analogous arrangement, directing the chanter to raise his voice for the introduction; however, since the September 3 reading begins with a formulaic inscription – as seen on the metal plaque – here the chanter undulates his voice for "I am the door," both to emphasize this section and to heighten anticipation. The drop into the somber and lower-pitched σωθήσεται is hence more pronounced, and then the short pause of an interpunct allows the verb to resonate in space. In this particular example, the pitch drops once again for "And they shall enter," stressing again the chain of causal verbs – going in, going out, and finding pasture and salvation. The promise of salvation is thus equated with the spatial passage through the doorway of Christ. Though "and they shall come out" features another lowering in pitch, the phrase is devoid of emphasis and is immediately followed by the discovery of pasture – spoken in the same pitch at which the lection began. The process is similar for the verse when spoken on November 13, though here *apostrophoi* are used to lower the pitch without emphasis for the word εὑρήσει before the conclusion of the lection. Thus, the verse is handled similarly in the lectionary and on the metal relief, as scribe and epigrapher have both chosen to stress movement in and out while equating salvation with pasture.

The Jaharis Lectionary was composed around 1100, but similar ekphonetic glosses are found in manuscripts that can be securely dated as roughly contemporary with Hagia Sophia's late tenth-century plaque. Only four extant lectionaries predate the eleventh century: Sinai gr. 213 (along with Leningrad, Public Library, gr. 283), from 967; London, British Library, Add. Cod. 39602, from 980; Vatican City, Biblioteca Apostolica Vaticana,

[28] See Pentcheva, *Hagia Sophia*, 7.

gr. 1238, from 991; and London, British Library, Harley 5598, from 995.[29] Though these examples vary in their place of origin and use, they all deploy the same sonic play in the verses in question.[30]

A lectionary in the British Library's collection is useful to us. The manuscript, known now as Harley 5787, was produced in Bursa and dated on paleographic grounds to around 900. In this lectionary, the chant marks for the reading of the lection of John 10:9–16 for September 3 are analogous to (though not exactly the same as) those of the Jaharis Lectionary. In Harley 5787, both the text and ekphonetic notations are done in the same ink, and we can assume that both were done by the same scribe (as is also true of Sinai gr. 213 from 967). The text on fol. 136r reads:

Εἶπεν ὁ κ̄ς+ ἐγώ εἰμὴ ἡ θύρα+ δι᾽ ἐμοῦ ἐάν τις εἰσέλθῃ. σωθήσεται.

{Καὶ εἰσελεύσεται} καὶ ἐξελεύσεται · καὶ νομὴν εὑρήσει+

Here, the scribe has periods on either side of σωθήσεται to indicate a rest even longer than that found in the Jaharis Lectionary, which uses interpuncts. Nevertheless, the phonetic logic here is quite similar, corroborating the simultaneous uniformity and relative flexibility of the ekphonetic system's chant scheme. It is evident that scribes, particularly in the earlier examples, chose to clearly set apart the term σωθήσεται.[31]

Beyond the specifics of the manuscript evidence, we must consider the instructions of the *Typikon of the Great Church*, produced at the end of the

[29] See Dolezal, "Middle Byzantine Lectionary," 1:81n15; cf. Lowden, *Jaharis Gospel Lectionary*, 122n5.

[30] Closest in time to the plaque at Hagia Sophia is the British Library's Add. 39602 from 980, which was made for the bishop of Caesarea in Cappadocia; its majuscule script is comparable to that found on the plaque at Hagia Sophia. But in the manuscript, the passage for September 3 from John 10:9–16 (fol. 145v) was accidentally abridged by the scribe. Normally, if a lection has already been included in full, only the first verse or so is written out, and a reference is given as to where in the manuscript one may find the full text. Here, the text is abridged as if it had already been included in the manuscript elsewhere. After the error was noted, the passage was written on the margin in a minuscule script without any ekphonetic notations. The same reading reappears for October 30 (fol. 164r) and November 13 (fol. 166r), again abridged with an indication that the reader look to the September 3 entry. Hence, this manuscript provides little evidence relevant to our purposes.

[31] On contemporary ekphonetic notations related to the dated tenth-century manuscripts, see Sandra Martani, "Das ekphonetische Notationssystem in den datierten Evangeliarien des 10. Jahrhunderts," in Gerda Wolfram (ed.), *Palaeobyzantine Notations III: Acts of the Congress Held at Hemen Castle, The Netherlands, in March 2001* (Leuven: Peeters, 2004), 27–47.

ninth or early tenth century for Hagia Sophia in Constantinople. The text describes the services for each calendar date, as well as for the movable feast days, and among other details lists the Gospel lections that are to be read on each day. John 10:9–16 is one of the most frequently prescribed Gospel readings, assigned to ten dates – October 30, November 13, December 28, March 22, April 6, May 12, June 2, June 4, August 9, and August 23 – and also recommended for the commemoration of a bishop.[32] This number of readings is rivaled only by Matthew 5:14–19 from the Sermon on the Mount (eleven times), John 15:17–16:3 on Christ's commandment (twelve), and Luke 1:46–47 on the Theotokos (sixteen) in various textual contexts (e.g., as part of a longer reading for the daily Gospel lection and also as a short excerpt in the prokeimenon). The *Typikon* makes clear that at the time when the metal plaque was set over the Imperial Doorway, the John 10:9 text played a far more important role in the liturgical calendar – and thus in the lectionary – than did most other readings.

It is also telling that among the most popular texts is Matthew 5:14–19, which begins "You all are the light of the world" (Ὑμεῖς ἐστε τὸ φῶς τοῦ κόσμου), from Christ's Sermon on the Mount. This would have resonated with the other image above the Imperial Doorway in the narthex: that on the mosaic of Christ with the open book, reading from John 8:12: "Peace onto you all. I am the light of the world" (Εἰρήνη ὑμῖν. Ἐγώ εἶμι τὸ φῶς τοῦ κόσμου). While in the image Christ's "I" (Ἐγώ) is the light of the world, in the liturgy it is his addressee – the congregation gathered around him, "You all" (Ὑμεῖς) – that becomes the light of the world. In other words, much as salvation finds its sonic manifestation within the space of Hagia Sophia, so Christ's greeting at the doorway is projected onto the congregation. As they become united with Christ, they become united to him as the "light of the world" (τὸ φῶς τοῦ κόσμου).

Salvation Regained

Returning to the metal relief in the narthex over the Imperial Doorway, we might say that the omitted term finds its manifestation in the acoustic

[32] As there is relative flexibility as to the readings prescribed for any given day, note that this *Typikon* does not prescribe this lection for September 3, putting Matthew 4:25–5:12 on the Sermon on the Mount in its place. This is comparable to the manner in which the Jaharis Lectionary deploys John 10:1–9 for November 13, rather than John 10:9–16 as the *Typikon* recommends and as occurs in the earlier, dated pre-eleventh-century, lectionaries. Anonymous, *Typicon Magnae Ecclesiae*, ed. Mateos, *Typicon de la Grande Église*, 1:82–83, 100–01, 166–67, 252–53, 264–65, 290–91, 304–05, 366–67, 382–83; 2:190–91 (cf. 1:14–15).

Figure 97 Opus sectile panel over Imperial Doorway in the nave of Hagia Sophia, Constantinople (Istanbul, Turkey).
(Photo: Roland Betancourt)

space of the naos, where the future tense of salvation is enacted in the present performance of the Divine Liturgy. On the obverse of this wall stands another enigmatic plaque: a simple opus sectile panel above the Imperial Doorway (Figure 97).[33] This image, displaying a bejeweled cross set upon an aedicula between parted curtains, is part of the Justinianic iconography of Hagia Sophia. Unlike the metal plaque that was added later,

[33] Underwood, "Notes on the Work," 206–08.

this image almost seems to echo or mirror the naos. Note in particular the conch-shaped dome atop the structure, which is inset with a small cross – an architectural element riffing on the program of the Justinianic Hagia Sophia, which was wholly nonfigural.[34] As the late sixth-century ekphrasis of Paul the Silentiary attests, the central dome over the naos featured a cross set within a circle at the zenith, through which the Savior of the world protected the church.[35] This plaque may have echoed the original apse mosaic, which would probably have depicted a simple cross on a three-stepped base, much like the one in the panel or in the apse of Hagia Eirene. Likewise, the structure of the aedicula might be taken as the type of chancel screen of the early Church with the parted curtains revealing the cross; that cross resonates symbolically both with the Eucharistic manifestation of Christ on earth and with the large jeweled processional cross used in the Little Entrance, which would have been set within the sanctuary during the liturgy.[36] In these various ways, the image might bear witness, as the congregation exited the church, to the liturgical ritual as a whole enacted within that space, yet its precise reading fluctuates between a number of possible meanings.[37]

As the congregation exits, the term that once resonated in the space and was imagined by the devoted listeners intently following the Gospel lection is made manifest in the image on the opus sectile panel, which shows the paradise-pasture that has been guaranteed in the present. In this sense, the image of the radiant cross in the aedicula, which initially appeared to be

[34] See Robin Cormack, "Interpreting the Mosaics of S. Sophia at Istanbul," *Art History* 4:2 (1981): 131–49, esp. 133–34. See also Cyril Mango and Ernest J.W. Hawkins, "The Apse Mosaics of St. Sophia at Istanbul: Report on Work Carried Out in 1964," *Dumbarton Oaks Papers* 19 (1965): 113–51.

[35] Paul Silentiarios, *Descriptio Sanctae Sophiae*, 489–92, ed. Otto Veh, *Prokop. Bauten* (Munich: Heimeran, 1977), 330; partial trans. Cyril Mango, *The Art of the Byzantine Empire, 312–1453: Sources and Documents* (Toronto: University of Toronto Press, 1986), 80–91, at 83. See also full Spanish trans. José M. Egea, *Paulo el Silenciario: Un poeta de la corte de Justiniano* (Granada: Centro de Estudios Bizantinos, Neogriegos y Chipriotas, 2007), 46–105, at 74–75. For the most recent critical edition, see Claudio de Stefani, *Descriptio Sanctae Sophiae. Descriptio ambonis* (Leipzig: Teubner, 2011).

[36] On the use and display of processional crosses in Hagia Sophia, see John Cotsonis, *Byzantine Figural Procession Crosses* (Washington, DC: Dumbarton Oaks, 1994), esp. 24–26; Karl Ayers Sandin, "Middle Byzantine Bronze Crosses of Intermediate Size: Form, Use and Meaning," PhD Dissertation, Rutgers University (1992), 72–113. See also Evan Freeman, "Entry, Offering, and Intercession: The Problem of Iconographic Programming on the Middle Byzantine Processional Cross at the Musée de Cluny in Paris," ThM Thesis, St. Vladimir's Orthodox Theological Seminary (2012).

[37] This panel is discussed in much greater detail in Chapter 6.

operating within a radically different logic than the metal relief, begins to work proleptically – manifesting in advance the soteriological realities that are now guaranteed, while building on the conditions that were established by the metal relief panel seen before it. Therefore, we here encounter the plaque functioning as a temporal foreshadowing and perceptual prefiguration. These unfolding chains of image stage sound, liturgy, and the lectionary's recitation from the site of the ambo as a unified aesthetic experience in Hagia Sophia.

The ambo's place as a device pointing toward the Holy Sepulcher – in the apse, but also presumably in this image – heightens the connections between the opus sectile panel in the naos and the metal relief plaque in the narthex. We have already examined how the metal panel manifests the inspirited nature of the Gospel's composition and recitation through its depiction of the descending Holy Spirit, as well as its clever play with the missing σωθήσεται – a verb that, not surprisingly, recurs frequently in the Gospels as a future-tense guarantee of salvation and that is given sonic emphasis when it is chanted. These various metaphors begin to orbit around the Gospel as a life-giving (ζωοποιός) and life-bearing (ζωηφόρος) object: divinely inspired in its creation, and divinely possessed in its recitation.

Perhaps the best visualization of the interplay between inspiration, recitation, hearing, and ingestion appears in a twelfth-century manuscript of John Chrysostom's homilies on the Pauline epistles (Milan, Biblioteca Ambrosiana, A 172 sup., fol. 263^{v}; Figure 98). The illumination opens the first homily on Ephesians, featuring John Chrysostom in the style of an Evangelist author portrait with Paul speaking to him from behind his seat. The figure of Christ in the heavenly sphere gestures down toward John, and the ray of light shining from his hand animates John's hand writing the opening words of the homily. Over his slanted writing desk the scroll trails off, transforming into streams of water from which a huddled congregation drinks. In this way, the scene carefully structures the divine inspiration of John Chrysostom from Paul and Christ, while it is the grace of God that animates his hand to write the text. The written format of this homily, on a scroll similar to those used by priests for the recitation of prayers in the liturgy, is a cue for speech that is to be made manifest through its recitation in the liturgy before a congregation that is tightly huddled around John's desk.

John Chrysostom was in fact known for preaching his homily from the ambo, rather than from the synthronon as was customary, so that he could be better understood – a detail observed by Sokrates Scholastikos in his

Figure 98 Homilies of John Chrysostom (Milan, Biblioteca Ambrosiana, A. 172 sup.), fol. 263^{v}. (Photo: Veneranda Biblioteca Ambrosiana / Mondadori Portfolio)

Ecclesiastical History.[38] Sozomenos's *Ecclesiastical History* likewise notes that he placed himself in the midst of the people, who pressed against one another as they eagerly crowded around him.[39] The image in the manuscript of the huddled masses bumping up against his desk can be understood as referring to just this circumstance. Paul the Silentiary, for instance, vividly describes how the people huddled around the ambo and the solea, particularly as the priest passed on his return from the ambo holding the Gospel book in hand: as they try to kiss and touch the manuscript, "the countless waves of the surging people break around" (κύματα κινυμένων περιάγνυται ἄσπετα δήμων).[40] In this image, the flowing waters of John's divinely inspired homily spill onto the multitudes, just as those multitudes crash back onto him as waves.

The artist in the Ambrosiana miniature has cleverly slanted John's writing desk so that it might resonate with the act of reading and recitation – rather than the act of writing itself. In the late antique world and perhaps up until the ninth century, scribes usually wrote on a wooden tablet held either on their laps or on their knees. This custom is attested by colophons that make reference to the work's production in stating that "the reed wrote me, right hand and knee" (κάλαμος μ' ἔγραψε, δεξιὰ χεὶρ καὶ γόνυ);[41] it is also a common visual motif in portraits of Evangelists who rest the blank or in-progress folio on their knees, while the text being copied stands upon the lectern. Because reading – even by an Evangelist in his study – would have been understood as an oral act, such lecterns seem to point to an oral recitation. A miniature of Christ speaking to the Apostles from such a lectern appears in an eleventh-century lectionary (Florence, Biblioteca Medicea Laurenziana, Palat. 244, fol. 30v; Figure 99).

[38] "Ὁ οὖν ἐπίσκοπος. . .καθεσθεὶς ἐπὶ τοῦ ἄμβωνος, ὅθεν εἰώθει καὶ πρότερον ὁμιλεῖν χάριν τοῦ ἐξακούεσθαι . . ." Sokrates of Constantinople (Scholastikos), *Historia ecclesiastica*, 6.5.5, ed. Pierre Maraval and Pierre Périchon, *Histoire ecclésiastique*, vol. 3, Sources chrétiennes 505 (Paris: Éditions du Cerf, 2006), 272.

[39] "τοσοῦτον δὲ πρὸς αὐτὸν τὸ πλῆθος ἐκεχήνεσαν καὶ τῶν αὐτοῦ λόγων κόρον οὐκ εἶχον, ὥστε, ἐπεὶ ὠστιζόμενοι καὶ περιθλίβοντες ἀλλήλους ἐκινδύνευον, ἕκαστος προσωτέρω ἰέναι βιαζόμενος ὅπως ἐγγὺς παρεστὼς ἀκριβέστερον αὐτοῦ λέγοντος ἀκούοι, μέσον ἑαυτὸν πᾶσι παρέχων ἐπὶ τοῦ βήματος τῶν ἀναγνωστῶν καθεζόμενος ἐδίδασκεν." Sozomenos, *Historia ecclesiastica*, 8.5.2–3, ed. Jospeh Bidez and Günther C. Hansen, *Kirchengeschichte*, Die griechischen christlichen Schriftsteller 50 (Berlin: Akademie Verlag, 1960), 357.

[40] "ἔνθεν ὑποτροπάδην χρυσέην εὐάγγελος ἀνὴρ/βίβλον ἀερτάζων διανίσσεται. ἱεμένης δὲ πληθύος, ἀχράντοιο θεοῦ κατὰ μύστιδα τιμήν, χείλεα καὶ παλάμας ἱερὴν περὶ βίβλον ἐρεῖσαι, κύματα κινυμένων περιάγνυται ἄσπετα δήμων." Paul Silentiarios, *Descriptio ambonis*, 247–51, ed. Otto Veh, *Prokop. Bauten*, 370; trans. Mango, *Art of the Byzantine Empire*, 95.

[41] Bruce Metzger, "When Did Scribes Begin to Use Writing Desks?," *Historical and Literary Studies: Pagan, Jewish, and Christian* (Leiden: Brill, 1968), 121–37.

Figure 99 Lectionary (Florence, Biblioteca Medicea Laurenziana, Ms. Palat. 244), fol. 30^{v}.
(Photo: GAP srl Firenze / Biblioteca Medicea Laurenziana, foto Donato Pineider. Reproduced with permission of MiBAC. Reproductions in any other medium are prohibited)

Robert Nelson has discussed this image at length, focusing precisely on the manner in which the unique miniature self-reflexively references the lectionary's recitation, here with Christ performing as reader.[42] John Chrysostom's lectern stand has the same spiraling woodwork and resembles the wooden stands from which the Evangelists read, suggesting that they were often used for the recitation of texts in contemporary churches. We can therefore surmise that here the artist is capturing the doubled act of writing and reciting, as the text that John has put down on paper flows off his desk in waves for his listeners to consume. In this way, the image plays not only with these intricate understandings of writing and reciting but also with John's personal history as a famed orator and his association with the trope of the Fount of Wisdom.[43]

Sound and Christian Community

The image of a fountain – often flanked by two or more birds, along with other small animals – is pervasive in Gospel books and lectionaries (Figures 100–04). The scene usually appears above the main headpieces, such as those that open the readings for each of the four Gospels, and the fountain itself ranges in shape from a minimal square basin to a multitiered vase-like structure spouting forth numerous streams. Thick, fleshy tendrils and other vegetation often spring from the fountain, mimicking the decorative flourishes of similar leaves and plants that often are included at the top corners and bases of such headpieces. These hints of a paradisiacal pasture suggest that this imagery can be interconnected with the Fountain of Life trope, which has a prominent place in middle and late Byzantine Gospel illuminations. In certain instances, the fountain's jets of water are themselves replaced by elaborate tendrils that echo the fountain's streams, thereby literalizing the notion of the life-giving waters. While the iconography of these images may be subtler than that of the more elaborate and easily categorized architectural representations of the Fountain of Life, so that to an untrained eye they seem to be mere decorative flourishes, the frequency with which this simple, nondescript fountain appears in Gospel manuscripts suggests that it may be identified with the Fountain of Life.

[42] Robert S. Nelson, "Empathetic Vision: Looking at and with a Performative Byzantine Miniature," *Art History* 30:4 (2007): 489–502.

[43] Andreas Xyngopoulos, "'Άγιος Ἰωάννης ὁ Χρυσόστομος 'Πηγὴ τῆς Σοφίας,'" *Αρχαιολογική Εφημερίς* 81–83 (1942–44): 1–36.

Figure 100 Lectionary (Florence, Biblioteca Medicea Laurenziana, Ms. Palat. 244), fol. 6r.
(Photo: GAP srl Firenze / Biblioteca Medicea Laurenziana, foto Donato Pineider. Reproduced with permission of MiBAC. Reproductions in any other medium are prohibited)

Such an identification would emphasize the interrelations between the act of biblical recitation and the flowing waters of the Fountain of Life.

In an appendix to his article on the Fountain of Life, Paul Underwood demonstrates that the depiction of the four rivers flowing from their

Figure 101 Gospel lectionary (Mount Athos, Dionysiou Monastery, Cod. 14), fol. 214^{r}.
(Photo: after Pelekanidis et al., *Treasures of Mount Athos*, 67, fig. 45)

Figure 102 Gospel lectionary (Mount Athos, Dionysiou Monastery, Cod. 13), fol. 2^{r}.
(Photo: Patriarchal Institute for Patristic Studies in Thessaloniki)

common source, the Fountain of Life, may be understood as an image of the symphony (συμφωνία) of the Gospels of the Four Evangelists,[44] an image of particular relevance to a lectionary, whose text is meant to be chanted melodically. We can build further on Underwood's work by exploring precisely how Christian communities were constructed on these

[44] Paul Underwood, "The Fountain of Life in Manuscripts of the Gospels," *Dumbarton Oaks Papers* 5 (1950): 41–138, esp. 118–31.

Figure 103 Lectionary (Athens, National Library of Greece, Cod. 2645), fol. 68[r].
(Photo: National Library of Greece / The Center for the Study of New Testament Manuscripts, www.csntm.org, digitized NLG 2645 at the National Library of Greece)

Figure 104 Lectionary (Athens, National Library of Greece, Cod. 163), fol. 140[r].
(Photo: National Library of Greece / The Center for the Study of New Testament Manuscripts, www.csntm.org, digitized NLG 163 at the National Library of Greece)

various, yet intricately interconnected, notions of symphony, divine inspiration, and divine possession tied to acts of recitation.[45]

Consider, for example, Ignatios of Antioch's statements in his letter to the Ephesians on the importance of the Christian community's harmonious operation as one:

> Thus it is proper for you to run together in harmony with the mind of the bishop, as you are in fact doing. For your council of presbyters, which is worthy of its name and worthy of God, is attuned to the bishop as strings to a lyre. Therefore in your unanimity and harmonious love Jesus Christ is sung. You must join this chorus, every one of you, so that by being harmonious in unanimity and taking your pitch from God you may sing in unison with one voice through Jesus Christ to the Father, in order that he may both hear you and, on the basis of what you do well, acknowledge that you are members of his Son. It is, therefore, advantageous for you to be in perfect unity, in order that you may always have a share in God.[46]

Here, Ignatios depicts the Christian community using metaphors of sonic entanglement, as the community harmonizes with the mind of the bishop. Such a text demonstrates a model of divine inspiration and possession analogous to the ones set forth already. But rather than being articulated through magnetized chains, as in the *Ion* dialogue, or through the literal ingestion of words, as in the case of Romanos the Melodist and John Chrysostom, such networks of community are constructed through a form of tuning. Such tuning retains traces of possession, since the chanters take on a single voice, speaking through Christ and rejecting individual agency and improvised harmony to embrace the symphony of the communal tune.

[45] As Gilbert Rouget has demonstrated in his cross-cultural theory of music and possession, in the ancient Greek world, music and trance were deeply interconnected in religious life as modes of reinserting oneself into a community and also into a broader cosmos. These complex connections extended into the Byzantine world (not considered by Rouget) through a basic orientation toward the ideas of authorship, reading, and performance, as early Christian writers came to terms with the implications and consequences of these orientations. See Gilbert Rouget, *Music and Trance: A Theory of the Relations between Music and Possession*, trans. Brunhilde Biebuyck (University of Chicago Press, 1985), esp. 187–26.

[46] "Ὅθεν πρέπει ὑμῖν συντρέχειν τῇ τοῦ ἐπισκόπου γνώμῃ, ὅπερ καὶ ποιεῖτε. Τὸ γὰρ ἀξιονόμαστον ὑμῶν πρεσβυτέριον τοῦ θεοῦ ἄξιον, οὕτως συνήρμοσται τῷ ἐπισκόπῳ, ὡς χορδαὶ κιθάρᾳ. Διὰ τοῦτο ἐν τῇ ὁμονοίᾳ ὑμῶν καὶ συμφώνῳ ἀγάπῃ Ἰησοῦς Χριστὸς ᾄδεται. Καὶ οἱ κατ᾽ ἄνδρα δὲ χορὸς γίνεσθε, ἵνα σύμφωνοι ὄντες ἐν ὁμονοίᾳ, χρῶμα θεοῦ λαβόντες ἐν ἑνότητι, ᾄδητε ἐν φωνῇ μιᾷ διὰ Ἰησοῦ Χριστοῦ τῷ πατρί, ἵνα ὑμῶν καὶ ἀκούσῃ καὶ ἐπιγινώσκῃ δι᾽ ὧν εὖ πράσσετε, μέλη ὄντας τοῦ υἱοῦ αὐτοῦ. Χρήσιμον οὖν ἐστὶν ὑμᾶς ἐν ἀμώμῳ ἑνότητι εἶναι, ἵνα καὶ θεοῦ πάντοτε μετέχητε." Ignatios of Antioch, *Epistulae vii genuinae*, 1.4.1–2, ed. and trans. Michael Holmes, "The Letter of Ignatius to the Ephesians," *The Apostolic Fathers: Greek Texts and English Translations*, 3rd edition (Grand Rapids, MI: Baker Academic, 2007), 182–201, at 186–87.

This process of creating a sonic community has been addressed by a number of scholars, most notably by R. Murray Schafer in his classic *The Tuning of the World* (1977).[47] More recently, Steven Feld has explained the foundational importance of such actions in what he calls an "acoustemology."[48] He offers a concise definition of acoustemology as encompassing the "local conditions of acoustic sensation, knowledge, and imagination embodied in the culturally particular sense of place."[49] The acousteme enables us to navigate through an environment and our placement in a physical space through its soundscape, as we identify familiar and foreign territories by their sonic qualities rather than by visual cues. What Feld's theory articulates is a form of being-in-the-world that relies on the sonic environment to know and interact with the world, rather than being centered on vision or logocentricism.

For the Church Fathers, the acoustemology of Eastern Orthodoxy was quite clear. On the one hand, to be "out of tune" (πλημμέλημα) literally meant to be sinning, or trespassing – language used in Athanasios of Alexandria's early fourth-century *On the Incarnation*, for example.[50] On the other hand, Clement of Alexandria's late second-century *Protreptikos* had set up the coming of Christ as the rise of a new musical form (καινῆς ἁρμονίας) and Jesus himself as the "new song" (τὸ ᾆσμα τὸ καινόν).[51] This is

[47] R. Murray Schafer, *The Tuning of the World* (New York: Knopf, 1977).

[48] Feld defines this at length as follows: "Acoustemology, acousteme: I'm adding to the vocabulary of sensorial-sonic studies to argue the potential of acoustic knowing, of sounding as a condition of and for knowing, of sonic presence and awareness as potent shaping forces in how people make sense of experiences . . . Acoustemology means that as a sensual space-time, the experience of place potentially can always be grounded in an acoustic dimension. This is so because space indexes the distribution of sounds and time indexes the motion of sounds. Yet acoustic time is always spatialized; sounds are sensed as connecting points up and down, in and out, echo and reverb, point-source and diffuse. And acoustic space is likewise temporalized; sounds are heard moving, locating, placing points in time . . . What these rather abstract formulations suggest, in simple terms, is that experiencing and knowing place – the idea of place as sensed, place as sensation – can proceed through a complex interplay of the auditory and the visual, as well as through other intersensory perceptual processes." See Steven Feld, "Places Sensed, Senses Placed: Toward a Sensuous Epistemology of Environments," in David Howes (ed.), *Empire of the Senses: The Sensual Culture Reader* (New York: Berg, 2005), 179–91, esp. 185. See also Steven Feld, "A Poetics of Place: Ecological and Aesthetic Co-evolution in a Papua New Guinea Rainforest Community," in R. Ellen and K. Fukui (eds.), *Redefining Nature: Ecology, Culture, and Domestication* (New York: Berg, 1996), 61–87; Feld, "Waterfalls of Song."

[49] Feld, "Waterfalls of Song," 91.

[50] Athanasios of Alexandria, *De incarnatione verbi*, 7.4 (cf. 5.3), ed. and trans. Behr, *On the Incarnation*, 64–65 (cf. 60–61).

[51] Clement of Alexandria, *Protrepticus*, 1.2.4 (cf. 1.4.4, 1.6.1, 1.7.3), ed. and trans. G.W. Butterworth, *The Exhortation to the Greeks*, Loeb Classical Library 92 (Cambridge, MA: Harvard University Press, 1919), 6–7.

a relatively common metaphor that stresses the orality of the conception of the Logos, which has come to tune the souls of men together with the harmonious arrangement of the universe.[52] The attention given by Byzantine architects to acoustics in church architecture speaks to the importance that they placed on the soundscape. Because most of the Divine Liturgy was chanted and interwoven with hymns,[53] architectural innovations were deployed to manage church acoustics along with meeting the demands of the liturgy. Such adjustments occurred not only in Hagia Sophia but also in monastic settings, such as on Mount Athos, where bilateral choirs were added to naves for the purpose of antiphonal chanting, notably examples in the late tenth-century Lavra Monastery.[54]

When we take even a cursory look at the Byzantine literature on music and hymnography, we find the epistemological consequences of acoustics. In the late fifth/early sixth century, Pseudo-Dionysios the Areopagite speaks of the material world as an echo (ἀπήχημα) of the divine harmony and of the celestial hierarchy as being likewise echoed on earth by the ecclesiastical hierarchy.[55] Pseudo-Dionysios explicitly states that it is through matter as "some echo of intelligible beauty" (ἀπηχήματά τινα τῆς νοερᾶς εὐπρεπείας) that one can be led "to the immaterial archetypes" (πρὸς τὰς ἀΰλους ἀρχετυπτίας).[56] As it develops in the intervening centuries, the acoustemology of the middle Byzantine world is marked by this rigorous appreciation of sonic metaphors that articulate aspects of both Christ, Christian community, and divine perception. Therefore, it is not surprising that acoustic and sonic play works as richly and complexly as that encountered in its visual counterparts – the initials, marginalia, and miniatures of the lectionary – and that both the visual and the sonic would work together. These are not simply parallel systems but, as this chapter shows,

[52] "Furthermore, it is this which composed the entire creation into melodious order, and tuned into concert the discord of the elements, that the whole universe might be in harmony with it" (Τοῦτό τοι καὶ τὸ πᾶν ἐκόσμησεν ἐμμελῶς καὶ τῶν στοιχείων τὴν διαφωνίαν εἰς τάξιν ἐνέτεινε συμφωνίας, ἵνα δὴ ὅλος ὁ κόσμος αὐτῷ ἁρμονία γένηται). Clement of Alexandria, *Protrepticus*, 1.5.1, ed. and trans. Butterworth, *Exhortation to the Greeks*, 10–11.

[53] Lingas, "How Musical was the 'Sung Office'?"; see also Lingas, "Medieval Byzantine Chant."

[54] See Papalexandrou, "Perceptions of Sound"; Robert Ousterhout, "The Holy Space: Architecture and the Liturgy," in Safran (ed.), *Heaven on Earth*, 81–120, esp. 102–07. See also Papalexandrou, "Text in Context," esp. 267–68.

[55] Pseudo-Dionysios the Areopagite, *De coelesti hierarchia*, 2.4, ed. Günter Heil and Adolf M. Ritter, *De coelesti hierarchia*, Patristische Texte und Studien 36 (Berlin: De Gruyter, 1991), 15–16; trans. Colm Luibheid, "The Celestial Hierarchy," *Pseudo-Dionysius: The Complete Works* (New York: Paulist Press, 1987), 144–91, at 152.

[56] Pseudo-Dionysios the Areopagite, *De coelesti hierarchia*, 2.4, ed. Heil and Ritter, 15; trans. Luibheid, 152.

parts of a holistic approach to representational modes of rhetoric, art, performance, ritual, and so on. Our concern then is not simply an acoustemology but rather a whole perceptual epistemology that involves all the senses, accounting for the various sensory dimensions of words and images.

For the world of the middle Byzantine liturgical experience, the ambo manifests the locus of this perceptual epistemology as the site within which reader, viewer, and listener must mediate between these various senses to make manifest the noetic and perceptual images that arise from the inscriptive arts of writing, painting, sculpture, architecture, and so on. Throughout the liturgy, these various modes of sensory representation operate in sync with other crucial images that are manifest through the senses and perceptions often left unacknowledged, such as the smell from the incense, which symbolizes the grace of God, or the kinesthetic actions of the liturgical rites, which likewise signify images of the deeds of Christ. The reading of the Gospel lectionary from the ambo and the reader-chanter's interaction with its images, which must be similarly imagined in the minds of the listeners, makes especially palpable the logic of the system across various media. Hence, in the recitation of the Gospel all notions of separate media of representation give way to a single understanding of a perceptual epistemology that is procedurally unfolding and being made manifest in time as a temporal event. The plaque above the Imperial Doorway operates as a case study of this perceptual epistemology, branding the space and functioning as a procedural image that slowly unfolds across the various senses to gradually reveal spectrums of meanings and interrelations between texts, images, and sounds. In the concluding chapter that follows, I shall turn to the adjoining plaque in the naos, over the Imperial Doorway, to consider how its meaning was shaped by the sonic and iconographic fluxes we have discussed throughout this book.

6 | Polyvalent Images

Iconography Shaped by Image, Space, and Sound

Over the Imperial Doorway, on the western wall of the naos of Hagia Sophia, is an opus sectile panel that depicts an aedicula in one-point perspective (as noted in Chapter 5). There, two fluted Corinthian columns in the foreground and two Ionic columns in the back seem to support a canopy, or an apse-like cupola, over the recessed space (see Figure 97).[1] A curtain rod is set between the two recessed Ionic columns, and two curtains, each hung on three rings, are parted and knotted to reveal a jeweled cross. The cross, which resembles a processional cross, has large inset gems and three teardrop pearls dangling from each arm.[2] It seems to hover over a three-stepped base, a usual iconographic image of a cross in pre-iconoclastic and iconoclastic churches, as can be seen in the nearby Hagia Eirene. As already noted, the panel appears to depict a heavenly, paradisiacal scene, with the enthroned cross manifesting to its viewers the promise of salvation as pasture that is suggested by the inscription on the plaque on the narthex. However, the ambiguity and polyvalence of this panel support a variety of readings and possible interpretations, suggesting an interesting site through which to consider how the interplay of text, image, and sound upset the stable iconographic reading of art.

Building on the previous chapter's interests in the narthex's bronze panel, its depiction of a lectionary, and the liturgical use of the lectionary in the space, this chapter follows through on these concerns by focusing on an image in the space of Hagia Sophia that ostensibly has nothing to do with the lectionary itself, but which nevertheless generatively responds to the sonic associations, narrative imagery, and liturgical movements that the lectionary motivated during the daily Gospel reading at Hagia Sophia. My desire here is to look at an image that is quite unrelated to the subject matter at hand in this book, precisely to give credit and articulation to how images latch on to meaning as ritual and practice unfurl beside them, beyond the skill or will of the artist.

[1] See Underwood, "Work of the Byzantine Institute," esp. 206–08.

[2] See Kurt Weitzmann and Ihor Ševčenko, "The Moses Cross at Sinai," *Dumbarton Oaks Papers* 17 (1963): 385–98, esp. 397.

The Panel's Iconographies

Throughout this volume, the challenge has been to successfully communicate through conventional narrative structures the iterative and permutating unfolding of readings that exceed the stability of an iconography, while also pushing beyond a model of mere semiotic "play" – a word to which I have often resorted to convey the procedurality of the images I have been looking at. In this chapter, the challenge is instead to make a simple argument: that elements of the decorative program of Hagia Sophia responded to the perpetual unfolding of art and ritual in its space. In other words, like marginalia or the bodies of chanters, the image is constantly caught in chains or networks of successive associations and meanings: the result is not only nested images but the coexistence of understandings in a cacophony of signification. However, this "simple" argument requires me repeatedly to go back to sources I have already examined, to return to issues I have already brought up, and to make lateral as well as conventional narrative shifts as I try to present all the variables that enable the whole system to operate. This is a rhetorical challenge, and at times it becomes simply impossible to adhere to linear narratives, which take for granted normative systems of representation that could easily be described by something akin to a single catalogue entry or captured in such established modes as rising action, climax, and resolution.

For that reason, this chapter presents the reader with a series of analyses of the opus sectile panel mentioned in the previous chapter. By serving as a counterpoint to the metal relief on the other side of the Imperial Doorway, the panel enables us to explore how text, image, and sound constantly alter and shape our understandings of static images and their iconographies. My goal here is to demonstrate how this system of thought manifests itself not just within the lectionary but in various and extensive spaces of Byzantine artistic production. I have therefore structured this chapter as a litany of possibilities connected in the subsection titles through the transitive "as," which links these various readings of iconographies and ritual contexts into coherent chains. But, I ask the reader now to consider these possibilities not as points in an argument but rather as a network of potential associations and permutations.

Panel as Heavenly Jerusalem

The iconography of the opus sectile panel, as Finbarr Barry Flood discusses in his study of the Great Mosque of Damascus, resonates with Justinianic representations of the Heavenly Jerusalem as described in the Book of Revelation (21:19–20),[3] but also as typified by the prophecies of Isaiah (1:26, 2:1–5, 60:1–22) and Ezekiel (40–48) as well as in Hebrews (12:22–23). While the idea of the apocalypse was not central in Byzantium as it was in the West, there is ample evidence that the image of the Heavenly Jerusalem was pervasive in late antique imperial thought, indicating an eschatological future that could already be seen in the process of being fulfilled on earth.[4] For instance, Maria Cristina Carile has explored the late antique interconnections between imperial palaces and the city of the Heavenly Jerusalem; and Alexei Lidov has investigated the image of the Heavenly Jerusalem as an expanded representational category, as well as the Pharos Chapel's own resonances with the ideated space of the Holy Sepulcher.[5] In the Great Mosque of Damascus, we can see how the configuration of the aedicula, with its one-point perspective and schematizing delineations of architectural structures, plays out in a large-scale monumental decorative program used to represent the Heavenly Jerusalem (Figure 105).

This paradisiacal cityscape can be compared with the fifth-century rotunda mosaics of Hagios Georgios in Thessaloniki.[6] There, martyrs labeled with their names and months of martyrdom stand before monumental architectural spaces that bear liturgical imagery. The two-storey buildings feature a series of details that resonate with those on the panel: small birds and peacocks punctuate rooftops, parted and knotted curtains are frequent, and hanging jewels decorate buildings and crosses. Closer inspection reveals more striking resemblances. For instance, on the

3 Finbarr Barry Flood, *The Great Mosque of Damascus: Studies on the Makings of an Umayyad Visual Culture* (Leiden: Brill, 2001), 15–56, esp. 25–27.

4 Paul J. Alexander, *The Byzantine Apocalyptic Tradition* (Berkeley: University of California Press, 1985); Paul Magdalino, "The History of the Future and Its Uses: Prophecy, Policy, and Propaganda," in Roderick Beaton and Charlotte Roueché (eds.), *The Making of Byzantine History: Studies Dedicated to Donald M. Nicol* (Aldershot: Varorium, 1993), 1–34; David Olster, "Byzantine Apocalypses," in Bernard J. McGinn, John J. Collins, and Stephen J. Stein (eds.), *The Continuum History of Apocalypticism* (New York: Continuum, 2003), 254–72.

5 Maria Cristina Carile, "Imperial Palaces and Heavenly Jerusalems: Real and Ideal Palaces in Late Antiquity," in Alexei Lidov (ed.), *New Jerusalems: Hierotopy and Iconography of Sacred Spaces* (Moscow: Indrik, 2009), 78–102, esp. 90–97. See also Maria Cristina Carile, *The Vision of the Palace of the Byzantine Emperors as a Heavenly Jerusalem* (Spoleto: Fondazione Centro Italiano di studi sull'alto Medioevo, 2012), esp. 40–46; Alexei Lidov, "Heavenly Jerusalem: The Byzantine Approach," *Jewish Art* 23–24 (1997–98): 340–53; Alexei Lidov, "A Byzantine Jerusalem: The Imperial Pharos Chapel as the Holy Sepulcher," in Annette Hoffmann and Gerhard Wolf (eds.), *Jerusalem as Narrative Space* (Leiden: Brill, 2012), 63–104.

6 See Charalambos Bakirtzis et al., *Mosaics of Thessaloniki: 4th to 14th Century*, trans. Alexandra Doumas (Athens: Kapon, 2012), 51–127.

Figure 105 Courtyard mosaics of the Great Mosque, Damascus, Syria.
(Photo: Judith McKenzie / Manar al-Athar)

northwest panel (Figure 106) there are two crosses on the rooftop, one on each side of the building. The crosses are quite simple (Figure 107): each has a small rho-like flourish at its top, and from both ends of each crossbar one teardrop pearl hangs on a chain, like the teardrops on the image on the Hagia Sophia panel (see Figure 97). The mosaicists have even interspersed the gold tesserae with silver tesserae to make the crosses shimmer differently than the rest of the gold-wrought structures and the scene's gold ground, thereby lending these depictions a materiality that recalls the actual objects. Both crosses are flanked by small birds that look intently in veneration at the cross, just as the two birds in the opus sectile relief flank the small architectural cross on the roof of the aedicula. On the second level of the Hagios Georgios mosaic, one's eye is drawn to a small glass lamp in the center of this panel (Figure 108). It is flanked by two columns on each side, and – just as in the Hagia Sophia relief – the two front columns are Corinthian and the other two, recessed in this aedicula-like space, are Ionic. Furthermore, on either side of this balcony-like area is

Figure 106 Northwest panel, Hagios Georgios, Thessaloniki, Greece.
(Photo: Ephorate of Antiquities of Thessaloniki, Hellenic Ministry of Culture & Sports – Archaeological Resources Fund)

a parted curtain. Like the two curtains in the relief, those in the mosaic are tied to the side, which the artist again has indicated with a small bulbous loop that is stylized as two folds of fabric curving at the knot; and again the curtains each hang from three metallic rings on a rod.

All these architectural vignettes at Hagios Georgios frame a central tholos- or canopy-like structure on the first storey. This focal point appears to serve as an altar: the small structure is flanked by long, tapered candles and contains either a praying figure, an enthroned Gospel book, or a jeweled and mounted processional cross. The monumental cross in the southern panel has been severely damaged and is all but gone, but the one in the northern panel is better preserved (Figure 109). Here Basiliskos and Priskos, both soldiers, stand beside the canopy; immediately in front of the

Figure 107 Detail of northwest panel, Hagios Georgios, Thessaloniki, Greece.
(Photo: Ephorate of Antiquities of Thessaloniki, Hellenic Ministry of Culture & Sports – Archaeological Resources Fund)

canopy is a massive cross, larger than both soldiers, that has been studded with large jewels, most oval but two rectangular (Figure 110). This is strikingly similar to the decorative use of the large jewels, oval and rectangular, on the cross in the Hagia Sophia panel. In Hagios Georgios, the cross is punctuated by a round, gold disc containing the Holy Spirit descending upon the cross.

While there is no consensus on how to read the rotunda mosaics, because of their unique iconographic program, some have viewed the cityscape as a scene of paradise at the end of time. Hjalmar Torp, for instance, has argued that the program should be understood as a representation of the Heavenly Jerusalem, a reading which has been advanced by Alexei Lidov.[7] Taking into consideration both this understanding of Hagios Georgios's imagery and its striking resonances with the Hagia Sophia opus

[7] Hjalmar Torp, "Dogmatic Themes in the Mosaics of the Rotunda at Thessaloniki," *Arte Medievale* n.s. 1 (2002): 11–34. See Lidov, "Heavenly Jerusalem," esp. 341–44.

Figure 108 Detail of northwest panel, Hagios Georgios, Thessaloniki, Greece. (Photo: Ephorate of Antiquities of Thessaloniki, Hellenic Ministry of Culture & Sports – Archaeological Resources Fund)

sectile relief, we should explore the consequences of seeing the relief as a manifestation of the Heavenly Jerusalem within the context of the Imperial Doorway.

As we keep in mind the play on the articulation of entering and exiting in the metal relief in the narthex, it is useful to read the panels on opposing sides of the Imperial Doorway against one another. By the tenth century, the lectionary as a book appears to be coming into the relatively stable form that appears in the eleventh century, at least as a distinct manuscript type with a fairly standardized logic in relation to its incipit formulas and layout – even if the included lections and their rubrics always showed great variety.[8] Having replaced whatever image once stood upon the lintel, the

[8] See Nelson, "Patriarchal Lectionaries of Constantinople."

Figure 109 Northern panel, Hagios Georgios, Thessaloniki, Greece.
(Photo: Ephorate of Antiquities of Thessaloniki, Hellenic Ministry of Culture & Sports – Archaeological Resources Fund)

image of the enthroned lectionary was certainly intended to operate within the context of the renovations to the church; but it was also playing with the preexisting art and architecture, and the sixth-century opus sectile panel on its obverse would have surely been a prime interlocutor. Following the action of the metal relief – that is, entering and primarily here *exiting* the naos – we can see the promise of salvation having been granted, as the jeweled cross depicted in the opus sectile panel is shorthand for the Heavenly Jerusalem.

The metal relief engages specifically with the movement of bodies through space and time in the Little Entrance, rewarding salvation on the obverse in an image of the Heavenly Jerusalem at the end of terrestrial time. This is an apt manner of manifesting a soteriological promise that had already – in the plaque – been promised similarly through movement through time and space in the line "I am the door of the sheep, through me, if anyone enters, [they will be saved], they will go in, and they will go out,

Figure 110 Detail of northern panel, Hagios Georgios, Thessaloniki, Greece.
(Photo: Ephorate of Antiquities of Thessaloniki, Hellenic Ministry of Culture & Sports – Archaeological Resources Fund)

and pasture they shall find." In this way, the artist of the metal relief appears to have been directly engaging with the sixth-century panel in order to metonymically represent salvation through the sight of the Heavenly Jerusalem as that promised pasture. Even if the image of the jeweled cross in the aedicula in the Justinianic construction did not explicitly refer to the Heavenly Jerusalem, this meaning would have been given greater salience both by the development of this iconography and by the visual interplay between the two plaques. The missing "to be saved" (σωθήσεται) from John 10:9 in the metal relief not only is fulfilled by the sonic reverberation of the word and its deeds in the space of the naos but also is made visually manifest by the image of the enthroned cross in the aedicula, standing – potentially – at the end of time within the Heavenly Jerusalem.

Panel as Heavenly Jerusalem as Holy Sepulcher

This Heavenly Jerusalem at the end of time would have resonated with the contemporary reality of the earthly Jerusalem – that is, the understanding that the future that is to come is already prefigured on earth in the material city of Jerusalem, and that the resurrection at the end of time has already occurred in Jesus Christ. Both these aspects were stressed by the image of the Holy Sepulcher, set in the earthly Jerusalem. Iconographically, the figure of the jeweled cross on steps would have made the connection to the earthly Jerusalem. According to legend, Theodosius II erected a cross on Golgotha during his rule, thereby associating the monumentalized cross with its presence at the site of the Crucifixion.[9] Although the actual presence of this cross in Jerusalem before the seventh century has been questioned, clearly in Byzantine art from the fifth and sixth centuries such a motif could serve as a synecdoche for the terrestrial and celestial Jerusalem, particularly through the

9 On the cross on Golgotha, see Anatole Frolow, "Numismatique byzantine et archéologie des lieux saints, au sujet d'une monnaie de l'impératrice Eudocia (Ve siècle)," in *Mémorial Louis Petit: Mélanges d'histoire et d'archéologie byzantines* (Bucharest: Institute Français d'Études Byzantines, 1948), 78–94; André Grabar, "A propos des mosaïques de la coupole de Saint-Georges a Salonique," *Cahiers Archéologiques* 17 (1967): 59–81, esp. 73–75; Julian Raby, "In Vitro Veritas: Glass Pilgrim Vessels from 7th-century Jerusalem," in Jeremy Johns (ed.), *Bayt al-Maqdis, Part Two: Jerusalem and Early Islam* (Oxford University Press, 2000), 113–83, esp. 137. On Islamic representations of the cross, see Nadia Jamil, "Caliph and *Qutb*: Poetry as a Source for Interpreting the Transformation of the Byzantine Cross on Steps on Umayyad Coinage," in Johns (ed.), *Bayt al-Maqdis*, 11–57.

Figure 111 Detail of an ampulla from Palestine (Monza, Treasury of the Cathedral of St. John the Baptist, No. 13).
(Photo: © Museo e Tesoro del Duomo di Monza, foto Piero Pozzi)

image of the Holy Sepulcher.[10] This connection would have been strengthened in the opus sectile panel by the architectural structure of the aedicula, which resembles diagrams of the Holy Sepulcher itself, as evidenced by sixth-century pilgrim ampullae and various forms of liturgical furnishings. For example, this imagery can be seen in a pilgrim ampulla from Palestine (Monza, no. 13; Figure 111). There, the Holy Sepulcher is depicted as a small building topped by a cross.[11] The structure is delineated by four columns, two on each side of its opening, and a conch-like enclosure, rendered much like the one in the Hagia Sophia panel. The structure contains within it another smaller edifice, also topped by a cross, and thus resembles a recessed aedicula, again much like the opus sectile relief.

Similar depictions of the Holy Sepulcher were also popular across sixth- and seventh-century liturgical furnishings, as in the fragment of the

[10] Christine Milner, "'Lignum Vitae' or 'Crux Gemmata'? The Cross of Golgotha in the Early Byzantine Period," *Byzantine and Modern Greek Studies* 20 (1996): 77–99, esp. 96–97.

[11] André Grabar, *Ampoules de Terre Sainte* (Paris: Klincksieck, 1958), 36–37.

chancel barrier depicting the Holy Sepulcher as a canopied structure with four columns and monumental cross (Washington, DC, Dumbarton Oaks, BZ.1938.56; Figure 112). There, the artist has ensured that the image is read as the tomb of Christ, depicting the removed door of the tomb as a perspectival, lozenge-shaped rhombus falling down to reveal the rectangular emptiness of Christ's burial. A staider depiction of the Sepulcher finds its place upon a fine glass chalice from the same period, identifiable as a liturgical chalice, with a scene of the Adoration of the Cross set within a curtained and stepped aedicula (Washington, DC, Dumbarton Oaks, BZ.1937.21; Figure 113). The sepulchral resonances of this motif were unmistakable and consequently popular on tombstones as well, as seen in the contemporaneous sixth-/seventh-century Coptic grave stele of Theodote (Berlin, Staatliche Museen zu Berlin, No. 4483; Figure 114).[12] The placement of the Holy Sepulcher on a tombstone is direct: the grave marker is as much an imitation of the Savior's burial as it is a guarantee of the dead's eventual resurrection. The burial site is therefore not so much a sealed tomb, as it is the fountainhead of eternal life.

Panel as Heavenly Jerusalem as Holy Sepulcher as Fountain of Life

The Holy Sepulcher is consequently tied to the iconography of the aedicula, particularly in its typological connection to a trope that has already been discussed here: namely, the Fountain of Life, which is found in many textual and visual sources. In his extensive study of Fountain of Life iconography, Paul Underwood has demonstrated the complex permutations of the motif in its associations with baptism, paradise, and the Holy Sepulcher.[13] The pool, eight columns, and the dome serve as the crucial elements of the Fountain of Life iconography.[14] As Tania Velmans notes in

[12] On grave stele, see Nezih Fıratlı, *Les stèles funéraires de Byzance gréco-romaine* (Paris: A. Maisonneuve, 1964).

[13] Underwood, "Fountain of Life."

[14] We might compare the Western example of the Carolingian Gospel lectionary of Godescalc (Paris, Bibliothèque nationale de France, nouv. acq. lat. 1203, fol. 3^{v}), commissioned by Charlemagne for his son's baptism, with the Justinianic panel in Hagia Sophia. In the Godescalc Lectionary, the fountain is depicted as a flattened circular building with eight columns – four in the foreground and four in the rear – with a large canopy above it topped by a squat golden cross. At the bottom, between the columns, a shallow enclosure forms the pool of the fountain. The whole edifice is surrounded by animals and vegetation that animate the scene, embodying the idea of the life-giving fountain.

Compare this representation with a very similar one in the contemporaneous Gospel of Saint-Médard de Soissons (Paris, Bibliothèque nationale de France, lat. 8850, fol. 6^{v}). Here a similar structure is represented, yet it is set against a recessed architectural background, which

Figure 112 Fragment of chancel barrier with Holy Sepulcher (Washington, DC, Dumbarton Oaks, BZ.1938.56).
(Photo: © Dumbarton Oaks, Byzantine Collection, Washington, DC)

Figure 113 Chalice with scenes of the Adoration of the Cross (Washington, DC, Dumbarton Oaks, BZ.1937.21).
(Photo: © Dumbarton Oaks, Byzantine Collection, Washington, DC)

Figure 114 Coptic grave stele of Theodote, Egypt (Berlin, Staatliche Museen zu Berlin, No. 4483). (Photo: Skulpturensammlung und Museum für Byzantinische Kunst der Staatlichen Museen zu Berlin – Preußischer Kulturbesitz. SBM Arbeitsfoto)

her own study of the motif, which focuses on its appearance in post-iconoclastic Byzantine art, representations of the Fountain of Life were common on the walls of churches in the early Christian and Justinian periods, yet it ceased to appear there by the Macedonian and Komnenian periods.[15]

Thus its depiction over the Imperial Door of Hagia Sophia would not be surprising, given the panel's date, if we are to read it as an iteration of the Fountain of Life motif. We should therefore pay particular attention to the structures in the Hagios Georgios mosaics, which feature a series of fountains interspersed throughout the edifices. The focal canopy- or tholos-like enclosures that punctuate each arrangement also seem to follow the type of the architectural fountain. Some of these structures even feature low parapets between the columns, as if alluding to a chancel barrier or to the structure of the Fountain of Life's basin – specifically, the enclosure, open in the front only, appears in the northern and southern panels, where the monumental cross is featured with diamond-patterned parapets visible behind it. In his study of the mosaics, Hjalmar Torp has attempted to draw connections between baptismal basins, with their imagery of the cross, and the descending Holy Spirit, which could allude to the moment of Christ's baptism.[16]

appears to recede in the same angular manner as the aedicula of the Hagia Sophia panel. The four frontal Corinthian columns in the Soissons Gospel hark back to the plaque as well, along with its cross-tipped canopy. Note in particular the two birds flanking the canopy of the panel, which are located in precisely the same location as the flanking peacocks evidenced in both the Godescalc Lectionary and the Soissons Gospel book. These seem to operate in the panel as a shorthand for the various animals often shown surrounding the Fountain of Life. Nevertheless, as Underwood demonstrates over the course of his compendium of examples, the tholos-like structure indicating the Fountain of Life appears in Ethiopian and Armenian Gospel books from the late Byzantine period without a fountain basin. While these examples are quite distant from the initial iconography, they nevertheless play with the location of the Fountain of Life in the Canon Tables of Latin Gospel books, such as in the Soissons Gospel (fol. 11). In the Table for Canons 6, 7, and 8, the Fountain of Life appears inset into the tympanum of the quasi-architectural space of the table. Here, the fountain is flanked by two curtains, hanging each from five rings off a rod, which is vaguely reminiscent of the aedicula. On the Godescalc Lectionary, see Bruno Reudenbach, *Das Godescalc-Evangelistar: Ein Buch für die Reformpolitik Karls des Großen* (Frankfurt: Fischer Taschenbuch, 1998). See also C.M. Kauffmann, "The Sainte-Chapelle Lectionaries and the Illustration of the Parables in the Middle Ages," *Journal of the Warburg and Courtauld Institutes* 67 (2004): 1–22. On the Cross and the Gospels in the Carolingian world, see Beatrice E. Kitzinger, *The Cross, the Gospels, and the Work of Art in the Carolingian Age* (Cambridge University Press, 2019).

15 Velmans, "L'iconographie de la 'Fontaine de Vie.'"

16 For instance, a cross with a similar descending Holy Spirit appears in the ambo that is built into the pool of the Orthodox Baptistery in Ravenna – clearly drawing a connection between a baptismal basin, the circular enclosure of the canopy (perhaps potentially, as the Fountain of Life), and an ambo. In the one other instance in Hagios Georgios that these low parapets emerge, on the western panel with Romanos and Eukarpion, the banisters feature a scalloped

Interestingly, as Underwood demonstrates, the iconography of setting the Fountain of Life within an octagonal, domed building came to be associated not only with baptism – a natural link for a life-giving fountain – but also with the Holy Sepulcher, since it manifested the life-giving powers of the True Cross and the rebirth granted through Christ's resurrection.[17] For example, in the early eighth century, John of Damascus, while writing in his First Treatise on icons of the veneration given to objects through which and in whom God worked for humanity's salvation, describes the Sepulcher as "the Holy Tomb, the fountain head of our resurrection" (ὁ τάφος ὁ ἅγιος ἡ πηγὴ τῆς ἡμῶν ἀναστάσεως).[18] In the late ninth century, Photios would also come to describe it as "the sepulcher, fountain of our immortality" (ἥ γε πηγὴ τῆς ἡμῶν ἀθανασίας, ὁ τάφος), as in the *Amphilochia*.[19] Thus, we may see a connection between the jeweled cross that represents the one set upon Golgotha and the representation on the Hagia Sophia panel of a celestial or terrestrial Jerusalem, while also understanding the life-giving cross itself as a manifestation of the life-giving fountain of the Resurrection, which the Holy Sepulcher manifests.

In the context of Hagia Sophia, however, we must first note that the Fountain of Life was believed to have its roots in Eden, which, as described in Genesis 2:6–10 and in the *Christian Topography* of Kosmas Indikopleustes, was believed to have been the source (πηγή) from which flowed the four rivers of Paradise.[20] In its position over the entryway of the church, the opus sectile panel, if understood as a fountain, could be considered as the source of the water for the marble floors of the church, which have been exhaustively analyzed in the work of Fabio Barry as a

pattern that even seems to riff on the idea of containing water – an idea encouraged by the presence in the building of small fountains flanking this scene. See Torp, "Dogmatic Themes," 14–19. On the ambo in the church of Hagios Georgios, see Nino Zchomelidse, "The Epiphany of the *Logos* in the Ambo in the Rotunda (Hagios Georgios) in Thessaloniki," in Manuela De Giorgi, Annette Hoffmann, and Nicola Suthor (eds.), *Synergies in Visual Culture* (Munich: Fink Verlag, 2013), 85–96.

17 Underwood, "Fountain of Life," 96–97.

18 John of Damascus, *Orationes de imaginibus tres*, 1.16 (cf. 2.14) and 3.34, ed. Kotter, *Die Schriften des Johannes von Damaskos*, 90 (cf. 106) and 139; trans. Louth, *Three Treatises on the Divine Images*, 29 (cf. 71) and 108.

19 Photios, *Epistulae et Amphilochia*, Amph.316, ed. L.G. Westerink, *Epistulae et Amphilochia*, vol. 6.1 (Leipzig: Teubner, 1987), 122–24, esp. 123; trans. John Wilkinson, "Question 107 to Amphilochius," *Jerusalem Pilgrims before the Crusades* (Warminster: Aris & Phillips, 1977), 146.

20 Kosmas Indikopleustes, *Topographia Christiana*, 2.82, ed. and trans. E.O. Winstedt, *The Christian Topography* (Cambridge University Press, 1909), 83.

manifestation of cosmic waters.[21] Paul the Silentiary and Michael, in their respective sixth- and twelfth-century ekphrases, both describe the ambo with maritime metaphors, characterizing the structure variously as an isthmus or as a cargo ship lashed by the tumultuous waves of the marble and the congregation. According to the authors of the *Protheoria*, in the Little Entrance the coming of the archpriest represents the manifestation of Christ upon the Jordan at the moment of the baptism.[22] But notably, the text does not identify the floor's bands just with the river Jordan or with any single river, instead using the plural ποταμοὶ. At the moment of the Little Entrance, the rivers on the floor follow the type of the Jordan, allowing the rivers in this particular moment to serve as its signifiers. But we can admire how the *Protheoria*'s authors, in keeping with its polysemy, do not limit them to representing the Jordan alone. Thus, these rivers could also represent the rivers of paradise, seen in the context of the panel over the entryway as flowing forth from the life-giving fountainhead of the Holy Sepulcher in the opus sectile panel and the Imperial Doorway below it.

In this way, the panel would have evoked the various associations of the Fountain of Life, deploying the iconography of the celestial Jerusalem through the terrestrial realities of the jeweled cross set upon Golgotha

21 Fabio Barry, "Walking on Water: Cosmic Floors in Antiquity and the Middle Ages," *Art Bulletin* 89:4 (2007): 627–56. Extensive work has been done on the pavements of Constantinople and the early Byzantine period: see Federico Guidobaldi and Silvia Pedone, "Il viraggio delle scelte decorative nei rivestimenti pavimentali e parietali in età constantiniana: dagli antefatti agli esiti," *Musiva & Sectilia* 8 (2011): 35–162; Alessandra Guiglia Guidobaldi and Claudia Barsanti, "Il progetto di ricercar sui marmi della Santa Sofia," in Augusta Acconcia Longo et al. (eds.), *La sapienza bizantina: Un secolo di ricerche sulla civiltà di Bisanzio all'Universita di Roma* (Rome: Campisano, 2012), 55–78; Urs Peschlow, "Zum byzantinischen opus sectile-Boden," in R.M. Boehmer and H. Hauptmann, *Beiträge zur Altertumskunde Kleinasiens: Festschrift für Kurt Bittel* (Mainz: Zabern, 1983), 435–47; Alessandra Guiglia Guidobaldi, "L'opus sectile pavimentale in area bizantina," in Raffaella Farioli Campanati (ed.), *Atti del I Colloquio dell' Associazione Italiana per lo Studio e la Conservazione del Mosaico* (Ravenna: Edizioni del Girasole, 1994), 643–63; Alessandra Guiglia Guidobaldi, "Note preliminari per una definizione dell'arte pavimentale costantinopolitana dei primi secoli," *Jahrbuch der österreichischen Byzantinistik* 32:4 (1982): 403–13; Eugenio Russo, *Le decorazioni di Isidoro il Giovane per S. Sofia di Constantinopoli* (Rome: Viella, 2011).

22 "Δοκοῦμεν γὰρ τὴν ἐπὶ τοῦ Ἰορδάνου ἀνάδειξιν καὶ φανέρωσιν τοῦ Χριστοῦ καὶ Θεοῦ ἡμῶν τὴν τοῦ ἀρ[χ]ιερέως εἴσοδον ὑπαινίττεσθαι. Ἐκ τούτου οὖν, ὡς ἔοικε, ποταμοὶ ὀνομάζονται τὰ ἐν τῷ ἐδάφει τῆς Μεγάλης Ἐκκλησίας κείμενα μα[ρ]μάρινα στενὰ καὶ μέλανα δίκην ὀρδίνων, καὶ μεταξὺ μετρίων διαστημάτων ἀλλήλων διαιρούμενα: μέχρι γὰρ τῆς εἰσόδου, εἰ καὶ ἦν ἀρχιερεύς, ἀλλ᾿ οὐχὶ πᾶσι δῆλος καὶ γνώριμος: εἰ δὲ εἰς μέσον ἑστώς, καὶ τὰ ὑπερφυῆ καὶ ἐξαίσια διατελῶν: ἀλλ᾿ ὁ τὸν καιρὸν λαβὼν ἱερεύς, [ὁ] καὶ μέσον τοῦ θυσιαστηρίου ἱστάμενος, πρὸ τῆς εἰσόδου τοῦ ἀρχιερέως, ὡς Πρόδρομος ἐνήργει τὸ διὰ μετανοίας βάπτισμα: ὃς εἰσελθόντα ἰδῶν τὸν ἀρχιερέα, μεθίσταται: μονονουχὶ τοῦτ᾿ ἐκεῖνο ἡμέρα διαλεγόμενος, ὅπερ ἔφησε καὶ Ἰωάννης, 'Τοῦτον δεῖ αὐξάνεσθαι, ἐμὲ δὲ ἐλαττοῦσθαι.'" Nicholas and Theodore of Andida, *Προθεωρία Κεφαλαιώδης*, 14, ed. PG 140:436.

and thus manifesting a vision of paradise that has been guaranteed through the fountainhead of Christ's burial. Seeing the Holy Sepulcher as an analogy for the rebirth enabled through baptism, we can understand how the reading of Hagia Sophia's "rivers" as a manifestation both of the Jordan and also of the Four Rivers of paradise is consistent with the Fountain of Life's association with Jerusalem, the Sepulcher, and baptism. Here, the polysemy of the rivers not only provides alternative readings but also, by doing so, produces a more complex image of the Fountain of Life: it is both the site of the baptism and the source of the Four Rivers that flow from Eden.[23]

When both the Imperial Doorway and the door beyond it in the narthex were open to the atrium, an observer would have seen the fountain of the courtyard of Hagia Sophia framed by the doorway and the opus sectile panel positioned over it, and would have directly linked the panel and the court's fountain. Paul the Silentiary provides a stirring description of the water feature:

> At the prized center of the wide court stands a spacious fountain, cleft from the Iasian peaks; from it a burbling stream of water, forced by a brazen pipe, leaps into the air, a stream that drives away all suffering.[24]

In other words, much as from the narthex the bronze plaque foreshadowed and diagrammed the liturgical spaces inside the naos, so the opus sectile panel explains the symbolism of the monumental fountain at the center of the courtyard, replacing its healing waters with the restorative powers of the cross. The lush garden of the courtyard would thus have been a compelling image of paradise, granting to those gazing outward at the end of the liturgy the deliverance into the pasture that they had earlier been promised by the bronze plaque.

The sixth-century doors of the narthex of Hagia Sophia are replete with similar allusions to a paradisiacal pasture and to other metonyms of salvation that allude to the life-giving fountain: the bronze door to the inner narthex, south of the central door, features the motif of the living cross as crosses are

[23] On the rivers of paradise in early Byzantine art and liturgy, see Brooke Shilling, "Fountains of Paradise in Early Byzantine Art, Homilies, and Hymns," in Brooke Shilling and Paul Stephenson (eds.), *Fountains and Water Culture in Byzantium* (Cambridge University Press, 2016), 208–28. On the post-iconoclastic history of this imagery and its associations with the Virgin, see Henry Maguire, "Where Did the Waters of Paradise Go After Iconoclasm?," in Shilling and Stephenson (eds.), *Fountains and Water Culture*, 229–45.

[24] "μηκεδανῆς δ᾽ ἐρίτιμον ἐς ὀμφαλὸν ἵσταται αὐλῆς / εὐρυτάτη φιάλη τις, Ἰασσίδος ἔκτομος ἄκρης, / ἔνθα ῥόος κελαδῶν ἀναπάλλεται ἠέρι πέμπειν / ὁλκὸν ἀναθρώσκοντα βίῃ χαλκήρεος αὐλοῦ, / ὁλκὸν ὅλων παθέων ἐλατήριον." Paul Silentiarios, *Descriptio Sanctae Sophiae*, 594–98, ed. Veh, 336; trans. Mango, 85.

depicted upon a chalice-like fountain, sprouting tendrils; the central door into the inner narthex features vegetation and birds feeding, in addition to lambs of God in proskynesis.[25] Such imagery suggests a paradisiacal pasture where vegetation and food are abundant, nurturing life; and it also engages directly with the imagery of the Imperial Doorway's metal relief plaque. The doors, like the opus sectile panel, manifest a paradise that has been guaranteed and is now being fulfilled through the images that cover them. On the sixth-century plaque, the life-giving cross flanked by birds could be read in this context as a synecdoche for the fountainhead of the life-giving waters. Such a reading is supported by the imagery on the bronze doors in the subsequent passageways, which depict flowering crosses sprouting out of fountain-like vessels. The tenth-century metal plaque and its earlier opus sectile counterpart, through their own spectrums of signification and through the meaning that they dialogically construct within their particular spaces, thus become part of an ever more unified program. They elicit a remembrance of the paradise lost, as well as a prefiguration of the paradise that will be regained at the end time and that is already proleptically being fulfilled in human time.[26]

Beyond their paradisiacal connotations, fountains in the Byzantine world were also recognized as sonic instruments. Paul the Silentiary's description stresses the dazzling aural effects of the courtyard fountain's "burbling stream" (ῥόος κελαδῶν). Eunice Dauterman Maguire has explored the visual and aural impact of such fountains in Byzantine daily life, noting that the depiction of a fountain within the context of a Gospel book, lectionary, or book of homilies would have brought to mind the varying sounds that such fountains made, determined by their different streams.[27] Moreover, the inclusion of birds alongside these fountains, as in the opus sectile panel, would similarly have encouraged the viewer to imagine the rushing of streams and the chirping of birds.

[25] See Margaret English Frazer, "Church Doors and the Gates of Paradise: Byzantine Bronze Doors in Italy," *Dumbarton Oaks Papers* 27 (1973): 145–62, esp. 162. See also Carl D. Sheppard, "Byzantine Carved Marble Slabs," *Art Bulletin* 51:1 (1969): 65–71.

[26] See Roland Betancourt, "Prolepsis and Anticipation: The Apocalyptic Futurity of the Now, East and West," in Michael A. Ryan (ed.), *A Companion to the Premodern Apocalypse*, Brill's Companions to the Christian Tradition series (Leiden: Brill, 2015), 176–204.

[27] Eunice Dauterman Maguire, "Spouts and Finials Defining Fountains by Giving Water Shape and Sound," in Shilling and Stephenson (eds.), *Fountains and Water Culture*, 182–207, esp. 189–95.

Panel as Heavenly Jerusalem as Holy Sepulcher as Fountain of Life as Ambo

Having considered the panel's image of the cross as fostering sonic manifestations and suggesting the paradisiacal pasture promised by the open Gospel lectionary, we should also consider how it mirrored the monumental ambo of Hagia Sophia that stood before it. In a sense, the opus sectile plaque stands between two sonic monuments: the courtyard's fountain and the naos's ambo.[28] Late antique and Byzantine literature, particularly in the eleventh and twelfth centuries, is full of associations between water and speech, stressing the melodic nature of poetic speech and chant.[29] And, as Paul Magdalino has noted, a poet praising in verse the baths built circa 900 by Leo the Wise used an anacreontic to mimic the undulating sound of flowing water.[30] The melodious flow of water was repeatedly associated with the flow of the human voice, a connection surely accentuated in the Gospel text's recitation during the Divine Liturgy by the vocal undulations directed by the lectionaries' ekphonetic notations.

Interestingly, as Flood has aptly observed, the opus sectile would also have brought to mind the actual jeweled cross set into the ambo of Hagia Sophia,[31] thereby mirroring the space of the naos and its features. This jeweled cross is described in the *Patria*'s account of medieval Constantinople, which includes a semi-legendary account of the construction of Hagia Sophia. The author writes:

[28] Although ambo production seems to have stopped sometime in the middle Byzantine period – largely to reflect monastic custom, according to Jean-Pierre Sodini – Hagia Sophia as well as many of the other churches in Constantinople retained their ambos; and they continued to be used into the late Byzantine period, as is attested repeatedly by the liturgical sources surveyed in this volume. See Alexander Kazhdan, "A Note on the 'Middle-Byzantine' Ambo," *Byzantion* 57 (1987): 422–26; Jean-Pierre Sodini, "Les ambons médiévaux à Byzance: Vestiges et problèmes," in M. Vassilaki, E. Georgoula, A. Delivorrias, and A. Markopoulos (eds.), *Θυμίαμα στη μνήμη της Λασκαρίνας Μπούρα*, 2 vols. (Athens: Benaki Museum, 1994), 1:303–07; Urs Peschlow, "Der mittelbyzantinische Ambo aus archäologischer Sicht," in Vassiliki et al., *Θυμίαμα στη μνήμη της Λασκαρίνας Μπούρα*, 1:255–60; Martin Dennert, "Mittelbyzantinische Ambone in Kleinasien," *Mitteilungen des deutschen archäologischen Instituts. Abteilung Istanbul* 45 (1995): 137–47. See also Vasileios Marinis, *Architecture and Ritual in the Churches of Constantinople: Ninth to Fifteenth Centuries* (Cambridge University Press, 2014), esp. 54–55.

[29] For a survey of such appearances, see Ingela Nilsson, "Words, Water, and Power: Literary Fountains and Metaphors of Patronage in Eleventh- and Twelfth-Century Byzantium," in Shilling and Stephenson (eds.), *Fountains and Water Culture*, 265–80.

[30] Paul Magdalino, "The Bath of Leo the Wise and the 'Macedonian Renaissance' Revisited: Topography, Iconography, Ceremonial, Ideology," *Dumbarton Oaks Papers* 42 (1988): 97–118, esp. 116–17.

[31] Flood, *Great Mosque*, 26.

Figure 115 'Menologion' of Basil II (Vatican, Biblioteca Apostolica Vaticana, gr. 1613), fol. 142. (photo: © 2019 Biblioteca Apostolica Vaticana. Reproduced by permission of Biblioteca Apostolica Vaticana, all rights reserved)

> [The ambo] had a golden dome with pearls, rubies and emeralds. The golden cross of the ambo weighed one hundred pounds; it also had pendants of rubies and pear-shaped pearls. Instead of parapets, the ambo had a canopy of pure gold on top.[32]

In addition, the image on the opus sectile would have recalled the large processional crosses that would have been used in the Little Entrance alongside the Gospel book, as depicted in the tenth-century Menologion of Basil II (fol. 142^r; Figure 115).[33] Without discrediting, obscuring, or detracting from the claim above that the Justinianic panel should be

[32] "εἶχε δὲ τροῦλον χρυσοῦν μετὰ μαργαριταρίων καὶ λυχνιταρίων καὶ σμαράγδων. Ὁ δὲ σταυρὸς τοῦ ἄμβωνος ἔστενε χρυσοῦ λίτρας ρ'· εἶχε δὲ καὶ σειστὰ καὶ λυχνίτας σὺν μαργαριταρίων ἀπιδωτῶν· ὁλόχρυσα δὲ πετάσια ἀντὶ στηθέων εἶχεν ἄνω ὁ ἄμβων." Anonymous, *Patria Constantinopoleos*, 4.21, ed. and trans. Albrect Berger, *Accounts of Medieval Constantinople: The Patria* (Washington, DC: Dumbarton Oaks Medieval Library, 2013), 260–61.

[33] On the 'Menologion' of Basil II, see Ihor Ševčenko, "The Illuminators of the Menologion of Basil II," *Dumbarton Oaks Papers* 16 (1962): 245–76; Ihor Ševčenko, "On Pantoleon the Painter," *Jahrbuch der Österreichischen Byzantinistik* 21 (1972): 241–49; Anna Zakharova,

understood as a synecdochal depiction of the Heavenly Jerusalem, the Holy Sepulcher, and so on, we can also see the plaque as unifying these elements of the Divine Liturgy, a coming together of the past, present, and future. These various temporalities must be seen as coexisting in and through the plaque's depiction. Architecturally, we might even sketch a connection between the aedicula on the panel and the function of the ambo – particularly when we consider the addition of the metal relief plaque over the entryway, which effectively revised how the earlier panel was originally understood.

Moreover, although it was omitted from many representations of the ambo in manuscript illuminations, including the one in the Dionysiou 587, fol. 119^{v} (Figure 116), a canopy surmounted the ambo of Hagia Sophia.[34] It would have resonated not only with the altar's canopy but also with the panel's aedicula. Perhaps the best representation of the ambo of Hagia Sophia that has come down to us is found in the Menologion of Basil II, in its depiction of the martyrdom of James the Brother of the Lord (fol. 131; Figure 117), who is cast from the height of the temple and clubbed to death.[35] There his assailant descends from the ambo as the fallen James bleeds while being beaten with a long rod. This canopied ambo matches Paul the Silentiary's description of the ambo of Hagia Sophia. The variegated marble of the ambo is inset with a handsome gold cross above the arch under which the choir stands, a space that itself echoes the depiction of the aedicula: it has the two large columns on its outer sides and two smaller inset columns within, below a subtle decorative cornice.[36] Moreover, the canopy of this ambo features a small cross on its pinnacle,

"Gli otto artisti del 'Menologio de Basilio II,'" *Miscellanea Bibliothecae Apostolicae Vaticanae*, vol. 10, Studi e Testi 416 (Vatican, 2003), 379–432.

34 See also the illustration for the elevation of the cross in the Panteleimon Lectionary (Mount Athos, Panteleimon Monastery, Cod. 2, fol. 189^{v}). On the canopy on the ambo, see Jelena Bogdanović, *The Framing of Sacred Space: The Canopy and the Byzantine Church (ca. 300–1500)* (Oxford University Press, 2017), esp. 74–77, 141–52.

35 In one twelfth-century Gospel Lectionary we see a similar ambo in the miniature depicting the elevation of the cross (Mt. Athos, Panteleimon Monastery, cod. 2, fol. 189^{v}). Beneath it is a large cavernous opening, as in descriptions of the ambo of Hagia Sophia, and the monumental ambo is topped with a canopy standing on four columns. The whole structure is made of marble, rendered in the lectionary with exuberant striations and colors. At the top of the ambo's canopy is a gold cross, now blurred into the rest of the adjoining gold background.

36 For a careful reconstruction of the layout of the choir of Hagia Sophia under and around the ambo, see Neil Moran, "The Musical 'Gestaltung' of the Great Entrance Ceremony in the 12th Century in Accordance with the Rite of Hagia Sophia," *Jahrbuch der Österreichischen Byzantinistik* 28 (1979): 167–93. On the practices and training of the choir, see Moran, *Singers*, esp. 14–50.

Figure 116 Dionysiou Lectionary (Mount Athos, Dionysiou Monastery, Cod. 587), fol. 119v.
(Photo: after Pelekanidis et al., *Treasures of Mount Athos*, 193, fig. 239)

just like the one at the tip of the aedicula. Comparing the panel and this ambo, we can observe that the larger cross beneath on the rampart of the ambo parallels that enthroned in the aedicula, as well as the smaller cross finial in both domed structures. In the panel, the cross finial does not visually sit at the top of the dome; instead, the dome seems to be formed around it, which appears to have been the artist's way of emphasizing that it rested on the top not of a rounded arch or scalloped niche but of a three-dimensional dome. The opus sectile plaque thus would have had strong visual resonances with the ambo itself, perhaps even to the point of being confusable with an image of the ambo.

While the panel functioned as a mirror image of the Justinianic apse through a schematic flattening, the apse of the church itself is described in Germanos's liturgical commentary as a manifestation of both the cave of

Figure 117 'Menologion' of Basil II (Vatican, Biblioteca Apostolica Vaticana, gr. 1613), fol. 131.
(Photo: © 2019 Biblioteca Apostolica Vaticana. Reproduced by permission of Biblioteca Apostolica Vaticana, all rights reserved)

the Nativity and the cave of the Sepulcher. Constructing an even more nuanced relationship between the apse and the ambo, he compares them both to parts of the Holy Sepulcher:

> The apse corresponds to the cave in Bethlehem where Christ was born, as well as the cave in which he was buried, as the evangelist Mark says: "There was a cave hewn of rock; there they placed Jesus" (cf. Mark 15:46).[37]

> The ambo manifests the shape of the stone at the Holy Sepulcher [on which the angel sat after he rolled it away from the doors of the tomb] proclaiming the resurrection of the Lord to the myrrhbearing women

[37] "Κόγχην ἐστὶ κατὰ τὸ ἐν Βηθλεὲμ σπήλαιον, ὅπου ἐγεννήθη ὁ Χριστός· καὶ κατὰ τὸ σπήλαιον ὅπου ἐτάφη, καθὼς φησὶν ὁ εὐαγγελιστὴς Μᾶρκος ὅτι «ἦν σπήλαιον λελατομημένον ἐκ πέτρας, ἐκεῖ καὶ ἔθηκαν τὸν Ἰησοῦν»." Germanos I, *Historia mystica ecclesiae catholicae*, 3, ed. and trans. Meyendorff, 58–59. Similar doubling is attested in the *Protheoria*, when the Andidan authors characterize the altar in the sanctuary as both the table of the Last Supper and the Sepulcher of Christ. See Nicholas and Theodore of Andida, *Προθεωρία Κεφαλαιώδης*, 4, ed. PG 140:421.

> (cf. Matthew 28:2–7). This is according to the words of the prophet, ["On a bare hill raise a signal," Isaiah 13:2] "Climb, O herald of good tidings, lift up your voice with strength" (Isaiah 40:9). For the ambo is a mountain situated in a flat and level place.[38]

The ambo in Germanos's view follows the type of the rolled-away stone at the Holy Tomb upon which the angel sat proclaiming the Anastasis, for it is from this site that the deacon reading the Gospel from the lectionary proclaims the deeds of Christ, bearing witness to the future resurrection of humanity at the end of time and making manifest that the resurrection has already occurred in terrestrial time through Christ.[39]

The dialogic relationship between the ambo and the apse is manifested by the liturgical rite: the Gospel is read from the ambo and then is followed by the homily, which is recited from within the sanctuary by the patriarch sitting upon his throne on the synthronon, as confirmed by various sources (including the *Protheoria*). At the same time, the ambo is a deictic vessel pointing toward the Holy Sepulcher as it is both represented by the apse and depicted in the opus sectile panel, which visually mirrors the apse. This entanglement would have been further echoed by the circular shape of the ambo – as Germanos notes; it is also crucial that the ambo is encircled by eight columns and thus resonates with images of the Fountain of Life and the Holy Sepulcher, as well as with early Christian octagonal baptisteries.[40]

The use of an aedicula with a monumental cross is similarly found upon Gospel book covers, as is seen in the silver and gold late sixth-century book covers at Dumbarton Oaks (Washington, DC, Dumbarton Oaks, BZ.1963.36.10 and BZ.1963.36.9; Figure 118). In this regard, the opus sectile panel not only had conceptual and theological resonances with the ambo and the Gospel book, but its iconography directly mirrored the

38 "Ὁ ἄμβων ἐστὶν ἐμφαίνων τὸ σχῆμα τοῦ λίθου τοῦ ἁγίου μνήματος [ὃν ὁ ἄγγελος ἀποκυλίσας ἐκ τῆς θύρας ἐκάθητο ἐπάνω αὐτοῦ πλησίον τῆς θύρας τοῦ μνήματος] ἀναβοῶν τὴν ἀνάστασιν τοῦ Κυρίου ταῖς μυροφόροις. Ἐστὶ δὲ καὶ κατὰ τὸν προφήτην τὸν λέγοντα: [«ἐπ' ὄρους πεδινοῦ ἄρατε σημεῖον»], ἀνάβηθι ὁ εὐαγγελιζόμενος καὶ «ὕψωσον φωνήν»: ὄρος γάρ ἐστὶν (ὁ ἄμβων) εἰς τόπον πεδινὸν καὶ ὁμαλὸν κείμενος." Germanos I, *Historia mystica ecclesiae catholicae*, 10, ed. and trans. Meyendorff, 62–63.

39 In the context of southern Italy, but relying heavily on Byzantine and Syriac sources, Nino Zchomelidse has similarly connected the early medieval ambo as manifesting the tomb of Christ, an association heightened in the Easter rites. See Nino Zchomelidse, *Art, Ritual, and Civic Identity in Medieval Southern Italy* (University Park: Pennsylvania State University Press, 2013), 8–33.

40 On baptistery architecture and its iconography, see Richard Krautheimer, "Introduction to an 'Iconography of Medieval Architecture,'" *Journal of the Warburg and Courtauld Institutes* 5 (1942): 1–33.

Figure 118 Gospel book covers (Washington, DC, Dumbarton Oaks, BZ.1963.36.10 and BZ.1963.36.9). (Photo: © Dumbarton Oaks, Byzantine Collection, Washington, DC)

images that would have been found upon the Gospel book itself. This connection would have been made explicitly clear for the reader standing upon the ambo, facing out toward the congregation and the western wall of the nave. The Gospel book's ornate covers would stand before him, duplicating the exact image of the Holy Sepulcher that stood before him above the Imperial Doorway from whence the Gospel book had come. Thus, the ambo cleverly enjoyed these associations, allowing itself to be read as Sepulcher, fountain, and baptismal font – the same associations as those connected with the opus sectile plaque. In this manner, the plaque mirrors the ambo; I will therefore now turn to consider the various implications of these polyvalent ties for the unified, multimedia aesthetic space of Hagia Sophia.

The Image in Contexts

Beyond the polyvalence of its imagery and its resonances with the larger space of the church, the image also functioned within the contexts provided by its location. Today, the opus sectile panel sits high above the threshold; it abuts the cornice below the gallery in the space over the Imperial Doorway on the western wall of the naos, above a large swathe of verde antique marble (Figure 119). The plaque is nestled between two square porphyry panels with a simple circular design, which lie above two other opus sectile panels bearing dolphins around porphyry disks.[41] Close inspection, however, provides evidence that the present configuration is an alteration from the earlier Justinian program (Figure 120): the opus sectile panel breaks the upper border of the church's revetment, a feature that appears nowhere elsewhere in the church's decorative program. The two porphyry panels beside it also appear to have been inserted later, or at least moved outward to accommodate the insertion of the opus sectile panel between them. In this area alone, on their outward edges there are thinner bands of green marble that appear to be imperfectly matched replacements, lighter in color than the adjoining bands. The physical evidence clearly suggests that although these elements may be contemporaneous with the sixth-century church, they no longer have their original arrangement.

The Icon of Christ

In the thirteenth and fourteenth centuries, Russian travelers to the city of Constantinople recount seeing an image of Christ the Savior, similar to that seen upon the Chalke Gate of the imperial palace.[42] According to these sources, a large miracle-working icon stood above the Imperial Doorway in the naos. In Stephen of Novgorod's account from 1349, the author conflates the image over the doorway with that of the Chalke Gate itself:

> Going a little farther, and turning toward the west, you will see an icon of the holy Savior standing high up over the doors there. The story of this

[41] On porphyry disks, see Isobel J. Baade and Eric C. Baade, "The Red Stones Speak: Porphyry Discs in the Pavements of Roman Churches," in Gareth Schmeling and Jon D. Mikalson (eds.), *Qui miscuit utile dulci. Festschrift Essays for Paul Lachlan MacKendrick* (Wauconda, IL: Bolchazy-Carducci, 1998), 1–15.

[42] George P. Majeska, "The Image of the Chalke Savior in Saint Sophia," *Byzantinoslavica* 32:2 (1971): 284–95. See also George P. Majeska, *Russian Travelers to Constantinople in the Fourteenth and Fifteenth Centuries* (Washington, DC: Dumbarton Oaks, 1984); Alexei Lidov, "Leo the Wise and the Miraculous Icons in Hagia Sophia," in E. Kountura-Galaki (ed.), *The Heroes of the Orthodox Church: The New Saints, 8th to 16th Century* (Athens: Ethniko Hidryma Ereunōn, 2004), 393–432; Cyril Mango, *The Brazen House: A Study of the Vestibule of the Imperial Palace of Constantinople* (Copenhagen: Munksgaard, 1959), esp. 61–72.

Figure 119 Western wall of the nave, Hagia Sophia, Constantinople (Istanbul, Turkey). (Photo: Michael Kelleher)

Figure 120 Detail of the western wall of the nave, Hagia Sophia, Constantinople (Istanbul, Turkey). (Photo: Roland Betancourt)

icon is recounted in books which we cannot quote, but, [briefly,] a pagan iconoclast put up a ladder, hoping to rip the golden crown off [the icon]. St. Theodosia overturned the ladder and killed the pagan, and the saint was killed there with a goat horn.[43]

43 "и пощед мало обратитися на запад и възрѣти горѣ на двери: ту стоит икоиа святы Спасъ; о той икоиѣ рѣч в' книгах пищется, того мы не можем исписати, ту бо поганыи иконоборец лѣствицю пристави, въсхотѣ съдрати вѣнець златы, и святая Феодосиа опроверже лѣствицю и разби поганина, и ту святую заклаща погом козьим." Stephen of Novgorod, *Wanderer*, ed. M.N. Speranskij, *Из старинной Новгородской литературы XIV века* (Leningrad: USSR Academy of Sciences, 1934), 51; trans. Majeska, *Russian Travelers*, 28.

And both Anthony of Novgorod, who refers to it as a mosaic in 1200, and the Russian anonymous descriptions from 1390 to 1391 report similar sightings of an icon of Christ the Savior high above the door.[44] However, Stephen of Novgorod's account is more revealing, because of the insights it offers into the image's insertion into Hagia Sophia's program and its association with the Chalke Gate, given its allusion to the iconoclastic narrative of Theodosia. In citing St. Theodosia's defense of the image of Christ upon the Chalke Gate from the imperial soldier deployed to remove it – for which action she was swiftly executed in the Forum of the Ox, as Stephen cursorily relates – he suggests a connection between that icon and the image of Christ above the doorway.[45]

We can extrapolate that the imagery of the Christ above the doorway followed the iconography of the Chalke type, which depicts a full-length figure of Christ with a cruciform halo, standing upon a footstool and blessing the viewer with his right hand while holding a closed Gospel book in his left.[46] An extant example of this iconography in Constantinople can be found in the inner narthex of the early fourteenth-century church of the Chora Monastery. There, we find an image of Christ and one of the Virgin with two benefactors kneeling before them; the Christ figure is labeled "The Brazen One" (Ὁ Χαλκίτης) (Figure 121).[47] Though the Christ here lacks a closed Gospel book, his iconography is closely in keeping with what would be expected of the Chalke type. Note that as his hand grasps the folds of his himation, his bent arm looks as if it were cradling an invisible Gospel book toward which his other hand is making a gesture of blessing. We might

See also Ihor Ševčenko, "Notes on Stephen, the Novgorodian Pilgrim to Constantinople in the XIV Century," *Südostforschungen* 12 (1953): 165–75.

44 See Majeska, *Russian Travelers*, 209–12.

45 Anonymous, *Vita sanctae Theodosiae*, ed. S. Kotzabassi, *Das hagiographische Dossier der heiligen Theodosia von Konstantinopel*, Byzantinisches Archiv 21 (Berlin: De Gruyter, 2009), 84–98; trans. Nicholas Constas, "Life of St. Theodosia of Constantinople," in Alice-Mary Talbot (ed.), *Byzantine Defenders of Images: Eight Saints' Lives in English Translation* (Washington, DC: Dumbarton Oaks, 1998), 3–7.

46 Mango, *Brazen House*, 108–42; Leslie Brubaker, "The Chalke Gate, the Construction of the Past, and the Trier Ivory," *Byzantine and Modern Greek Studies* 23 (1999): 258–85; Marie-France Auzépy, "La destruction de l'icône du Christ de la Chalcé par Léon III: Propagande ou réalité?," *Byzantion* 60 (1990): 445–92; Anatole Frolow, "Le Christ de la Chalcè," *Byzantion* 33 (1963): 107–20. See also Paul Speck, *Kaiser Konstantin VI: Die Legitimation einer Fremden und der Versuch einer eigenen Herrschaft* (Munich: Wilhelm Fink Verlag, 1978), 616–19.

47 Robert Ousterhout, *The Art of the Kariye Camii* (London: Scala, 2002), 23; Paul Underwood, "The Deisis Mosaic in the Kahrie Cami at Istanbul," in Kurt Weitzmann (ed.), *Late Classical and Medieval Studies in Honor of A.M. Friend, Jr.* (Princeton University Press, 1955), 254–60.

Figure 121 Mosaic of Christ in the narthex, Chora Monastery, Constantinople (Istanbul, Turkey). (Photo: Roland Betancourt)

imagine that a similar iconographic type once graced the space above the Imperial Doorway in Hagia Sophia.

In his study of the Hagia Sophia image, George P. Majeska observes that while the travelers' chronicles all document an image of Christ in that space, there appears to be no physical evidence that a monumental icon, probably done in mosaic, could have been hung there, since no dowel holes or brackets are visible.[48] As observed earlier, the whole area has clearly been altered: apparently the opus sectile panel with the cross was moved upward at some point, a relocation that necessitated the rearrangement of the entire section. Majeska convincingly proposes that the image of the Chalke-type Christ was displayed where the empty panel of verde antique marble now stands, and that the original image of the cross had to be moved upward to make space for it. The proportions of the sheet of verde antique in Hagia Sophia (1.215 m by 3.150 m) would well accommodate an image of Christ.

In the eastern part of the naos of the Chora Monastery upon the left pillar, we can observe an image of Christ of strikingly similar proportions and similar iconography to that of the Chalke type: he stands upon a footstool, blessing with his right hand and holding a Gospel book in his left (Figure 122). His Gospel book is opened to Matthew 11:28: "Come to me, all you who are weary and burdened, and I [will give you rest]" (Δεῦτε πρός με πάντες οἱ κοπιῶντες καὶ πεφορτισμένοι, κἀγὼ ἀ[ναπαύσω ὑμᾶς]). Like the excerpt on the bronze lectionary in the narthex of Hagia Sophia, or in the Gospel book in the imperial mosaic above it, this line acknowledges the promise of salvation through the viewer's movements within the liturgical space, thereby playing with the site of its placement. As was the case in Chora, the viewer who approaches the image in the eastern part of the naos not only comes toward the sanctuary but likewise comes toward Christ, who guarantees their solace. The same play with Matthew 11:28 is found in the images of Christ in the *proskynetaria* of St. Nicholas Orphanos in Thessaloniki and St. George in Staro Nagoričino.[49] Thus, we can reasonably follow Majeska's suggestion that the image of Christ the Savior would have been placed in the space that is currently occupied only by the verde antique slab, immediately below the image of the aedicula and the

[48] Majeska, "Image of the Chalke," 289.

[49] See Sophia Kalopissi-Verti, "The Proskynetaria of the Templon and the Narthex: Form, Imagery, Spatial Connections, and Reception," in Sharon E.J. Gerstel (ed.), *Thresholds of the Sacred: Architectural, Art Historical, Liturgical, and Theological Perspectives on Religious Screens, East and West* (Washington, DC: Dumbarton Oaks, 2006), 106–32, esp. 120.

Figure 122 Mosaic of Christ in the nave, Chora Monastery, Constantinople (Istanbul, Turkey).
(Photo: Roland Betancourt)

cross, uniting into one composition Christ's representation and the cross, his image, and his symbol.

In his fourteenth-century commentary on how the clergy enter Hagia Sophia, Symeon of Thessaloniki recounts the treatment and veneration of this panel during the Entrance of the Patriarch. After having entered through the Imperial Doorway, the "beautiful doors" (ὡραίων πυλῶν), and having bowed three times in the direction of the altar, the patriarch

> advances to the first river, turns around facing westward and venerates three times the holy image of the Savior that is found above the beautiful doors, saying: "We venerate your immaculate image." Four lines are sung in a low voice: "Our master and patriarch, O Lord, protect."[50]

Walking toward the altar, the patriarch stops on one of the first colored bands in Hagia Sophia – presumably the westernmost, the closest to the Imperial Doors. From that place on the "river" (ποτάμιον), he then turns to venerate the image of Christ the Savior above the doors through which he had entered, below the opus sectile panel with its resonances with the paradisiacal Fountain of Life.

Furthermore, the image's associations with the Chalke Gate and the iconoclastic controversies are made explicit by the troparion that the archpriest is said to recite before it: "We venerate your immaculate icon" (Τὴν ἄχραντον εἰκόνα σου προσκυνοῦμεν). This troparion is specifically associated with the Triumph of Orthodoxy in 843, and in the lives of various saints this hymn signifies resistance against the iconoclasts. The Vita of the martyr St. Stephen the Younger recounts that when he was imprisoned in the late eighth century, he proudly sang this troparion in defiance; and according to the Vita of Theodore the Studite, on Palm Sunday he commanded the monks to sing it throughout the monastery alongside icons.[51] Furthermore, the synaxarion of the Monastery of the Theotokos Evergetis specifies that it is proclaimed on August 16 when the feast of the Mandylion is commemorated, celebrating the miraculous icon

50 "Ἀπελθὼν δὲ εἰς τὸ ἀπὸ τῶν πυλῶν πρῶτον ποτάμιον στρέφεται πρὸς δυσμὰς καὶ προσκυνῶν τρὶς τὴν ἐπάνω τῶν ὡραίων πυλῶν <τοῦ Σωτῆρος> ἁγίαν εἰκόνα, λέγει· Τὴν ἄχραντον εἰκόνα σου προσκυνοῦμεν <… ψάλλοντες χθα>|μαλωτέρᾳ φωνῇ· Τὸν δεσπότην καὶ ἀρχιερέα ἡμῶν, Κύριε, φύλαττε." Symeon of Thessaloniki, *On the Rite of the Great Church*, ed. Jean Darrouzès, "Sainte-Sophie de Thessalonique d'après un ritual," *Revue des études byzantines* 34 (1976): 45–78, esp. 46–49. For a classic study on ritual and the space of Hagia Sophia, see Jean Ebersolt, *Sainte-Sophie de Constantinople: Étude de topographie d'après les cérémonies* (Paris: E. Leroux, 1910).

51 Nancy Ševčenko, "Icons in the Liturgy," *Dumbarton Oaks Papers* 45 (1991): 45–57, esp. 45. See also *Vita S. Stephani Junioris* (PG 100:1125A), and *Vita Theodori Studitae* (PG 99:185B–C).

of Christ not-made-by-human-hands.[52] These uses all further connect the image with St. Theodosia and the defense of icons.

Thus, we can reasonably posit that the image of Christ the Savior was added to the program of Hagia Sophia during one of the restorations to the church after the Triumph of Orthodoxy, a suggestion with which Majeska agrees.[53] It may even have been done at the same time that the bronze plaque on the obverse of the western wall was added, along with the imperial mosaic in the narthex. Not only have some, including Marie-France Auzépy, argued that the toppling of the image on the Chalke Gate was a political fiction invented around 800 to magnify the injustices suffered by the iconophiles, but it has also been suggested, in light of the nonfigural decorative program of the sixth-century church, that the so-called restoration of images in Hagia Sophia was similarly fictive.[54] Some have even proposed that the inscription on the similarly restored icon upon the Chalke Gate was simply a version of the epigram on the apse of Hagia Sophia: "The images that the impostors had cast down here pious emperors have again set up."[55] The addition of the image of Christ the Savior, with contemporary and later folkloric associations with the Chalke Gate, would have played into imperial policy and its desire for a pseudo-restoration of Hagia Sophia's images: an image of a nonfigural aedicula with a cross would have required the addition of a figural image of Christ.

Imperial Female Piety

Crucially, the image resonates in important ways with female imperial piety. The Chalke icon and its restoration were intimately tied to imperial policy, and the gate was also the entryway into the "Brazen House" of the emperor. We can thus see an association not only between the images of Christ on the Chalke Gate and on the Imperial Doorway of Hagia Sophia,

[52] Anonymous, *Synaxarium*, ed. Robert H. Jordan, *The Synaxarion of the monastery of the Theotokos Evergetis (March-August, The Movable Cycle)* (Queen's University of Belfast, 2005), 266–67.

[53] Majeska, "Image of the Chalke," 293.

[54] See Auzépy, "Destruction de l'icône." On Hagia Sophia, see Mango and Hawkins, "Apse Mosaics of St. Sophia"; Nicolas Oikonomides, "Some Remarks on the Apse Mosaic of St. Sophia," *Dumbarton Oaks Papers* 39 (1985): 111–15.

[55] "Ἃς οἱ πλάνοι καθεῖλον ἐνθάδ' εἰκόνας ἄνακτες ἐστήλωσαν εὐσεβεῖς πάλιν." Mango and Hawkins, "Apse Mosaics of St. Sophia," 125. See also Mango, *Brazen House*, 121; Silvio G. Mercati, "Sulle iscrizioni di Santa Sofia," *Bessarione* 26 (1922): 200–18, esp. 204–05; Robin Cormack, "Women and Icons, and Women in Icons," in Liz James (ed.), *Women, Men and Eunuchs: Gender in Byzantium* (London: Routledge, 1997), 24–51.

in that both involve imperial thresholds, but also with the image of the aedicula insofar as it represents an image of the imperial palace in the guise of the Heavenly Jerusalem, a fortified and divine city authorizing imperial rule and imperial doctrine. That St. Theodosia, along with female companions, defended the icon upon the Chalke Gate, and that icons, including the Chalke Christ, were restored under the oversight of Empress Eirene in 787, suggest a connection with imperial women. In this regard the placement of the image and plaque is significant: they appear immediately below the gallery level, where the imperial gynaeceum was located.

The arrangement on the western wall indicates notable imperial associations despite the simplicity of its plaques. First, the circle-in-square panels beside the aedicula use imperial porphyry as a way to monumentalize the space and draw attention to its composition. Second, the corresponding opus sectile plaques below them similarly bear inset porphyry disks; they carry images of two pairs of dolphins each, which appear to have an imperial association. Within the context of Hagia Sophia, dolphins appear in the fabric of the church in only one other place: namely, on the bas reliefs that decorate the space of the metatorion (the emperor's oratory and changing room), where the emperor retreated during key moments during the rite and partook in the liturgy from there, located in the southeastern exedra on the ground floor of the church (Figures 123 and 124).[56] There appears to be a second metatorion on the second floor in the galleries. This, according to the *Book of Ceremonies*, is the imperial gynaeceum from which the empress participated in the Divine Liturgy.[57] As the text explains:

> It should be known that when the Divine Liturgy begins, the members of the *kouboukleion* immediately go up into the gallery and the *augousta* goes out from the metatorion which is in the gallery (μητατωρίου, τοῦ

[56] The location of the metatorion and whether there was more than one have been debated. See George P. Majeska, "The Emperor in His Church: Imperial Ritual in the Church of St. Sophia," in Henry Maguire (ed.), *Byzantine Court Culture from 829 to 1204* (Washington, DC: Dumbarton Oaks, 1997), 1–12, esp. 6; J.-B. Papadopoulos, "Le mutatorion des églises byzantines," *Mémorial Louis Petit: Mélanges d'histoire et d'archéologie byzantines* (Bucharest: Institut Français d'Études Byzantines, 1948), 366–72; Mango, *Brazen House*, 60–70. See also Rowland J. Mainstone, *Hagia Sophia: Architecture, Structure and Liturgy of Justinian's Great Church* (New York: Thames & Hudson, 1988), 223–26; Gilbert Dagron, *Emperor and Priest: The Imperial Office in Byzantium*, trans. Jean Birrell (Cambridge University Press, 2003), 92–97, esp. 96n25. See also Ken Dark and Jan Kostenec, *Hagia Sophia in Context: An Archaeological Re-examination of the Cathedral of Byzantine Constantinople* (Oxford: Oxbow, 2019), esp. 69.

[57] See Robert F. Taft, "Women at the Church in Byzantium: Where, When – and Why?," *Dumbarton Oaks Papers* 52 (1998): 27–87, esp. 40–42.

Figure 123 Dolphins from northeastern pillar in the imperial metatorion in the southeastern exedra of Hagia Sophia, Constantinople (Istanbul, Turkey).
(Photo: Roland Betancourt)

> ὄντος ἐν τοῖς κατηχουμενίοις) and sits on a chair, and all the members of the *koubouklelon* stand to either side while the eunuch *protospatharioi* stand behind the *augousta* ... After the *augousta* has given them all the kiss ... [she] stands up and goes into the metatorion with her household *koubikoulariai* while the rest of the *koubouklelon* go down to the emperor.[58]

This passage, describing the feast of Pentecost, offers some information that is key to identifying where the empress was located during this rite. First, the text speaks of this second metatorion as "in the galleries" (or, the catechumena; literally, the place where the catechumens stand) from which

[58] "Χρὴ δὲ εἰδέναι ὅτι ἡνίκα ἄρξηται ἡ θεία λειτουργία, εὐθέως ἀνέρχονται οἱ τοῦ κουβουκλείου ἐν τοῖς κατηχουμενίοις, καὶ ἐξέρχεται ἡ αὐγοῦστα ἐκ τοῦ μητατωρίου, τοῦ ὄντος ἐν τοῖς κατηχουμενίοις, καὶ καθέζεται ἐπὶ σελλίου καὶ ἵστανται οἱ τοῦ κουβουκλείου ἅπαντες ἔνθεν κἀκεῖσε, οἱ δὲ εὐνοῦχοι πρωτοσπαθάριοι ἵστανται ὄπισθεν τῆς αὐγούστης ... Καὶ μετὰ τὸ δοῦναι πάσαις τὴν ἀγάπην τὴν αὐγοῦσταν ... Ἀναστᾶσα δὲ ἡ αὐγοῦστα, εἰσέρχεται ἐν τῷ μητατωρίῳ μετὰ τῶν οἰκειακῶν αὐτῆς κουβικουλαρίων, οἱ δὲ λοιποὶ τοῦ κουβουκλείου κατέρχονται εἰς τὸν βασιλέα." Constantine VII Porphyrogennetos, *De cerimoniis aulae Byzantinae*, 1.9, ed. and trans. Moffatt and Tall, 67–68. See Taft, "Women at the Church," 41.

Figure 124 Dolphins from southeastern pillar in the imperial metatorion in the southeastern exedra of Hagia Sophia, Constantinople (Istanbul, Turkey). (Photo: Roland Betancourt)

we know the empress participated in the ritual; we thus can understand other mentions of it in the text as referring to this site, from which the emperor also at times partook in the rite. But second, the text also establishes that while the imperial metatorion for the empress might well have been located in the southeast gallery, directly above the emperor's metatorion, she exited this site at the beginning of the liturgy and sat upon her little throne (σελλίου) as she welcomed the delegations.

The location of this throne is important for our purposes here, since it likely was located in the western gallery, above the narthex of the church, where four bands of green marble (much like the "rivers" on the floor below), with scalloped decorative borders, delineate this space overlooking the naos.[59] At its eastern end, a circular disk of marble intersects one band of the square, a later replacement of the sixth-century flooring. Notably,

[59] On the green marble bands, see George P. Majeska, "Notes on the Archaeology of St. Sophia at Constantinople: The Green Marble Bands on the Floor," *Dumbarton Oaks Papers* 32 (1978): 299–308. See Robert L. Van Nice, *St. Sophia in Istanbul: An Architectural Survey* (Washington, DC: Dumbarton Oaks, 1966), plate 17; William R. Lethaby and Harold Swainson, *The Church of*

circular porphyry disks were often associated in late antique spaces with imperial ritual and ceremony, as several studies have articulated.[60] In his ekphrasis of Hagia Sophia, Paul the Silentiary describes the imperial metatorion on the lower floor, and immediately afterward indirectly describes the galleries of the church:

> And whoever mounts up will find that the women's aisles on either side are similar to those below; but the one that runs above the narthex, to the west, is not like the other two.[61]

Paul's passing mention is frustratingly terse. But even if there is no mention in this sixth-century text of a metatorion in the southern gallery and no explanation of the western gallery's uniqueness, it is clear that the western space was different in character from the side aisles of the gallery. It appears to have taken its present appearance later through the mutual interaction of its form, decoration, and function.

The floor arrangement here demonstrates that there was a desire to monumentalize this space (Figure 125), which is located directly above the Imperial Doorway, immediately above the opus sectile plaque and the icon of Christ the Savior. Thus, we might surmise that the throne of the empress was set up in this space, accommodating her large retinue and enabling her to sit upon or step forth onto the marble disk to observe the start of the Divine Liturgy and welcome the delegations. Only after she had done so would she retreat to the imperial metatorion to her right, which is cordoned off by a gateway framed by walled-up marble doors (Figure 126), the rightmost of which bears the image of two dolphins on its bottom register (Figure 127).

Sancta Sophia: A Study of a Byzantine Building (London: Macmillan, 1894), 81; Emerson H. Swift, *Hagia Sophia* (New York: Columbia University Press, 1940), 72–73 and 197–98.

60 On the porphyry disk or *omphalos* near the Emperor's metatorion, see Silvia Pedone, "The Marble Omphalos of Saint Sophia in Constantinople: An Analysis of an Opus Sectile Pavement of Middle Byzantine Age," in M. Şhain (ed.), *11th International Colloquium on Ancient Mosaics, October 16th–20th 2009, Bursa Turkey* (Istanbul: Uludağ University Press, 2011), 749–68. See also André Piganiol, "L'hémisphairion et l'omphalos des lieux saints," *Cahiers archéologiques* 1 (1945): 7–14; P. Schreiner, "Omphalion und Rota Porphyretica: Zum Kaiserzeremoniell in Konstantinopel und Rom," in Ivan Dujčev (ed.), *Byzance et les Slaves: Études de civilization* (Paris: Association des amis des études archéologiques des mondes byzantino-slaves et du christianisme oriental, 1979), 401–10.

61 "Ἶσα δὲ τοῖς ὑπένερθε καὶ ὑψόθι πάντα νοήσει/ θηλυτέρην αἴθουσαν ἐς ἀμφοτέρας τις ἀνελθών·/ ἡ γὰρ ὑπερτέλλουσα πρὸς ἕσπερον οὐκέτι δοιαῖς/ ἴση ταῖς ἑτέρῃσιν, ὑπὲρ νάρθηκος ἰοῦσα." Paul Silentiarios, *Descriptio Sanctae Sophiae*, 594–98, ed. Veh, 336; trans. Mango, 85.

Figure 125 West gallery of Hagia Sophia, Constantinople (Istanbul, Turkey). (Photo: © Vanni Archive / Art Resource, NY)

The Sunday of Orthodoxy

The *Book of Ceremonies* explains that on the First Sunday of Lent – also known as the Sunday of Orthodoxy that commemorates the Triumph of Orthodoxy, first celebrated on March 11, 843 – the emperor attends the service from the "metatorion of the catechumena" (μητατωρίου τῶν κατηχουμενίων), where the emperor and his entourage also dine with the patriarch afterward.[62] This observation suggests that the emperor may have participated from the same space as the empress, above the Imperial Doorway, on the day that commemorates the restoration of icons. The post-iconoclastic associations suggested by Stephen of Novgorod's account, which connected the Christ image above the Imperial Doorway with that of the Chalke Gate and the story of Theodosia, may not by themselves be persuasive, but the case is strengthened by Symeon of Thessaloniki's claim

[62] Constantine VII Porphyrogennetos, *De cerimoniis aulae Byzantinae*, 1.28, ed. and trans. Moffatt and Tall, 157.

Figure 126 Marble doors in southeast gallery of Hagia Sophia, Constantinople (Istanbul, Turkey). (Photo: Roland Betancourt)

that the icon is venerated with the troparion "We venerate your immaculate icon," which is also used on the Sunday of Orthodoxy.

The tenth-century *Typikon* of Hagia Sophia does not include the feast of the Triumph of Orthodoxy, because the second portion of the text appears to have been derived from an earlier, probably pre-iconoclastic, source.[63] The first mention of the feast appears in the *Kletorologion* of Philotheos from 899;[64] it is described fully in the *Book of Ceremonies* and in the late eleventh-century Dresden Praxapostolos (Dresden, Sächsische Landesbibliothek, cod. A 104).[65] These sources evidence the importance of the feast, its development, and the involvement of the city and its

[63] See Anonymous, *Typicon Magnae Ecclesiae*, ed. Mateos, *Typicon de la Grande Église*, 1:x–xiv, 2:20–23.

[64] See Nicolas Oikonomides, *Les listes de préséance byzantines des IXe et Xe siècle* (Paris: Éditions du Centre National de la Recherche Scientifique, 1972), 195.

[65] Anonymous, *Dresden Praxapostolos*, ed. A.A. Dmitrievskii, *Древнейшие патриаршие типиконы: Святогорский Иерусалимский и Великой Константинопольской Церкви* (Kiev: Tip. I.I. Gorbunova, 1907). The Dresden Praxapostolos is usually referred to erroneously as the Dresden Typikon. See also Parenti, "Cathedral Rite of Constantinople," esp. 461–63; K.K. Akent'ev, *Типикон Великой Церкви. Cod. Dresde A 104. Реконструкция текста по*

Figure 127 Dolphins on the marble doors in southeast gallery of Hagia Sophia, Constantinople (Istanbul, Turkey).
(Photo: Roland Betancourt)

monuments:[66] the celebrations begin with a vigil at the Blachernai church, followed by a procession to Hagia Sophia. There the Divine Liturgy takes place and includes the reading of the Synodikon, proclaiming the defense of icons from the ambo of the church; after it ends, the emperor dined with the patriarch. According to the eleventh-century Vita of Saints David, Symeon, and George, the procession celebrating the Triumph of Orthodoxy, which took place a few days before the first Sunday of Lent and was the model for the later Lenten commemorations, concluded at the

материалам архива А.А. Дмитриевского, Subsidia Byzantinorossica 5 (Saint Petersburg: Vizantinorossica, 2008).

[66] On the Sunday of Orthodoxy, see Bernard Flusin, "Le triomphe des images et la nouvelle définition de l'Orthodoxie: À propos d'un chapitre du *De cerimoniis* (I. 37)," in Antonio Rigo and Pavel Ermilov (eds.), *Orthodoxy and Heresy in Byzantium: The Definition and the Notion of Orthodoxy and Some Other Studies on the Heresies and the Non-Christian Religions* (Rome: Università degli Studi di Roma, 2010), 3–20. See also Dimitra Kotoula, "The British Museum Triumph of Orthodoxy Icon," in Louth and Casiday (eds.), *Byzantine Orthodoxies*, 121–30.

imperial palace after passing through the Chalke Gate, where praises to Christ were exclaimed.[67] Thus, we see that the images of the aedicula and of Christ on the western wall not only responded to the imperial associations of the site and the role of women in the restoration of icons but also were caught in a series of spatial associations, just as polyvalent as their iconographies, with the monuments in the city of Constantinople that were linked with the defense of icons. Notably, these included the Blachernai church – famous for the Usual Miracle, where the image of the Theotokos revealed itself to the congregation on a weekly basis – and the restored image of the Christ at the imperial palace's Chalke Gate, through which, the *Book of Ceremonies* tells us, the emperor passed during his procession on the Sunday of Orthodoxy (and on countless other occasions).[68]

The kontakia and troparia sung by the crowds all proclaim the triumph of orthodoxy in ways that would resonate with the images on the western wall of Hagia Sophia. The Dresden Praxapostolos and the *Book of Ceremonies* both tell us that the procession moves from the Blachernai to Hagia Sophia singing a troparion, now lost to the modern rite but often reproduced in full in the manuscript tradition:

> Your church, being ornamented by your cross, boasts the brilliance of true doctrines and the fair representation of icons, O Christ, our God, and through these things we are led into a single faith and glorify your ungraspable majesty.[69]

It is repeated up to the arrival at Hagia Sophia, where all the clerics and monks of the churches and monasteries convene "with the cross" (μετὰ τοῦ σταυροῦ) – which the *Book of Ceremonies* helpfully clarifies as the veneration of "the precious cross" (τὸν τίμιον σταυρόν) – and the Gospel when the emperor meets with the patriarch, greeting him and the two objects with a kiss.[70] This occurs in front of the church, prefiguring the imperial

[67] Anonymous, *Vita sanctorum Davidis, Symeonis et Georgii Mitylenae*, 30, ed. J. van den Gheyn, "Acta Graeca ss. Davidis, Symeonis et Georgii Mitylenae in insula Lesbo," *Analecta Bollandiana* 18 (1899): 211–59, at 249; trans. Dorothy Abrahamse and Douglas Domingo-Forasté, "Life of Sts. David, Symeon, and George of Lesbos," in Talbot (ed.), *Byzantine Defenders of Images*, 143–242, at 224.

[68] Constantine VII Porphyrogennetos, *De cerimoniis aulae Byzantinae*, 1.28, ed. and trans. Moffatt and Tall, 159.

[69] "Τὴν τῶν ἀληθινῶν δογμάτων φαιδρότητα καὶ τὴν εὐπρεπῆ τῶν εἰκόνων ἀνατύπωσιν ἡ ἐκκλησία σου κεκοσμημένη τῷ σταυρῷ σου κεκαύχηται, Χριστὲ ὁ Θεός, καὶ δι᾽ αὐτῶν εἰς μίαν ἀναγόμενοι πίστιν, δοξάζομεν τὴν ἀκατάληπτόν σου μεγαλειότητα." Reproduced in Flusin, "Triomphe des images," 15 (from manuscripts: Sinai gr. 737, fol. 102 and Sinai gr. 734, fol. 83^{v}).

[70] Anonymous, *Dresden Praxapostolos*, ed. Dmitrievskii, 194; Constantine VII Porphyrogennetos, *De cerimoniis aulae Byzantinae*, 1.28, ed. and trans. Moffatt and Tall, 158.

procession's greeting of the Gospel book in the narthex. The emperor then enters the narthex; when he comes before the Imperial Doorway with the patriarch, he is given a candle for his proskynesis before the Gospel book and the patriarch completes the prayer of the Little Entrance. After entering into the middle of the naos, they ascend through the ambo and go into the solea to the Holy Doors of the sanctuary.[71] There, the emperor again performs proskynesis before the altar; but he on this day does not enter it, instead retreating to the metatorion.[72]

The Dresden Praxapostolos helps to fill in some of the further gaps regarding rites, particularly those in which the emperor himself does not participate but which are occurring at the same time. For example, it mentions the reading of the kontakion associated with Patriarch Tarasios (d. 806), who recanted his iconoclastic beliefs and became a fervent supporter of images. This kontakion, which figures as part of the Sunday of Orthodoxy to this day, goes as follows:

> The uncircumscribed Word of the Father became circumscribed, taking flesh from you, O Theotokos, and he has restored the sullied image to its ancient glory, filling it with the divine beauty. This our salvation we confess in deed and word.[73]

It is sung by the congregation in front of Hagia Sophia until the patriarch and the emperor arrive from the imperial palace, having traversed various imperial sites, as the *Book of Ceremonies* elucidates, including the Chalke Gate. The Praxapostolos recounts that when the cross and the Gospel lectionary are greeted, they enter into the narthex, they venerate the Holy Doors, and the emperor retreats to the metatorion, as already noted.[74]

[71] On the role of singers and the choir in the exaltation of the cross, see Moran, *Singers*, 59–65.

[72] Constantine VII Porphyrogennetos, *De cerimoniis aulae Byzantinae*, 1.28, ed. and trans. Moffatt and Tall, 157–60. On the veneration of the cross, see Bernard Flusin, "Les cérémonies de l'exaltation de la Croix à Constantinople au XIe siècle d'après le Dresdensis," in Jannic Durand and Bernard Flusin (eds.), *Byzance et les reliques du Christ* (Paris: Centre de Recherche d'Histoire et Civilisation de Byzance, 2004), 61–89.

[73] "'Ο ἀπερίγραπτος Λόγος τοῦ Πατρός, ἐκ σοῦ Θεοτόκε περιεγράφη σαρκούμενος, καὶ τὴν ῥυπωθεῖσαν εἰκόνα, εἰς τὸ ἀρχαῖον ἀναμορφώσας, τῷ θείῳ κάλλει συγκατέμιξεν. Ἀλλ' ὁμολογοῦντες τὴν σωτηρίαν, ἔργῳ καὶ λόγῳ ταύτην ἀνιστοροῦμεν." Anonymous, *Triodion*, ed. Anonymous, *ΤΡΙῼΔΙΟΝ*, 4th edn (Venice: Hellēnikou Typographeiou Ho Phoinix, 1876), 126; trans. Mother Mary and Kallistos Ware, *The Lenten Triodion* (London: Faber and Faber, 1978), 306. On the Triodion, see Gabriel Bertonière, *The Sundays of Lent in the Tridion: The Sundays without a Commemoration* (Rome: Pont. Institutum Orientalium Studiorum, 1997).

[74] Anonymous, *Dresden Praxapostolos*, ed. Dmitrievskii, 194–95. For a close study of the emperor's actions on the Sunday of Orthodoxy, see Flusin, "Triomphe des images," esp. 8–11.

While the *Book of Ceremonies* only sketches the rest of the rite, skipping to the events occurring at its completion, the Dresden manuscript describes the events that follow: the readings from the ambo, including the Synodikon. But first, the apolytikion (troparion) "We venerate your immaculate icon" is read:

> We venerate your holy icon, loving Lord, asking you to pardon our transgressions, Christ our God. For you of your own will were pleased in the flesh to ascend upon the Cross, so to deliver from the bondage of the enemy those whom you have fashioned. Therefore in thanksgiving we cry aloud to you: You have filled all things with joy, our Savior, when you came to save the world.[75]

After the singing of this troparion, the Dresden Praxapostolos tells us, the kontakion would have been sung, followed by the Thrice-Holy Hymn and then the reading of the Synodikon, proclaimed as usual.[76]

This troparion would have well suited the image of the Christ upon the western wall of the naos, given both that image's association with the iconoclastic import of the Chalke Gate and its appellation "Christ the Savior," and given that the hymn not only makes reference to the veneration of icons but also addresses Christ as "our Savior" (ὁ Σωτὴρ ἡμῶν). That address nicely meshes as well with the play around the term missing from the bronze plaque in the narthex, salvation (σωθήσεσθαι). In the troparion, this salvation is rhetorically staged "to deliver from the bondage of the enemy those whom you have fashioned": it is God's breaking of the chains of those whom he fashioned in his own image, thereby recalling humanity's own iconic relation to God. We should also note that chains of the Apostle Paul were said by the Russian anonymous description from the late fourteenth century to be near the Imperial Doors; a commemoration of

[75] "Τὴν ἄχραντον Εἰκόνα σου προσκυνοῦμεν Ἀγαθέ, αἰτούμενοι συγχώρησιν τῶν πταισμάτων ἡμῶν, Χριστὲ ὁ Θεός· βουλήσει γὰρ ηὐδόκησας σαρκὶ ἀνελθεῖν ἐν τῷ Σταυρῷ, ἵνα ῥύσῃ οὓς ἔπλασας ἐκ τῆς δουλείας τοῦ ἐχθροῦ· ὅθεν εὐχαρίστως βοῶμέν σοι· Χαρᾶς ἐπλήρωσας τὰ πάντα, ὁ Σωτὴρ ἡμῶν, παραγενόμενος εἰς τὸ σῶσαι τὸν Κόσμον." Anonymous, *Triodion*, ed. Anonymous, 123 (cf. 133); modified trans. Mother Mary and Ware, 302. See also Loukas of Messina, *Acoluthia sanctae quadragesimae monasterii Christi Salvatoris in Messenae*, 15, ed. Miguel Arranz, *Le Typicon du monastère du Saint-Sauveur à Messine*, Orientalia Christiana Analecta 185 (Rome: Pont. Institutum Orientalium Studiorum, 1969). This verse became associated with specific images, like the Mandylion; see Venance Grumel, "Léon de Chalcédoine et le canon de la fête du saint Mandylion," *Analecta Bollandiana* 68 (1950), 135–52, esp. 139–40.

[76] Anonymous, *Synodicon orthodoxiae*, ed. Jean Gouillard, "Le *Synodikon de l'Orthodoxie*: Édition et commentaire," *Travaux et Mémoires* 2 (1967): 1–316, esp. 6–7. On the reading of the Synodikon, see Charles Barber, "The *Synodikon of Orthodoxy* and the Ground of Painting," *Contesting the Logic of Painting*, 1–22.

this relic is listed by another source for January 16 in the Peter Chapel of Hagia Sophia, though a late eleventh- or early twelfth-century Latin text mentions them as being in the imperial palace.[77] Thus, while this context may not have always been available to those experiencing this rite, the association surely seems to have been possible in the fourteenth and fifteenth centuries.

Returning to the troparion, we observe that this freeing from bondage occurs precisely through Christ's willing consent "to ascend upon the cross" (ἀνελθεῖν ἐν τῷ Σταυρῷ). Not only has the True Cross been honored in the rites of the feast for the Sunday of Orthodoxy, but likewise upon the reconfigured wall above the Imperial Doorway, the image of Christ the Savior is immediately below the monumentalized cross in the aedicula: its stepped entryway is presented to the image below, which can ascend its steps into the glory and salvation that the symbol represents. In these rites for the Sunday of Orthodoxy, we can see an interest in the True Cross and its veneration, as the first troparion stresses. That troparion praises the church decorated in the cross, while also advocating for the triumph of orthodoxy and the representation of the icon – as do the kontakion and second troparion. Hence, we can understand how the audience would have heard these hymns stressing the importance of the icon and the cross together as one, a fusion made visible to them in the combination of the icon of Christ and the primitive aedicula upon the western wall.

Conclusion

The image configures and reconfigures the promise of salvation through allusions to the Heavenly Jerusalem, the Holy Sepulcher, the Fountain of Life, and the ambo – themselves images that mirror one another, as when Germanos states that the ambo is an image of the Holy Sepulcher and of the angel's proclamation of Christ's deeds. The Synodikon, which like the Gospel lectionary was chanted from the ambo, would have strengthened the associations discussed above between the aedicula image and its dialogic exchanges with the sound of the lectionary. Thus, the western wall's decoration is shown even more clearly to work as a procedural image, which reveals itself variously day to day and according to different liturgical

[77] For a concise description of the various accounts, see Majeska, *Russian Travelers*, 210.

events, incorporating the sacred topography of Constantinople and the actions of the congregation in the church.

This troparion was certainly not composed in response to this decorative program, but its use in this context would have actively resonated with these various visual associations and permutations. To be sure, that context would have changed throughout the troparion's use: thus an important factor is the exact date of when the Christ icon was added, which may have been considerably later than the tenth century given that it is most clearly attested in fourteenth-century sources. Furthermore, the context would have depended on the ever-changing imperial practices in these various rites. As Symeon of Thessaloniki's account suggests, this troparion was not used exclusively on the Sunday of Orthodoxy, but rather was habitually deployed in the space of Hagia Sophia to venerate this image of Christ the Savior above the Imperial Doorway. Its resonances with the Sunday of Orthodoxy were surely not lost, however, and must have contributed to the strengthening of the image's post-iconoclastic associations with the Chalke Gate, Theodosia, and both female and imperial piety.

The most unusual aspect of the operation of the western wall's images is precisely that they are not unique. As this volume has shown, Byzantine art in service of the Divine Liturgy fueled itself and thrived on these forms of seeing, reading, and hearing, which understood the liturgical space and its objects as pulsating across a series of typologies that are always in the process of divine and hermeneutic revelation. I close this volume with the opus sectile panel precisely because it appears so trite and simple at first glance. But it also neatly articulates for us a deep and thick understanding of the experiences of the image, which can appear simultaneously as a symphony and a cacophony, exciting its users through a series of permutations that bring them to the edge of confusion and misdirection. This is how text, image, and sound operate in service of the Divine Liturgy: through the construction of the perpetually polyvalent image.

+ ΕΙΡ
ΗΝΗ
ΥΜΙΝ
ΕΓΩ
ΕΙΜΙ
ΤΟ Φ
ΩΣ ΤΟΥ
ΚΟΣΜ

Epilogue

Following networks of iconographic iterations, semiotic permutations, and contextual associations, this volume has repeatedly traced ways in which image, text, and sound actively respond to a variety of contexts in the Divine Liturgy. I do not mean to suggest that all such meanings were prescribed by the original image or that they were evident to all audiences; rather, my point is that they unfolded procedurally through repeated use, flashing different facets of their polyvalence to various users over different times. This experience of slowly unfolding and of partial revelation is what I have attempted to convey through this volume's litany of permutations, iterations, and nested chains of iconographic readings. This study provides a space for the transcription of a series of representations that emerge only through the contemplation of images, texts, and sound over time and in different contexts – at some times, as the result of long and studious contemplation; at other times, as the result of the cursory glance of someone in the process of reciting a text. My hope is that this volume has constantly expected and demanded that the reader make connections and associations between different works and viewing conditions, so that together they may all make possible the diverse understandings of these artworks' spectrums of meaning. The lessons of these polyvalent and faltering images should spur us to think about the ever-withdrawing and perpetually complex nature of Byzantine art, demanding that we all become skeptical readers as we articulate the many possibilities that these images offer.

Methodologically, this project has been oriented around the role of the art historian in elucidating and mapping out the networks of meanings and possibilities offered up by these faltering and polyvalent images. As a provocation to the reader, I wish to declare now that I cannot definitively argue many of the points made in this volume, nor can I convince you beyond question that my unique observations are anything else than my own idiosyncratic failures in the reading of iconography. I say this not to dismiss my belief in the argument that has been expounded, nor to deny the rigor and diligence of this research. Instead, my hope is to cultivate a certain critical nuance that aspires to foreground the art historian as the interpreter. The so-called faults and permutations that have been explored here open up spaces where slippages, confusions, and misdirection are possible, even if they were not specifically intended or always consciously perceived as such. It is this space of and for possibility that has most interested me in this work – a space that often is overlooked, ignored, or subdued in academic writing.

The critical importance of this disclaimer is that it allows me to foreground the manner in which Byzantine artists somehow cultivated ample room for iconographic possibilities precisely by pushing and pulling at the strictures of what our contemporary field of art history has come to articulate as the contours of iconography. At stake in this outlook is an approach to writing art history in which Byzantine artists can themselves respond to the discussions and categories of a scholarly field they never knew.

My methodological approach to this project thus arose from the bifurcation of two temporalities: that of the Byzantine artist-scribes and that of my present subject position as an art historian of Byzantine visual culture, trained in its methods and narratives. By procedurally unfolding these possibilities of meaning through close readings of texts and images that have long been dismissed as failures or banalities, I have articulated for us a dialogue between a historical subject and the field that now studies it. In this way, my analyses of these images and texts are as much an unfolding of a Byzantine creator's skill as they are the cause and effect of a critical, analytic skepticism engendered through my art-historical training in close looking and formal analysis.

Bibliography

Primary Sources

PG = Patrologiae cursus completus, series graeca

Al-Ghazali, *The Recitation and Interpretation of the Qur'an.*
Trans. Muhammad Abul Quasem, *The Recitation and Interpretation of the Qur'an: Al-Ghazali's Theory* (London: Kegan Paul International, 1982).

Anonymous, *Anthologia Marciana.*
Ed. S. Lampros, "Ὁ Μαρκιανὸς κῶδιξ 524," *Neos Hellenomnemon* 8:2 (1911): 2–59, 123–92.
Trans. Paul Magdalino, "The Liturgical Poetics of an Elite Religious Confraternity," in Teresa Shawcross and Ida Toth (eds.), *Reading in the Byzantine Empire and Beyond* (Cambridge University Press, 2018), 116–32.

Anonymous, *Byzantine Book Epigrams.*
Ed. Maria Tomadaki and Paulien Lemay, "Occurrence 23121," in Kristoffel Demoen et al. (eds.), *Database of Byzantine Book Epigrams*, www.dbbe.ugent.be/occurrences/23121.

Anonymous, *Concilium universale Chalcedonense anno 451.*
Ed. E. Schwartz, *Acta conciliorum oecumenicorum*, vol. 2.1.2 (Berlin: De Gruyter, 1933).
Trans. Edward Rochie Hardy, "The Chalcedonian Decree," in Edward Rochie Hardy (ed.), *Christology of the Later Fathers* (Louisville, KY: Westminster John Knox Press, 1954; repr., 2006), 371–77.

Anonymous, *Dresden Praxapostolos.*
Ed. A.A. Dmitrievskii, *Древнейшие патриаршие типиконы: Святогорский Иерусалимский и Великой Константинопольской Церкви* (Kiev: Tip. I.I. Gorbunova, 1907).

Anonymous, *Patria Constantinopoleos.*
Ed. and trans. Albrect Berger, *Accounts of Medieval Constantinople: The Patria* (Washington, DC: Dumbarton Oaks Medieval Library, 2013).

Anonymous, *Synaxarium.*
Ed. Robert H. Jordan, *The Synaxarion of the Monastery of the Theotokos Evergetis*, 2 vols. (Queen's University of Belfast, 2000–05).

Anonymous, *Synodicon orthodoxiae*.
Ed. Jean Gouillard, "Le *Synodikon de l'Orthodoxie*: Édition et commentaire," *Travaux et Mémoires* 2 (1967): 1–316.

Anonymous, *Triodion*.
Ed. Anonymous, *ΤΡΙΩΔΙΟΝ*, 4th edn (Venice: Hellēnikou Typographeiou Ho Phoinix, 1876).
Trans. Mother Mary and Kallistos Ware, *The Lenten Triodion* (London: Faber and Faber, 1978).

Anonymous, *Typicon Magnae Ecclesiae*.
Ed. Juan Mateos, *Le Typicon de la Grande Église*, 2 vols. (Rome: Pont. Institutum Orientalium Studiorum, 1963–64).

Anonymous, *Vita S. Stephani Junioris*.
Ed. PG 100:1070–1186.

Anonymous, *Vita sanctae Theodosiae*.
Ed. S. Kotzabassi, *Das hagiographische Dossier der heiligen Theodosia von Konstantinopel*, Byzantinisches Archiv 21 (Berlin: De Gruyter, 2009).
Trans. Nicholas Constas, "Life of St. Theodosia of Constantinople," in Alice-Mary Talbot (ed.), *Byzantine Defenders of Images: Eight Saints' Lives in English Translation* (Washington, DC: Dumbarton Oaks, 1998), 3–7.

Anonymous, *Vita sanctorum Davidis, Symeonis et Georgii Mitylenae*.
Ed. J. van den Gheyn, "Acta Graeca ss. Davidis, Symeonis et Georgii Mitylenae in insula Lesbo," *Analecta Bollandiana* 18 (1899): 211–59.
Trans. Dorothy Abrahamse and Douglas Domingo-Forasté, "Life of Sts. David, Symeon, and George of Lesbos," in Alice-Mary Talbot (ed.), *Byzantine Defenders of Images: Eight Saints' Lives in English Translation* (Washington, DC: Dumbarton Oaks, 1998), 143–242.

Anonymous, *Vita Theodori Studitae*.
Ed. PG 99:114–232.

Aphthonios, *Progymnasmata*, 216.20–24.
Ed. Hugo Rabe, *Progymnasmata*, Rhetores Graeci 10 (Leipzig: Teubner, 1926).
Trans. George A. Kennedy, *Progymnasmata: Greek Textbooks of Prose Composition and Rhetoric* (Atlanta, GA: Society of Biblical Literature, 2003).

Athanasios of Alexandria, *De incarnatione verbi*.
Ed. Charles Kannengiesser, *Sur l'incarnation du Verbe*, Sources chrétiennes 199 (Paris: Éditions du Cerf, 1973).
Trans. John Behr, *On the Incarnation* (Yonkers, NY: St. Vladimir's Seminary Press, 2011).

Clement of Alexandria, *Protrepticus*.
Ed. and trans. G.W. Butterworth, *The Exhortation to the Greeks*, Loeb Classical Library 92 (Cambridge, MA: Harvard University Press, 1919).

Constantine VII Porphyrogennetos, *De cerimoniis aulae Byzantinae*.
Ed. and trans. Ann Moffatt and Maxeme Tall, *The Book of Ceremonies*, 2 vols. (Canberra: Australian Association for Byzantine Studies, 2012).
Ed. and French trans. A. Vogt, *Le livre des cérémonies*, 4 vols. (Paris: Les Belles Lettres, 1935–39).

Cyril of Alexandria, *Apologeticus ad Theodosium*.
Ed. E. Schwartz, *Acta conciliorum oecumenicorum 1.1.3* (Berlin: De Gruyter, 1927).

Germanos I, *Epistula domaticae*, 2 (or, *Epistula Germani ad Joannem episcopum Synadensem*).
Ed. J.D. Mansi, *Sacrorum conciliorum nova et amplissima collectio*, vol. 13 (Paris: H. Welter, 1902), 99–106.

Germanos I, *Historia mystica ecclesiae catholicae*.
Ed. and trans. Paul Meyendorff, *On the Divine Liturgy* (Crestwood, NY: St. Vladimir's Seminary Press, 1984).

Gregory of Nazianzus, *Funebris oratio in laudem Basilii Magni Caesareae in Cappadocia episcopi*.
Ed. F. Boulenger, *Discours funèbres en l'honneur de son frère Césaire et de Basile de Césarée* (Paris: Picard, 1908).

Ignatios of Antioch, *Epistulae vii genuinae*.
Ed. and trans. Michael Holmes "The Letter of Ignatius to the Ephesians," *The Apostolic Fathers: Greek Texts and English Translations*, 3rd ed. (Grand Rapids, MI: Baker Academic, 2007), 182–201.

Indikopleustes, Kosmas, *Topographia Christiana*, 2.82.
Ed. and trans. E.O. Winstedt, *The Christian Topography* (Cambridge University Press, 1909).

John of Damascus, *Orationes de imaginibus tres*.
Ed. P. Bonifatius Kotter, *Die Schriften des Johannes von Damaskos*, vol. 3, Patristische Texte und Studien 17 (Berlin: De Gruyter, 1975).
Trans. Andrew Louth, *Three Treatises on the Divine Images* (Crestwood, NY: St. Vladimir's Seminary Press, 2003).

Komnene, Anna, *Alexias*.
Ed. A. Kambylis and D.R. Reinsch, *Alexias*, Corpus Fontium Historiae Byzantinae, Series Berolinensis 60.1 (Berlin: De Gruyter, 2001).
Trans. E.R.A. Sewter, *The Alexiad* (New York: Penguin, 1969).

Loukas of Messina, *Acoluthia sanctae quadragesimae monasterii Christi Salvatoris in Messenae.*
Ed. Miguel Arranz, *Le Typicon du monastère du Saint-Sauveur à Messine*, Orientalia Christiana Analecta 185 (Rome: Pont. Institutum Orientalium Studiorum, 1969).

Michael the Deacon, *Ekphrasis of Hagia Sophia.*
Ed. and trans. Cyril Mango and John Parker, "A Twelfth-Century Description of St. Sophia," *Dumbarton Oaks Papers* 14 (1960): 233–45.

Nicholas of Myra, *Progymnasmata.*
Ed. J. Felten, *Progymnasmata*, Rhetores Graeci 11 (Leipzig: Teubner, 1913).
Trans. George A. Kennedy, *Progymnasmata: Greek Textbooks of Prose Composition and Rhetoric* (Atlanta, GA: Society of Biblical Literature, 2003).

Nicholas and Theodore of Andida, *Προθεωρία Κεφαλαιώδης.*
Ed. PG 140:413–68.

Nikephoros I, *Antirrheticus.*
Ed. PG 100:202–534.

Philes, Manuel, *Carmina.*
Ed. E. Miller, *Carmina*, vol. 1 (Paris: Excusum in Typographeo Imperiali, 1855).

Photios, *Epistulae et Amphilochia.*
Ed. L.G. Westerink, *Epistulae et Amphilochia*, vol. 6.1 (Leipzig: Teubner, 1987).
Trans. John Wilkinson, "Question 107 to Amphilochius," *Jerusalem Pilgrims before the Crusades* (Warminster: Aris & Phillips, 1977).

Photios, *Homiliae.*
Ed. Basileiou Laourdas, *ΟΜΙΛΙΑΙ* (Thessaloniki: Hetaireia Makedonikōn Spoudōn, 1959).
Trans. Cyril Mango, *The Homilies of Photius Patriarch of Constantinople* (Cambridge, MA: Harvard University Press, 1958).

Plato, *Ion.*
Ed. Albert Rijksbaron, *Ion, Or: On the Iliad* (Leiden: Brill, 2007).
Ed. and trans. W.R.M. Lamb, *Statesman. Philebus. Ion*, Loeb Classical Library 164 (Cambridge, MA: Harvard University Press, 1925).

Psellos, Michael, *Epistulae.*
Ed. Stratis Papaioannou, *Epistulae* (Leipzig: Teubner, 2019).

Psellos, Michael, *Oratoria minora*, 37 (or, Encomium for the Monk Ioannes Kroustoulas).

Ed. A. R. Littlewood, *Oratoria minora* (Leipzig: Teubner, 1985), 137–51.
Trans. Stratis Papaioannou, "Encomium for the Monk Ioannes Kroustoulas Who Read Aloud at the Holy Soros," in Charles Barber and Stratis Papaioannou (eds.), *Michael Psellos on Literature and Art: A Byzantine Perspective on Aesthetics* (Notre Dame University Press, 2017), 218–44.

Pseudo-Dionysios the Areopagite, *De coelesti hierarchia.*
Ed. Günter Heil and Adolf M. Ritter, *De coelesti hierarchia*, Patristische Texte und Studien 36 (Berlin: De Gruyter, 1991).
Trans. Colm Luibheid, "The Celestial Hierarchy," *Pseudo-Dionysius: The Complete Works* (New York: Paulist Press, 1987), 144–91.

Romanos the Melodist (dub.), *Ἀκάθιστος ὕμνος.*
Ed. and trans. Leena Peltomaa, *The Image of the Virgin Mary in the Akathistos Hymn* (Leiden: Brill, 2001).

Romanos the Melodist, *Cantica.*
Ed. José Grosdidier de Matons, *Romanos le Mélode: Hymnes*, 5 vols., Sources chrétiennes 99, 110, 114, 128, 283 (Paris: Éditions du Cerf, 1964–81).
Trans. Ephrem Lash, *On the Life of Christ: Kontakia* (San Francisco, CA: Harper Collins, 1995), 129–38.

Sikeliotes, John, *Vita Nicephori archiepiscopi Mileti.*
Ed. H. Delehaye, "Vita S. Nicephori," *Der Latmos. Milet* 3.1 (Berlin: Reimer, 1913), 157–71.

Silentiarios, Paul, *Descriptio ambonis*, 247–51.
Ed. Otto Veh, *Prokop. Bauten* (Munich: Heimeran, 1977), 358–75.
Cf. ed. Claudio de Stefani, *Descriptio ambonis* (Leipzig: Teubner, 2011).
Partial trans. Cyril Mango, *The Art of the Byzantine Empire, 312–1453: Sources and Documents* (University of Toronto Press, 1986), 91–96.

Silentiarios, Paul, *Descriptio Sanctae Sophiae.*
Ed. Otto Veh, *Prokop. Bauten* (Munich: Heimeran, 1977), 306–58.
Cf. ed. Claudio de Stefani, *Descriptio Sanctae Sophiae* (Leipzig: Teubner, 2011).
Partial trans. Cyril Mango, *The Art of the Byzantine Empire, 312–1453: Sources and Documents* (University of Toronto Press, 1986), 80–91.
Cf. Spanish trans. José M. Egea, *Paulo el Silenciario: Un poeta de la corte de Justiniano* (Granada: Centro de Estudios Bizantinos, Neogriegos y Chipriotas, 2007).

Sokrates of Constantinople (Scholastikos), *Historia ecclesiastica.*
Ed. Pierre Maraval and Pierre Périchon, *Histoire ecclésiastique*, vol. 3, Sources chrétiennes 505 (Paris: Éditions du Cerf, 2006).
Sozomenos, *Historia ecclesiastica.*

Ed. Jospeh Bidez and Günther C. Hansen, *Kirchengeschichte*, Die griechischen christlichen Schriftsteller 50 (Berlin: Akademie Verlag, 1960).

Stephen of Novgorod, *Wanderer*.
Ed. and trans. George P. Majeska, *Russian Travelers to Constantinople in the Fourteenth and Fifteenth Centuries* (Washington, DC: Dumbarton Oaks, 1984), 28–46.
Ed. M. N. Speranskij, *Из старинной Новгородской литературы XIV века* (Leningrad: USSR Academy of Sciences, 1934).

Symeon the Theologian, *Orationes ethicae*.
Ed. Jean Darrouzès, *Syméon le Nouveau Théologien, Traites théologiques et éthiques*, Sources chrétiennes 122 (Paris: Éditions du Cerf, 1966).
Trans. Alexander Golitzin, *On the Mystical Life: The Ethical Discourses*, vol. 1: *The Church and the Last Things* (Crestwood, NY: St. Vladimir's Seminary Press, 1995–97).

Symeon of Thessaloniki, *On the Rite of the Great Church*.
Ed. Jean Darrouzès, "Sainte-Sophie de Thessalonique d'après un ritual," *Revue des études byzantines* 34 (1976): 45–78.

Theodore of Stoudios, *Antirrhetici adversus iconomachus*.
Ed. PG 99:327–436.
Trans. Catharine Roth, *On the Holy Icons* (Crestwood, NY: St. Vladimir's Seminary Press, 1981).

Theodore of Stoudios, *Refutatio poematum iconomachorum*.
Ed. PG 99:435–78.

Secondary Sources

Abel, Jonathan et al., "Estimating Room Impulse Responses from Recorded Balloon Pops," paper presented at Audio Engineering Society Convention (November 2010), www.aes.org/e-lib/browse.cfm?elib=15594.

Ahmed, Sara, *Queer Phenomenology: Orientations, Objects, Others* (Durham, NC: Duke University Press, 2006).

Akent'ev, K. K., *Типикон Великой Церкви. Cod. Dresde A 104. Реконструкция текста по материалам архива А.А. Дмитриевского*, Subsidia Byzantinorossica 5 (Saint Petersburg: Vizantinorossica, 2008).

Alexander, Paul J., *The Byzantine Apocalyptic Tradition* (Berkeley: University of California Press, 1985).

Alpers, Svetlana, "Is Art History?," *Daedalus* 106:3 (Summer 1977): 1–13.

Altripp, Michael, "Remarks on the Synthronon and Episcopal Throne in the Byzantine Churches of Greece," *Bulletin de correspondence hellénique* 124:1 (2000): 377–412.

Anastos, Milton, "The Ethical Theory of Images Formulated by the Iconoclasts in 754 and 815," *Dumbarton Oaks Papers* 8 (1954): 153–60.

Anderson, Jeffrey C., "Cod. Vat. gr. 463 and an Eleventh-Century Byzantine Painting Center," *Dumbarton Oaks Papers* 32 (1978): 175–96.

"The Date and Purpose of the Barberini Psalter," *Cahiers archéologiques* 31 (1983): 35–67.

"The Illustrated Sermons of James the Monk: Their Dates, Order, and Place in the History of Byzantine Art," *Viator* 22 (1991): 69–120.

"The Illustration of Cod. Sinai. Gr. 339," *Art Bulletin* 61:2 (1979): 167–85.

The New York Cruciform Lectionary (University Park, PA: Pennsylvania State University Press, 1992).

"On the Nature of the Theodore Psalter," *Art Bulletin* 70:4 (1988): 550–68.

"The Palimpsest Psalter, Pantokrator Cod. 61: Its Content and Relationship to the Bristol Psalter," *Dumbarton Oaks Papers* 48 (1994): 199–220.

"The Seraglio Octateuch and the Kokkinobaphos Master," *Dumbarton Oaks Papers* 36 (1982): 83–114.

"The Walters Praxapostolos and Liturgical Illustration," *Δελτίον Χριστιανικής Αρχαιολογικής Εταιρείας* 19 (1997): 9–38.

Anderson, Jeffrey C., and Stephano Parenti, *A Byzantine Monastic Office, 1105 A.D.* (Washington, DC: Catholic University of America Press, 2016).

Antonopoulos, Spyridon, Sharon E.J. Gerstel, Chris Kyriakakis, Konstantinos T. Raptis, and James Donahue, "Soundscapes of Byzantium," *Speculum* 92:S1 (2017): S321–35.

Appadurai, Arjun (ed.), *The Social Life of Things: Commodities in Cultural Perspective* (Cambridge University Press, 1986).

Atkinson, Niall, *The Noisy Renaissance: Sound, Architecture, and Florentine Urban Life* (University Park: Pennsylvania State University Press, 2016).

Atsalos, Basilios, *La terminologie du livre-manuscrit à l'époque byzantine: Termes désignant le livre-manuscrit e l'écriture* (Thessaloniki: Hetaireia Makedonikōn Spoudōn, 1971).

Auzépy, Marie-France, "La destruction de l'icône du Christ de la Chalcé par Léon III: Propagande ou réalité?," *Byzantion* 60 (1990): 445–92.

Baade, Isobel J. and Eric C. Baade, "The Red Stones Speak: Porphyry Discs in the Pavements of Roman Churches," in Gareth Schmeling and Jon D. Mikalson (eds.), *Qui miscuit utile dulci: Festschrift Essays for Paul Lachlan MacKendrick* (Wauconda, IL: Bolchazy-Carducci, 1998), 1–15.

Bakirtzis, Charalambos et al., *Mosaics of Thessaloniki: 4th to 14th Century*, trans. Alexandra Doumas (Athens: Kapon, 2012).

Bakirtzis, Charalambos, and Pelli Mastora, "Are the Mosaics in the Rotunda into Thessaloniki Linked to its Conversion as a Christian Church?," in

Miša Rakocija (ed.), *Niš and Byzantium* (University of Niš, 2011), 33–45.

Barad, Karen, *Meeting the Universe Halfway: Quantum Physics and the Entanglement of Matter and Meaning* (Durham, NC: Duke University Press, 2007).

"Posthumanist Performativity: Toward an Understanding of How Matter Comes to Matter," *Signs: Journal of Women in Culture and Society* 28:3 (Spring 2003): 801–31.

Barber, Charles, *Contesting the Logic of Painting: Art and Understanding in Eleventh-Century Byzantium* (Leiden: Brill, 2007).

Figure and Likeness: On the Limits of Representation in Byzantine Iconoclasm (Princeton University Press, 2002).

"The Koimesis Church, Nicaea: The Limits of Representation on the Eve of Iconoclasm," *Jahrbuch der Österreichischen Byzantinistik* 41 (1991): 43–60.

Barbour, Ruth, "Summary Description of the Greek Manuscripts from the Library at Holkham Hall," *Bodleian Library Record* 6 (1960): 591–613.

Barry, Fabio, "Walking on Water: Cosmic Floors in Antiquity and the Middle Ages," *Art Bulletin* 89:4 (2007): 627–56.

Barthes, Roland, "The Grain of the Voice," *Image-Music-Text*, trans. Stephen Heath (New York: Hill & Wang, 1977), 179–89.

Bassett, Sarah, *The Urban Image of Late Antique Constantinople* (Cambridge University Press, 2004).

Bauer, Franz Alto, "Urban Space and Ritual: Constantinople in Late Antiquity," *Acta ad archaeologiam et artium historiam pertinentia* 15 (2001): 27–61.

Bennett, Jane, *Vibrant Matter: A Political Ecology of Things* (Durham, NC: Duke University Press, 2010).

Bernard, Floris, *Writing and Reading Byzantine Secular Poetry, 1025–1081* (Oxford University Press, 2014).

Bertonière, Gabriel, *The Sundays of Lent in the Tridion: The Sundays without a Commemoration* (Rome: Pont. Institutum Orientalium Studiorum, 1997).

Betancourt, Roland, "A Byzantine Liturgical Commentary in Verse: Introduction and Translation," *Orientalia Christiana Periodica* 81:2 (2015): 433–72.

"Extended in the Imagination: The Representation of Architectural Space in Byzantium," in Vasileios Marinis, Amy Papalexandrou, and Jordan Pickett (eds.), *Architecture and Visual Culture in the Late Antique and Medieval Mediterranean. Studies in Honor of Robert G. Ousterhout* (Turnhout: Brepols, 2020).

"Faltering Images: Failure and Error in Byzantine Manuscript Illumination," *Word & Image* 32:1 (2016): 1–20.

"Medieval Art after Duchamp: Hans Belting's *Likeness and Presence* at 25," *Gesta* 55:1 (2016): 5–17.

"Prolepsis and Anticipation: The Apocalyptic Futurity of the Now, East and West," in Michael A. Ryan (ed.), *A Companion to the Premodern*

Apocalypse, Brill's Companions to the Christian Tradition series (Leiden: Brill, 2015), 176–204.

"Representation as Indwelling: Contextualizing Michael Psellos's *empsychos graphe* across Artistic, Liturgical, and Literary Theory," *Byzantine and Modern Greek Studies* (forthcoming).

"Review of Bissera Pentcheva's Hagia Sophia: Sound, Space, and Spirit in Byzantium (University Park: Pennsylvania State University Press, 2017)," *Art Bulletin*, 101:4 (2019): 142–45.

Sight, Touch, and Imagination in Byzantium (Cambridge University Press, 2018).

"Why Sight Is Not Touch: Reconsidering the Tactility of Vision in Byzantium," *Dumbarton Oaks Papers* 70 (2016): 1–23.

Bettini, Maurizio, *Voci: Antropologia sonora del mondo antico* (Turin: Einaudi, 2008).

Bingham, Steven, *The Image of God the Father in Orthodox Theology and Iconography: And Other Studies* (Crestwood, NY: St. Vladimir's Seminary Press, 1995).

Boeck, Elena, *Imagining the Byzantine Past: The Perception of History in the Illustrated Manuscripts of Skylitzes and Manasses* (Cambridge University Press, 2015).

Bogdanović, Jelena, *The Framing of Sacred Space: The Canopy and the Byzantine Church (ca. 300–1500)* (Oxford University Press, 2017).

Bogost, Ian, *Alien Phenomenology, or What It's Like to Be a Thing* (Minneapolis: University of Minnesota Press, 2012).

Persuasive Games: The Expressive Power of Videogames (Cambridge, MA: MIT Press, 2007).

Bolter, Jay David, and Richard Grusin, *Remediation: Understanding New Media* (Cambridge, MA: MIT Press, 1998).

Bouras, Laskarina, and Maria Parani, "The Lighting System of Hagia Sophia in Constantinople," in Laskarina Bouras and Maria Parani (eds.), *Lighting in Early Byzantium* (Washington, DC: Dumbarton Oaks, 2008), 31–36.

Bourbouhakis, Emmanuel, "Rhetoric and Performance," in Paul Stephenson (ed.), *The Byzantine World* (London: Routledge, 2010), 175–87.

(organizer), "The Sound of Sense: Orality/Aurality in Byzantine Texts and Contexts," Symposium, Princeton University, May 16–17, 2015.

Boynton, Susan, and Diane J. Reilly (eds.), *Resounding Images: Medieval Intersections of Art, Music, and Sound* (Turnhout: Brepols, 2015).

Brightman, Frank Edward, *Liturgies Eastern and Western*, vol. 1: *Eastern Liturgies* (Oxford: Clarendon Press, 1896).

Brown, Bill, "Thing Theory," *Critical Inquiry* 28:1 (2001): 1–22.

Browning, Robert, *Medieval and Modern Greek*, 2nd edn (Cambridge University Press, 1983).

Brubaker, Leslie, "The Chalke Gate, the Construction of the Past, and the Trier Ivory," *Byzantine and Modern Greek Studies* 23 (1999): 258–85.

"Image, Meta-Text and Text in Byzantium," in Shoishi Sato (ed.), *Herméneutique du texte d'histoire: orientation, interprétation et questions nouvelles* (Nagoya University, 2009), 93–100.

"The Introduction of Painted Initials in Byzantium," *Scriptorium* 45:1 (1991): 22–46.

"Pictures are Good to Think With: Looking at Byzantium," in Paolo Odorico, Panagiotis A. Agapitos, and Martin Hinterberger (eds.), *L'écriture de la mémoire: La littérarité de l'historiographie* (Paris: École des Hautes Études en Sciences Sociales, 2006), 221–52.

"Politics, Patronage, and Art in the Ninth Century: The Homilies of Gregory Nazianzus in Paris (B.N. gr. 510)," *Dumbarton Oaks Papers* 39 (1985): 1–13.

Vision and Meaning in Ninth-Century Byzantium (Cambridge University Press, 1998).

Bruns, Gerald L., *Hermeneutics Ancient and Modern* (New Haven, CT: Yale University Press, 1992).

Burns, Yvonne, "The Historical Events that Occasioned the Inception of the Byzantine Gospel Lectionary," *Jahrbuch der Österreichischen Byzantinistik* 32:4 (1982): 119–27.

"The Lectionary of the Patriarch of Constantinople," *Studia Patristica* 15:1 (1984): 515–20.

Butler, Shane, *The Ancient Phonograph* (Brooklyn: Zone, 2015).

Butler, Shane, and Alex Purves (eds.), *Synaesthesia and the Ancient Senses* (Durham, NC: Acumen, 2013).

Camille, Michael, *Image on the Edge: The Margins of Medieval Art* (London: Reaktion, 1992).

"Seeing and Reading: Some Visual Implications of Medieval Literacy and Illiteracy," *Art History* 8 (1985), 26–49.

Carile, Maria Cristina, "Imperial Palaces and Heavenly Jerusalems: Real and Ideal Palaces in Late Antiquity," in Alexei Lidov (ed.), *New Jerusalems: Hierotopy and Iconography of Sacred Spaces* (Moscow: Indrik, 2009), 78–102.

The Vision of the Palace of the Byzantine Emperors as a Heavenly Jerusalem (Spoleto: Fondazione Centro Italiano di studi sull'alto Medioevo, 2012).

Carruthers, Mary, *The Book of Memory: A Study of Memory in Medieval Culture*, 2nd edn (Cambridge University Press, 2008).

Casey, Maurice, *Son of Man: The Interpretation and Influence of Daniel* (London: Society for Promoting Christian Knowledge, 1979).

Cavallo, Guglielmo, *Lire à Byzance*, trans. P. Odorico and A. Segonds (Paris: Belles Lettres, 2006).

Chen, Mel Y., *Animacies: Biopolitics, Racial Mattering, and Queer Affect* (Durham, NC: Duke University Press, 2012).

Chion, Michel, *Audio-Vision: Sound on Screen*, trans. Claudia Gorbman (New York: Columbia University Press, 1994).

Collins, John, *Daniel: A Commentary on the Book of Daniel* (Minneapolis: Fortress, 1993).

Cormack, Robin, "Interpreting the Mosaics of S. Sophia at Istanbul," *Art History* 4:2 (1981): 131–49.

"Women and Icons, and Women in Icons," in Liz James (ed.), *Women, Men and Eunuchs: Gender in Byzantium* (London: Routledge, 1997), 24–51.

Writing in Gold: Byzantine Society and Its Icons (Oxford University Press, 1985).

Corrigan, Kathleen, "Visualizing the Divine: An Early Byzantine Icon of the 'Ancient of Days' at Mount Sinai," in Sharon E.J. Gerstel and Robert S. Nelson (eds.), *Approaching the Holy Mountain: Art and Liturgy at St. Catherine's Monastery in the Sinai* (Turnhout: Brepols, 2010), 285–303.

Cotsonis, John, *Byzantine Figural Procession Crosses* (Washington, DC: Dumbarton Oaks, 1994).

"New Light on the Dionysiou Lectionary," MA thesis, Pennsylvania State University (1986).

"On Some Illustrations in the Lectionary, Athos, Dionysiou 587," *Byzantion* 59 (1989): 5–19.

Cunningham, Mary B., "Messages in Context: The Reading of Sermons in Byzantine Churches and Monasteries," in Angeliki Lymberopoulou (ed.), *Images of the Byzantine World: Visions, Messages and Meanings: Studies Presented to Leslie Brubaker* (Burlington, VT: Ashgate, 2011), 83–98.

Cutler, Anthony, "Liturgical Strata in the Marginal Psalters," *Dumbarton Oaks Papers* 34–35 (1980–81): 17–30.

Dagron, Gilbert, *Emperor and Priest: The Imperial Office in Byzantium*, trans. Jean Birrell (Cambridge University Press, 2003).

Dale, Thomas E.A., "Monsters, Corporeal Deformities, and Phantasms in the Cloister of St-Michel-de-Cuxa," *Art Bulletin* 83:3 (September 2001): 402–36.

Daley, Brian, *Gregory of Nazianzus* (London: Routledge, 2006).

Dark, Ken, and Jan Kostenec, "The Byzantine Patriarchate in Constantinople and the Baptistery of the Church of Hagia Sophia," *Architectura* 36 (2006): 113–30.

Hagia Sophia in Context: An Archaeological Re-examination of the Cathedral of Byzantine Constantinople (Oxford: Oxbow, 2019).

"Paul the Silentiary's Description of Hagia Sophia in the Light of New Archaeological Evidence," *Byzantinoslavica* 69:3 (2011): 88–105.

De Vries, Irmgard, *The Epistles, Gospels, and the Tones of the Byzantine Liturgical Year* (Antwerp: Vita et Pax, 1954).

Demarrais, Elizabeth, "The Materialisation of Culture," in Elizabeth Demarrais, Chris Godsen, and A. Colin Renfrew (eds.), *Rethinking Materiality: The Engagement of Mind with the Material World* (Cambridge: McDonald Institute, 2004), 11–22.

Dennert, Martin, "Mittelbyzantinische Ambone in Kleinasien," *Mitteilungen des deutschen archäologischen Instituts. Abteilung Istanbul* 45 (1995):137–47.

Denny, Frederick, "The *Adab* of Quran Recitation: Text and Context," in A.H. Johns (ed.), *International Congress for the Study of the Quran* (Canberra: Australian National University, 1981), 143–60.

"Exegesis and Recitation: Their Development as Classical Forms of Quranic Piety," in Frank E. Reynolds and Theodore M. Ludwig (eds.), *Transitions and Transformations in the History of Religions* (Leiden: Brill, 1980), 91–123.

Der Nersessian, Sirarpie, "The Illustrations of the Homilies of Gregory of Nazianzus, Paris gr. 510," *Dumbarton Oaks Papers* 16 (1962): 197–228.

"A Psalter and New Testament Manuscript at Dumbarton Oaks," *Dumbarton Oaks Papers* 19 (1965): 153–83.

Derrida, Jacques, "Différance," *Speech and Phenomena, and Other Essays on Husserl's Theory of Signs*, trans. David Allison (Evanston, IL: Northwestern University Press, 1973), 129–60.

Dirimtekin, Feridun, "Le local de Patriarcat à Sainte Sophie," *Istanbuler Mitteilungen* 13–14 (1963–64): 113–27.

"Le skeuophylakion de Sainte-Sophie," *Revue des études byzantines* 19 (1961): 390–400.

Dolezal, Mary-Lyon, "Illuminating the Liturgical Word: Text and Image in a Decorated Lectionary (Mount Athos, Dionysiou Monastery, cod. 587)," *Word & Image* 12:1 (1996): 23–60.

"The Middle Byzantine Lectionary: Textual and Pictorial Expression of Liturgical Ritual," 2 vols., PhD dissertation, University of Chicago (1991).

Downey, Glanville, "Earthquakes at Constantinople and Vicinity, A.D. 342–1454," *Speculum* 30:4 (1955): 596–600.

Drpić, Ivan, *Epigram, Art, and Devotion in Later Byzantium* (Cambridge University Press, 2016).

Dufrenne, Suzy, *L'illustration des Psautiers grecs du Moyen Âge*, vol. 1 (Paris: C. Klincksieck, 1966).

Ebersolt, Jean, *Sainte-Sophie de Constantinople: Étude de topographie d'après les cérémonies* (Paris: E. Leroux, 1910).

Elkins, James, "On Some Limits of Materiality in Art History," *31: Das Magazin des Instituts für Theorie* [Zürich] 12 (2008): 24–30.

Emerson, William, and Robert L. Van Nice, "Hagia Sophia: Construction of the Second Dome and Its Later Repairs," *Archaeology* 4:3 (1951): 162–71.

Engberg, Sysse Gudrun, "Greek Ekphonetic Notation: The Classical and the Pre-Classical Systems," in Jørgen Raasted and Christian Troelsgård (eds.), *Palaeobyzantine Notations: A Reconsideration of the Source Material* (Hernen: A.A. Bredius Foundation, 1995), 33–55.

"The Greek Old Testament Lectionary as a Liturgical Book," *Cahiers de l'Insititut de Moyen Age grec et latin* 54 (1986): 39–48.

Erlmann, Veit, *Reason and Resonance: A History of Modern Aurality* (Brooklyn: Zone, 2010).

Evangelatou, Maria, "From Word into Image: The Visualization of Ulcer in Byzantine Illustrated Manuscripts of the Book of Job," *Gesta* 48:1 (2009): 19–36.

"Liturgy and the Illustration of the Ninth-Century Byzantine Marginal Psalters," *Dumbarton Oaks Papers* 63 (2011): 59–116.

Fanar, Emma Maayan, *Revelation through the Alphabet: Aniconism and Illuminated Initial Letters in Byzantine Artistic Imagination* (Geneva: La Pomme d'Or, 2011).

Featherstone, Michael, "Der Große Palast von Konstantinopel: Tradition oder Erfindung?," *Byzantinische Zeitschrift* 106:1 (2013): 19–38.

Feld, Steven, "Places Sensed, Senses Placed: Toward a Sensuous Epistemology of Environments," in David Howes (ed.), *Empire of the Senses: The Sensual Culture Reader* (New York: Berg, 2005), 179–91.

"A Poetics of Place: Ecological and Aesthetic Co-evolution in a Papua New Guinea Rainforest Community," in R. Ellen and K. Fukui (eds.), *Redefining Nature: Ecology, Culture, and Domestication* (New York: Berg, 1996), 61–87.

Sound and Sentiment: Birds, Weeping, Poetics, and Song in Kaluli Expression, 2nd ed. (Philadelphia: University of Pennsylvania Press, 1990).

"Waterfalls of Song: An Acoustemology of Place Resounding in Bosavi, Papua New Guinea," in Steven Feld and Keith H. Basso (eds.), *Senses of Place* (Santa Fe, NM: School of American Research Press, 1996), 91–135.

Feuillet, A., "Le Fils de l'homme de Daniel et la tradition biblique," *Revue biblique* 60 (1953): 170–202.

Fıratlı, Nezih, *Les stèles funéraires de Byzance gréco-romaine* (Paris: A. Maisonneuve, 1964).

Fisher, Susannah, "Formulating Viewer Response: Early Medieval Treasury Bindings," in Elise Louviot (ed.), *La formule au Moyen Âge* (Turnhout: Brepols, 2012), 295–313.

Flood, Finbarr Barry, *The Great Mosque of Damascus: Studies on the Makings of an Umayyad Visual Culture* (Leiden: Brill, 2001).

Flusin, Bernard, "Les cérémonies de l'exaltation de la Croix à Constantinople au XIe siècle d'après le Dresdensis," in Jannic Durand and Bernard Flusin (eds.), *Byzance et les reliques du Christ* (Paris: Centre de Recherche d'Histoire et Civilisation de Byzance, 2004), 61–89.

"Le Triomphe des images et la nouvelle définition de l'Orthodoxie: À propos d'un chapitre du *De cerimoniis* (I. 37)," in Antonio Rigo and Pavel Ermilov (eds.), *Orthodoxy and Heresy in Byzantium: The Definition and the Notion of Orthodoxy and Some Other Studies on the Heresies and the Non-Christian Religions* (Rome: Università degli Studi di Roma, 2010), 3–20.

Fonkitch, Boris L., "Notes paléographiques sur les manuscrits grecs de bibliothèques italiennes," *Thesaurismata* 16 (1979): 153–57.

Foucault, Michel, "The Discourse on Language," *The Archaeology of Knowledge; and, The Discourse on Language*, trans. A.M. Sheridan Smith (New York: Pantheon, 1972), 215–38.

Franc-Sgourdeou, Catherine, "Les initiales historiées dans les manuscrits byzantins aux XIe–XIIe siècles," *Byzantinoslavica* 2 (1967): 336–54.

Franses, Rico, "When All that Is Gold Does Not Glitter: On the Strange History of Looking at Byzantine Art," in Antony Eastmond and Liz James (eds.), *Icon and Word: The Power of Images in Byzantium. Studies Presented to Robin Cormack* (Aldershot: Ashgate, 2003), 13–24.

Frazer, Margaret English, "Church Doors and the Gates of Paradise: Byzantine Bronze Doors in Italy," *Dumbarton Oaks Papers* 27 (1973): 145–62.

Freeman, Evan, "Entry, Offering, and Intercession: The Problem of Iconographic Programming on the Middle Byzantine Processional Cross at the Musée de Cluny in Paris," ThM Thesis, St. Vladimir's Orthodox Theological Seminary (2012).

Fricke, Beate, "Jesus Wept! On the History of Anthropophagy: A New Reading of a Miniature from the Gospel Book of Otto III as *Kippfigur*," *RES: Anthropology and Aesthetics* 59–60 (2011): 192–205.

Frolow, Anatole, "Le Christ de la Chalcè," *Byzantion* 33 (1963): 107–20.

"Numismatique byzantine et archéologie des lieux saints, au sujet d'une monnaie de l'impératrice Eudocia (Ve siècle)," in *Mémorial Louis Petit: Mélanges d'histoire et d'archéologie byzantines* (Bucharest: Institute Français d'Études Byzantines, 1948), 78–94.

Gadamer, Hans-Georg, *Truth and Method*, 2nd edn, trans. Joel Weinsheimer and Donald G. Marshall (New York: Crossroad, 1989).

Gade, Anna M., *Perfection Makes Practice: Learning, Emotion, and the Recited Qur'ān in Indonesia* (Honolulu: University of Hawai'i Press, 2004).

Galadza, Daniel, "A Greek Source of the Jerusalem Lectionary: Sinai Gr. N.E. MΓ 8 (10th c.)," in Diliana Atanassova and Tinatin Chronz (eds.), *Synaxis Katholike: Beiträge zu Gottesdienst und Geschichte der fünf altkirchlichen Patriarchate für Heinzgerd Brakmann zum 70. Geburtstag* (Vienna: Lit Verlag, 2014), 213–28.

"The Jerusalem Lectionary and the Byzantine Rite," in Bert Groen, Daniel Galadza, Nina Glibetić, and Gabriel Radle (eds.), *Rites and Rituals of the Christian East* (Leuven: Peeters, 2014), 181–99.

Liturgy and Byzantinization in Jerusalem (Oxford University Press, 2018).

Galavaris, George, "'Christ the King': A Miniature in a Byzantine Gospels and Its Significance," *Jahrbuch der Österreichischen Byzantinistik* 21 (1972): 119–26.

The Illustrations of the Liturgical Homilies of Gregory Nazianzenus (Princeton University Press, 1969).

"Manuscripts and the Liturgy," in G. Vikan (ed.), *Illuminated Greek Manuscripts from American Collections: An Exhibition in Honor of Kurt Weitzmann* (Princeton University Press, 1973), 20–25.

Gamillscheg, Ernst, "Die Lektüre der Bibel in Byzanz: Kurze Beobachtungen zu einigen griechischen Handschriften mit Bibelkatenen," in Claudia Rapp and Andreas Külzer (eds.), *The Bible in Byzantium: Appropriation, Adaptation, Interpretation* (Göttingen: Vandenhoeck & Ruprecht, 2018), 39–46.

Ganz, David, *Buch-Gewänder: Prachteinbände im Mittelalter* (Berlin: Reimer, 2015).

Gaul, Niels, "The Letter in the *Theatron*: Epistolary Voice, Character, Soul and Their Audience," in Alexander Riehle (ed.), *A Companion to Byzantine Epistolary* (Leiden: Brill, forthcoming).

"Performative Reading in the Late Byzantine *Theatron*," in Shawcross and Toth (eds.), *Reading in the Byzantine Empire*, 215–33.

Gell, Alfred, *Art and Agency: An Anthropological Theory* (Oxford: Clarendon Press, 1998).

Gerstel, Sharon, *Beholding the Sacred Mysteries: Programs of the Byzantine Sanctuary* (Seattle: University of Washington Press, 1999).

"Liturgical Scrolls in the Byzantine Sanctuary," *Greek, Roman and Byzantine Studies* 35:2 (1994): 195–204.

Gerstel, Sharon E.J., Chris Kyriakakis, Konstantinos T. Raptis, Spyridon Antonopoulos, and James Donahue, "Soundscapes of Byzantium: The Acheiropoietos Basilica and the Cathedral of Hagia Sophia in Thessaloniki," *Hesperia: The Journal of the American School of Classical Studies at Athens* 87:1 (2018): 177–213.

Getcha, Job, "Le système des lectures bibliques du rite byzantin," in A.M. Triacca and A. Pistoia (eds.), *La liturgie, interprète de l'écriture*, vol. 1 (Rome: Edizioni Liturgiche, 2003), 25–56.

Gitelman, Lisa, *Always Already New: Media, History, and the Data of Culture* (Cambridge, MA: MIT Press, 2006).

Godsen, Chris, "What Do Objects Want?," *Journal of Archaeological Method and Theory* 12:3 (2005): 193–211.

Grabar, André, "A propos des mosaïques de la coupole de Saint-Georges a Salonique," *Cahiers Archéologiques* 17 (1967): 59–81.

Ampoules de Terre Sainte (Paris: Klincksieck, 1958).

Christian Iconography: A Study of Its Origins, trans. Terry Grabar (Princeton University Press, 1968).

"La représentation de l'intelligible dans l'art byzantin du Moyen Âge," in André Grabar (ed.), *L'art de la fin de l'antiquité et du Moyen Âge*, vol. 1 (Paris: Collège de France, 1968), 51–62.

Graham, William A., *Beyond the Written Word: Oral Aspects of Scripture in the History of Religion* (Cambridge University Press, 1987).

"Quran as Spoken Word: An Islamic Contribution to the Understanding of Scripture," in Richard C. Martin (ed.), *Approaches to Islam in Religious Studies* (Tucson: University of Arizona Press, 1985), 23–40.

Grosdidier de Matons, José, "Liturgie et hymnographie: Kontakion et canon," *Dumbarton Oaks Papers* 34–35 (1980–81): 31–43.

Romanos le Mélode: Hymnes, vol. 4, Sources chrétiennes 128 (Paris: Éditions du Cerf, 1967).

Grumel, Venance, "Léon de Chalcédoine et le canon de la fête du saint Mandylion," *Analecta Bollandiana* 68 (1950), 135–52.

Guidobaldi, Alessandra Guiglia, "Note preliminari per una definizione dell'arte pavimentale costantinopolitana dei primi secoli," *Jahrbuch der österreichischen Byzantinistik* 32:4 (1982): 403–13.

"L'opus sectile pavimentale in area bizantina," in Raffaella Farioli Campanati (ed.), *Atti del I Colloquio dell' Associazione Italiana per lo Studio e la Conservazione del Mosaico* (Ravenna: Edizioni del Girasole, 1994), 643–63.

Guidobaldi, Alessandra Guiglia and Claudia Barsanti, "Il progetto di ricercar sui marmi della Santa Sofia," in Augusta Acconcia Longo et al. (eds.), *La sapienza bizantina: un secolo di ricerche sulla civiltà di Bisanzio all'Universita di Roma* (Rome: Campisano, 2012), 55–78.

Guidobaldi, Federico and Silvia Pedone, "Il viraggio delle scelte decorative nei rivestimenti pavimentali e parietali in età constantiniana: dagli antefatti agli esiti," *Musiva & Sectilia* 8 (2011): 35–162.

Harman, Graham, *Tool-Being: Heidegger and the Metaphysics of Objects* (Chicago: Open Court, 2002).

Hawkins, Ernest J.W., "Further Observations on the Narthex Mosaic in St. Sophia at Istanbul," *Dumbarton Oaks Papers* 22 (1968): 151–66.

Heidegger, Martin, *Being and Time*, trans. John Macquarrie and Edward Robinson (New York: Harper, 1962).

Heller-Roazen, Daniel, *The Fifth Hammer: Pythagoras and the Disharmony of the World* (Brooklyn: Zone, 2011).

Hirschkind, Charles, *The Ethical Soundscape: Cassette Sermons and Islamic Counterpublics* (New York: Columbia University Press, 2006).

"The Ethics of Listening: Cassette-Sermon Audition in Contemporary Egypt," *American Ethnologist* 28:3 (2001): 623–49.

Hodder, Ian, *Entangled: An Archaeology of the Relationships between Humans and Things* (Malden, MA: Wiley-Blackwell, 2012).

Høeg, Carsten, *La notation ekphonétique* (Copenhagen: Levin & Munksgaard, 1935).

Hörandner, Wolfram, *Der Prosarhythmus in der rhetorischen Literatur der Byzantiner* (Vienna: Verlag der Osterreichischen Akademie der Wissenschaften, 1981).

Howard, Deborah, *Sound and Space in Renaissance Venice* (New Haven, CT: Yale University Press, 2010).

Huang, P. et al., "Reverberation Echo Density of Psychoacoustics," paper presented at Audio Engineering Society Convention (November 2008), www.aes.org/e-lib/browse.cfm?elib=14735.

Hunger, Herbert, *Schreiben und Lesen in Byzanz: Die byzantinische Buchkultur* (Munich: C.H. Beck, 1989).

Hutter, Irmgard, "Decorative Systems in Byzantine Manuscripts, and the Scribe as Artist: Evidence from Manuscripts in Oxford," *Word & Image* 12:1 (1996): 4–22.

"Die Homilien des Mönches Jakobos und ihre Illustrationen," PhD dissertation, University of Vienna (1970).

"Some Aspects of Byzantine Manuscript Illumination Reconsidered," in E.N. Dobrynina (ed.), *Drevnerusskoe iskusstvo: Iskusstvo rukopisnoi knigi: Vizantiia, Drevniaia Rus'* (Saint Petersburg: Dmitrii Bulanin, 2004), 21–43.

Hutter, Irmgard and Paul Canart, *Das Marienhomiliar des Mönches Jakobos von Kokkinobaphos, Codex Vaticanus graecus 1162*, 2 vols. (Vatican, 1991).

Ingold, Tim, "Materials against Materiality," *Archaeological Dialogues* 14:1 (2007): 1–16.

Jamil, Nadia, "Caliph and *Qutb*: Poetry as a Source for Interpreting the Transformation of the Byzantine Cross on Steps on Umayyad Coinage," in Jeremy Johns (ed.), *Bayt al-Maqdis, Part Two: Jerusalem and Early Islam* (Oxford University Press, 2000), 11–57.

Janin, Raymond, *La géographie ecclésiastique de l'Empire byzantin*, 3 vols. (Paris: Institut Français d'Études Byzantines, 1953).

Jantzen, H. *Die Hagia Sophia des Kaisers Justinian in Konstantinopel* (Cologne: DuMont Schauberg, 1967).

Jeffreys, Elizabeth, "The Sevastokratorissa Eirene as Literary Patroness: The Monk Iakovos," *Jahrbuch der Österreichischen Byzantinistik* 32:3 (1982): 63–71.

Jenkins, Henry, *Convergence Culture: Where Old and New Media Collide* (New York: NYU Press, 2006).

Jenkins, Romilly J.H. and Cyril Mango, "A Synodicon of Antioch and Lacedaemonia," *Dumbarton Oaks Papers* 15 (1961): 225–42.

Juack, K., "Zu den griechischen Lektionaren und ihrer Überlieferung der Katholischen Briefe," in Kurt Aland (ed.), *Die alten Übersetzungen des Neuen Testaments, die Kirchenväterzitate und Lektionare*, Arbeiten zur neutestamentlichen Textforschung 5 (Berlin: De Gruyter, 1972), 498–589.

Kakoulidi, Eleni D., "Κατάλογος τῶν ἑλληνικῶν χειρογράφων τοῦ Ἑλληνικοῦ Ἰνστιτούτου Βενετίας," *Thesaurismata* 8 (1971): 249–73.

Kalopissi-Verti, Sophia, "The Proskynetaria of the Templon and the Narthex: Form, Imagery, Spatial Connections, and Reception," in Sharon E.J. Gerstel (ed.), *Thresholds of the Sacred: Architectural, Art Historical, Liturgical, and Theological Perspectives on Religious Screens, East and West* (Washington, DC: Dumbarton Oaks, 2006), 106–32.

Kane, Brian, *Sound Unseen: Acousmatic Sound in Theory and Practice* (New York: Oxford University Press, 2014).

Kauffmann, C.M., "The Sainte-Chapelle Lectionaries and the Illustration of the Parables in the Middle Ages," *Journal of the Warburg and Courtauld Institutes* 67 (2004): 1–22.

Kavrus-Hoffmann, Nadia, "Catalogue of Greek Medieval and Renaissance Manuscripts in the Collections of the United States of America. Part V.1: Harvard University, The Houghton Library," *Manuscripta* 54 (2010): 64–147.

Kazhdan, Alexander, "A Note on the 'Middle-Byzantine' Ambo," *Byzantion* 57 (1987): 422–26.

Keogh, Brendan, *A Play of Bodies: How We Perceive Videogames* (Cambridge, MA: MIT Press, 2018).

Kessler, Herb, "The Psalter," in Gary Vikan (ed.), *Illuminated Greek Manuscripts from American Collections: An Exhibition in Honor of Kurt Weitzmann* (Princeton University Press, 1973), 31–33.

Kislinger, Ewald, "Nikolaos Episkopos Lakedaimonias: Chronologische Präzisierungen zur Bischofsliste im Bodleianus Holkham gr. 6," *Jahrbuch der Österreichischen Byzantinistik* 57 (2007): 27–33.

Kitzinger, Beatrice E., *The Cross, the Gospels, and the Work of Art in the Carolingian Age* (Cambridge University Press, 2019).

Knappett, Carl, "Materiality," in Ian Hodder (ed.), *Archaeological Theory Today*, 2nd edn (Cambridge: Polity Press, 2012), 188–207.

"Materiality in Archaeological Theory," in Claire Smith (ed.), *Encyclopedia of Global Archaeology* (New York: Springer, 2014), 4700–08.

Kniazeff, Alexis, "Le lecture de l'Ancien et du Nouveau Testament dans le rite byzantin," in Bishop Cassien and Bernard Botte (eds.), *Le Prière des heures*, Lex Orandi 35 (Paris: Éditions du Cerf, 1963), 201–51.

Knight, David J., "The Archaeoacoustics of a Sixth-Century Christian Structure: San Vitale, Ravenna," in Raquel Jiménez, Rupert Till, and Mark Howell (eds.), *Music and Ritual: Bridging Material and Living Cultures* (Berlin: Publications of the ICTM Study Group on Music Archaeology, 2013), 133–46.

Kominis, A., "Συναγωγὴ ἐπιγραμμάτων εἰς τοὺς τέσσαρας Εὐαγγελιστάς," *Ἐπετηρὶς Ἑταιρείας Βυζαντινῶν Σπουδῶν* 21 (1951): 254–79.

Kopytoff, Igor, "The Cultural Biography of Things: Commoditization as Process," in Appadurai (ed.), *Social Life of Things*, 64–92.

Kostof, Spiro, *The Orthodox Baptistery of Ravenna* (New Haven, CT: Yale University Press, 1965).

Kotoula, Dimitra, "The British Museum Triumph of Orthodoxy Icon," in Andrew Louth and Augustine Casiday (eds.), *Byzantine Orthodoxies: Papers from the 36th Spring Symposium of Byzantine Studies* (Aldershot: Ashgate, 2006), 121–30.

Krapp, Peter, *Noise Channels: Glitch and Error in Digital Culture* (Minneapolis: University of Minnesota Press, 2011).

Krauss, Rosalind, *Under Blue Cup* (Cambridge, MA: MIT Press, 2011).

Krautheimer, Richard, "Introduction to an 'Iconography of Medieval Architecture,'" *Journal of the Warburg and Courtauld Institutes* 5 (1942): 1–33.

Krueger, Derek, *Writing and Holiness: The Practice of Authorship in the Early Christian East* (Philadelphia: University of Pennsylvania Press, 2004).

Kun, Josh, *Audiotopia: Music, Race, and America* (Berkeley: University of California Press, 2005).

Lachenaud, Guy, *Les routes de la voix: L'antiquité grecque et le mystère de la voix* (Paris: Belles Lettres, 2013).

Lampsidis, Odysseus, "Zur Sebastokratorissa Eirene," *Jahrbuch der Österreichischen Byzantinistik* 34 (1984): 91–105.

Latour, Bruno, *Reassembling the Social: An Introduction to Actor-Network-Theory* (Oxford University Press, 2005).

Laugerud, Henning, Hans Henrik Lohfert Jorgensen, and Laura Katrine Skinnebach (eds.), *The Saturated Sensorium: Principles of Perception and Mediation in the Middle Ages* (Aarhus University Press, 2015).

Lazarev, Viktor, *Storia della pittura bizantina*, Italian trans. Gildo Fossati (Turin: G. Einaudi, 1967).

Lethaby, William R. and Harold Swainson, *The Church of Sancta Sophia: A Study of a Byzantine Building* (London: Macmillan, 1894).

Lidov, Alexei, "A Byzantine Jerusalem: The Imperial Pharos Chapel as the Holy Sepulcher," in Annette Hoffmann and Gerhard Wolf (eds.), *Jerusalem as Narrative Space* (Leiden: Brill, 2012), 63–104.

"Heavenly Jerusalem: The Byzantine Approach," Jewish Art 23–24 (1997–98): 340–53.

"Leo the Wise and the Miraculous Icons in Hagia Sophia," in E. Kountura-Galaki (ed.), *The Heroes of the Orthodox Church: The New Saints, 8th to 16th Century* (Athens: Ethniko Hidryma Ereunōn, 2004), 393–432.

Linardou, Kallirroe, "The Kokkinobaphos Manuscripts Revisited: The Internal Evidence of the Books," *Scriptorium* 61:2 (2007): 384–407.

"Reading Two Byzantine Illustrated Books: The Kokkinobaphos Manuscripts (Vaticanus graecus 1162 and Parisinus graecus 1208)," PhD dissertation, University of Birmingham (2004).

Lingas, Alexander, "From Earth to Heaven: The Changing Soundscape of Byzantine Liturgy," in Mark Jackson and Claire Nesbitt (eds.), *Experiencing Byzantium: Papers from the 44th Spring Symposium of the Society for the Promotion of Byzantine Studies* (Aldershot: Ashgate, 2013), 311–58.

"How Musical was the 'Sung Office'? Some Observations on the Ethos of the Byzantine Cathedral Rite," in Ivan Moody and Maria Takala-Roszczenko (eds.), *The Traditions of Orthodox Music: Proceedings of the First International Conference on Orthodox Church Music, University of Joensuu, Finland, 13–19 June 2005* (Joensuu: University of Joensuu & International Society for Orthodox Church Music, 2007), 217–34.

"The Liturgical Place of the Kontakion in Constantinople," in Constantine C. Akentiev (ed.), *Liturgy, Architecture, and Art in the Byzantine World: Papers of the XVIII International Byzantine Congress (Moscow, 8–15 August 1991) and Other Essays Dedicated to the Memory of Fr. John Meyendorff* (Publications of the Saint Petersburg Society for Byzantine and Slavic Studies, 1995), 50–57.

"Medieval Byzantine Chant and the Sound of Orthodoxy," in Andrew Louth and Augustine Casiday (eds.), *Byzantine Orthodoxies: Papers from the 36th Spring Symposium of Byzantine Studies* (Aldershot: Ashgate, 2006), 131–50.

Lowden, John, "Book Production," in Elizabeth Jeffreys, John Haldon, and Robin Cormack (eds.), *Oxford Handbook of Byzantine Studies* (Oxford University Press, 2008), 462–72.

Illuminated Prophet Books: A Study of Byzantine Manuscripts of the Major and Minor Prophets (University Park: Pennsylvania State University Press, 1988).

"Illustrated Octateuch Manuscripts: A Byzantine Phenomenon," in Paul Magdalino and Robert Nelson (eds.), *The Old Testament in Byzantium* (Washington, DC: Dumbarton Oaks, 2010), 107–52.

The Jaharis Gospel Lectionary: The Story of a Byzantine Book (New York: Metropolitan Museum of Art, 2009).

"The Luxury Book as a Diplomatic Gift," in J. Shepard et al. (eds.), *Byzantine Diplomacy* (Aldershot: Variorum, 1992), 249–60.

"Luxury and Liturgy: The Function of Books," in R. Morris (ed.), *Church and People in Byzantium* (Centre for Byzantine, Ottoman and Modern Greek Studies, University of Birmingham, 1990), 263–80.

The Octateuchs: A Study in Byzantine Manuscript Illustration (University Park: Pennsylvania State University Press, 1992).

"The Word Made Visible: The Exterior of the Early Christian Book as Visual Argument," in W.E. Klingshirn and L. Safran (eds.), *The Early Christian Book* (Washington, DC: Catholic University of America, 2007), 13–47.

Macrides, Ruth, and Paul Magdalino, "The Architecture of Ekphrasis: Construction and Context of Paul the Silentiary's Poem on Hagia Sophia," *Byzantine and Modern Greek Studies* 12:1 (1988): 47–82.

Macridy-Bey, Th., and Jean Ebersolt, "Monuments funéraires de Constantinople," *Bulletin de correspondance héllenique* 46 (1923): 363–93.

Magdalino, Paul, "The Bath of Leo the Wise and the 'Macedonian Renaissance' Revisited: Topography, Iconography, Ceremonial, Ideology," *Dumbarton Oaks Papers* 42 (1988): 97–118.

"The History of the Future and Its Uses: Prophecy, Policy, and Propaganda," in Roderick Beaton and Charlotte Roueché (eds.), *The Making of Byzantine History: Studies Dedicated to Donald M. Nicol* (Aldershot: Varorium, 1993), 1–34.

"The Liturgical Poetics of an Elite Religious Confraternity," in Shawcross and Toth (eds.), *Reading in the Byzantine Empire*, 116–32.

Maguire, Eunice Dauterman, "Spouts and Finials Defining Fountains by Giving Water Shape and Sound," in Shilling and Stephenson (eds.), *Fountains and Water Culture*, 182–207.

Maguire, Henry, *Earth and Ocean: The Terrestrial World in Early Byzantine Art* (University Park: Pennsylvania State University Press, 1987).

"Medieval Art without 'Art'?: Introduction," *Gesta* 34:1 (1995): 3–4.

Nectar and Illusion: Nature in Byzantine Art and Literature (Oxford University Press, 2012).

"Where Did the Waters of Paradise Go after Iconoclasm?," in Shilling and Stephenson (eds.), *Fountains and Water Culture*, 229–45.

Mainstone, Rowland J., *Hagia Sophia: Architecture, Structure and Liturgy of Justinian's Great Church* (New York: Thames & Hudson, 1988).

Majeska, George P., "The Emperor in His Church: Imperial Ritual in the Church of St. Sophia," in Henry Maguire (ed.), *Byzantine Court Culture from 829 to 1204* (Washington, DC: Dumbarton Oaks, 1997), 1–12.

"The Image of the Chalke Savior in Saint Sophia," *Byzantinoslavica* 32:2 (1971): 284–95.

"Notes on the Archaeology of St. Sophia at Constantinople: The Green Marble Bands on the Floor," *Dumbarton Oaks Papers* 32 (1978): 299–308.

"Notes on the *Skeuophylakion* of St. Sophia," *Византийский временник* 55:80 (1998): 212–15.

Russian Travelers to Constantinople in the Fourteenth and Fifteenth Centuries (Washington, DC: Dumbarton Oaks, 1984).

Malickij, Nicolas, "Le Psautier byzantine à illustrations marginales du type Chludov est-il de provenance monastique?," in Gabriel Millet (ed.), *L'art byzantin chez les Slaves: L'ancienne Russie, les Slaves catholiques*, vol. 2 (Paris: P. Guenther, 1932), 235–43.

Manafis, Konstantinos, *Sinai: Treasures of the Monastery of Saint Catherine* (Athens: Ekdotikē Athēnōn, 1990).

Mango, Cyril, *The Brazen House: A Study of the Vestibule of the Imperial Palace of Constantinople* (Copenhagen: Munksgaard, 1959).

"The Date of the Narthex Mosaics of the Church of the Dormition at Nicaea," *Dumbarton Oaks Papers* 13 (1959): 245–52.

The Homilies of Photius Patriarch of Constantinople (Cambridge, MA: Harvard University Press, 1958).

Materials for the Study of the Mosaics of St. Sophia at Istanbul (Washington, DC: Dumbarton Oaks, 1962).

Mango, Cyril and Ernest J.W. Hawkins, "The Apse Mosaics of St. Sophia at Istanbul: Report on Work Carried Out in 1964," *Dumbarton Oaks Papers* 19 (1965): 113–51.

Manieri, Alessandra, *L'immagine poetica nella teoria degli antichi: Phantasia ed enargeia* (Pisa: Istituti editoriali e poligrafici internazionali, 1998).

Manolessou, Io, "On Historical Linguistics, Linguistic Variation and Medieval Greek," *Byzantine and Modern Greek Studies* 32:1 (2008): 63–79.

Manovich, Lev, *The Language of New Media* (Cambridge, MA: MIT Press, 2001).

Marinis, Vasileios, *Architecture and Ritual in the Churches of Constantinople: Ninth to Fifteenth Centuries* (Cambridge University Press, 2014).

Mark, Robert and Ahmet Ş. Çakmak (eds.), *Hagia Sophia from the Age of Justinian to the Present* (Cambridge University Press, 1992).

Martani, Sandra, "Das Ekphonetische Notationssystem in den datierten Evangeliarien des 10. Jahrhunderts," in Gerda Wolfram (ed.), *Palaeobyzantine Notations III: Acts of the Congress Held at Hemen Castle, The Netherlands, in March 2001* (Leuven: Peeters, 2004), 27–47.

"The Theory and Practice of Ekphonetic Notation: The Manuscript, Sinait. Gr. 213," *Plainsong and Medieval Music* 12 (2003): 15–42.

"Words and Music in the Greek Gospel Lectionaries," in Nina-Maria Wanek (ed.), *Psaltike: Neue Studien zur byzantinischen Musik. Festschrift für Gerda Wolfram* (Vienna: Praesens, 2011), 219–31.

Mastora, Pelli, "Ο ψηφιδωτός διάκοσμος στις φωτιστικές θυρίδες της Ροτόντας Θεσσαλονίκης," *Αρχαιολογική Εφημερίς* 149 (2010): 83–107.

Mateos, Juan, *La célébration de la parole dans la liturgie byzantine: Étude historique* (Rome: Pont. Institutum Studiorum Orientalium, 1971).

Le Typicon de la Grande Église, 2 vols. (Rome: Pontifical Oriental Institute, 1962–64).

Mathews, Thomas, *The Clash of Gods: A Reinterpretation of Early Christian Art*, 2nd edn (Princeton University Press, 1999).

The Early Churches of Constantinople: Architecture and Liturgy (University Park: Pennsylvania State University Press, 1971).

May, Regine, "The Metamorphosis of Pantomime: Apuleius's *Judgment of Paris* (*Met.* 10:30–34)," in Edith Hall and Rosie Wyles (eds.), *New Directions in Ancient Pantomime* (Oxford University Press, 2008), 338–62.

McKay, Gretchen Kreahling, "Christ's Polymorphism in Jerusalem, Taphou 14: An Examination of Text and Image," *Apocrypha* 14 (2003): 177–91.

"The Eastern Christian Exegetical Tradition of Daniel's Vision of the Ancient of Days," *Journal of Early Christian Studies* 7:1 (1999): 139–61.

"Illustrating the Gospel of John: The Exegesis of John Chrysostom and Images of the Ancient of Days in Eleventh-Century Byzantine Manuscripts," *Studies in Iconography* 31 (2010): 51–68.

"Imaging the Divine: A Study of the Representations of the Ancient of Days in Byzantine Manuscripts," PhD dissertation, University of Virginia (1997).

Meijering, Roos, *Literary and Rhetorical Theories in Greek Scholia* (Groningen: Egbert Forsten, 1987).

Mellas, Andrew, "Melismatic Events," *Phronema* 23 (2008): 67–85.

Mercati, Silvio G., "Sulle iscrizioni di Santa Sofia," *Bessarione* 26 (1922): 200–18.

Meskell, Lynn, *Object Worlds in Ancient Egypt: Material Biographies Past and Present* (Oxford: Berg, 2004).

Metzger, Bruce, "Greek Lectionaries and a Critical Edition of the New Testament," in Kurt Aland (ed.), *Die alten Übersetzungen des Neuen Testaments, die Kirchenväterzitate und Lektionare*, Arbeiten zur neutestamentlichen Textforschung 5 (Berlin: De Gruyter, 1972), 479–97.

"When Did Scribes Begin to Use Writing Desks?," *Historical and Literary Studies: Pagan, Jewish, and Christian* (Leiden: Brill, 1968), 121–37.

Miller, Daniel (ed.), *Materiality* (Durham, NC: Duke University Press, 2005).

Milner, Christine, "'Lignum Vitae' or 'Crux Gemmata'? The Cross of Golgotha in the Early Byzantine Period," *Byzantine and Modern Greek Studies* 20 (1996): 77–99.

Mitchell, Margaret, *The Heavenly Trumpet: John Chrysostom and the Art of Pauline Interpretation* (Louisville, KY: Westminster John Knox Press, 2002).

Moore, John D., "The Dating of Plato's *Ion*," *Roman and Byzantine Studies* 15:5 (1974): 421–39.

Moran, Neil, "The Choir of Hagia Sophia," *Oriens Christianus* 89 (2005): 1–7.

"The Musical 'Gestaltung' of the Great Entrance Ceremony in the 12th Century in Accordance with the Rite of Hagia Sophia," *Jahrbuch der Österreichischen Byzantinistik* 28 (1979): 167–93.

Singers in Late Byzantine and Slavonic Painting (Leiden: Brill, 1986).

"The Skeuophylakion of the Hagia Sophia," *Cahiers archéologiques* 34 (1986): 29–32.

Morgenstern, Julian, "The 'Son of Man' of Daniel 7:13f.: A New Interpretation," *Journal of Biblical Literature* 80:1 (1961): 65–77.

Morton, Timothy, *Hyperobjects: Philosophy and Ecology after the End of the World* (Minneapolis: University of Minnesota Press, 2013).

Murray, Janet, *Hamlet on the Holodeck: The Future of Narrative in Cyberspace* (New York: Free Press, 1997).

Nelson, Kristina, *The Art of Reciting the Quran* (Austin: University of Texas Press, 1985).

Nelson, Robert S., "The Discourse of Icons, Then and Now," *Art History* 12:2 (1989): 144–57.

"Dressing and Undressing Greek Lectionaries in Byzantium and Italy," in David Ganz and Barbara Schellewald (eds.), *Clothing Sacred Scriptures: Book Art and Book Religion in Christian, Islamic, and Jewish Cultures* (Berlin: De Gruyter, 2018), 107–21.

"Empathetic Vision: Looking at and with a Performative Byzantine Miniature," *Art History* 30:4 (2007): 489–502.

Hagia Sophia, 1850–1950: Holy Wisdom Modern Monument (University of Chicago Press, 2004).

"Image and Inscription: Pleas for Salvation in Spaces of Devotion," in Liz James (ed.), *Art and Text in Byzantine Culture* (Cambridge University Press, 2007), 100–19.

"The Manuscripts of Antonios Malakes and the Collecting and Appreciation of Illuminated Books in the Early Palaeologan Period," *Jahrbuch der Österreichischen Byzantinistik* 36 (1986): 229–54.

"Michael the Monk and His Gospel Book," *Actes du XVe congrès international d'études byzantines*, vol. 2 (Athens: Association Internationale des Études Byzantines, 1981), 575–82.

"Patriarchal Lectionaries of Constantinople: History, Attributions, and Prospects," in Derek Krueger and Robert S. Nelson (eds.), *The New Testament in Byzantium* (Washington, DC: Dumbarton Oaks, 2016), 87–115.

"Theoktistos and Associates in Twelfth-Century Constantinople: An Illustrated New Testament of A.D. 1133," *J. Paul Getty Museum Journal* 15 (1987): 53–78.

"A Thirteenth-Century Byzantine Miniature in the Vatican Library," *Gesta* 20:1 (1981): 213–22.

Nesbitt, Claire, "Shaping the Sacred: Light and the Experience of Worship in Middle Byzantine Churches," *Byzantine and Modern Greek Studies* 36:2 (2012): 139–60.

Nilsson, Ingela, "Words, Water, and Power: Literary Fountains and Metaphors of Patronage in Eleventh- and Twelfth-Century Byzantium," in Shilling and Stephenson (eds.), *Fountains and Water Culture*, 265–80.

Nünlist, René, *The Ancient Critic at Work: Terms and Concepts of Literary Criticism in Greek Scholia* (Cambridge University Press, 2009).

Oikonomides, Nicolas, "Leo VI and the Narthex Mosaic of Saint Sophia," *Dumbarton Oaks Papers* 30 (1976): 151–72.

Les listes de préséance byzantines des IXe et Xe siècle (Paris: Éditions du Centre National de la Recherche Scientifique, 1972).

"Some Remarks on the Apse Mosaic of St. Sophia," *Dumbarton Oaks Papers* 39 (1985): 111–15.

Olsen, Bjørnar, "Material Culture after Text: Re-membering Things," *Norwegian Archaeological Review* 36:3 (2003): 87–104.

Olster, David, "Byzantine Apocalypses," in Bernard J. McGinn, John J. Collins, and Stephen J. Stein (eds.), *The Continuum History of Apocalypticism* (New York: Continuum, 2003), 254–72.

Osburn, Carroll, "The Greek Lectionaries of the New Testament," in Bart D. Ehrman and Michael W. Holmes (eds.), *The Text of the New Testament in Contemporary Research: Essays on the Status Quaestionis*, 2nd edn (Leiden: Brill, 2013), 93–114.

Otto, Nina, *Enargeia: Untersuchung zur Charakteristik alexandrinischer Dichtung* (Stuttgart: Franz Steiner Verlag, 2009).

Ousterhout, Robert, *The Art of the Kariye Camii* (London: Scala, 2002).

"The Holy Space: Architecture and the Liturgy," in Linda Safran (ed.), *Heaven on Earth: Art and the Church in Byzantium* (University Park: Pennsylvania State University Press, 1998), 81–120.

Master Builders of Byzantium (Princeton University Press, 1999).

Özügül, A., "The Doorframes of Late Antique Buildings in Anatolia (Fifth and Sixth Centuries)," in Çiğdem Özkan Aygün (ed.), *Soma 2007: Proceedings of the XI Symposium on Mediterranean Archaeology* (Oxford: Archaeopress, 2009), 301–08.

Papadopoulos, J.-B., "Le mutatorion des églises byzantines," *Mémorial Louis Petit: Mélanges d'histoire et d'archéologie byzantines* (Bucharest: Institut Français d'Études Byzantines, 1948), 366–72.

Papaioannou, Stratis, "Byzantine *Enargeia* and Theories of Representation," *Byzantinoslavica* 3 (2011): 48–60.

"Encomium for the Monk Ioannes Kroustoulas Who Read Aloud at the Holy Soros," in Charles Barber and Stratis Papaioannou (eds.), *Michael Psellos on Literature and Art: A Byzantine Perspective on Aesthetics* (Notre Dame University Press, 2017), 218–44.

"Fragile Literature: Byzantine Letter-Collections and the Case of Michael Psellos," in Paolo Odorico (ed.), *La face cachée de la littérature byzantine: Le texte en tant que message immédiat* (Paris: Centre d'études byzantines, néo-helléniques et sud-est européennes, École des Hautes Études en Sciences Sociales, 2012), 289–328.

"Readers and Their Pleasures," in Stratis Papaioannou (ed.), *Oxford Handbook of Byzantine Literature* (Oxford University Press, forthcoming).

Papaioannou, Stratis, "Readers and Their Pleasures," in Stratis Papaioannou "Sicily, Constantinople, Miletos: The Life of a Eunuch and the History of Byzantine Humanism," in Theodora Antonopoulou, Sofia Kotzabassi, and Marina Loukaki (eds.), *Myriobiblos: Essays on Byzantine Literature and Culture* (Berlin: De Gruyter, 2015), 261–84.

Papalexandrou, Amy, "The Past Is Noise: Architectural Contexts and the Soundways of Byzantium," paper presented at Byzantine Studies Conference, University of Pennsylvania, 2010.

"Perceptions of Sound and Sonic Environments across the Byzantine Acoustic Horizon," in Susan Ashbrook Harvey and Margaret Mullett (eds.), *Knowing Bodies, Passionate Souls: Sense Perception in Byzantium* (Washington, DC: Dumbarton Oaks, 2017), 67–85.

"Text in Context: Eloquent Monuments and the Byzantine Beholder," *Word & Image* 17:3 (2001): 259–83.

Parenti, Stefano, "The Cathedral Rite of Constantinople: Evolution of a Local Tradition," *Orientalia Christiana Periodica* 77 (2011): 449–69.

Parmenter, Dorina Miller, "The Iconic Book: The Image of the Bible in Early Christian Rituals," in James W. Watts (ed.), *Iconic Books and Texts* (Sheffield: Equinox, 2013), 63–92.

Parpulov, Georgi, "The Psalms and Personal Piety in Byzantium," in Paul Magdalino and Robert Nelson (eds.), *The Old Testament in Byzantium* (Washington, DC: Dumbarton Oaks, 2010), 77–105.

"Toward a History of Byzantine Psalters," PhD dissertation, University of Chicago (2004).

Pedone, Silvia, "The Marble Omphalos of Saint Sophia in Constantinople: An Analysis of an Opus Sectile Pavement of Middle Byzantine Age," in M. Șhain (ed.), *11th International Colloquium on Ancient Mosaics, October 16th–20th 2009, Bursa Turkey* (Istanbul: Uludağ University Press, 2011), 749–68.

Peers, Glenn, "Breathless, Speechless Images: On the Chalke Gate Epigram," in L. Finnete and A.P. Booth *Hommages Margaret Thomson*, Cahiers des études anciennes 34 (Quebec: Université Laval, 1998), 109–12.

Sacred Shock: Framing Visual Experience in Byzantium (University Park: Pennsylvania State University Press, 2004).

Subtle Bodies: Representing Angels in Byzantium (Berkeley: University of California Press, 2001).

Pelekanidis, S.M. et al., *The Treasures of Mount Athos: Illuminated Manuscripts*, vol. 1 (Athens: Ekdotikē Athēnōn, 1974).

Pentcheva, Bissera, "Hagia Sophia and Multisensory Aesthetics," *Gesta* 50:2 (2011): 93–111.

Hagia Sophia: Sound, Space, and Spirit in Byzantium (University Park: Pennsylvania State University Press, 2017).

"Moving Eyes: Surface and Shadow in the Byzantine Mixed-Media Relief Icon," *RES: Anthropology and Aesthetics* 53 (2009): 223–34.

The Sensual Icon: Space, Ritual, and the Senses in Byzantium (University Park: Pennsylvania State University Press, 2010).

"Visual Textuality: The Logos as Pregnant Body and Building," *RES: Aesthetics and Anthropology* 45 (2004): 225–38.

(ed.), *Aural Architecture in Byzantium: Music, Acoustics, and Ritual* (London: Routledge, 2018).

Peschlow, Urs, "Der mittelbyzantinische Ambo aus archäologischer Sicht," in M. Vassilaki, E. Georgoula, A. Delivorrias, and A. Markopoulos (eds.), *Θυμίαμα στη μνήμη της Λασκαρίνας Μπούρα*, 2 vols. (Athens: Benaki Museum, 1994), 1:255–60.

"Observations in the So-called Skeuophylakion of Ayasofya in Istanbul," *Araştırma Sonuçları Toplantısı* 26:2 (2008): 391–96.

"Zum byzantinischen opus sectile-Boden," in R.M. Boehmer and H. Hauptmann, *Beiträge zur Altertumskunde Kleinasiens: Festschrift für Kurt Bittel* (Mainz: Zabern, 1983), 435–47.

Pietersma, A. and B.G. Wright (eds.), *A New English Translation of the Septuagint* (Oxford University Press, 2007).

Piganiol, André, "L'hémisphairion et l'omphalos des lieux saints," *Cahiers archéologiques* 1 (1945): 7–14.

Pingree, Geoffrey B. and Lisa Gitelman, "What's New about New Media?," in Geoffrey B. Pingree and Lisa Gitelman (eds.), *New Media, 1740–1915* (Cambridge, MA: MIT Press, 2003), xi–xxii.

Preda, Alex, "The Turn to Things: Arguments for a Sociological Theory of Things," *Sociological Quarterly* 40:2 (1999): 347–66.

Pyatnitsky, Yury and Nadezhda Kavrus-Hoffmann, *The Hermitage Psalter: The Amazing Journey of an Exceptional Byzantine Manuscript* (Ann Arbor, MI: Legacy Press, forthcoming).

Raby, Julian, "In Vitro Veritas: Glass Pilgrim Vessels from 7th-century Jerusalem," in Jeremy Johns (ed.), *Bayt al-Maqdis, Part Two: Jerusalem and Early Islam* (Oxford University Press, 2000), 113–83.

Rancière, Jacques, *Aisthesis: Scenes from the Aesthetic Regime of Art*, trans. Zakir Paul (London: Verso, 2013).

Randall, Lilian, *Images in the Margins of Gothic Manuscripts* (Berkeley: University of California Press, 1966).

Rapp, Claudia, "Holy Texts, Holy Men and Holy Scribes: Aspects of Scriptural Holiness in Late Antiquity," in William Klingshirn and Linda Safran (eds.), *The Early Christian Book* (Washington, DC: Catholic University of America Press, 2007), 194–222.

Ray, Walter D., *Tasting Heaven on Earth: Worship in Sixth-Century Constantinople* (Grand Rapids, MI: W.B. Eerdmans, 2012).

Reinsch, Diether Roderich, "The History of Editing Byzantine Historiographical Texts," in Paul Stephenson (ed.), *The Byzantine World* (London: Routledge, 2010), 435–44.

Reiske, J.J., *De ceremoniis byzantini*, 3 vols. (Bonn: Weber, 1829–40).

Reudenbach, Bruno, *Das Godescalc-Evangelistar: Ein Buch für die Reformpolitik Karls des Großen* (Frankfurt: Fischer Taschenbuch, 1998).

Rigo, Antonio, "Le *Synodikon de l'Orthodoxie* et le Palamisme: La forme primitive de P (1351 – avant 1360): Les sources et les témoins," in I.A. Biliarsky (ed.), *Laudator temporis acti: Studia in memoriam Ioannis a. Božilov*, vol. 2 (Sofia: Gutenberg, 2018), 227–41.

Robinson, Cynthia, "Marginal Ornament: Poetics, Mimesis, and Devotion in the Palace of the Lions," *Muqarnas* 25 (2008): 185–214.

"Seeing Paradise: Metaphor and Vision in the *Taifa* Palace Architecture," *Gesta* 36:2 (1997): 145–55.

Roby, Courtney, *Technical Ekphrasis in Ancient Science and Literature: The Written Machine between Alexandria and Rome* (Cambridge University Press, 2016).

Rosenberg, Jordy, "The Molecularization of Sexuality: On Some Primitivisms of the Present," *Theory & Event* 17:2 (2014): n.p.

Rouget, Gilbert, *Music and Trance: A Theory of the Relations between Music and Possession*, trans. Brunhilde Biebuyck (University of Chicago Press, 1985).

Rubin, Arnold, *Art as Technology: The Arts of Africa, Oceania, Native America, and Southern California* (Catskill, NY: Hillcrest Press, 1989).

Russo, Eugenio, *Le decorazioni di Isidoro il Giovane per S. Sofia di Constantinopoli* (Rome: Viella, 2011).

Sandin, Karl Ayers, "Middle Byzantine Bronze Crosses of Intermediate Size: Form, Use and Meaning," PhD Dissertation, Rutgers University (1992).

Sandler, Lucy Freeman, *Studies in Manuscript Illumination, 1200–1400* (London: Pindar Press, 2008).

Schafer, R. Murray, *The Tuning of the World* (New York: Knopf, 1977).

Schibille, Nadine, *Hagia Sophia and the Byzantine Aesthetic Experience* (Burlington, VT: Ashgate, 2014).

Schreiner, P., "Omphalion und Rota Porphyretica: Zum Kaiserzeremoniell in Konstantinopel und Rom," in Ivan Dujčev (ed.), *Byzance et les Slaves: Études de civilization* (Paris: Association des amis des études archéologiques des mondes byzantino-slaves et du christianisme oriental, 1979), 401–10.

Schulz, Hans-Joachim, *The Byzantine Liturgy: Symbolic Structure and Faith Expression*, trans. Matthew J. O'Connell (New York: Pueblo, 1986).

Schwartz, Hillel, *Making Noise: From Babel to the Big Bang & Beyond* (Brooklyn: Zone, 2011).

Sells, Michael, *Approaching the Qur'an: The Early Revelations* (Ashland, OR: White Cloud Press, 1999).

Ševčenko, Ihor, "The Illuminators of the Menologion of Basil II," *Dumbarton Oaks Papers* 16 (1962): 245–76.

"Notes on Stephen, the Novgorodian Pilgrim to Constantinople in the XIV Century," *Südostforschungen* 12 (1953): 165–75.

"On Pantoleon the Painter," *Jahrbuch der Österreichischen Byzantinistik* 21 (1972): 241–49.

Ševčenko, Nancy, "Icons in the Liturgy," *Dumbarton Oaks Papers* 45 (1991): 45–57.

"Illuminating the Liturgy: Illustrated Service Books in Byzantium," in Linda Safran (ed.), *Heaven on Earth: Art and the Church in Byzantium* (University Park: Pennsylvania State University Press, 1998), 186–228.

Shaviro, Steven, *The Universe of Things: On Speculative Realism* (Minneapolis: University of Minnesota Press, 2014).

Shawcross, Teresa and Ida Toth (eds.), *Reading in the Byzantine Empire and Beyond* (Cambridge University Press, 2018).

Sheldon, Rebekah, "You Can't Have Me: Feminist Infiltrations in Object-Oriented Ontology," *Los Angeles Review of Books*, April 8, 2017, https://lareviewofbooks.org/article/you-cant-have-me-feminist-infiltrations-in-object-oriented-ontology.

Sheppard, Carl D., "Byzantine Carved Marble Slabs," *Art Bulletin* 51:1 (1969): 65–71.

Shilling, Brooke, "Fountains of Paradise in Early Byzantine Art, Homilies, and Hymns," in Shilling and Stephenson (eds.), *Fountains and Water Culture*, 208–28.

Shilling, Brooke and Paul Stephenson (eds.), *Fountains and Water Culture in Byzantium* (Cambridge University Press, 2016).

Shipp, G.P., "The Phonology of Modern Greek," *Glotta* 37 (1958): 233–58.

Snyder, James, "The Meaning of the Maiestas Domini in Hosios David," *Byzantion* 37 (1967): 143–52.

Sodini, Jean-Pierre, "Les ambons médiévaux à Byzance: Vestiges et problèmes," in M. Vassilaki, E. Georgoula, A. Delivorrias, and A. Markopoulos (eds.), *Θυμίαμα στη μνήμη της Λασκαρίνας Μπούρα*, 2 vols. (Athens: Benaki Museum, 1994), I:303–07.

Spatharakis, Ioannis, *Corpus of Dated Illuminated Greek Manuscripts to the Year 1453*, vol. 1 (Leiden: Brill, 1981).

"An Illuminated Greek Grammar Manuscript in Jerusalem: A Contribution to the Study of Comnenian Illuminated Ornament," *Jahrbuch der Österreichischen Byzantinistik* 35 (1985): 231–52.

Speck, Paul, *Kaiser Konstantin VI: Die Legitimation einer Fremden und der Versuch einer eigenen Herrschaft* (Munich: Wilhelm Fink Verlag, 1978).

Stock, Brian, *The Implications of Literacy: Written Language and Models of Interpretation in the Eleventh and Twelfth Centuries* (Princeton University Press, 1983).

Strunk, Oliver, "The Byzantine Office at Hagia Sophia," *Dumbarton Oaks Papers* 9–10 (1955–56): 175–202.

Stuhlfauth, Georg, "A Greek Psalter with Byzantine Miniatures," *Art Bulletin* 15:4 (1933): 311–26.

Svenbro, Jesper, *Phrasikleia: An Anthropology of Reading in Ancient Greece*, trans. Janet Lloyd (Ithaca, NY: Cornell University Press, 1993).

Swift, Emerson H., *Hagia Sophia* (New York: Columbia University Press, 1940).

"The Bronze Doors of the Gate of the Horologium at Hagia Sophia," *Art Bulletin* 19:2 (1937): 137–47.

Taft, Robert F., "The Dialogue before the Anaphora in the Byzantine Eucharistic Liturgy, I: The Opening Greeting," *Orientalia Christiana Periodica* 52 (1986): 299–324.

"The Dialogue before the Anaphora in the Byzantine Eucharistic Liturgy, II: The Sursum Corda," *Orientalia Christiana Periodica* 54 (1988): 47–77.

"The Dialogue before the Anaphora in the Byzantine Eucharistic Liturgy, III: 'Let us give thanks to the Lord – It is fitting and right,'" *Orientalia Christiana Periodica* 55 (1989): 63–74.

The Great Entrance: A History of the Transfer of Gifts and Other Pre-anaphoral Rites of the Liturgy of St. John Chrysostom, Orientalia Christiana Analecta 200 (Rome: Pont. Institutum Studiorum Orientalium, 1975).

A History of the Liturgy of St. John Chrysostom, vol. 4: *The Diptychs*, Orientalia Christiana Analecta 238 (Rome: Pont. Institutum Studiorum Orientalium, 1991).

A History of the Liturgy of St. John Chrysostom, vol. 5: The *Precommunion Rites*, Orientalia Christiana Analecta 261 (Rome: Pont. Institutum Studiorum Orientalium, 2000).

A History of the Liturgy of St. John Chrysostom, vol. 6: *The Communion, Thanksgiving, and Concluding Rites*, Orientalia Christiana Analecta 281 (Rome: Pont. Institutum Studiorum Orientalium, 2008).

"The Liturgy of the Great Church: An Initial Synthesis of Structure and Interpretation on the Eve of Iconoclasm," *Dumbarton Oaks Papers* 34 (1980): 45–75.

"*Questiones disputatae*: The Skeuophylakion of Hagia Sophia and the Entrances of the Liturgy Revisited," *Oriens Christianus* 81 (1997): 1–35.

"Textual Problems in the Diaconal Admonition before the Anaphora in the Byzantine Tradition," *Orientalia Christiana Periodica* 49 (1983): 340–65.

"Women at the Church in Byzantium: Where, When – and Why?," *Dumbarton Oaks Papers* 52 (1998): 27–87.

Talbot, Alice-Mary, "Epigrams of Manuel Philes on the Theotokos tes Peges and Its Art," *Dumbarton Oaks Papers* 48 (1994): 135–65.

Teteriatnikov, Natalia, "Devotional Crosses in the Columns and Walls of Hagia Sophia," *Byzantion* 68:2 (1998): 419–45.

Justinianic Mosaics of Hagia Sophia and Their Aftermath (Washington, DC: Dumbarton Oaks, 2017).

"The Mosaics of the Eastern Arch of Hagia Sophia in Constantinople: Program and Liturgy," *Gesta* 52:1 (2013): 61–84.

Thibaut, Jean-Baptiste, *Monuments de la notation ekphonétique et hagiopolite de l'Église grecque* (Saint Petersburg: Kügelgen, Glitsch, 1913).

Origine byzantine de la notation neumatique de l'Église latine (Paris: A. Picard et Fils, 1907).

Tilley, Christopher, *A Phenomenology of Landscape: Places, Paths and Monuments* (Oxford: Berg, 1997).

Tillyard, H.J.W., *Handbook of the Middle Byzantine Musical Notation* (Copenhagen: Levin & Munksgaard, 1935).

"The Problem of Byzantine Neumes," *Journal of Hellenic Studies* 41:1 (1921): 29–49.

Torp, Hjalmar, "Dogmatic Themes in the Mosaics of the Rotunda at Thessaloniki," *Arte Medievale* n.s. 1 (2002): 11–34.

Touliatos, Diane, "Henry Julius Wetenhall Tillyard," in Helen Damico (ed.), *Medieval Scholarship: Biographical Studies on the Formation of a Discipline*, vol. 3 (New York: Garland, 2000), 153–64.

Troelsgård, Christian, *Byzantine Neumes: A New Introduction to the Middle Byzantine Musical Notation* (Copenhagen: Museum Tusculanum Press, 2011).

"Psalm: III. Byzantine Psalmody," in Stanley Sadie (ed.), *The New Grove Dictionary of Music and Musicians*, 29 vols., 2nd edn (London: Macmillan, 2001), 20:463–66.

Underwood, Paul, "The Deisis Mosaic in the Kahrie Cami at Istanbul," in Kurt Weitzmann (ed.), *Late Classical and Medieval Studies in Honor of A.M. Friend, Jr.* (Princeton University Press, 1955), 254–60.

"The Evidence of Restorations in the Sanctuary Mosaics of the Church of the Dormition at Nicaea," *Dumbarton Oaks Papers* 13 (1959): 235–43.

"The Fountain of Life in Manuscripts of the Gospels," *Dumbarton Oaks Papers* 5 (1950): 41–138.

"Notes on the Work of the Byzantine Institute in Istanbul: 1957–1959," *Dumbarton Oaks Papers* 14 (1960): 205–22.

Valivitcharska, Vessela, *Rhetoric and Rhythm in Byzantium: The Sound of Persuasion* (Cambridge University Press, 2013).

Van Nice, Robert L., *St. Sophia in Istanbul: An Architectural Survey* (Washington, DC: Dumbarton Oaks, 1966).

Velimirović, Miloš, "Egon Wellesz and the Study of Byzantine Chant," *Musical Quarterly* 62:2 (1976): 265–77.

Velkovska, Elena, "Il lezionario patriarcale Ottoboni gr. 175," in Marco D'Agostino and Paola Degni (eds.), *Alethes Philia: Studi in onore di Giancarlo Prato*, vol. 2 (Spoleto: Fondazione Centro italiano di studi sull'alto Medioevo, 2010), 687–94.

Velmans, Tania, "L'iconographie de la 'Fontaine de Vie' dans la tradition byzantine a la fin du Moyen Âge," in André Grabar and Jean Hubert (eds.), *Synthronon* (Paris: C. Klincksieck, 1968), 119–34.

Walter, Christopher, "The Date and Content of the Dionysiou Lectionary," *Δελτίον Χριστιανικής Αρχαιολογικής Εταιρείας* 4:13 (1985–86): 181–89.

L'iconographie des conciles dans la tradition byzantine, Archives de l'orient chrétien 13 (Paris: Institut Français d'Études Byzantines, 1970).

"Icons of the First Council of Nicaea," *Δελτίον Χριστιανικής Αρχαιολογικής Εταιρείας* 16 (1991–92): 209–18.

"Liturgy and the Illustration of Gregory of Nazianzen's Homilies: An Essay in Iconographical Methodology," *Revue des études byzantine* 29 (1971): 183–212.

Webb, Ruth, *Demons and Dancers: Performance in Late Antiquity* (Cambridge, MA: Harvard University Press, 2008).

Weitze, Christoffer et al, "The Acoustical History of Hagia Sophia Revived through Computer Simulation" (2002), accessed 1 November 2009, www.odeon.dk/pdf/ForumAcousticum2002.pdf.

Weitzmann, Kurt, *Byzantine Liturgical Psalters and Gospels* (London: Variorum Reprints, 1980).

"The Constantinopolitan Lectionary, Morgan 639," in Dorothy Miner (ed.), *Studies in Art and Literature for Belle da Costa Greene* (Princeton University Press, 1954), 358–73.

Illustrations in Roll and Codex: A Study of the Origin and Method of Text Illustration (Princeton University Press, 1947).

"An Imperial Lectionary in the Monastery of Dionysiou on Mount Athos: Its Origins and Its Wanderings," *Revue des études sud-est européennes* 7 (1969): 239–53.

The Miniatures of the Sacra Parallela Parisinus graecus 923 (Princeton University Press, 1979).

The Monastery of St. Catharine, The Icons (Princeton University Press, 1976).

Weitzmann, Kurt and Ihor Ševčenko, "The Moses Cross at Sinai," *Dumbarton Oaks Papers* 17 (1963): 385–98.

Weitzmann, Kurt and Massimo Bernabò, *The Byzantine Octateuchs*, 2 vols. (Princeton University Press, 1999).

Wellesz, Egon, *A History of Byzantine Music and Hymnography*, 2nd edn (Oxford: Clarendon Press, 1961).

Westbrook, Nigel, "The Chalkê: The Bronze Gate of the Byzantine Great Palace," *Cultural Crossroads: Proceedings of the 26th International SAHANZ Conference* (University of Auckland, 2009), 1–15.

Whitby, Mary, "The Occasion of Paul the Silentiary's *Ekphrasis* of S. Sophia," *Classical Quarterly* 35:1 (1985): 215–28.

White, Andrew Walker, *Performing Orthodox Ritual in Byzantium* (Cambridge University Press, 2015).

Woszczyk, Wieslaw, "Acoustics of Hagia Sophia: A Scientific Approach to the Humanities and Sacred Space," in Pentcheva (ed.), *Aural Architecture in Byzantium*, 176–97.

Wybrew, Hugh, *The Orthodox Liturgy: The Development of the Eucharistic Liturgy in the Byzantine Rite* (Crestwood, NY: St. Vladimir's Seminary Press, 1990).

Xydis, Stephen G., "The Chancel Barrier, Solea, and Ambo of Hagia Sophia," *Art Bulletin* 29:1 (1947): 1–24.

Xyngopoulos, Andreas, "Τὸ ἱστορημένο εὐαγγέλιον τοῦ Ἑλληνικοῦ Ἰνστιτούτου Βενετίας," *Thesaurismata* 1 (1962): 63–88.

"'Ἅγιος Ἰωάννης ὁ Χρυσόστομος 'Πηγὴ τῆς Σοφίας,'" *Αρχαιολογική Εφημερίς* 81–83 (1942–44): 1–36.

Yota, Elisabeth, "The Lectionary," in Vasiliki Tsamakda (ed.), *A Companion to Byzantine Illustrated Manuscripts* (Leiden: Brill, 2017), 287–99.

Zagklas, Nikolaos, "A Byzantine Grammar Treatise Attributed to Theodoros Prodromos," *Graeco-Latina Brunensia* 16:1 (2011): 77–86.

Zakharova, Anna, "Gli otto artisti del 'Menologio de Basilio II,'" *Miscellanea Bibliothecae Apostolicae Vaticanae*, vol. 10, Studi e Testi 416 (Vatican, 2003), 379–432.

"The Relationship between Text and Image in Byzantine Illuminated Gospel Lectionaries," in Karin Krause and Barbara Schellewald (eds.), *Bild und Text im Mittelalter* (Cologne: Böhlau, 2011), 283–311.

Zchomelidse, Nino, *Art, Ritual, and Civic Identity in Medieval Southern Italy* (University Park: Pennsylvania State University Press, 2013).

"The Epiphany of the *logos* in the Ambo in the Rotunda (Hagios Georgios) in Thessaloniki," in Manuela De Giorgi, Annette Hoffmann, and Nicola Suthor (eds.), *Synergies in Visual Culture* (Munich: Fink Verlag, 2013), 85–96.

Index

Page numbers in *italics* indicate illustrations. Manuscripts and objects will be found under city and institution (e.g. New York, Morgan Library); they are also indexed by name (Dionysiou Lectionary) and specific object type (chancel barrier). Buildings are listed by name, if well-known, and by location.